Everyday Memory

This book presents an authoritative overview of memory in everyday contexts. Written by an expert team of international authors, it gathers together research on some of the more neglected but revealing areas of memory, to provide a comprehensive overview of remembering in real-life situations.

Contributions from leading experts deal with a variety of important questions concerning everyday memory, from under-researched areas such as memory for odours to more well-known areas, like collective memory. Topics covered also include:

- beliefs about memory and the metaphors used to discuss memory
- the relation between self-referent beliefs and actual memory performance
- the development of autobiographical memory.

Everyday Memory summarizes current knowledge and presents new interpretations and hypotheses to be explored by future research. It discusses aspects of human memory that are frequently ignored or dealt with only very briefly by ordinary textbooks and as a result will have a broad appeal for researchers and students.

Svein Magnussen and **Tore Helstrup** are at the Centre for Advanced Study, the Norwegian Academy of Science and Letters, and the Department of Psychology, University of Oslo.

D0082077

Everyday Memory

**Edited by Svein Magnussen and
Tore Helstrup**

Psychology Press
Taylor & Francis Group

HOVE AND NEW YORK

First published 2007 by Psychology Press
27 Church Road, Hove, East Sussex, BN3 2FA

Simultaneously published in the USA and Canada
by Psychology Press
270 Madison Avenue, New York, NY 10016

*Psychology Press is an imprint of the Taylor & Francis Group,
an informa business*

© 2007 Psychology Press

Typeset in Times by RefineCatch Limited, Bungay, Suffolk
Printed and bound in Great Britain by
MPG Books Ltd, Bodmin, Cornwall
Cover design by Lisa Dynan

This publication has been produced with paper manufactured to strict
environmental standards and with pulp derived from sustainable forests.

British Library Cataloguing in Publication Data
A catalogue record for this book is available from the British Library

Library of Congress Cataloging in Publication Data
Everyday memory / edited by Svein Magnussen and Tore Helstrup.
  p. cm.
ISBN 1–84169–579–3 (hardback)
1. Memory. I. Magnussen, Svein. II. Helstrup, Tore.
BF371.E838 2007
153.1′2–dc22

               2006017755

ISBN 978–1–84169–579–2

Contents

Tables

Figures

Contributors

Jan Andersson Swedish Defense Research Agency, Box 1165, SE-581 11 Linköping, Sweden (E-mail: jan.andersson@foi.se)

Cesare Cornoldi Department of Psychology, University of Padua, Via Venezia 8, 35131 Padua, Italy (E-mail: cesare.cornoldi@unipd.it)

Rossana De Beni Department of Psychology, University of Padua, Via Venezia 8, 35131 Padua, Italy (E-mail: rossana.debeni@unipd.it)

Tor Endestad University of Oslo, Box 1904 Blindern, 0317 Oslo, Norway

Gail S. Goodman Department of Psychology, University of California, 1 Shields Avenue, Davis, CA 95616, USA (E-mail: ggoodman@ucdavis.edu) and University of Oslo, Box 1094 Blindern, 0317 Oslo, Norway

Tore Helstrup Department of Psychology, University of Oslo, Box 1094 Blindern, 0317 Oslo, Norway (E-mail: tore.helstrup@psykologi.uio.no)

Asher Koriat Department of Psychology, University of Haifa, Haifa, Israel (E-mail: akoriat@research.haifa.ac.il)

Maria Larsson Department of Psychology, Stockholm University, Frescati Hagväg 14, SE-106 91 Stockholm, Sweden (E-mail: maria.larsson@psychology.su.se)

Lene Løkken University of Oslo, Box 1904 Blindern, 0317 Oslo, Norway

Svein Magnussen Department of Psychology, University of Oslo, Box 1094 Blindern, 0317 Oslo, Norway (E-mail: s.j.magnussen@psykologi.uio.no)

Annika Melinder Department of Psychology, University of Oslo, Box 1094 Blindern, 0317 Oslo, Norway (E-mail: a.m.d.melinder@psykologi.uio.no)

Agnes Cathrine Moestue University of Oslo, Box 1094 Blindern, 0317 Oslo, Norway

Lars-Göran Nilsson Department of Psychology, Stockholm University, SE-106 91 Stockholm, Sweden (E-mail: lgn@psychology.su.se)

Jerker Rönnberg Department of Behavioural Sciences and the Swedish Institute for Disability Research, Linkøping University, S-581 83 Linkøping, Sweden (E-mail: jr@ibv.liu.se)

Mary Rudner Linkøping University, S-581 83 Linkøping, Sweden

Hubert D. Zimmer Department of Psychology, Saarland University, Postfach 151150, D–66041 Saarbrücken, Germany (E-mail: huzimmer@mx.uni-saarland.de)

Foreword

During the academic year 2003–2004, an international group of cognitive psychologists was invited to the Centre of Advanced Study (CAS) at the Norwegian Academy of Science and Letters in Oslo. The editors of the present volume, whose proposal "Towards a comprehensive model of human memory" had been selected by CAS, organized the group. Being of modest size in comparison with advanced study centres in many other countries in Europe and the USA, it is the policy of CAS to invite groups rather than individual researchers to ascertain that the fellows of CAS share a familiar scientific milieu during their stay. The editors spent the entire academic year at CAS; the other members of the group joined CAS for periods of varying duration depending upon individual work schedules, and all of us assembled for joint workshops four times during the year. CAS provides office facilities and administrative support, but leaves the individual groups free to organize their work. The groups may choose to proceed in terms of parallel individual projects, collaborate on a joint project, or a mixture of both. The memory group decided on the latter solution, and the present volume is the result of the joint effort.

It soon turned out, as it often does in the course of a project in progress, that the focus of the project changed from a "comprehensive model" to "everyday memory". Representing a broad range of research portfolios, a joint interest of the members of the group was the application of basic research to memory in everyday contexts, and precisely because of the range of interests, we decided that a volume written by the group might cover topics that are not usually covered by books on human memory. The present volume was broadly conceived by the editors and planned in detail by the entire group in the initial workshops, during which the various chapters were assigned to author teams. In the final versions, a couple of the author teams recruited collaborators who originally were not associated with CAS (Chapters 2 and 7). Choices of themes, as well as chapter drafts, were discussed in joint sessions. Thus, the present volume should be considered a shared responsibility of the group.

In writing the book we had in mind the general reader of cognitive psychology and memory, a reader interested in how memory works in everyday situations, familiar with the basics of current psychology of cognition but not necessarily familiar with the technical details of the research. Yet, the book does not abstain from going into details when required or introducing new ideas and viewpoints. As a textbook it might be useful for courses targeting everyday memory and those discussing limits and applications of current memory research.

We thank CAS for the unique opportunity to bring together this distinguished group of fellow memory researchers under exceptionally favourable conditions. We will always remember the friendly and relaxed atmosphere at CAS; the interesting daily lunches interacting with the other research groups, and the late dinner parties of the memory group at the beautiful premises of the Academy of Science. Warm thanks go to the staff at CAS – Unn Haaheim Hagen, Maria Sætre, Marit Finnemyhr Strøm and scientific director Willy Østreng – for enthusiastic support. We also thank the University of Oslo for granting us a sabbatical leave out of turn.

Finally, we thank the editors and the reviewers of Psychology Press for advice, help and support, and for constructive and helpful comments on the various chapters of the book.

Svein Magnussen and **Tore Helstrup**
Oslo, April 2006

Introduction

Svein Magnussen and Tore Helstrup

During the four decades that have passed since the "cognitive revolution" in psychology, research on human memory has grown extensively, and memory is by now one of the most intensively investigated areas in psychology, and perhaps in neuroscience in general. Cognitive psychology, joining forces with theoretically motivated patient studies of cognitive neuropsychology, and with the brain imaging of cognitive processes by PET and fMRI technology, has produced a wealth of knowledge about the organization of human memory and the brain mechanisms involved in the encoding, storage and retrieval processes. This research is covered by most textbooks on memory and cognitive neuroscience, and will only be touched on in passing in the present volume. The focus of the present volume is on the more general aspects of memory that emanate from examinations of memory in everyday contexts. Thirty years ago, Neisser (1976, 1978) recommended that researchers focus on the relation between the theoretical and the practical questions in the cognitive explorations of memory. In the wake of Neisser's critique, there followed many efforts to examine issues of everyday memory scientifically. Examples of this line of research are studies of autobiographical memory, studies of the memory for past and prospective actions and events, and studies of the memory of witnesses to dramatic and mundane complex events. And gradually, the study of memory in everyday contexts changed from studying the quantity of memory performance – how much is remembered – to studying the quality of the memory performance and the distortions and errors contained in the memory reports. These themes will pop up in several places in this volume.

In planning the book, it soon became clear that we should not aim to cover all aspects of everyday memory, but rather to cover some aspects of everyday memory that are not covered by other texts, reflecting the research interests and expertise of this particular team of authors. We have selected memory domains where the members of the project group at the Centre of Advanced Study (CAS), at the Norwegian Academy of Science and Letters 2003–2004, have the research background required to match the questions of everyday memory with the corresponding laboratory research. The answers to a large-scale survey study, cited in Chapter 1, suggest a folk psychology of everyday memory. The chapters reviewing and discussing relevant everyday memory research demonstrate some overlap but also some disagreements between scientists and lay people. Where there is agreement, science may serve to explain why common sense is right; where there are disagreements, research may correct folk psychology.

The ideas we have and the ways we think about memory will guide us, not only in scientific research, but also in the choices and decisions we make in everyday life about the possibilities and limitations of development and change, in ourselves and in others. We know something about how memory researchers think about memory, but we know little about the ideas and opinions that people have in general. There are two ways of finding this out: We can ask people what they believe about memory or we can examine how people talk about memory. Chapter 1 does both, analysing first the memory metaphors of daily language and of science, and second, discussing the results of a large-scale public opinion poll carried out during the planning stage of this book. In this study, a representative sample of 1000 adult Norwegians were asked some of the questions about memory that memory researchers are frequently asked privately in social settings, and by the media. The three chapters closing the volume follow up the themes introduced by the opening chapter. Chapter 11 discusses meta-cognitive aspects of memory, the planning and monitoring of learning, and memory challenges, controlled by our own conceptions of cognitive capacities and limitations. Chapter 12 reports the results of a study of the relationship between beliefs about the capacity of own memory performance and the actual memory performance on relevant memory tasks, measured in the ageing population, and Chapter 13 concludes the volume by introducing a new memory metaphor, the concept of memory pathways. The metaphor is based on the observation that episodic memories sometimes simply pop out, at times against one's will and wishes, while at other times they can be surprisingly hard, or even impossible, to get at, even when one knows that these memories are not lost.

Four chapters on types of memory and five chapters on individual and social factors in memory follow the opening chapter. Starting with some typical problems of cognition and memory in everyday life – reading assembly instructions supplied with flat-packs of furniture from a major Nordic furniture distributor – Chapter 2 discusses different ways of using visual information, examines different cognitive systems for processing such information, and looks specifically at visual aspects of memory and thinking. A similar approach is taken in Chapter 3, which, following a discussion of how people perceive and understand action events, goes on to examine research on memory for actions, in particular whether we remember actions in the same way that we remember visually or verbally presented information. Chapter 4 deals with an aspect of memory that has received little attention in cognitive psychology, olfactory memory, and discusses the possible usefulness of olfactory memory tests in forensic contexts, especially with children. The eyewitness angle is followed up in Chapter 5, which reviews research on the development of autobiographical memory and presents a new model of memory development.

Everyday memory episodes may be recorded privately or under social conditions, and retrieved privately or under social conditions. Social context factors may thus affect memory encoding as well as retrieval, and social factors may or may not be reflected in the content, quality and accuracy of episodic memory. Chapter 6 on collaborative memory examines the theoretical and practical implications of research on the episodic memory performances by dyads and small groups, guided by the question of whether we remember better or worse when tested with fellow eyewitnesses. Chapter 7 discusses how memory illusions and false memories may arise in everyday contexts under the influence of social factors.

It is a common observation that people like to reminisce about their common past, but there is little systematic research on the dynamics of this activity. Chapter 8 presents research based on a new questionnaire constructed to measure proneness to reminiscence. Chapter 9 takes a different approach to individual differences in memory, discussing various conceptions of memory skill and different types of memory expertise, with examples from several areas that are usually not covered in treatments of expertise, such as visual learning, orienteering and speech reading. And what happens when memory fails? This is the topic of Chapter 10, which discusses different types of compensatory mechanisms, used by special populations of people who for various reasons have memory problems.

The authors of this volume come from six different countries; thus illustrations of everyday memories could be drawn from and checked against different sociocultural and linguistic backgrounds. The illustrations cited were chosen to be representative of everyday situations we all are familiar with, but there is, in many of the chapters, a distinct Scandinavian-European leaning in the choice of illustrative examples – examples that might be novel for the general reader. That should not be a disadvantage.

REFERENCES

Neisser, U. (1976). *Cognition and reality*. San Francisco: Freeman.

Neisser, U. (1978). Memory: What are the important questions? In M.M. Gruneberg, P.E. Morris, & R.N. Sykes (Eds.), *Practical aspects of memory*. London: Academic Press.

1   What do people believe about memory and how do they talk about memory?

Svein Magnussen, Tor Endestad,
Asher Koriat and Tore Helstrup

Memory is a central part of the brain's attempt to make sense of experience, and to tell coherent stories about it. These tales are all we have of our past, so they are potent determinants of how we view ourselves and what we do. Yet our stories are built from many ingredients. Snippets of what actually happened, thoughts about what might have happened, and beliefs that guide us as we attempt to remember. Our memories are the powerful but fragile products of what we recall from the past, believe about the present, and imagine about the future.

Schacter, 1996, p. 308

INTRODUCTION

A Norwegian newspaper (Dagbladet, Magasinet, 27 March, 2004) recently told the story of Dodo, a young man of Asian origin who in January 2003 woke up on the freezing ground in a small village in Switzerland with his well-equipped rucksack nearby, stuffed with expensive clothes and a money belt containing $5000, but no identity papers or tickets and with absolutely no personal memory. Dodo wandered around in Europe for some weeks, and somehow managed to travel to Oslo, Norway, for reasons he cannot explain; there he is currently being studied at the University Hospital. His memory loss of the time before he woke up in Switzerland is massive; he has no idea who he is, and he did not recognize his own face in the mirror. He has even lost his native language – he speaks heavily accented English but not any Asian language. All he has is a picture of a young girl, taken in Paris, but he has no idea who she is. Dodo's memory now goes back roughly a year – the rest is speculation. The only thing he knows about himself is that he smokes Camel and likes pop music. "I was nobody", Dodo says, "Now I tell myself I was born one year ago".

The story of Dodo, fanciful as it may seem, illustrates well the central role of memory in human life. This young man has lost not only his personal past – his autobiographical memories – but he has also lost large parts of his general knowledge of the world and even his ability to speak his native language.

Thus, the systems or forms of memory that we term episodic and semantic memory are, in Dodo's case, heavily affected. True, there is more to memory than general knowledge and the recollection of personal episodes, but episodic memory is assigned a special role in human life. Episodic memory is unique in that memories are associated with a place and a time, an association that even if incorrect gives the memories a sense of personal historical truth, and contributes to the person's self-identity. Episodic memory is, in the words of Tulving (2002), the only known example of a process where the arrow of time is turned back and the past can be re-experienced. While some form of episode-like memory may be demonstrated in non-human primates (Hampton & Schwartz, 2004), genuine episodic memory is probably unique to humans as it may depend upon linguistic capacities. Without episodic memory, the mental representation that psychologists call the self – the organization of personal memories in a historical context – is lost. Apparently this is what has happened to Dodo.

Dodo suffers from the condition of retrograde amnesia. That is, he has lost his memory in the sense people usually use the term memory. When we talk about memory in everyday life we refer to the recollection of private experiences and facts we have learned about the world. But obviously Dodo remembered many things; he remembered what cigarettes were for, the workings of photographic equipment, he understood the value of money, was able to buy food, and mastered the skill of travelling by public transport. So he could make use of many of the things he had learned. This type of selective memory impairment, which has been reported in many patients exhibiting large individual differences in memory profiles, is the main evidence cited by memory researchers in support of the idea that memory, rather than being a single cognitive process or system, is a collective term for a family of neuro-cognitive systems that store information in different formats (Schacter, Wagner, & Buckner, 2000; Tulving, 2002).

Varieties of human memory

Most current taxonomies of human memory (see Figure 1.1) distinguish between several forms of memory. For example, most memory researchers agree that in addition to episodic-semantic memory, which supports explicit recollection of previous episodes and previously acquired knowledge, there exists another system that allows previous experiences to express themselves directly but implicitly, as for example in skill learning, emotional conditioning and perceptual learning. These distinctions will be further discussed and elaborated in subsequent chapters, and will only briefly be reviewed here.

Motor learning is responsible for all the procedural skills that we have acquired throughout life, from knowing how to eat with a fork and knife (or sticks) to the mastery of swimming, bicycling or driving a car, as well as the advanced skills of playing billiards or playing a saxophone. Memory is

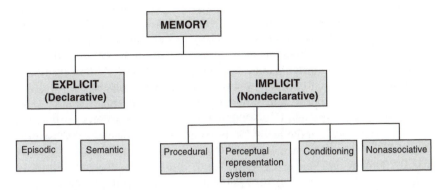

Figure 1.1 A taxonomy of human memory systems.

implicit in the sense that the effects of previous experiences and exercises manifest themselves directly in behaviour; the individual training sessions may be vaguely remembered or may be completely inaccessible to conscious recollection, but the mastery of the skill is there. In a broad sense, motor skills also include what is referred to as procedures – linguistic as well as academic and social skills.

Conditioning represents a basic memory system (Squire & Kandel, 1999) that, in humans, is particularly important in tying emotional reactions to external stimuli or situations. For example, in phobic reactions, anxiety is triggered by the phobic stimuli but the person is typically not aware of the learning episodes in which the connection between the emotion and stimulus was established. Similarly, a piece of music, or a specific odour, may evoke romantic feelings without an accompanying experienced memory episode.

Perceptual learning, or the perceptual representation system, enables us to perceive the world as consisting of meaningful entities, because in order to produce a perceptual experience, on-line sensory signals must join stored representations, and this linking is part of the perceptual process itself. To see is to recognize, or to realize that you do not recognize.

We could go on to list a variety of identified memory types or typical memory tasks. One reason why many memory researchers were led to postulate the existence of separate memory systems is that lesions to the brain may impair some forms of memory while leaving other forms intact; such dissociations have been described for several memory systems.

An important feature of the memory-systems concept is the idea that the various systems store information in different formats, and that the information stored in one format is not directly translatable into others. This implies that the information stored in one system is not immediately accessible to other systems. Assuming that the memory systems operate independently and in parallel, this would imply that most experiences are recorded and stored in parallel in different formats, and can be accessed with the assistance of several memory systems working in concert (Tulving, 2002). Memory researchers disagree, however, as to whether the distinction between episodic and semantic memory indeed reflects separate systems or only different manifestations of one and the same system. When memory is tested in the laboratory, it may be difficult to distinguish episodic from semantic memories. Most memories will contain aspects of both. For example, when a particular picture is recognized as having been presented earlier, is it because the participant *remembers* it or because the participant *knows* that it was there? In the first case it would be episodic memory, in the second it might be semantic memory that governs the choice – or perhaps it is guessing based on yet another *implicit* memory system? Tulving and Schacter (1990) identified *priming* as a separate memory system in implicit memory. In priming, the person's performance on a specific recognition or production task is facilitated (or inhibited) by the previous presentation of related information.

This idea has also been debated, however. There is little disagreement between memory researchers that human memory covers a vast array of memories of different types, and that some of these can be functionally lost because of failures of systems or processes while others remain intact. There is an ongoing discussion, however, as to whether memory is a set of systems or a set of processes or classes of memory operations (Bowers & Marsolek, 2003; Foster & Jelicic, 1999; Tulving, 2002). The treatment of human memory in everyday contexts in this book is neutral with regard to this debate.

The importance of memory in human life is testified by the widespread public interest in memory-related questions. It is a popular theme in party conversations: Many people wonder about memory either because they notice absentmindedness or forgetfulness in everyday life, or because they have relatives who have become disoriented or have bizarre memory problems. The reliability of memory and eyewitness reports is discussed in the media. Articles on memory-enhancing techniques are frequently published in the press, "therapeutic" groups and techniques for recovering near-birth memories are advertised, and topics such as memory and emotion are among the most popular ones for visits to neuroscience websites (Herculano-Houzel, 2003) – just to mention a few examples. People have various ideas about memory, about how we remember and why we forget, and about ways to improve memory. These ideas are sometimes disclosed in the way we speak about memory – the metaphors of memory. A question of interest is whether the folk psychology of everyday memory constitutes just a set of loose metaphors, or are these metaphors actually based on firm common sense? If the latter is true, then to what extent has modern memory research exchanged old metaphors for new ones, which today are invading everyday memory conceptions? In what follows, we discuss lay beliefs about memory, focusing first on the way people talk about memory, and then looking at the specific ideas people have about memory.

HOW WE TALK ABOUT MEMORY –
MEMORY METAPHORS

In attempting to understand memory, scientists as well as laymen are forced to try to describe something that is not directly observable. We are aware of the processes that take place during learning, and of the processes that take place in attempting to search for a piece of information in memory, but we have little access to the processes that mediate between encoding and retrieval. In order to make sense of the phenomena to which we have little access, both laypeople and researchers tend to use metaphors and analogies borrowed from the physical world. The use of metaphors is very widespread in communication: When describing a man's bravery we might say "he is a lion" or if he is coward, "he is a mouse". What is physical and known is used to describe what is abstract or unknown. This use of analogies and metaphors is not only characteristic of everyday communication; memory researchers sometimes also resort to metaphors in communicating their ideas. Furthermore, these metaphors also guide them in formulating their questions and designing their experimental paradigms. In his classic article on reaction time research, Saul Sternberg (1969) described a process termed "memory scanning". In a task used to investigate that process, Sternberg had people study lists of letters or digits and then indicate whether a subsequently presented target letter or digit had been included in the study list. Implicit in the Sternberg paradigm is the notion that a list, represented as a mental image, is processed by something like a beam scanner, a mechanism that searches the image in order to carry out the task of recognition. The scanner metaphor accords with participants' post-experimental reports of what they did in order to perform the task, and is commonly described by laypeople in terms of the notion of a memory "search". "Wait a moment; I need to search my memory for that name."

Metaphors are quite frequent in everyday descriptions of memory. However, as illustrated by the previous example, memory researchers also use metaphors to guide investigations. The metaphor in the Sternberg case is not just an "as if" conceptualization of a phenomenon. By utilizing the metaphor, Sternberg postulated a mechanism that could either operate the scanner or examine the content of memory, but could not do both at the same time. He further assumed that it takes a fixed amount of time to switch from one operation to the other; each step of encoding and matching takes a certain time for each item in the list. If scanning involves searching the list of items one at a time, the pattern of reaction times would be different to that if all items were scanned simultaneously. Thus, the metaphor, when specified, permits scientists to derive testable hypotheses; the metaphor serves as a working model for scientific tests (Fernandez-Duque & Johnson, 1999).

In many cases, the metaphors used by scientists are simply ways to talk about and think about phenomena at a pre-theoretical stage. Many such metaphors have been proposed to guide our understanding of memory. Thus, memory has been compared to a wax tablet, an encyclopaedia, a muscle, a telephone switchboard, a computer and a hologram (Roediger, 1980). Theorists have proposed core-context units, cognitive maps, memory tags, kernels and loops (Underwood, 1972). Common to most memory metaphors, in science and in everyday life, is that they are based on the idea of an organized space; a physical store of some sort. This space might have a structure of networks with nodes or paths or hierarchies with localizations and classifications. The nodes or localizations may represent verbal, perceptual, propositional or other entities of memory. These metaphors affect both the scientific investigation of memory and how we talk about and understand memory in everyday life.

One can talk about "storing" memories, "searching" them and "accessing" them. Memories and thoughts can be "organized", memories that have been "lost" can be "looked for" and, if we are lucky, they can be "found". More broadly, ideas in our minds are described as objects in a space, and the mind is a place that keeps "things". We can "keep" ideas "in mind", or ideas might be in the "front" or at the "back" or on "top" of our mind, or in the dark corners or "dim recesses" of the mind. They can be difficult to "grasp" or encounter difficulties "penetrating" into our mind. We even speak of people as of being "broad", "deep" or "open" minded whereas others are "narrow, "shallow" or "closed". Metaphors like these imply that humans think and talk of memory processes in terms of concrete, physical analogues. The Norwegian word for memory, "*hukommelse*", derives from the word "hug", which has as its etymological origin a name for a small bag in which to keep important things when travelling.

The physical store metaphor implies that anything that has entered the store will remain there until it is removed. One might fail to retrieve a piece of information from memory but it is nevertheless available there; an idea reflected, for example, in Tulving and Pearlstone's (1966) distinction between availability and accessibility. The metaphor has inspired speculative theories that memories might disturb us and create psychological problems, without conscious awareness, and it implies that the important areas to look at for explanations of poor memory performance are linked to encoding and retrieval, rather than to the memory store in itself.

A good example of how metaphors might provide us with ideas on how memory works is the muscle metaphor, first suggested by Woodworth (1929). According to this view, memory can be trained and developed in more or less the same way as muscular systems can be trained. Just as muscles have strength, memories can be regarded as varying in strength. Muscles can gain or lose strength. Can memory too? This is still a moot question that nonetheless has instigated much theorizing and empirical research on learning and memory. Everyday memory statements like "my brain works slowly today", "ask me again when I am not so worn out", or "I feel sharp" all suggest an organ metaphor of memory.

Metaphors like these are widespread both in everyday language and in science. But because metaphors tend to highlight certain aspects of an issue while hiding others, the metaphor chosen will steer research in a certain direction. In the following section we discuss some of the most prominent metaphors in current memory research. Memory metaphors will be encountered in several of the following chapters, and new ones will be introduced (see, for example, Chapter 13).

The theatre metaphor

The theatre metaphor can be traced to David Hume (1939–40/1978): "The mind is a kind of theatre, where several perceptions successively make their appearance; pass, re-pass, glide away, and mingle in an infinite variety of postures and situations. There is properly no simplicity in it at one time, nor identity in different; whatever natural propensity we may have to imagine that simplicity and identity. The comparison of the theatre must not mislead us. They are the successive perceptions only, that constitute the mind, where these scenes are represented, or of the materials, of which it is composed" (p. 253). The metaphor accords with Hume's meta-theoretical empiristic stand, in which the mind is conceived as a stage at which mental processes take place along associative links rather than being guided by an active agent.

In the scientific study of cognition, theatrical analogies have continued to guide research. Mental phenomena have been regarded as representations ("*Vorstellungen*") that are displayed in front of inner perceptions of thoughts, analogous to the way a work of art is staged before an audience. Accordingly, to remember is viewed as a representation of events or knowledge, and conscious awareness resembles a spectator who is only partly aware of what is going on "backstage" or below awareness. The theatre metaphor provides a rich analogy, inviting inferences about the mind, and allusions to the theatre metaphor persist in memory research. A script in the theatre is a recipe of the prescribed actions of actors during the performance. According to Schank and Abelson (1977) scripts are "long-term memory representations of some complex event such as going to a restaurant". The idea is that people record in memory a generalized representation of events they have experienced and these experiences are invoked, or retrieved, when a new event matches an old script. An important feature of a script is that it is a structure that reduces the burden on memory for all details of events. At the same time it represents a framework or context within which new experiences can be understood and a variety of inferences can be drawn to complete the understanding of a new event (Abbott, Black, & Smith, 1985).

In everyday language, the terms schemata and scripts are rarely used. This is not surprising, because schemata and scripts are assumed to function without conscious awareness. We suggest, however, that expressions such as "we are programmed to behave in this way", "it is difficult to stop giving tips after being abroad", or "I have to get back to my routine", point towards a folk realization of script-like structures. The script notion belongs to a class of models with emphasis on the constructive nature of memory.

The multiple store metaphor

By conceiving memories as being like physical objects and the mind as operating on programs in multiple stores, the multiple store model has guided theoretical research on memory over the last 40 years. Inspired by the rapidly developing computer technology, the emerging information-processing psychology proposed a distinction between a primary short-term store and a secondary long-term store (e.g., Atkinson & Shiffrin, 1968; Waugh & Norman, 1965), in addition, a separate transient sensory store was recognized (Sperling, 1963). The short-term store is assumed to hold information over a short period of time. During this time the information has a certain probability of being transferred into the long-term store. In the earlier models this transfer was linked to the kind of processing that was performed on the information. Maintenance rehearsal was considered to be a holding operation, whereas elaboration rehearsal would increase the probability that information became transferred. The long-term store was thought of as unlimited. Retrieval of information from the long-term to the short-term store was conceived of as a re-presentational process, with long-term stored information temporarily activated in a short-term working memory space.

Although the idea of distinct memory stores has a long history, it received its strongest impetus from the computer metaphor and from the various memory stores that are installed in computers. This has had implications for how researchers conceptualized the kind of units that are stored in memory. Emphasis has been on verbal, word-like material, with units not unlike those found in high-level computer programs, and a number of stores have been suggested (Tulving, 1972). One implication of this conceptualization is that memory traces are viewed as static structures with active processes working on information in the stores. For example, to retrieve is to locate a memory and select the appropriate information. Memories are viewed as complete, with all information in a trace available simultaneously.

The store metaphor has inspired laboratory research to the extent that the Atkinson and Shiffrin model is often called "the modal model" for human memory. Atkinson and Shiffrin outlined the model, allowing for the inclusion of a multitude of stores and substores, with various control processes connected to the stores. The model has been a huge success in accounting for the available empirical findings, but the price has been that the model is difficult to refute. As a metaphor it has served more like a conceptual framework than a strict theory to be tested for its precise propositions.

One of the important features of the store model is that it implies limited capacity. It is impossible to conceive of a physical store that would not be filled up at some point in time. Thus, the metaphor has implications for how we understand the forgetting process. A common misconception is related to assumptions about short-term storage. In everyday language we sometimes hear statements like "I cannot remember what happened yesterday because my short-term memory is no longer working properly", suggesting that the general public has picked up the idea of distinct memory stores, but not in the same way that memory researchers meant. The departure from scientific conceptions derives, perhaps, from the lack of introspective access to cognitive mechanisms like forgetting over the short term. People tend to understand short-term memory as extending over hours and days, and long-term memory as being measured in months and years. Interestingly, several researchers have recently begun to go along with this folk conception of short-term memory, and debate the usefulness of the modal model.

The multiple store metaphor calls for some mechanism by which information "moves" between stores. In some descriptions, the multiple store metaphor implies that when information is "transferred" from short- to long-term memory (through some sort of "stamping"), it no longer exists in short-term memory. This is an example of a situation in which researchers employ a metaphor without committing themselves to all the features of that metaphor. An alternative solution, sometimes proposed, is that of implicating a kind of copy-machine at the interface between stores: A "copy" of the information is transferred from short- to long-term memory or vice versa. But a metaphor may also force researchers to consider aspects of the metaphor that have not been intended. For example, if short-term memory is a gateway to long-term memory, we must change our conception of short-term memory to accommodate the observations that information in long-term memory appears to be represented in a variety of formats, such as acoustic, visual and enactive.

Multiple store models have also been criticized for not capturing important memory phenomena, such as false and incomplete memories. Although these models have inspired ingenious laboratory experiments, researchers concerned with observing memory phenomena in "real life" have questioned the usefulness of storage-inspired research. Neisser (1967), for example, proposed a different metaphor to account for everyday memory.

Memory as archaeology

The store metaphor has not reigned alone. A metaphor covering other aspects of memory was developed by Bartlett (1932), who observed that episodes are remembered in terms of common, culturally shared knowledge. This common knowledge, Bartlett believed, had a structure similar to schemata. The basic assumption of the metaphor is that remembering is a reconstruction of memories from available information rather than a verbatim reproduction of the contents of memory. The assumption is that from the memory of a general theme plus a few memory details we reconstruct the event, much like a story that has been told. "Schema refers to an active organization of past reactions or of past experiences, which must be supposed to be operating in any well-adapted organic response" (Bartlett, 1932, p. 213).

Neisser subsequently adopted the constructionist view, suggesting that remembering ". . . likens the constructive work of a palaeontologist who uses a small set of bone fragments as well as general knowledge about dinosaurs and other similar animals in order to reconstruct and piece together the skeleton: out of a few bone chips, we remember the dinosaur" (Neisser, 1967, p. 285), and more recently Schacter consider the constructive view of memory to provide a useful framework for conceptualizing a variety of phenomena observed in the study of memory intrusions and memory distortions (Schacter, 1996, 2001; Schacter, Norman, & Koutstaal, 1998).

Archaeology is the study of the cultural past. From pieces and fragments the archaeologist reconstructs old cultural constructions. The past is thus regained (cf. Proust, 1932/1938). In analogy, the study of memory might be conceived as an attempt to reconstruct a person's individual memories, with remembering viewed as a process of reconstruction, like putting together a whole picture based on a few pieces. This process entails "filling in" of the missing parts, a process well known in perceptual processing (Spillmann & De Weerd, 2003; Spillmann, Otte, Hamburger & Magnussen, 2006). The implications of the archaeology metaphor, then, are that memory traces are incomplete as opposed to the "all-in-one" structure of the store model. Remembering is a process where memories are constructed rather than found or selected. To remember is a question of the fit between an event and what is remembered (Koriat & Goldsmith, 1996a).

Memory as perception

A third metaphor proposed as an alternative to the store model is the depth of processing model (Craik & Lockhart, 1972). Within this framework, memory is regarded as a product of perceptual processing. Rather than assuming different stores processing different kinds of information, Craik and Lockhart suggested that it is the level of information processing that characterizes memories. Preliminary, shallow levels deal with sensory and physical properties and pattern recognition, while deep levels of processing deal with meaning and more elaborate processing. Craik and Lockhart argued that this model was a literal interpretation compared to the meta-phorical store model. However, the model can be easily understood in terms of metaphors of orientation or metaphors of trace strength. Like items being embedded on a riverbank leaving traces, levels of processing can be seen as more or less "deep" imprints of the items to be remembered. At this point a few comments on the metaphorical aspects of the trace concept are appropri-ate. Although memory researchers at times refer to "memory traces" as if they should be observable entities, the concept of a memory trace was intro-duced as a hypothetical construct, as a metaphor of a memory's material substrate. No one has ever observed a memory trace, and perhaps never will, despite the impressive advances of modern brain imaging, Thus, there is some dissatisfaction with the concept of a "memory trace", particularly when it implies a "full-blown entity" (see below).

The correspondence metaphor

Koriat and Goldsmith (1996b) pointed out that the storehouse metaphor invites an interest in the number of stored items. An effective store is one that can contain many items, that can retain these items for long periods of time, and that allows easy access to the stored items. Memory, then, is evaluated in terms of its *quantity* – how much is retained, how much is lost. Quantitative aspects of memory are frequently of great interest in everyday life but often, in forensic contexts, the focus is on accuracy. When people disagree on questions of memory, it is frequently a question of nuances: was her dress green or blue, was the party arranged in the beginning, in the middle or at the end of which month? A high-quality memory is more faithful to the remembered event than an inferior memory is. However, sometimes people remember events that never happened (see Chapter 7). The assessment of memory correspondence should therefore start with the output – what the person reports – rather than with the input – what actually happened. An output-bound assessment reflects the accuracy of what is remembered – how much of what the person reports did in fact occur. Indeed, in many real-life situations, such as in court, there is greater concern with the accuracy of the report than with the amount of information reported.

The value of memory metaphors

There is no way to prove a metaphor wrong or right. Metaphors are conceptual tools that help us to understand phenomena in a more or less appropriate way (see Koriat & Goldsmith, 1996b). They provide conceptual frameworks within which memory phenomena can be analysed and explained. Metaphors highlight some aspects of a phenomenon and hide others. Thus scientific research may be guided by metaphors, but may miss important attributes of a phenomenon. Both the multiple store metaphor and the archaeology metaphor capture important aspects of memory. The store metaphor has guided laboratory research whereas the archaeology metaphor survives in the context of everyday memory. The two types of metaphor reflect fundamentally different ways of thinking about memory. As Koriat and Goldsmith (1996b, p. 186) argue, "even if agreement could be reached about the memory phenomena that ought to be studied, the experimental procedures, and the appropriate context of enquiry, the two metaphors would still imply different perspectives for looking at and interpreting the data". However, nothing prevents us from being inspired by more than one metaphor; each metaphor has its own advantages and its focus of convenience.

WHAT PEOPLE BELIEVE ABOUT MEMORY

So far we have discussed the metaphors of memory that seem to be used in everyday communication about memory. These metaphors capture some of the beliefs that people hold about the working of memory. We turn next to an examination of some of the specific beliefs that people have about memory. These beliefs concern questions such as whether children's memories are less trustworthy than those of adults, the old-age impairment in memory, and why we forget. Beliefs are important because they govern social behaviour, explicitly or implicitly (Fazio & Olson, 2003; Ferguson & Bargh, 2004), and the ideas people have about memory guide their judgements and evaluations in many circumstances. Memory researchers have studied such questions for more than a century. To what degree have the results of scientific research been incorporated into the psychological folklore? Do people typically nurture ideas about memory that conflict with the current knowledge, or do they have scientifically realistic ideas about memory?

To obtain some tentative answers to these questions, the authors of the present volume carried out a nationwide telephone survey, asking three representative samples of 1000 adult Norwegians a set of general questions about memory (Magnussen et al., 2006). In selecting questions for study, the authors drew on their personal experience as memory researchers regarding the type of questions they had been asked by news media, the popular media and by individuals in informal settings.

The questions that were included in the survey are those that have been addressed in various chapters of this book. For some of the questions, science has a reasonably good answer, for some we have a tentative answer, and for some we still do not have an answer, although the individual researcher may express definite opinions. When people talk about memory, they usually refer to episodic and semantic memory; the recollection of the things they have learned and the experiences they have had. In the survey we avoided complicating the issue by calling people's attention to the various forms of memory that scientific taxonomies define, but accepted the assumption that memory is simply what people believe it is.

Table 1.1 lists some of the questions included in the survey (Magnussen et al., 2006). The first two are questions that memory experts are frequently asked privately and by the public media. First: Do you think it is possible to train memory? Weekly magazines frequently publish articles on memory enhancing techniques – how to improve your memory. Most of these rephrase the various mnemonic techniques, but sometimes the mnemonic techniques are presented as suitable for overall memory improvements. The scientific literature on memory expertise indicates that superior memory of experts in the various fields, such as chess and sports, is limited to domain-relevant information and does not carry over to other fields (Kimball & Holyak, 2000; see also Chapter 9). Thus scientists would tend to answer that memory cannot be trained in this way. However, when we probed this "muscle" concept of

Table 1.1 Some of the questions included in the survey

Question	Response %				
	A	B	C	D	E
Physical exercise makes the body stronger. Do you think it is possible to train memory in an analogous fashion? (a) Yes (b) No	94	4			
Most people receive large amounts of new information each day. Do you think there is a limit to the amount of information the brain is able to remember? (a) Yes (b) No	69	26			
Why do we forget? (a) Memory fades like tracks in snow (b) Memory capacity is limited and old memories are pushed out (c) New memories block old memories	31	9	38		
When small children tell about events they have experienced, do you think they remember better, as well as, or worse than adults? (a) Better (b) As well as (c) Worse	38	37	18		
Many people tell about memories from early childhood years. How far back in time do you believe people can remember? (a) 1 yr (b) 2 yr (c) 3 yr (d) 4 yr (e) 5 yr >	4	14	29	21	29
It is generally believed that the memory gets worse with age. When do you think the decline starts? (a) < 30 yr (b) 30–50 yr (c) 50–60 yr (d) 60–70 yr (e) > 70 yr	19	35	19	12	3
Sometimes people become witnesses to dramatic events. Do you think the memory for such events is (a) worse, (b) as good as or (c) better compared to the memory for everyday events?	70	12	11		
Sometimes people who have committed murder claim to have no memory of the crime. Do you think such memories can be repressed and (a) that the perpetrators are telling the truth, or (b) do you think they are lying?	39	45			

Notes
The table is based on data reported by Magnussen et al. (2006). Note that the percentages do not add up to 100; the missing value is the "uncertain" category.

memory, the results showed that an overwhelming majority of the participants believed that memory capacity can be trained in this way, and only 2% were sceptical.

Closely linked with the idea of memory exercising is the question of whether long-term memory has a limited storage capacity or whether it is limitless. This question specifically hinted at the storehouse metaphor of long-term memory (Koriat & Goldsmith, 1996b; Koriat, Goldsmith & Pansky, 2000), illustrated by the textbook anecdote of the professor of ornithology who stopped learning the names of his students because each time he learned the name of a student, he forgot the name of a bird. However, memory science is not aware of any limit to the amount of information the brain is able to store and retrieve; we do not know how many memories each of us have stored. Most classical papers on the memory for large amounts of information suggest that human long-term memory is virtually limitless (Landauer, 1986; Standing, 1973), and the wide distribution of memory-activated neural circuits in the brain (Cabeza & Nyberg, 2000), together with the evidence that the brain is continuously forming new synapses and even growing new neurons (Gould, Reeves, Graziano, & Gross, 1999), suggest a system that might be expanding according to need. Whatever memory researchers believe, the results of the survey show that two-thirds of the respondents believed there is a limit to memory, with a substantial minority disagreeing (Table 1.1).

If memory capacity is limited, is this the reason why we forget? We gave a third sample of participants three alternatives, illustrating theoretical explanations of forgetting, that are well known to memory researchers: first, memories fade like ski tracks in snow (in Norway everybody practises winter sports and cross-country skiing); second, memory capacity is limited and old memories are pushed out of the store; and third, memories do not disappear but new memories block the retrieval of old memories. A large minority of the respondents could not decide. The remaining respondents were divided between the fading and interference explanations, with a very small minority believing in the limited storehouse space explanation (Table 1.1). Thus, it appears that even if the majority of respondents believed in a limited storage capacity of memory, this is not believed to be the main cause of forgetting. Perhaps the answer to the capacity question may be based on a more philo-sophical approach to the question – for example, the brain contains a limited number of neurons – rather than on a belief in what are the limiting factors to one's own memory.

How does memory change across the lifespan? This is one of the main topics in current memory research, and the basic facts about the develop-ment, maintenance and decline of the various memory systems are now fairly well known (see also Chapters 5 and 12). We asked our respondents four questions. First, what do you believe about the memory of small children as compared with the memory of adults? The scientific evidence is quite clear: The memory reports of children at the age of 3–6 years are basically correct if children are questioned properly, but contain fewer details than do the stories of older children and adults (Fivush, 2002; Peterson, 2002; see Chapter 5). On this question, the public does not agree with science. A large majority believed that small children's memory is at least as good as the memory of adults, and close to 40% of the respondents even thought it was better. This is an interesting result, given most parents' experience that small children do not remember much of what has happened in kindergarten, and if asked, the answer is often "we played". Perhaps the belief in children's memory skills derives from our selective memory of the infrequent episodes where the child displays an extraordinary good recollection of a detail of a long-forgotten event; it is perhaps the surprising memory performance that we remember rather than the daily sketchy stories from the classroom (Magnussen et al., 2006).

How well do adults remember their own early childhood? The concept of childhood amnesia refers to the inability of adults to remember anything from the early years of life, usually before 3 years of age, depending upon their language capabilities at the time (Simcock & Hayne, 2002; see also Chapter 5). Each of us may nonetheless possess a grey zone with memory glimpses and vague images before genuine episodic memories emerge (Peterson, 2002). Rubin (2000) has published a meta-analysis indicating that a very small proportion of memories can be dated back to the second year of life, and that there is a steady growth in the proportion of memories from that time on. This curve is independent of the age of the informant, which indicates that it is not the time factor in storage – the age of the memory – that determines the fate of early memories. If the beliefs in early memories are influenced by the informant's own childhood memories, they should conform to the empirically established findings – which they did. Very few respondents (1%) believed it was possible to have memories from birth on, and only a few more believed that it was possible to have memories from the first year of life. In fact, the general public is more conservative than science, as more than 50% of the participants believed that no memories were available before the age of 4 years. This might be a little surprising, given the frequent reports about age regression in the popular media and the current popularity of various regression exercises offered in courses, seminars and non-professional therapies. Obviously, the overwhelming majority of the readers and listeners remain soundly unconvinced by such claims.

Episodic memory is most vulnerable in older age. This is the target of many jokes among adults when something has slipped from the mind. Obviously, the expected memory decline is an important part of the adult self-concept. We asked 1000 persons to judge their own memory performance during the last 5 years – whether it had become better or worse – and another 1000 participants to tell us at what age they believed memory started to decline. The results showed interesting discrepancies between the rating of their own memory, the general belief in time of memory decline, and the objective finding from large-scale studies on memory changes in the adult lifespan (Hedden & Gabrieli, 2004; Nilsson, 2003; see also Chapter 12). People have an unduly pessimistic view of their own memory. More than 40% of the respondents aged between 18–29 years reported that their memory had declined, a similar proportion of respondents between 30–44 years reported a decline, and this figure rose to 50% for participants aged 45–59 years and to more than 60% for participants above 70 years of age. However, when a similar sample of respondents were asked when they thought age decline stared, only 6% believed it started before 30 years of age, and more than 50% of the participants, independent of their own age, believed it started after 50 years (Table 1.1). The results of empirical research suggest that the general change in performance on episodic and semantic memory would not be noticeable until after that age. When healthy young to middle-aged people claim to have memory problems, it must be due to misattribution of the normal memory problems all people have, rather than genuine age changes, but probably inspired by the well-known fact that memory declines as a result of old-age degenerative brain diseases, and that memory problems are an early sign of such diseases (Hedden & Gabrieli, 2004; Nilsson, 2003).

On September 10, 2003, the Swedish foreign minister Anna Lindh was stabbed to death in a shopping mall in Stockholm in front of many people. How well will these witnesses remember this tragic and dramatic event later? How well do victims and witnesses to crimes, natural disasters and war remember the events they witnessed? This is a question of the relationship between emotional activation and memory: whether emotional events are remembered better or worse than ordinary events. In the history of science, two positions have been defended by philosophers and psychologists: Emotional memories were strong and vivid, "clinging to the mind" (Augustine, William James) or repressed from conscious recollection (Schopenhauer, Freud), in whole or in part (Porter & Birt, 2001). From a lay point of view, the answer is not obvious. For example, it might be argued that such events are frequently fast moving and that observations are therefore unreliable, or that the drama of the event would lead to emotional activation that might interfere with or block observational capacities and memory encoding. Therefore, the memories of emotional, dramatic events might be dim. Or it might be argued that such memories are so frightening that they are denied access to consciousness. In the terms of psychoanalysis, they become repressed. However, it might also be argued, as many memory researchers do, that emotional activation might act to focus attention and facilitate encoding of attended details, which would lead to enhanced memory for some aspects of the event at the expense of other aspects (Christianson, 1992; Ochsner & Schacter, 2000). This would lead to objectively superior memory for some aspects of the emotional event, and probably a subjectively vivid memory. Both of these aspects of memory might be further reinforced by frequent rehearsal of the event.

The experimental evidence tends to support the latter position. Studies in the flashbulb memory tradition show that memory for dramatic events is as good as, or better than, memory for ordinary events (Christianson & Engelberg, 2003; Talarico & Rubin, 2003), but is subject to similar distortions. Several studies of memory for war experiences, natural disasters and accidents (McNally, 2003) confirm this. The results of the survey show that two-thirds of the respondents agreed with scientists who hold emotional memory to be better, whereas only every tenth respondent answered "worse" on the simple question whether dramatic events were remembered better or worse than non-dramatic events. We also asked, of two different samples of 1000 persons each, questions that were directly aimed at probing the idea that frightening events might be repressed. One question stated that people who have had frightening and dramatic experiences sometimes claim memory loss, and asked the participants to indicate whether they believe that such loss is genuine. The second question specifically mentioned the example of the self-reported amnesic murderer – between 25 and 70% of persons committing violent murders claim to have no memory of the event (Christianson & Merckelbach, 2004; Parkin, 1997) – and asked whether the participants believed that such memory loss was real or faked (Table 1.1). On these specific questions the participants were more divided. A sizeable minority of about 15% in both samples refused to take sides on the issue, and the remaining participants were split. A closer analysis of the data revealed an interesting pattern, namely that the belief in genuine memory loss increased with the number of years of formal education. On the more general question of amnesia for dramatic events, about 30% of the respondents with elementary school education believed in the memory loss explanation compared to 46% of the respondents with a college or university degree. On the question of the amnesic murderer, only 20% of the low-education participants believed they spoke the truth, whereas 45% of respondents with a university degree expressed the belief that the amnesia was genuine (Magnussen et al., 2006).

The idea that traumatic memories are blocked from consciousness can be traced to the psychoanalytic concept of repression, originally formulated to explain the blocking of painful childhood memories from conscious recollection. However, in the psychological folklore this notion has been expanded and applied to the apparent forgetting of adult traumatic experiences such as having committed violent crimes. Psychoanalytically inspired thinking has been absorbed by society, especially by intellectuals, but detached from its theoretical basis and diluted. In Norwegian daily language, the concept of repression has become almost synonymous with forgetting but with special reference to unpleasant memories, such as remembering an appointment with the dentist. So the idea that extremely unpleasant memories can be completely blocked is readily available. The finding that the proportion of participants accepting the idea of repression increased with years of formal education is an indication that the belief derives from intellectual theory rather than from folk psychology. However, the ideas of folk psychology are consistent with science. The concept of repression has been difficult to support empirically (see, for example, Schacter, 2001; Tulving & Craik, 2000), as it does not stand the test of relevant real-life studies of traumatized individuals (Goodman et al., 2003; McNally, 2003). Indeed, trauma-induced psychogenic amnesia is extremely rare, if it exists at all (Christianson & Merckelbach, 2004; Kihlstrom & Schacter, 2000). Rather, studies of war veterans, some of whom may themselves have committed gruesome acts, and of victims to such acts, point in the opposite direction: These memories persist all too well (McNally, 2003).

The wisdom of everyday psychology

In general, the results of the present survey indicate that beliefs about memory among non-scientists in a Western European country are in good agreement in many respects with the findings of normal memory science, but in other respects the beliefs of the public deviate from current scientific knowledge, sometimes in ways that have implications for the interpretation of daily events. The reason for the shared opinions might be found, at least partly, to reflect shared memory metaphors. Where disagreements show up, scientists may have developed, or be on their way to developing, new or revised metaphors (see Chapter 13 for an example). These metaphors need not be more precise; they may leave space for different interpretations and beliefs, as we saw, for example, in connection with the memory training question in our survey.

In this chapter we have argued that memory science is heavily influenced by metaphorical thinking. Everyday memory conceptions are similarly saturated by metaphors. These metaphors help guide our thinking about memory. Although there are certain differences between the metaphors that are common in everyday conversations and those that are implicit in the scientific literature, both types of metaphors reflect accumulated knowledge about memory. What is clear is that each metaphor captures only some aspect of the phenomena of memory, neglecting others. Because metaphors are vehicles of thought that help us think about the phenomena, their worth depends entirely on their utility. There is no objection to entertain a variety of metaphors in order to capture the richness of memory phenomena. In the spirit of Koriat and Goldsmith's (1996b) plea for "metaphorical pluralism", this book attempts to combine metaphors from both the scientific study of memory and everyday conceptions.

REFERENCES

Abbott, V., Black, J.H., & Smith, E.E. (1985). The representation of scripts in memory. *Journal of Memory and Language, 24*, 179–199.

Atkinson, R.C., & Shiffrin, R.M. (1968). Human memory: A proposed system and its control processes. In K.W. Spence & J.T. Spence (Eds.), *The psychology of learning and motivation, Vol. 1*. New York: Academic Press.

Bartlett, F. (1932). *Remembering*. Cambridge, UK: Cambridge University Press.

Bowers, J.S., & Marsolek, C.J. (2003). *Rethinking implicit memory*. Oxford, UK: Oxford University Press.

Cabeza, R.. & Nyberg, L. (2000). Imaging cognition II: An empirical review of 275 PET and fMRI studies. *Journal of Cognitive Neuroscience, 12*, 1–47.

Christianson, S.-Å. (1992). Emotional stress and eyewitness memory: A critical review. *Psychological Bulletin, 112*, 284–309.

Christianson, S.-Å., & Engelberg, E. (1999). Memory and emotional consistency: The MS Estonia ferry disaster. *Memory, 7*, 471–482.

Christianson, S.-Å., & Merckelbach, H. (2004). Crime-related amnesia as a form of deception. In P.A. Granhag & L.A. Strömwall (Eds.), *The detection of deception in forensic contexts* (pp. 195–225). Cambridge, UK: Cambridge University Press.

Craik, F.I., & Lockhart, R.S. (1972). Levels of processing: A framework for memory research. *Journal of Verbal Learning and Verbal Behavior, 11*, 671–684.

Dagbladet. (March 27, 2004). *Magasinet.* http://www.dagbladet.no/magasinet/2004/03/27/39442.html Web page (in Norwegian).

Fazio, R.H., & Olson, M.A. (2003). Implicit measures of social cognition. *Annual Review of Psychology, 54*, 297–327.

Ferguson, M., & Bargh, J.A. (2004). How social perception can automatically influence behavior. *Trends in Cognitive Sciences, 8*, 33–39.

Fernandez-Duque, D., & Johnson, M.L. (1999). Attention metaphors: How metaphors guide the cognitive psychology of attention. *Cognitive Science, 23*, 83–116.

Fivush, R. (2002). The development of autobiographical memory. In H.L. Westcott, G.H. Davies, & R.H.C. Bull (Eds.), *Children's testimony: A handbook of psychological research and forensic practice* (pp. 55–68). Chichester, UK: Wiley

Foster, J.K., & Jelicic, M. (Eds.) (1999). *Memory: Systems, process, or function?* Oxford, UK: Oxford University Press.

Goodman, G.S., Ghetti, S., Quas, J.A., Edelstein, R.S., Alexander, K.W., Redlich, A.D., Cordon, I.M., & Jones, D.P.H. (2003). A prospective study of memory for child abuse. New findings relevant to the repressed-memory controversy. *Psychological Science, 14*, 113–118.

Gould, E., Reeves, A.J., Graziano, M.S.A., & Gross, C.G. (1999). Neurogenesis in the neocortex of adult primates. *Science, 286*, 548–552.

Hampton, R.R., & Schwartz, B.L. (2004). Episodic memory in nonhumans: What, where and when. *Current Opinion in Neurobiology, 14*, 192–197.

Hedden, T., & Gabrieli, J.D. (2004). Insights into the ageing mind: A view from cognitive neuroscience. *Nature Neuroscience Reviews, 5*, 87–96.

Herculano-Houzel, S. (2003). What does the public want to know about the brain? *Nature Neuroscience, 6*, 325.

Hume, D. (1978). *A treatise of human nature* (H. Nidditch, Ed.). Oxford, UK: Clarendon Press (Original work published 1939–40).

Kihlstrom, J.E., & Schacter, D.L. (2000). Functional amnesia. In F. Bollner & J. Grafman (Eds.), *Handbook of neuropsychology, Vol. 2* (2nd ed., pp. 409–427). Amsterdam: Elsevier.

Kimball, D.R., & Holyak, K.J. (2000). Transfer and expertise. In E. Tulving & F.I.M. Craik (Eds.), *The Oxford handbook of memory* (pp. 109–122). Oxford, UK: Oxford University Press.

Koriat, A., & Goldsmith, M. (1996a). Memory as something that can be counted vs. memory as something that can be counted on. In D.J. Herrmann, C. McEvoy, C. Hertzog, P. Hertel, & M.K. Johnson (Eds.), *Basic and applied memory research: Practical applications, Vol. 2* (pp. 3–18). Hillsdale, NJ: Lawrence Erlbaum Associates, Inc.

Koriat, A., & Goldsmith, M. (1996b). Memory metaphors and the real life/laboratory controversy: Correspondence versus storehouse conceptions of memory. *Behavioral and Brain Sciences, 19*, 167–228.

Koriat, A., Goldsmith, M., & Pansky, A. (2000). Toward a psychology of memory accuracy. *Annual Review of Psychology, 51*, 481–537.

Landauer, T.K. (1986). How much do people remember? Some estimates of the quantity of learned information in long-term memory. *Cognitive Science, 10,* 477–493.

Magnussen, S., Andersson, J., Cornoldi, C., De Beni, R., Endestad, T., Goodman, G., Helstrup, T., Koriat, A., Larsson, M., Melinder, A., Nilsson, L.G., Rönnberg, S., & Zimmer, H. (2006). What people believe about memory. *Memory, 14,* 595–594.

McNally, R.J. (2003). *Remembering trauma.* Cambridge, MA: Harvard University Press.

Neisser, U. (1967). *Cognitive psychology.* New York: Appleton-Centruy-Crofts.

Nilsson, L.-G. (2003). Memory function in normal aging. *Acta Neurologica Scandinavia, 107* (Suppl 179), 7–13.

Ochsner, K.N., & Schacter, D.L. (2000). Constructing the emotional past: A social-cognitive neuroscience approach to emotion and memory. In J.C. Borod (Ed.), *The neuropsychology of emotion* (pp. 75–143). New York: Oxford University Press.

Parkin, A.J. (1997). *Memory and amnesia.* Oxford: Blackwell Publishers

Peterson, C. (2002). Children's long-term memory for autobiographical events. *Developmental Review, 22,* 370–402.

Porter, S., & Birt, A.R. (2001). Is traumatic memory special? A comparison of traumatic memory characteristics with memory of other emotional life experiences. *Applied Cognitive Psychology, 15,* 101–117.

Proust, M. (1932/1938). *A la recherché du temps perdu.* Paris: Gallimard.

Roediger, H. (1980). Memory metaphors in cognitive psychology. *Memory and Cognition, 8,* 231–246.

Rubin, D.C. (2000). The distribution of early childhood memories. *Memory, 8,* 265–269.

Schacter, D.L. (1996). *Searching for memory: The brain, the mind, and the past.* New York: Basic Books.

Schacter, D.L. (2001). *The seven sins of memory: How the mind forgets and remembers.* Boston, MA: Houghton Mifflin.

Schacter, D.L., Norman, K.A., & Koutstaal, W. (1998). The cognitive neuroscience of constructive memory. *Annual Review of Psychology, 49,* 289–318.

Schacter, D.L., Wagner, A.D., & Buckner, R.L. (2000). Memory systems of 1999. In E. Tulving & F.I.M. Craik (Eds.), *The Oxford handbook of memory* (pp. 627–643). Oxford, UK: Oxford University Press.

Schank, R.C., & Abelson, R. (1977). *Scripts, plans, goals and understanding.* Hillsdale, NJ: Lawrence Erlbaum Associates, Inc.

Simcock, G., & Hayne, H. (2002). Breaking the barrier? Children fail to translate their preverbal memories into language. *Psychological Science, 13,* 225–231.

Soyland, A.J. (1994a). After Lashley: Neuropsychology, metaphors, promissory notes. *Theory and Psychology, 4,* 227–244.

Soyland, A.J. (1994b). *Psychology as metaphor.* London: Sage.

Sperling, G. (1963). A model for visual memory tasks. *Human Factors, 5,* 19–30.

Spillmann L., & De Weerd, P. (2003) Mechanisms of surface completion: Perceptual filling-in of texture. In L. Pessoa & P. de Weerd (Eds.), *Filling-in: From perceptual completion to cortical reorganization* (pp. 81–95). Oxford, UK: Oxford University Press.

Spillmann, L., Otte, T., Hamburger, K., & Magnussen, S. (in press). Filling-in from the edge of the blind spot. *Vision Research.*

Squire, L., & Kandel, E.R. (1999). *Memory. From mind to molecules.* New York: Freeman.

Standing, L. (1973). Learning 10,000 pictures. *Quarterly Journal of Experimental Psychology, 25*, 207–222.

Sternberg, S. (1966). High-speed scanning in human memory. *Science, 153*, 652–654.

Sternberg, S. (1969). Memory scanning: Mental processes revealed by reaction time experiments. *American Scientist, 57*, 421–457.

Talarico, J.M., & Rubin, D.C. (2003). Confidence, not consistency, characterizes flashbulb memories. *Psychological Science, 14*, 455–461.

Tulving, E. (1972). Episodic and semantic memory. In E. Tulving & W. Donaldson (Eds.), *Organization of memory*. New York: Academic Press.

Tulving, E. (2002). Episodic memory: From mind to brain. *Annual Review of Psychology, 53*, 1–25.

Tulving, E., & Craik, F.I.M. (2000). *The Oxford handbook of memory*. Oxford, UK: Oxford University Press.

Tulving, E., & Pearlstone, Z. (1966). Availability versus accessibility of information in memory for words. *Journal of Verbal Learning and Verbal Behavior, 5*, 381–391.

Tulving, E., & Schacter, D. (1990). Priming and human memory systems. *Science, 247*, 301–306.

Underwood, B.J. (1972). Are we overloading memory? In A.W. Melton & E. Martin (Eds.), *Coding processes in human memory* (pp. 1–23). Washington, DC: Winston.

Waugh, N.C., & Norman, D.A. (1965). Primary memory. *Psychological Review, 72*, 89–104.

Woodworth, R.S. (1929). *Psychology*. New York: Holt.

2 Visuospatial thinking, imagination and remembering

Hubert D. Zimmer, Svein Magnussen,
Mary Rudner and Jerker Rönnberg

MAKING USE OF VISUAL INFORMATION

One of the exceptional accomplishments of humans is their ability to visually imagine objects and mentally simulate events that are physically absent. Sometimes this is done from memory, such as when we imagine the appearance of the beach where we have spent our last holiday. Sometimes it is done by combining perceptual input with stored knowledge, e.g., while inspecting rooms offered for sale, we consider their usefulness and may mentally furnish them. However, sometimes we even imagine doing things that we are unable to perform in reality, such as making a perfect drive at the first tee of the golf course. These tasks are the topic of this chapter, in which we present a selection of results concerning visuospatial thinking and imagining, and their explanation. We tackle the question of which mental device might perform these tasks and what kind of neural structures are likely candidates for them. We also discuss the construct of visuospatial working memory and its relationship with imagining and short-term memory. In order to provide an impression of the kind of tasks we refer to, we start with a few examples taken from everyday contexts.

A lively example of imagination is the understanding of fiction. Anyone who has ever followed a murder mystery on the radio will immediately agree that imagination plays an important role in understanding. Take the following example: A short person sneaked around the corner in a ducked posture. Silently, he slipped through the broken window into the dimly lit hall. In the back of the hall, one could sense the contour of the safe underneath the dirty curtain blowing slowly in the wind. The feeble beam of the torch threw light on the left-hand wall, revealing the ugly picture of a bloodhound baring its teeth. On the floor, a number of toppled chairs were scattered around a table, on top of which one could see an ashtray filled with butts and a dozen smudged beer glasses.

If we asked you, as the reader of these sentences, to describe your introspection, you would probably report that you imagined the place of this crime and that you actively constructed a visual image of the hall. This is the reason why following a radio play of a murder mystery is a much more powerful imaginative experience than watching a movie on TV. In the laboratory, these tasks are investigated under the heading of the construction of a situation model during text processing (e.g., Betgen & Dupont, 2003), and the role of imagery in this task.

The assembly instructions often supplied with do-it-yourself furniture are another example of the use of visuospatial imagery in everyday life. Flatpacks of furniture from a major Nordic furniture distributor usually enclose pictorial assembly instructions. For example, the pieces of a bookcase are depicted alongside the screws and devices that fit these elements together. Arrows indicate where the connections should be placed and a series of diagrams demonstrates the sequence of actions that needs to be performed in order to build the bookcase. In order to understand these pictures, it is necessary to transform visual images, to rotate constructional components mentally, to compose part images to new units, and to adopt different vantage points on the structural parts. In such situations, visual imagery ability is a key feature for the successful solution of the practical problem.

Comparable processes in the laboratory are mental construction tasks or mental synthesis tasks (Pearson & Logie, 2000). Participants are faced with a series of figures and are instructed to combine these figures into new ones. Other examples are spatial reasoning in navigation tasks (e.g., how to get from A to B) and technical reasoning (e.g., working out the direction that the lever of a machine consisting of a number of connected gears will move in, when the first wheel turns anticlockwise).

Two memory tasks are final illustrations of visuospatial thinking. Recall the hotel rooms of your last vacation. Where was the furniture located? Was the TV to the left or to the right of the mini bar? Was it on top of it or was it mounted at the wall? If it was at the wall, at what height was it? Can you draw the floor plan of the bathroom? In order to give answers to these tasks, you retrieve visual information from long-term memory and you probably imagine the rooms. You mentally inspect the "internal pictures" and "read out" the visual details from the images. The images are used in these tasks in a similar way to visual input during perception.

A somewhat different example can be found in the concentration game (Schumann-Hengsteler, Demmel, & Seitz, 1995). Several pictures are scattered in front of you. They are facing down, so you cannot see what symbol is depicted on them. If it is a difficult version of the game, the symbol is an arbitrary configuration of patterns in different colours and textures. The symbol is only briefly visible when the picture is turned during a move. There are two copies of each picture, and the task is to find the pair of images. With each turn, one learns the location of one symbol, and one has to keep this location in memory in order to return to it and hence to its picture when the second element of this pair is found in a later move. Both tasks are visuospatial memory tasks, but whereas visual long-term memory dominates the first one, spatial short-term memory is more important in the second.

In the laboratory, such performances are investigated in experiments on sensory memory. Participants learn visual stimuli and are later requested to remember the pictures. If the duration is only a few seconds, we are speaking of a working memory task and of long-term tasks when the delays are longer. Memory is tested for the depicted object or its sensory details, e.g., colour, size, orientation or location (e.g., Engelkamp, Zimmer, & de Vega, 2001). Very often it is a recognition experiment in which participants see old and new pictures, and they have to decide whether or not they have already seen the current picture. This is basic research, but it obviously has practical implications. An example of an everyday task in which detailed perceptual knowledge is usually relevant is eye-witnesses' memory. Witnesses, for example, have to specify the visual appearance of a suspect.

COGNITIVE SYSTEMS FOR VISUOSPATIAL THINKING AND REMEMBERING

Given that visual imagery plays such an important role in thinking, it is not remarkable that specialized mental (and neural) devices have been proposed for processing visuospatial information. Nearly 50 years ago, it was already being postulated that humans possess both a verbal and a non-verbal representation system. In the context of this dual-code theory (Paivio, 1971), many experiments on visual imagery and memory were performed between 1960 and 1990, which supported the concept of an independent visual-imaginal memory system. The core assumption of the dual-code theory is that humans possess two mental systems: verbal and non-verbal. The verbal system represents and processes verbal information. It is used for language understanding and production and it processes information serially. In contrast, the non-verbal system was thought of as being image-based and it was assumed to process pictorial information. Although in its early stages the non-verbal system was not restricted to the visual domain, experimental research almost exclusively investigated visual information. In many experiments, specific effects of mental images and memory advantages of encoding by imagination were demonstrated (for a review see Paivio, 1986).

People, for example, remember more when they generate images to verbal input, and associative information in particular is enhanced if the items to be associated are integrated into a unique mental picture (e.g., Bower, 1970). The memory advantage of imagining was explained by the activation of visual components (pictogens) in addition to verbal components (logogens), which are regularly activated during language processing. The memory advantage of pictures compared to words was explained in the same way – hence the concept of dual coding. Words are processed in the verbal system, which is responsible for language processing. Pictogens should be processed in a modality-specific visual system. The latter system processes visual-imaginal information and is also the memory store for this type of information.

In dual-code theory, therefore, no distinction was made between working memory and long-term memory. Verbal and visual systems performed both functions. The main focuses of this research were differences in the outcomes of verbal and visual encoding. The processes themselves, for example encoding and transforming of images, were not a central topic. This was different for those researchers who were interested in imagery, who wanted to know more about the processes themselves. A leading scientist in this field is Stephen Kosslyn, and his model of visual imagery within the visual buffer had a powerful impact on research.

The visual buffer as an imagery device

From the outset, Kosslyn suggested (e.g., 1975, 1981) that visual-imaginal processes operate on a visual buffer that has analogue qualities. The buffer – a blackboard metaphor – is spatially organized; it represents pictorial information in a quasi-analogue format "depicting" visual information in a medium that is functionally spatial. The latter means that processes running within this (mental) buffer behave as if they were operating in a medium with physical spatial qualities. These analogue qualities were highly controversial, leading to the so-called imagery debate (Kosslyn, 1981; Pylyshyn, 1973, 1981), and they remain controversial today, as recent publications demonstrate (Pylyshyn, 2002).

Researchers agree that human performance when solving visual imagery tasks looks like processes operating in a spatial medium. However, not all scientists accept that these effects are caused by structures that have functional spatial characteristics, i.e., that these characteristics are built-in features of the representation. In contrast, the spatial qualities might be simulated by mental processes in a completely different format. Kosslyn (1994) claimed that the debate is resolved because we now understand better the neural systems that perform these operations (Kosslyn, Ganis, & Thompson, 2001), but even this remains controversial (Pylyshyn, 2003). Postulating that the medium has spatial qualities demands results located at the physiological level (Zimmer, 1996), and such evidence is still lacking. However, in the context of this article, the effects of imaginal processes are more relevant than their explanation, for which reason we do not discuss this topic any further. On the other hand, we will later demonstrate some of the spatial effects; these provide insights into the characteristics of visual-imaginal processes, which can regularly be observed when people think about spatial information.

The visual-spatial sketch pad (VSSP)

Another approach that is relevant in the context of imagination is the tripartite model of working memory (Baddeley & Logie, 1999). In this model, it is postulated that within working memory two processing subsystems have to be distinguished – a verbal phonological loop and a visuospatial sketchpad – and both are controlled by a third system, the central executive (Baddeley &

Hitch, 1974). In this tradition, researchers mainly search for global evidence for the two independent subsystems. In consequence, nothing is said about the format of representation, but many experiments were performed with the aim of demonstrating that visual memory is different from verbal working memory. For that purpose, visual memory is investigated in the context of a verbal secondary task such as articulatory suppression (repeatedly articulating a word), or of a visual secondary task. A large body of results supports the independence of these two components. A verbal secondary task does not interfere with a visual main task but with a verbal main task, and a visual secondary task does vice versa (see Logie, 1995, for a review). For example, mentally inspecting an image and pointing to spatial locations interfere with each other (Brooks, 1967). This suggests that some components of visual working memory have limited capacities.

Visual cache versus inner scribe

More recently, the components of the visuospatial sketchpad have been further differentiated. Logie (1995) suggested that the VSSP comprises two components: a passive visual cache maintaining visual sensory information (colour, shape and static locations) and an active inner scribe maintaining dynamic visual information (movements). One reason for this differentiation is the selective interference between visual and spatial main tasks – for example, remembering colours versus remembering spatial sequences – and between visual and spatial secondary tasks – viewing pictures versus tapping a spatial sequence (Klauer & Rao, 2004; Logie & Marchetti, 1991). The visual cache temporarily stores visual material, and the inner scribe works as a refresh mechanism on this information. The inner scribe is necessary for remembering sequential spatial information, but it is also involved in the manipulation of visuospatial images (Logie, 2003; Logie & Salway, 1990). While the cache is closely linked to visual perception, the inner scribe is linked to the central executive and to planning movements (Logie, Engelkamp, Dehn, & Rudkin, 2001).

Although this suggestion sounds reasonable, it suffers from the flaw of ill-defined relationships between components, tasks and processes. For example, on the one hand, the inner scribe operates on visual information, while on the other hand the central executive should also perform this task, e.g. in an imagery situation. Similarly, it remains unclear where the manipulated visual information is stored. Logie and colleagues explicitly stated that the visual cache is not comparable to the visual buffer discussed by Kosslyn, and it therefore is not involved in a visual imagery task. The cache only stores the results of the manipulation; it does not execute it (Pearson & Logie, 2000). Hence, an additional representation that holds the image during manipulation ought to exist. Pearson therefore explicitly postulated a visual buffer as a third component (Pearson, 2001). The buffer represents consciously experienced visual images and is a workspace for manipulating images, whereas the transformation processes themselves are tied to the central executive. In contrast, Logie (2003) speculated in the light of some data from neglect-patients that the medium for visual-imaginal processing might have been damaged in some of these patients, and he mentioned the visual cache as a possible candidate. We therefore have to recognize that our actual knowledge of visual-imaginal processes is still rather limited. We know that these processes are different from verbal processes, but we only partially understand how they function and how visual working memory is operating (Baddeley, 2003). We also know that the capacities of visual and spatial processes are different and that they are limited, but unfortunately inconsistent results about which factors constrain visual working memory have been reported.

Capacity limitations of visual working memory

On the one hand, it was suggested that the number of entries in visual working memory is limited to four. Humans can remember about four simultaneously presented visual features, e.g., colours, but also four integrated objects, e.g., shapes in a specific colour and orientation (Luck & Vogel, 1997; Vogel, Woodman, & Luck, 2001; but see Wheeler & Treisman, 2002, for a different result). It was therefore assumed that visual working memory can keep four object files in view (Schneider, 1999). An object file is the representation of a perceived object that binds features provided by the sensory organs. Such a file is opened when an object is being attended to and it is updated when the perceptual input changes, for example when the object moves. Hence, the content of an object file represents the actual features of a perceived object, which includes its actual position in the environment, and four files can co-exist.

However, there is also evidence for another limit of one entry (Phillips, 1983; Walker, Hitch, & Duroe, 1993). This figure is usually inferred from enhanced memory for one specific item in a series of pictorial stimuli. Without additional instruction, it is the last picture of a series, but it can also be another serial position if that picture was marked as relevant during presentation. This suggests that the visual working memory can only hold one item at a time, but we should note that the stimuli in these experiments were complex and meaningless visual features.

Finally, a third kind of limitation is not caused by the number of items, but by their perceptual qualities. This is a structural interference due to visual similarity and complexity. Given that verbal recoding is prevented, working memory performance is reduced if the items to be remembered are visually similar to each other (Walker et al., 1993). The same mechanisms might explain the reduced performances reported when additional visual material was presented during retention of visual information in short-term memory (Klauer & Rao, 2004; Logie, 1986). In other words, if, during maintenance, the same type of material that has to be maintained is encoded, memory performances are reduced relative to an empty interval.

Such a structural interference was also reported in a number of imagery tasks. Visual imagery mnemonics were less efficient if, during maintenance, dynamic visual noise was present (e.g., Quinn & McConnell, 1996). In the dynamic visual noise condition, a checkerboard is presented and the fields of this board are randomly coloured in black and white with a high rate of change. Such a result is expected when visual imaginal and perceptual processes partially share the same structures (Farah, 1985). In line with this assumption, it was observed that verbal visual input (reading) impaired simultaneous mental imagery processes. When "perceptual" assertions are verified such as "the front wheels of a farm tractor are smaller than the rear wheels", a visual image should be inspected. Such assertions were thus less efficiently solved using a visual than an acoustic sentence presentation (Glass, Eddy, & Schwanenflugel, 1980). If that is a general principle, performing a visual perceptual and an imaging task at the same time is not recommended. However, it should be noted that, in contrast to these results, in some studies unattended visual input did not impair performance. For example, memory for locations of objects was not reduced when, during maintenance, additional not-to-be-remembered material was presented (Andrade, Kemps, Werniers, May, & Szmalec, 2002; Zimmer, Speiser, & Seidler, 2003). A critical variable for the absence or presence of interference effects might be whether the task requires active or passive usage of images (Cornoldi & Vecchi, 2000).

Visuospatial processing capacities

The above-mentioned approaches can be classified as system-oriented because they aim at finding domain-specific devices dedicated to the processing of specific types of information. Besides the system-oriented approach, capacity- or process-oriented approaches exist. In this tradition, scientists do not search for independent processing systems but for independent processing "capacities". These usually use individual differences and their correlations with visual or verbal tasks as indicators of independent processing facilities. Verbal processing capacity, for example, is measured as reading span, which is a serial word recall embedded in a sentence comprehension task (e.g., Daneman & Merikle, 1996). Participants have to verify sentences and then repeat one previously specified word from each sentence. The span is the number of words that can be repeated in their correct order without mistake. Visuospatial processing capacity, for example, is measured as spatial processing span (Shah & Miyake, 1996). In this task, participants are presented with a series of upper-case letters in different orientations (rotated and/or mirror reversed). For each picture, they have to decide whether this letter is mirror reversed or not. At the end of the series the spatial orientation of each letter also has to be indicated – more exactly, the spatial position of the top of the letter. The length of the series increases from trial to trial (from 2 to 5). The spatial span score is the total number of spatial orientations recalled in correct serial order.

Much of this research addressed the question whether processing capacities are domain general or domain specific. Considering the distinction between verbal and visual processes, the results suggests domain-specific capacities (Shah & Miyake, 1996). The answer is less clear for different processes within the visuospatial domain (Miyake, Friedman, Rettinger, Shah, & Hegarty, 2001). Interestingly, these results do not only support independent resources but have also supplied evidence for the relevance of visuospatial processing in several everyday tasks such as comprehending descriptive texts or spatial navigation. For example, individual abilities in visuospatial processing are correlated with performances in text comprehension if spatial models have to be constructed (Friedman & Miyake, 2000), and they are related to route learning (Garden, Cornoldi, & Logie, 2002; Marco, 2000).

This research also demonstrates that the introduction of part systems is not sufficient to explain everyday behaviour. We also have to consider inter-individual differences in the efficiency of the processing systems. Observed performance depends on the type of processes that are demanded by the task *and* on individual capacities. For example, elderly people are clearly impaired in a visual working memory task if active manipulations are necessary, but not if passive maintenance is sufficient (Vecchi & Cornoldi, 1999; for a detailed discussion of the active-passive dimension, see Cornoldi & Vecchi, 2000).

Neuropsychological evidence for non-verbal (working) memory systems

Although they differ in detail, the aforementioned models share the assumption of domain-specific processes and therefore probably the assumption of different neural processing structures. Hence, brain imaging techniques are obvious for testing these assumptions, and in fact, these data have confirmed that different neural structures are active according to the sensory modality of the stimuli and the task. This was frequently shown for perception (for a brief review, see Kanwisher, 2003). It has also been shown for imagery (Kosslyn et al., 2001; Thompson & Kosslyn, 2000) and has been demonstrated for working memory too (Jonides, Lacey, & Nee, 2005; Postle, Druzgal, & D'Espositio, 2003). These neuropsychological studies have greatly increased our understanding of the structures of visuospatial (working) memory. First, the already mentioned distinction between verbal and visual working memory was substantiated. Verbal tasks have a tendency to activate the brain areas in the left hemisphere more than in the right hemisphere, and visual tasks do vice versa (for a review, see Smith & Jonides, 1997). However, visual tasks can be further subdivided. From research on perception, we know that visual information processing is split into a dorsal (where) and a ventral (what) stream. The dorsal path – from occipital to parietal cortex – processes spatial information, whereas the ventral path – from occipital to temporal cortex – processes object information. Similarly, in working memory and imagery these two paths can be distinguished (Rämä, Sala, Gillen, Pekar, & Courtney, 2001; for a review see Wager & Smith, 2003).

However, not only brain-imaging data support this differentiation; electrophysiological data also suggest it. When a configuration of objects is presented, event-related potentials showed a different topography during maintenance in an object task than in a spatial configuration task (Bosch, Mecklinger, & Friederici, 2001; Mecklinger, 2000). It has also been shown that the amplitudes of the potentials are graded according to memory load. With an increase in memory load, amplitudes in the object task turned more negative at the mid-frontal electrodes, while in the spatial task the load effect was observed at the parietal electrodes (Mecklinger & Pfeifer, 1996). These results demonstrate that the electrophysiological effects really have something to do with working memory. We have recently been able to demonstrate similar results during maintenance in auditory spatial tasks – remembering locations of sound sources – and we observed this activation at the same parieto-occipital location as with visual input (Lehnert, Zimmer, & Mecklinger, 2006). This suggests a common supramodal spatial processing component. This assumption is further supported by the observation that auditory-spatial and visuospatial memory loads draw on the same capacity (Lehnert & Zimmer, in press). Independent of the modality of the input, it therefore seems that humans hold in a common spatial working memory a representation of the spatial environment, and that for this purpose occipitoparietal structures are used – probably triggered by frontal brain areas.

In view of these results, one should expect visual working memory to be located in parietal, and perhaps occipitotemporal, neural structures. If the visual buffer is a device for generating images, one might also expect activation of neural structures used in early vision, e.g., the secondary visual cortex (Kosslyn & Thompson, 2003). In their meta-analysis, Mazard and colleagues (Mazard, Tzourio-Mazoyer, Crivello, Mazoyer, & Mellet, 2004) reported that all kinds of imagery shared an occipitotemporal and occipitoparietal network. The superior parietal cortex, including the intraparietal sulcus, displayed higher activation during spatial tasks, while anterior areas in the ventral stream showed stronger activation during object tasks. Trojano et al. (2002) required their participants to judge the angle of the hands of a clock, which is a spatial imagery task, and they observed posterior parietal activation. The intraparietal sulcus in particular may be important for these tasks (Bosch et al., 2001). Even in language comprehension, it could be shown that the intraparietal sulcus is active in an imagery condition, e.g., when high-imagery sentences were being processed (Just, Newman, Keller, McEleney, & Carpenter, 2004). Furthermore, this structure was active when a stimulus retrieved from memory was mentally rotated (Jordan, Heinze, Lutz, Kanowski, & Jäncke, 2001), and it partially overlaps with structures that are active when rotating a perceived stimulus (Just, Carpenter, Maguire, Diwadkar, & McMains, 2001).

Interim conclusion

In summary, much evidence exists in support of the assumption that visuospatial processing is independent of verbal processing, and that domain-specific visual working memory structures are dedicated to this visual-imaginal process. Three components have been suggested as being parts of this working memory: (1) a visual cache, which is best described as a passive, temporary storage of visual information; (2) a visual buffer, which is a workspace for the transformation of images; and (3) an inner scribe, which is an active process that in our view can be understood as a series of shifts in spatial attention (cf. Zimmer & Speiser, 2001). Baddeley (2000) even discussed a fourth component that might also be involved in visuospatial processes. He suggested an episodic buffer, which comprises units that actively bind components from different modalities. This latter component is a kind of active episodic memory. The problem with this mainly system-oriented approach is that the list of components might not be exhaustive, nor does it specify how these components process visuospatial information, e.g., during mental rotation, mental scanning, or image generation. From a different perspective (e.g., Cowan, 1999), one might identify in these components information that is used by different (visual-imaginal) processes. The information remains active as long as it is used, i.e., bound to a specific type of process. Hence, in order to understand visual working memory it is necessary to understand the visual-imaginal processes and their specific characteristics.

From this point of view, we suggest that visual working memory is a network of neural structures in which those (posterior) areas that process the information are also the areas that maintain the information (Ungerleider, Courtney, & Haxby, 1998). However, because the stimuli have to be maintained, retrieved, re-integrated or manipulated, additional (frontal) structures are relevant. Working memory is therefore an anterior-posterior network (Fuster, 1997; Ruchkin, Grafman, Cameron, & Berndt, 2003), in which the anterior parts are the control structures of the posterior parts that represent the information. Within the posterior parts, ventrotemporal areas seem to be more relevant for objects and parietal areas for spatial information – with a special relevance of the intraparietal sulcus. However, other than visual modalities are relevant; other domain-specific areas are of importance (Kosslyn et al., 2001).

Finally, with active spatial rehearsal in working memory, spatial attention also plays an important role (Zimmer & Speiser, 2001). In general, spatial attention changes the visual representation of stimuli attended to (Postle, Awh, Jonides, Smith, & D'Esposito, 2004) and it may therefore influence working memory. The presence or absence of this attentional process might be the difference between active and passive storage. In imagery tasks, the control of action might play a similar role because attention is necessary for effective control of voluntary actions. This would explain why visual working memory is linked to the central executive, as has been suggested by some authors (e.g., Pearson, 2001).

REMEMBERING VISUAL-SENSORY INFORMATION

What happens with visual information that is no longer in working memory? Classical studies show that we have a truly extraordinary memory for pictures of natural scenes. Standing, Conezio, and Haber (1970) presented their subjects with 2560 pictures, each of which was viewed for 5–10 seconds, and found that 90% of the pictures were correctly recognized after an interval of 1½ days. Standing (1973) expanded this experiment to include 10,000 pictures and probed the recognition memory 2 days after the learning session. He found the recognition performance to be somewhat lower than with smaller sets, but when recognition was plotted against the size of the study set, there was no indication of a ceiling effect or even a levelling-off of memory performance, indicating an almost limitless capacity for remembering natural pictures. Comparisons between pictorial memory and memory for equally long lists of words show that pictorial memory is distinctly superior to verbal memory (Standing, 1973). This picture superiority effect (Shepard, 1967) has been replicated many times with simple memory designs for both individual and group recollection (Weldon & Bellinger, 1997), but is subject to a number of experimental factors (Vaidya & Gabrieli, 2000) and appears to be a property of explicit but not of implicit memory (Kinjo & Snodgrass, 2000; Weldon & Coyote, 1996). How can we explain the build-up of such a reservoir of pictorial and presumably ecological real-life visual memories? One possibility is indicated by the results of experiments on so-called perceptual memory, in which researchers study the memory for perceptual details.

Memory for perceptual features

In these experiments, the memory for visual features such as colour, orientation, spatial frequency or size, contrast and the speed of moving objects is measured using a design borrowed from visual psychophysics, in which the fidelity of our perceptual discriminations is measured in terms of thresholds. A discrimination threshold is the smallest difference between two stimuli that can be detected with a statistical probability midway between chance and perfect performance. In perceptual memory experiments, the two stimuli that are compared are separated in time, and the changes in the values of the discrimination threshold in this sort of delayed discrimination task is a measure of how well the information about the first stimulus has been retained in memory.

The results of such experiments have shown that information about elemental visual attributes or single features such as the size, orientation and motion of visual patterns is retained with very high accuracy across memory intervals in the short-term and quasi short-term range of 1 second to 3 minutes (Bennett & Cortese, 1996; Blake, Cepeda, & Hiris, 1997; Lalonde & Chaudhuri, 2002; Magnussen & Greenlee, 1992; Magnussen, Greenlee, Asplund, & Dyrnes, 1990), whereas information about colour and contrast decays across similar intervals (Magnussen, Greenlee, & Thomas, 1996). The memory for colour appears to be particularly poor; there is a sevenfold increase in discrimination threshold across intervals where the memory for spatial frequency (size) remains unaffected, and for some colours there is also a systematic shift in memory (Pérez-Carpinell, Baldovi, de Fez, & Castro, 1998). A number of studies have further shown that the different attributes are represented independently and may be independently accessed in memory (Magnussen et al., 1996; Magnussen & Greenlee, 1997; Xu, 2002), while other studies have shown that features such as shape and colour are stored independently of information about spatial location (Mecklinger, 1998; Vuontela, Rämä, Raninen, Aronen, & Carlson, 1999)

These results have led to the proposal of a special low-level perceptual memory mechanism, organized in a modular fashion and devoted to the storage of single features of visual stimuli (Magnussen, 2000; Magnussen & Greenlee, 1999). Such a feature-memory mechanism might contribute to pictorial memory by storing all the information necessary for the reconstruction of the memory image via the activation of central codes (Damasio, 1989), or it might be a temporary memory mechanism that stores information during the build-up and consolidation of higher-order pictorial representations (Magnussen, 2000). Interestingly, the attribute of colour, which is an unstable attribute in memory, does not contribute much to recognition memory for natural scenes (Wichman, Sharpe, & Gegenfurtner, 2002).

Memory for pictures

However, there is evidence that pure visual representations are less important in ecological visual memory than suggested by this model. First, slightly more complex abstract pictures such as black-and-white or colour block patterns (Cornelissen & Greenlee, 2000; Phillips, 1983), or block versions of naturalistic pictures where the colour and overall spatial structure of the original picture is maintained (Vogt & Magnussen, 2006), are very quickly forgotten. Although such results might be explained by interference or inhibitory interaction in short-term perceptual memory, real-life visual memories and naturalistic pictures would induce similar interference. Thus, although pictorial memory should be poor, it is not. Second, in a recent experiment, Vogt and Magnussen tested the memory for a study set of 400 pictures that had the same motif but were otherwise very different, namely colour photographs of front doors of Norwegian townhouses. They compared two versions of the pictures; the originals, and an edited version where elements such as nametags, signs or flowerpots were removed, and areas of worn-down paint were "repaired". The results of these experiments showed that removal of these small, nonsignificant details that the subjects hardly noticed had a large effect on memory. When tested shortly after the study session, participants who studied and were tested with the original pictures scored more than 80% correct, whereas the participants who studied and were tested with edited images scored around 65% correct, and these differences in memory performance were maintained across 2 weeks of testing.

Thus, it appears that recognition memory for pictures is strongly supported by the number of details or pictorial elements, as if the chance of remembering increases as the availability of possible cues increases. A.G. Goldstein and Chance (1974) argue that to recognize a naturalistic picture you do not need to remember the whole picture – just some elements of it. Informal observations suggest that this is true even for pictures we have seen many times. For example, most people are unable to recollect the background in Leonardo's painting of the Mona Lisa, even if they have seen hundreds of reproductions, but they vividly remember Salvador Dalí's version with moustache – that is, they remember the face with the moustache.

Recent experiments on change-blindness in naturalistic and quasi-naturalistic settings strongly suggest that people attend to only a part of the scene, and that many things go unnoticed. For example, Simons and Levin (1998) showed participants a video of two ladies conversing at a lunch table; the camera switched between the ladies and in each cut a number of changes were made in the arrangement of objects on the table and the ladies' looks, most of which went unnoticed by the participants. Other experiments have shown that people do not notice a person in a gorilla costume crossing a basketball field when they are engrossed in the game, or that the person to whom they are giving directions in the street is different from the person who asked about the direction, when they have been distracted for a moment (Simons & Chabris, 1999).

Perceptual memory for details is thus not the building block of ecological visual memory – the memories of natural scenes. Rather, memory for pictures and natural scenes is based on higher-level representations at the level of object descriptions (Tulving & Schacter, 1990), and picture recognition may be assisted by a number of independent representations of elements of the original scene. It is perhaps this complexity that accounts for the picture superiority effect. Images are supported by many subsystems of memory, whereas words are basically supported by one system. This is a more general version of the dual-coding principle (Paivio, 1995), according to which pictures are remembered better than words because pictorial memory is assisted by both verbal and visual representational systems whereas the memory for words is primarily based on verbal representations.

So what is the low-level perceptual memory mechanism for? Recent studies indicate that at least some of the elementary features of visual stimuli are extremely well retained across intervals of 24 hours (Magnussen, Greenlee, Aslaksen, & Kildebo, 2003), suggesting that it is not limited to short-term memory. Thus, in parallel with the high-capacity pictorial memory, we also have a long-term memory for certain perceptual details. It is the type of memory that allows us to notice immediately that a picture on the wall in the living room has been moved a few centimetres to the left or that one's spouse has put on a couple of kilos. In accordance with this assumption, it could be shown that such visual features influence our recognition of pictures. When we change visual features from study to test the size, orientation, etc. of a picture, for example, recognition of the picture is impaired relative to an unchanged condition (Cooper, Schacter, Ballesteros, & Moore, 1992; Jolicoeur, 1987; Zimmer, 1995; Zimmer & Steiner, 2003; for a review see Engelkamp, Zimmer, & de Vega, 2001). The sensory mismatch can be observed even when the sensory dimension has been declared not to be relevant for recognition. We have recently been able to demonstrate by event-related potentials that this visual mismatch reduces the familiarity of the picture during recognition (Groh-Bordin, Zimmer, & Mecklinger, 2005).

We therefore assume that pictures are represented in memory as a structural description at different levels of detail, including to some degree low-level visual information. However, it is a matter of active encoding so that only a selection of features is represented. Treisman has suggested that features are processed in parallel during perception, but that focal attention is necessary for binding of features (see Treisman, in press, for a review). This would explain why we have extremely good perceptual memory under some conditions, but poorer memory for certain visual aspects under others.

VISUOSPATIAL WORKING MEMORY IN USE

We have discussed several aspects of visuospatial working memory and visual memory in general. Now, we wish to enquire what this working memory is good for and what effects occur when people process information by mental visualization.

Processing visuospatial information

According to Kosslyn, visual images are processed in the visual buffer. For this buffer he has postulated a matrix-like structure with functional spatial qualities. The buffer has a spatial resolution, a specific size, and distances between objects are made explicit in the image representation. The representations in this buffer are processed by the same processes that analyse perceived images, so that we have to consider processes of *mental inspection* within a spatial medium. In many experiments, data were reported that are compatible with this spatial character of images. If, for example, we imagine two objects side by side, and one picture is larger than the other, it takes more time to verify a visual feature of a small than a large picture (Kosslyn, 1975). Similarly, if we mentally "look" at a visual detail in front of an object, and are subsequently asked about a detail to the rear of the object, the response time is a function of the distance we would have to pass through if we really moved around the object (for these and similar results, see Kosslyn, 1980).

Another well-known example is *mental scanning*. People learned a map of a fictitious island and they were asked mentally to scan from a verbally given starting point to another verbally given destination on the imagined map. They were required to push a button when they "arrived" at the destination. Hence, the mental scanning time could be measured. The result was that mental scanning time is a nearly linear function of the Euclidean distance between the locations (Kosslyn, Ball, & Reiser, 1978). This is an often-replicated result. Interestingly, it can also be observed when the maps were not learned from physical maps but only from verbal instructions (e.g., Denis & Zimmer, 1992). This was taken as evidence that people generate spatial mental models from a verbal description of a map. Denis and Kosslyn (1999) speculated that this scanning process is performed by neural structures within the dorsal stream (Kosslyn et al., 2001).

A third example is *mental rotation*. People view two pictures of objects and they are required to decide whether the second picture is a mirror image of the first one. The second picture is rotated by a certain number of degrees relative to the first one. The critical variable is the decision time as a function of the angle between the two pictures. It was observed that decision time is a linear function of the shortest angle of rotation that is necessary to align the two objects, i.e., between 0 and 180 degrees clockwise or anticlockwise (Shepard & Metzler, 1971). When the pictures are presented serially and people know the orientation of the target in advance, the decision time does not depend on the angle. However, when the time between the presentation of the first and second picture is reduced, so that it is too short to allow the rotation to be completed during the inter-stimulus interval, the decision time is a function of the remaining angle (see Finke & Shepard, 1986, for review). Mental rotation, too, should be performed in parietal brain areas (see above). A number of experiments have shown that parietal occipital ERPs became more negative when more rotation was necessary (see Heil, 2002, for a review). Furthermore, the observation that the amplitude of this effect occurs later, when the perceptual quality of the stimulus has been reduced, suggests that this component is really linked to the start of rotation (Heil & Rolke, 2002). However, we should note that it seems to be possible to rotate a figure in two different ways. People can either perform a visual task – they imagine a rotating figure – or they perform an internal action – they mentally manually turn the figure. The latter task activates the primary motor areas (Kosslyn, Thompson, Wraga, & Alpert, 2001).

Imagination as a memory aide

That memory is strongly enhanced if people imagine the information to be remembered has been known for a long time, and it has often been shown in the context of the dual-code theory (for a review, see Paivio, 1986). This way of encoding is therefore used by many mnemonic techniques.

One famous method is the *loci technique*. People select a route that they know perfectly well and that consists of a number of distinct loci, i.e., land-marks. During study, an image that is to be remembered is associated with each landmark. Later in the memory test the subject follows this route mentally, and at each landmark the generated mental picture is retrieved. This technique clearly enhances memory, especially if the order of the items is also relevant (e.g., Roediger, 1980), and it can be efficiently trained even with elderly people, though young people profit more from this method than the elderly (Lindenberger, Kliegl, & Baltes, 1992). The imagery component provides the association between the landmark and a mental picture of the item, and this association is probably based on a common pictorial representation of both elements within the visual buffer. This is supported by a visual interference effect that was observed by Quinn and McConnell (1996), when they combined the loci technique with dynamic visual noise. Visual interference would also explain why this method is more efficient with an oral than a visual presentation of items (DeBeni, Mò, & Cornoldi, 1997).

A related method is *peg-word mnemonics*. In this case, a mental route is not used as a retrieval path, but rather a learned series of peg-words is used. In a training phase, each peg-word is associated with a number, e.g., one is a bun, two is a shoe, three . . . After the learning stage, one can retrieve the words in a fixed order. During study, an image is generated for each item by pairing it with the object used as peg-word. During testing, the image can be used for retrieval. This method is very effective and it is likely that the memory advantage has something to do with visual imagery processes, too, because several experiments have shown that additional visual input causes interference effects (Quinn & McConnell, 1999).

In principle, all these methods make use of an integrated image that "depicts" both components; the cue and the target item. It is therefore hardly surprising that generating images in other types of relational encoding is also an effective encoding strategy. For example, the efficiency of mental images was demonstrated for pair-associate learning (Bower, 1970), and it was shown to be an effective memory aid in associating faces and names (Yesavage, Rose, & Bower, 1983). In the latter case, the phonological structure of the name was transformed into a related word for which an image could be generated, and this image was then associated with a salient feature of the face. Therefore, using visual information during encoding as real pictures or as mental images seems to be a good memory strategy in general.

Visuospatial thinking

In principle, all previously mentioned encoding tasks are in some sense tasks of visuoimaginal thinking. Participants generate images, transform them, inspect or scan them, etc. This is the reason why many of these tasks show a positive correlation with visuospatial processing capacities. In consequence, when participants are instructed to form images in absence of any visual input, brain areas are activated that are usually involved in visual processing (for a brief review, see Kosslyn et al., 2001). However, the level up to which this activation may take place is still a matter of controversy. Activation of parietal structures and of visual association cortex is likely, but it is a matter of discussion whether the primary visual cortex is also activated. For example, Knauff, Kassubek, Mulack, and Greenlee (2000) did not find any activation in primary visual cortex, whereas others did (Kosslyn, Thompson, Kim, & Alpert, 1995; see Kosslyn et al., 2001 for further references). On the basis of their meta-analysis of studies on visual imagery, Mazard et al. (2004) concluded that early visual structures are involved in imagery if detailed visual features are processed, but that this activation also shows high inter-individual variation.

However, explicit visual imagery tasks are not the only ones in which these imagery abilities are used. We wish to mention briefly only a few conditions in which imagery plays a role during reasoning. One occasion on which visual processes are used is text processing. When people comprehend texts that refer to spatial relationships, they generate something like a spatial model of the situation described (Friedman & Miyake, 2000; Glenberg & McDaniel, 1992). These mental models have spatial characteristics; for example, retrieval of information is a function of Euclidean distance. However, the models do not possess "real" space in a physical analogy because other dimensions, such as categorical structure, also influence retrieval time (Rinck & Bower, 2000; Rinck & Denis, 2004). These mental models are representations of spatial environments incorporating spatial constraints.

Other types of mental representations are models of technical systems. How does a specific machine work, or how do parts of a mechanical apparatus interact? Such questions often form part of technical intelligence tests. In order to solve these tasks it seems to be necessary to "use" these machines mentally and to allow the parts to move. In other words, one is mentally simulating the movements of the functional components of the machine. If that task is processed within visual working memory, one would expect processing to be subject to visual interference, which is exactly what has been observed. Participants were required to infer the motion of a component of a mechanical system when a connected component was moved in a given direction. Performance on this task was specifically lowered when it was combined with a secondary visual task (a memory load caused by remembering the locations of filled cells in a spatial grid; Sims & Hegarty, 1997). Mental animation, therefore, seems to be a task that is solved within visual working memory.

Other kinds of deductive reasoning, e.g., those that permit a visual-imaginal representation of relationships to be made, also seem to draw on visual imagery and hence on visuospatial working memory. It has been suggested that people construct mental models or even concrete mental images of instances for verbally presented reasoning tasks. For this generation process, visual working memory may be the workplace. Knauff and colleagues reported on such tasks in the absence of any visual input activation in an occipito-parietal-frontal network (e.g., Knauff, Fangmeier, Ruff, & Johnson-Laird, 2003; Knauff, Mulack, Kassubek, Salih, & Greenlee, 2002) that included the visual association cortex. In comparison with a visuospatial maintenance task with a dominant parietal activation, the reasoning task additionally activated medial frontal areas (Ruff, Knauff, Fangmeier, & Spreer, 2003). Hence, it is likely that in a surprisingly literal sense, people think in visual images when they solve logical problems that allow visual representation.

Last but not least, we should mention spatial navigation. Three different types of information are usually suggested as the basis of navigation: path integration, view-dependent place recognition with associated direction knowledge, and allocentric spatial maps (e.g., Mallot & Gillner, 2000; Wang & Spelke, 2002). The last of these components, in particular, might be related to visuospatial working memory. In accordance with this suggestion, spatial processing abilities (mental rotation) correlate positively with orienteering (Malinowski, 2001). Similarly, a spatial secondary task impaired route learning, but only in subjects who claimed to use survey knowledge or who had high scores in spatial ability tests (Garden et al., 2002). Similarly, when participants are oriented towards verbal processing (verbal overshadowing), the generation of survey knowledge was impaired (Fiore & Schooler, 2002). Taken together, these results suggest that visuospatial working memory is also used for the generation of survey knowledge.

The involvement of visuospatial processes might also explain why males show a preference for survey orientation whereas females prefer route orientation (Choi & Silverman, 2002; Cutmore, Hine, Maberly, Langford, & Hawgood, 2000). A route strategy uses landmark-direction knowledge and this knowledge, in some cases, could be verbally mediated. A hint of this is the observation that a verbal secondary task impaired route learning of females but not of males (Saucier, Bowman, & Elias, 2003). At the same time, males often had higher spatial ability scores than females. If that is correct, it might be that rather than gender, the critical variable is personal, in this case visuospatial, abilities. Everyone adapts to his or her personally optimal type of way-finding by using the mental method he or she can apply most effectively. However, on this point we need more empirical data.

Sign language and visual working memory

One particularly intriguing form of visuospatial processing is that involved in sign language, in which hand shapes, directions of hand movement and locations of the movements are used for communication. This gives sign language an obvious specific perceptual and production difference from speech processing. It characterizes this language modality as more strongly based on the visuospatial modality than speech, thus possibly enhancing the relevance of visual, and reducing the relevance of verbal, working memory for language understanding. Somewhat surprisingly, however, there are striking similarities in the neural organization of sign and vocal languages. For example, the origins of sign aphasia, like those of spoken aphasia, tend to be in the classical Broca and Wernicke language areas of the left side of the brain (Poizner, Bellugi, & Klima, 1990). Neuroimaging studies confirm the dominance of the left hemisphere in sign language processing (Neville et al., 1997, 1998; Rönnberg, Söderfeldt, & Risberg, 1998, 2000). There are also linguistic versus nonlinguistic dissociations, such that linguistic visuospatial information processing may be selectively spared while processing of non-linguistic information is impaired (e.g., impairment in the Corsi test while ASL (American sign language) performance remains intact, Corina, Kritchevsky, & Bellugi, 1996), but the dissociation may also go in the opposite direction (Hickok, Bellugi, & Klima, 1996). Yet another aspect of the language specificity is the fact that there are also production dissociations, such that sign language production is impaired while performance is normal on apraxia tests (Hickok, Klima, Kritchevsky, & Bellugi, 1995). Sign language processing thus shares more components with oral language than with visual or motor processing, even though it is highly reliant on visual input and uses hand movements for output, and compared to verbal encoding, it enhances memory as overt performance of actions (Zimmer & Engelkamp, 2003).

The language similarity is also shown by similarities in working memory for sign and speech. Behaviourally, working memory for signed input shows the same type of phonological similarity, word length, articulatory suppression and irrelevant input effects as for spoken input (Wilson & Emmorey, 1997a, b, 2003), suggesting some kind of "phonological loop" for signed materials as well. This kind of result cannot easily be explained in terms of the classical Baddeley and Hitch model. The same is true for related "inner scribe" notions (Baddeley & Logie, 1999), as the VSSP is assumed to be non-linguistic in nature. The functional similarities are more compatible with recent data concerning the selective interference for both signed and non-linguistic visual input on working memory for signs (Wilson & Emmorey, 2003). Therefore, the loop ought to be amodal and share the same neural correlates as the spoken phonological loop. Rönnberg, Rudner, and Ingvar (2004) directly tested this hypothesis in early bilinguals. They observed that the active part of the loop component was similar for signed input and audiovisual spoken input (i.e., left-sided Broca's, premotor, and supplementary motor areas). In contrast, working memory performance was rather associated with selective enhancement of bilateral temporal and parietal areas, corresponding to the storage component in working memory. This suggests a mixed model. Storage would be language-specific whereas the phonological representation is independent of modality. In other words, the sign language loop operates on a virtual visuospatial array (Rönnberg et al., 2004) and thus working memory for sign language is supported by a different anterior-posterior network than that for speech or spatial input. The components relevant for active rehearsal are similar to those areas used in the generation of speech, while the passive components are similar to areas found in spatial working memory, and this storage component appears to be spatially organized.

The mixed model is also supported by capacity measures. The total working memory capacity available for linguistic tasks can be measured by complex span tasks such as reading span (Daneman & Merikle, 1996) and production span (Daneman & Green, 1986). Overall capacity is comparable in deaf signers and hearing speakers (Boutla, Supalla, Newoport, & Bavelier, 2004). However, the working memory loops are consistently found to be shorter for sign than for speech when loop capacity is tested using simple span tasks such as digit span (Wechsler, 1955). This span deficit for signs is found in both deaf and hearing signers, indicating that the effect is related to language modality rather than deafness. One explanation is that differences in the capacities of the sign and speech loops are directly due to differences in articulation rates between modalities (Marschark & Mayer, 1998), as in oral language (Ellis & Hennelly, 1980). However, Rönnberg and co-workers (2004) found that sign loop size did not correlate with articulation rate, and this finding was replicated by Boutla and co-workers (2004). Two other suggestions have been made regarding the reasons for loop size discrepancies, both of which postulate inherent differences in cognitive systems due to reliance on different sensory modalities (Boutla et al., 2004). The first suggestion is that speech-like information decays at a slower rate than visually encoded information. This is supported by the unequal durations of the primary sensory memory stores for sound and vision. The longer duration of echoic memory compared to iconic memory would mean that words could be retained for longer than signs without rehearsal being required. The second suggestion is that apparent differences in loop size are really due to a measuring problem that highlights inherent differences in the retention of serial order information across modalities. The digit span test, which is used to measure simple span size, requires retention of serial order, but while the auditory system is known to be highly efficient in retaining the order of occurrence of sounds, the capacity of the visual system in this respect is more limited. Thus, the visuo-spatial array, which has been suggested as a storage component in working memory for sign (Rönnberg et al., 2004), would not be intrinsically suitable for the retention of temporal information, and in order to assess the capacity of the sign loop more adequately, a test must be devised that taps capacity and order without relying on temporal aspects (Emmorey & Wilson, 2004; Rudner & Rönnberg, 2006).

The issue of modifications in working memory due to practised sign language is further illuminated by a number of features of other types of cognitive and linguistic processing and their neural correlates in native sign language users. For example, signers are better at face discrimination (McCullough & Emmorey, 1997) and more accurate in identifying emotional facial expression (N. Goldstein & Feldman, 1996). Facial expressions have a grammatical function in sign language, and it has been shown that perception of linguistically meaningful facial expressions is left-lateralized in signers but not in non-signers (McCullough, Emmorey, & Sereno, 2005). Signers are more rapid at mental rotation and image generation (Emmorey, Klima, &

Hickok, 1998; Emmorey, Kosslyn, & Bellugi, 1993) and, unlike non-signers, they perform equally well in forward and reverse recall of serially presented stimuli (Wilson, Bettger, Niculae, & Klima, 1997), indicating that the memory representations on which recall is based are not serially ordered. Lexical retrieval in sign language has been shown to be supported by the same neural networks as word retrieval (Emmorey et al., 2003) and, despite the fact that some signs are iconic – in other words, gesturally similar to pantomime actions representing certain objects and actions – their retrieval is supported by neural networks related to linguistic rather than gestural processing (Emmorey et al., 2004). On the other hand, descriptions of spatial relationships in sign language, which in spoken languages are dealt with by prepositions (for example, *on, in, under*), do engage right superior parietal areas to a greater extent than the use of equivalent prepositions in oral language (Emmorey et al., 2005). Thus, it is not only working memory that shows a complex mix of modality-free and modality-specific effects; other aspects of cognition and language processing do so too.

In conclusion, it appears that working memory systems mediated by visuospatial language are functionally very similar to those mediated by spoken languages. Many of the components of working memory for sign seem to have the same structure and appear to be based on the same neural correlates as equivalent components for speech. This applies to executive functions and the rehearsal component of the language-supporting loop in both modalities. However, working memory for sign also differs from working memory for speech in a number of important respects relating to the temporary storage of memorized items, and these differences reflect the inherently visuospatial nature of sign language.

REFERENCES

Andrade, J., Kemps, E., Werniers, Y., May, J., & Szmalec, A. (2002). Insensitivity of visual short-term memory to irrelevant visual information. *The Quarterly Journal of Experimental Psychology, 55A*, 753–774.

Baddeley, A.D. (2000). The episodic buffer: A new component of working memory? *Trends in Cognitive Neurosciences, 4*, 417–423.

Baddeley, A.D. (2003). Working memory: Looking back and looking forward. *Nature Reviews: Neuroscience, 4*, 829–839.

Baddeley, A.D., & Hitch, G.J. (1974). Working memory. In G.A. Bower (Ed.), *Recent advances in learning and motivation, Vol. 8* (pp. 47–90). New York: Academic Press.

Baddeley, A.D., & Logie, R.H. (1999). Working memory: The multiple-component model. In A. Miyake & P. Shah (Eds.), *Models of working memory* (pp. 28–61). Cambridge, UK: Cambridge University Press.

Bennett, P.J., & Cortese, F. (1996). Masking of spatial frequency in visual memory depends upon distal, not retinal, frequency. *Vision Research, 36*, 233–238.

Bestgen, Y., & Dupont, V. (2003). The construction of spatial situation models during reading. *Psychological Research, 67*, 209–219.

Blake, R., Cepeda, N., & Hiris, E. (1997). Memory for visual motion. *Journal of Experimental Psychology: Human Perception and Performance, 22*, 353–369.

Bosch, V., Mecklinger, A., & Friederici, A.D. (2001). Slow cortical potentials during retention of object, spatial, and verbal information. *Cognitive Brain Research, 10*, 219–237.

Boutla, M., Supalla, T., Newoport, E.L., & Bavelier, D. (2004). Short-term memory span: Insights from sign language. *Nature Neuroscience, 7*, 997–1002.

Bower, G.H. (1970). Imagery as a relational organizer in associative learning. *Journal of Verbal Learning and Verbal Behavior, 9*, 529–533.

Brooks, L.R. (1967). The suppression of visualization by reading. *Quarterly Journal of Experimental Psychology, 19*, 289–299.

Choi, J., & Silverman, I. (2002). The relationship between testosterone and route-learning strategies in humans. *Brain and Cognition, 50*, 116–120.

Cooper, L.A., Schacter, D.L., Ballesteros, S., & Moore, C. (1992). Priming and recognition of transformed three-dimensional objects: Effects of size and reflection. *Journal of Experimental Psychology: Learning, Memory, and Cognition, 18*, 43–57.

Corina, D., Kritchevsky, M., & Bellugi, U. (1996). Visual language processing and unilateral neglect: Evidence from American Sign Language. *Cognitive Neuropsychology, 13*, 321–356.

Cornelissen, F., & Greenlee, M.W. (2000). Visual memory for random block patterns defined by luminance and color contrast. *Vision Research, 40*, 287–299.

Cornoldi, C., & Vecchi, T. (2000). *Visuospatial working memory and individual differences*. Hove, UK: Psychology Press.

Cowan, N. (1999). An embedded-processes model of working memory. In A. Miyake & P. Shah (Eds.), *Models of working memory: Mechanisms of active maintenance and executive control* (pp. 62–101). Cambridge, UK: Cambridge University Press.

Cutmore, T.R.H., Hine, T.J., Maberly, K.J., Langford, N.M., & Hawgood, G. (2000). Cognitive and gender factors influencing navigation in a virtual environment. *International Journal of Human-Computer Studies, 53*, 223–249.

Damasio, A.R. (1989). The brain binds entities and events by multiregional activation from convergence zones. *Neural Computation, 1*, 123–132.

Daneman, M., & Green, I. (1986). Individual differences in comprehending and producing words in context. *Journal of Memory and Language, 25*, 1–18.

Daneman, M., & Merikle, P.M. (1996). Working memory and language comprehension: A meta-analysis. *Psychonomic Bulletin and Review, 3*, 422–434.

De Beni, R., & Moè, A. (2003a). Imagery and rehearsal as study strategies for written or orally presented passages. *Psychonomic Bulletin and Review, 10*, 975–980.

De Beni, R., & Moè, A. (2003b) Presentation modality effects in studying passages. Are mental images always effective? *Applied Cognitive Psychology, 17*, 309–324.

De Beni, R., Moè, A., & Cornoldi, C. (1997). Learning from texts or lectures: Loci mnemonics can interfere with reading but not with listening. *European Journal of Cognitive Psychology, 9*, 401–415.

Denis, M., & Kosslyn, S.M. (1999). Scanning visual mental images: A window on the mind. *Cahiers de Psychologie Cognitive/Current Psychology of Cognition, 18*, 409–465.

Denis, M., & Zimmer, H.D. (1992). Analog properties of cognitive maps constructed from verbal descriptions. *Psychological Research, 54*, 286–298.

Ellis, N.C., & Hennelly, R.A. (1980). A bilingual word-length effect: Implications for intelligence testing and the relative ease of mental calculation in Welsh and English. *British Journal of Psychology, 71*, 43–51.

Emmorey, K., Grabowski, T., McCullough, S., Damasio, H., Ponto, L.L., Hichwa, R.D., & Bellugi, U. (2003). Neural systems underlying lexical retrieval for sign language. *Neuropsychologia, 41*, 85–95.

Emmorey, K., Grabowski, T., McCullough, S., Damasio, H., Ponto, L.L., Hichwa, R.D., & Bellugi, U. (2004). Motor-iconicity of sign language does not alter the neural systems underlying tool and action naming. *Brain and language, 89*, 27–37.

Emmorey, K., Grabowski, T., McCullough, S., Ponto, L.L., Hichwa, R.D., & Damasio, H. (2005). The neural correlates of spatial language in English and American Sign Language: A PET study with hearing bilinguals. *NeuroImage, 24*, 832–840.

Emmorey, K., Klima, E., & Hickok, G. (1998). Mental rotation within linguistic and non-linguistic domains in users of American sign language. *Cognition, 68*, 221–246.

Emmorey, K., Kosslyn, S.M., & Bellugi, U. (1993). Visual imagery and visual-spatial language: Enhanced imagery abilities in deaf and hearing ASL signers. *Cognition, 46*, 139–181.

Emmorey, K., & Wilson, M. (2004). The puzzle of working memory for sign language. *Trends in Cognitive Sciences, 8*, 521–523.

Engelkamp, J., Zimmer, H.D., & de Vega, M. (2001). Pictures in memory: The role of visual-imaginal information. In M. Denis, C. Cornoldi, R.H. Logie, M. DeVega, & J. Engelkamp (Eds.), *Imagery, language and visuospatial thinking* (pp. 59–80). Hove, UK: Psychology Press.

Farah, M.J. (1985). Psychophysical evidence for a shared representational medium for mental images and percepts. *Journal of Experimental Psychology: General, 114*, 91–103.

Finke, R.A., & Shepard, R.N. (1986). Visual functions of mental imagery. In K.R. Boff, I. Kaufman, & J. Thomas (Eds.), *Handbook of perception and human performance, Vol. 2* (pp. 37.1–37.55). New York: Wiley.

Fiore, S.M., & Schooler, J.W. (2002). How did you get here from there? Verbal over-shadowing of spatial mental models. *Applied Cognitive Psychology, 16*, 897–910.

Friedman, N.P., & Miyake, A. (2000). Differential roles for visuospatial and verbal working memory in situation model construction. *Journal of Experimental Psychology: General, 129*, 61–83.

Fuster, J.M. (1997). Network memory. *Trends in Neuroscience, 20*, 451–459.

Garden, S., Cornoldi, C., & Logie, R.H. (2002). Visuospatial working memory in navigation. *Applied Cognitive Psychology, 16*, 35–50.

Glass, A.L., Eddy, J.K., & Schwanenflugel, P.J. (1980). The verification of high and low imagery sentences. *Journal of Experimental Psychology: Human Learning and Memory, 6*, 692–704.

Glenberg, A.M., & McDaniel, M.A. (1992). Mental models, pictures, and text: Integration of spatial and verbal information. *Memory and Cognition, 20*, 458–460.

Goldstein, A.G., & Chance, J. (1974). Some factors in picture recognition memory. *Journal of General Psychology, 90*, 69–85.

Goldstein, N., & Feldman, R.S. (1996). Knowledge of American Sign Language and the ability of hearing individuals to decode facial expressions of emotion. *Journal of Nonverbal Behavior, 20*, 111–122.

Groh-Bordin, C., Zimmer, H.D., & Mecklinger, A. (2005). Feature binding in perceptual priming and in episodic object recognition: Evidence from event-related brain potentials. *Cognitive Brain Research, 24*, 556–567.

Heil, M. (2002). The functional significance of ERP effects during mental rotation. *Psychophysiology, 39*, 535–545.

Heil, M., & Rolke, B. (2002). Toward a chronopsychophysiology of mental rotation. *Psychophysiology, 39*, 414–422.

Hickok, G., Bellugi, U., & Klima, E.S. (1996). The neurobiology of sign language and its implications for the neural basis of language. *Nature, 381*, 699–702.

Hickok, G., Klima, E., Kritchevsky, M., & Bellugi, U. (1995). A case of "sign blindness" following left occipital damage in a deaf signer. *Neuropsychologia, 33*, 1597–1606.

Jolicoeur, P. (1987). A size-congruency effect in memory for visual shape. *Memory and Cognition, 15*, 531–543.

Jonides, J., Lacey, S.C., & Nee, D.E. (2005). Processes of working memory in mind and brain. *Current Directions in Psychological Science, 14*, 2–6.

Jordan, K., Heinze, H.J., Lutz, K., Kanowski, M., & Jäncke, L. (2001). Cortical activations during the mental rotation of different visual objects. *Neuroimage, 13*, 143–152.

Just, M.A., Carpenter, P.A., Maguire, M., Diwadkar, V., & McMains, S. (2001). Mental rotation of objects retrieved from memory: A functional MRI study of spatial processing. *Journal of Experimental Psychology: General, 130*, 493–504.

Just, M.A., Newman, S.D., Keller, T.A., McEleney, A., & Carpenter, P.A. (2004). Imagery in sentence comprehension: An fMRI study. *Neuroimage, 21*, 112–124.

Kanwisher, N. (2003) The ventral visual object pathway in humans: Evidence from fMRI. In L. Chalupa & J. Werner (Eds.), *The visual neurosciences* (pp. 1179–1189). Cambridge, MA: MIT Press.

Kinjo, H., & Snodgrass, J.G. (2000). Is there a picture superiority effect in perceptual implicit tasks? *European Journal of Cognitive Psychology, 12*, 145–164.

Klauer, K.C., & Rao, Z. (2004). Double dissociations in visual and spatial short-term memory. *Journal of Experimental Psychology: General, 133*, 355–381.

Knauff, M., Fangmeier, T., Ruff, C.C., & Johnson-Laird, P.N. (2003). Reasoning, models, and images: Behavioral measures and cortical activity. *Journal of Cognitive Neuroscience, 15*, 559–573.

Knauff, M., Kassubek, J., Mulack, T., & Greenlee, M.W. (2000). Cortical activation evoked by visual mental imagery as measured by fMRI. *Neuroreport, 11*, 3957–3962.

Knauff, M., Mulack, T., Kassubek, J., Salih, H.R., & Greenlee, M.W. (2002). Spatial imagery in deductive reasoning: A functional MRI study. *Brain Research: Cognitive Brain Research, 13*, 203–212.

Kosslyn, S.M. (1975). Information representation in visual images. *Cognitive Psychology, 7*, 341–370.

Kosslyn, S. (1980). *Image and mind.* Cambridge, MA: Harvard University Press.

Kosslyn, S.M. (1981). The medium and the message in mental imagery: A theory. *Psychological Review, 88*, 46–66.

Kosslyn, S.M. (1994). *Image and brain. The resolution of the imagery debate.* Cambridge, MA: MIT Press.

Kosslyn, S.M., Ball, T.M., & Reiser, B.J. (1978). Visual images preserve metric spatial information: Evidence from studies of image scanning. *Journal of Experimental Psychology: Human Perception and Performance, 4*, 47–60.

Kosslyn, S.M., Ganis, G., & Thompson, W.L. (2001). Neural foundations of imagery. *Nature Reviews – Neuroscience, 2*, 635–642.

Kosslyn, S.M., & Thompson, W.L. (2003). When is early visual cortex activated during visual mental imagery? *Psychological Bulletin, 129*, 723–746.

Kosslyn, S.M., Thompson, W.L., Kim, I.J., & Alpert, N.M. (1995). Topographical representations of mental images in primary visual cortex. *Nature, 378*, 496–498.

Kosslyn, S.M., Thompson, W.L., Wraga, M., & Alpert, N.M. (2001). Imagining rotation by endogenous versus exogenous forces: Distinct neural mechanisms. *Neuroreport: For Rapid Communication of Neuroscience Research, 12*, 2519–2525.

Lalonde, J., & Chaudhuri, A. (2002). Task-dependent transfer of perceptual memory representations during delayed spatial frequency discrimination. *Vision Research, 42*, 1759–1759.

Lehnert, G., & Zimmer, H. (in press). Auditory and visuo-spatial working memory. *Memory and Cognition.*

Lehnert, G., Zimmer, H., & Mecklinger, A. (2006). *Common coding of auditory and visual spatial information in working memory.* Manuscript under review.

Lindenberger, U., Kliegl, R., & Baltes, P.B. (1992). Professional expertise does not eliminate age differences in imagery-based memory performance during adulthood. *Psychology and Aging, 7*, 585–593.

Logie, R.H. (1986). Visuospatial processing in working memory. *Quarterly Journal of Experimental Psychology, 38A*, 229–247.

Logie, R.H. (1995). *Visuospatial working memory.* Hove, UK: Lawrence Erlbaum Associates.

Logie, R.H. (2003). Spatial and visual working memory: A mental workspace. *The Psychology of Learning and Motivation, 42*, 37–78.

Logie, R.H., Engelkamp, J., Dehn, D., & Rudkin, S. (2001). Actions, mental actions, and working memory. In M. Denis & R.H. Logie (Eds.), *Imagery, language and visuospatial thinking* (pp. 161–183). New York: Psychology Press.

Logie, R.H., & Marchetti, C. (1991). Visuospatial working memory: Visual, spatial or central executive. In R.H. Logie & M. Denis (Eds.), *Mental images in human cognition* (pp. 105–115). Amsterdam: North-Holland.

Logie, R.H., & Salway, A.F.S. (1990). Working memory and modes of thinking: A secondary task approach. In K.J. Gilhooly & M.T.G. Keane (Eds.), *Lines of thinking: Reflections on the psychology of thought, Vol 2: Skills, emotion, creative processes, individual differences and teaching thinking* (pp. 99–113). Oxford, UK: John Wiley.

Luck, S.J., & Vogel, E.K. (1997). The capacity of visual working memory for features and conjunctions. *Nature, 390*, 279–281.

Magnussen, S. (2000). Low-level memory processes in vision. *Trends in Neurosciences, 23*, 247–251.

Magnussen, S., & Greenlee, M.W. (1992). Retention and disruption of motion information in visual short-term memory. *Journal of Experimental Psychology: Learning, Memory, and Cognition, 18*, 151–157.

Magnussen, S., & Greenlee, M.W. (1997). Competition and sharing of processing resources in visual discrimination. *Journal of Experimental Psychology: Human Perception and Performance, 22*, 1603–1616.

Magnussen, S., & Greenlee, M.W. (1999). The psychophysics of perceptual memory. *Psychological Research, 62*, 81–92.

Magnussen, S., Greenlee, M.W., Aslaksen, P.M., & Kildebo, O.Ø. (2003). High-fidelity long-term memory for spatial frequency revisited – and confirmed. *Psychological Science*, *14*, 74–76.

Magnussen, S., Greenlee, M.W., Asplund, R., & Dyrnes, S. (1990). Perfect visual short-term memory for periodic patterns. *European Journal of Cognitive Psychology*, *4*, 345–362.

Magnussen, S., Greenlee, M.W., & Thomas, J.P. (1996). Parallel processing in visual short-term memory. *Journal of Experimental Psychology: Human Perception and Performance*, *22*, 202–212.

Malinowski, J.C. (2001). Mental rotation and real-world wayfinding. *Perceptual and Motor Skills*, *92*, 19–30.

Mallot, H.A., & Gillner, S. (2000). Route navigating without place recognition: What is recognized in recognition-triggered responses? *Perception*, *29*, 43–55.

Marco, P. (2000). Construzione di modelli spaziali di percorsi in memoria di lavoro: Il ruolo delle abilita visuospaziali. *Ricerche di Psicologia*, *24*, 81–104.

Marschark, M., & Mayer, T.S. (1998). Interactions of language and memory in deaf children and adults. *Scandinavian Journal of Psychology*, *39*, 145–148.

Mazard, A., Tzourio-Mazoyer, N., Crivello, F., Mazoyer, B., & Mellet, E. (2004). A PET meta-analysis of object and spatial mental imagery. *European Journal of Cognitive Psychology*, *16*, 673–695.

McCullough, S., & Emmorey, K. (1997). Face processing by deaf ASL signers: Evidence for expertise in distinguishing local features. *Journal of Deaf Studies and Deaf Education*, *2*, 212–222.

McCullough. S., Emmorey, K., & Sereno, M. (2005). Neural organization for recognition of grammatical and emotional facial expressions in deaf ASL signers and hearing nonsigners. *Cognitive Brain Research*, *22*, 193–203.

Mecklinger, A. (1998). On the modularity of recognition memory for object form and spatial location: A topographic ERP analysis. *Neuropsychologia*, *36*, 441–460.

Mecklinger, A. (2000). Interfacing mind and brain: A neurocognitive model of recognition memory. *Psychophysiology*, *37*, 1–18.

Mecklinger, A., & Pfeifer, E. (1996). Event-related potentials reveal topographical and temporal distinct neuronal activation patterns for spatial and object working memory. *Cognitive Brain Research*, *4*, 211–224.

Miyake, A., Friedman, N.P., Rettinger, D.A., Shah, P., & Hegarty, M. (2001). How are visuospatial working memory, executive functioning, and spatial abilities related? A latent-variable analysis. *Journal of Experimental Psychology: General*, *130*, 621–640.

Neville, H.J., Bavelier, D., Corina, D., Rauschecker, J., Karni, A., Lawani, A., Braun, A., Clark, V., Jezzard, P., & Turner, R. (1998). Cerebral organization for language in deaf and hearing subjects: Biological constraints and effects of experience. *Proceedings of the National Academy of Sciences*, *95*, 922–929.

Neville, H.J., Coffey, S.A., Lawson, D.S., Fischer, A., Emmorey, K., & Bellugi, U. (1997). Neural systems mediating American Sign Language: Effects of sensory experience and age of acquisition. *Brain and Language*, *57*, 285–308.

Paivio, A. (1971). *Imagery and verbal processes*. New York: Holt, Rinehard & Winston.

Paivio, A. (1986). *Mental representations. A dual coding approach*. New York: Oxford University Press.

Paivio, A. (1995). Imagery and memory. In M.S. Gazzaniga (Ed.), *The cognitive neurosciences* (pp. 977–986). Cambridge, MA: MIT Press.

Pearson, D.G. (2001). Imagery and the visuospatial sketchpad. In J. Andrade (Ed.), *Working memory in perspective*. Philadelphia, PA: Psychology Press.

Pearson, D.G., & Logie, R.H. (2000). Working memory and mental synthesis: A dual-task approach. In S.O. Nuallain (Ed.), *Spatial cognition: Foundations and applications: selected papers from Mind III, Annual Conference of the Cognitive Science Society of Ireland, 1998 – Advances in consciousness research*. Amsterdam: John Benjamins.

Pérez-Carpinell, J., Baldovi, R., de Fez, M.D., & Castro, J. (1998). Color memory matching: Time effect and other factors. *Color Research and Application, 23*, 234–247.

Phillips, W.A. (1983). Short-term visual memory. *Philosophical Transactions of the Royal Society of London, B302*, 295–309.

Poizner, H., Bellugi, U., & Klima, E.S. (1990). Biological foundation of language: Clues from sign language. *Annual Review of Neuroscience, 13*, 283–307.

Postle, B.R., Awh, E., Jonides, J., Smith, E.E., & D'Esposito, M. (2004). The where and how of attention-based rehearsal in spatial working memory. *Cognitive Brain Research, 20*, 194–205.

Postle, B.R., Druzgal, T.J., & D'Esposito, M. (2003). Seeking the neural substrates of visual working memory storage. *Cortex, 39*, 927–946.

Pylyshyn, Z.W. (1973). What the mind's eye tells the mind's brain: A critique of mental imagery. *Psychological Bulletin, 80*, 1–24.

Pylyshyn, Z.W. (1981). The imagery debate: Analogue media versus tacit knowledge. *Psychological Review, 88*, 16–45.

Pylyshyn, Z.W. (2002). Mental imagery: In search of a theory. *Behavioral and Brain Sciences, 25*, 157–238.

Pylyshyn, Z. (2003). Return of the mental image: Are there really pictures in the brain? *Trends in Cognitive Sciences, 7*, 113–118.

Quinn, J.G., & McConnell, J. (1996). Irrelevant pictures in visual working memory. *Quarterly Journal of Experimental Psychology Human Experimental Psychology, 49A*, 200–215.

Quinn, J.G., & McConnell, J. (1999). Manipulation of interference in the passive visual store. *European Journal of Cognitive Psychology, 11*, 373–389.

Rämä, P., Sala, J.B., Gillen, J.S., Pekar, J.J., & Courtney, S.M. (2001). Dissociation of the neural systems for working memory maintenance of verbal and nonspatial visual information. *Cognitive, Affective and Behavioral Neuroscience, 1*, 161–171.

Rinck, M., & Bower, G.H. (2000). Temporal and spatial distance in situation models. *Memory and Cognition, 28*, 1310–1320.

Rinck, M., & Denis, M. (2004). The metrics of spatial distance traversed during mental imagery. *Journal of Experimental Psychology: Learning, Memory, and Cognition, 30*, 1211–1218.

Roediger, H.L. (1980). Memory metaphors in cognitive psychology. *Memory and Cognition, 8*, 231–246.

Rönnberg, J. (2006). Cognitive and neuroscience perspectives on speech and sign processing: Evidence from persons with deafness, hearing impairment, and normal hearing. In Q. Jing, M.R. Rosenzweig, G. d'Ydewalk, H. Zhang, H.-C. Chen, & K. Zhang (Eds.), *Progress in psychological science around the world: Volume 1* (pp. 383–399). Hove, UK: Psychology Press.

Rönnberg, J., Rudner, M., & Ingvar, M. (2004). Neural correlates of working memory for sign language. *Cognitive Brain Research, 20*, 165–182.

Rönnberg, J., Söderfeldt, B., & Risberg, J. (1998). Regional cerebral blood flow during signed and heard episodic and semantic memory tasks. *Applied Neuropsychology, 5*, 132–138.

Rönnberg, J., Söderfeldt, B., & Risberg, J. (2000). The cognitive neuroscience of signed language. *Acta Psychologica, 105*, 237–254.

Ruchkin, D.S., Grafman, J., Cameron, K., & Berndt, R.S. (2003). Working memory retention systems: A state of activated long-term memory. *Behavioral and Brain Sciences, 26*, 709–777.

Rudner, M., & Rönnberg, J. (2006). *Space for compensation – further support for a visuospatial array for temporary storage in working memory for deaf native signers.* Manuscript in preparation.

Ruff, C.C., Knauff, M., Fangmeier, T., & Spreer, J. (2003). Reasoning and working memory: Common and distinct neural processes. *Neuropsychologia, 41*, 1241–1253.

Saucier, D., Bowman, M., & Elias, L. (2003). Sex differences in the effect of articulatory or spatial dual-task interference during navigation. *Brain and Cognition, 53*, 346–350.

Schneider, W.X. (1999). Visual-spatial working memory, attention, and scene representation: A neurocognitive theory. *Psychological Research, 62*, 220–236.

Schumann-Hengsteler, R., Demmel, U., & Seitz, K. (1995). Effekte des Darbietungsmodus auf die visuell-räumliche Arbeitsleistung bei Kindern und Erwachsenen. *Zeitschrift für Experimentelle Psychologie, 42*, 594–616.

Shah, P., & Miyake, A. (1996). The separability of working memory resources for spatial thinking and language processing: An individual differences approach. *Journal of Experimental Psychology: General, 125*, 4–27.

Shepard, R.N. (1967). Recognition memory for words, sentences and pictures. *Journal of Verbal Learning and Verbal Behavior, 6*, 156–163.

Shepard, R.N., & Metzler, J. (1971). Mental rotation of three-dimensional objects. *Science, 171*, 701–703.

Simons, D.J., & Chabris, D.F. (1999). Gorillas in our midst: Sustained inattentional blindness for dynamic events. *Perception, 28*, 1059–1074.

Simons, D.J., & Levin, D.T. (1998). Failure to detect changes to people during a real-world interaction. *Psychonomic Bulletin and Review, 5*, 644–649.

Sims, V.K., & Hegarty, M. (1997). Mental animation in the visuospatial sketchpad: Evidence from dual-task studies. *Memory and Cognition, 25*, 321–333.

Smith, E.E., & Jonides, J. (1997). Working memory: A view from neuroimaging. *Cognitive Psychology, 33*, 5–42.

Söderfeldt, B., Ingvar, M., Rönnberg, J., Eriksson, L., Serrander, M., & Stone-Elander, S. (1997). Signed and spoken language perception studied by positron emission tomography. *Neurology, 49*, 82–87.

Standing, L. (1973). Learning 10,000 pictures. *Quarterly Journal of Experimental Psychology, 25*, 207–222.

Standing, L., Conezio, J., & Haber, R.N. (1970). Perception and memory for pictures: Single-trial learning of 2500 visual stimuli. *Psychonomic Science, 19*, 73–74.

Thompson, W.L., & Kosslyn, S.M. (2000). Neural systems activated during visual mental imagery. In A.W. Toga & J.C. Mazziotta (Eds.), *Brain mapping: The systems* (pp. 535–560). San Diego, CA: Academic Press.

Treisman, A. (in press). Object tokens, binding, and visual memory. In H.D. Zimmer,

A. Mecklinger, & U. Lindenberger (Eds.), *Binding in human memory: A neurocognitive approach*. Oxford, UK: Oxford University Press.

Trojano, L., Grossi, D., Linden, D.E., Formisano, E., Goebel, R., Cirillo, S., Elefante, R., & Di Salle, F. (2002). Coordinate and categorical judgements in spatial imagery: An fMRI study. *Neuropsychologia, 40*, 1666–1674.

Tulving, E., & Schacter, D.L. (1990). Priming and human memory systems. *Science, 247*, 301–306.

Ungerleider, L.G., Courtney, S.M., & Haxby, J.V. (1998). A neural system for human visual working memory. *Proceedings of the National Academy of Sciences, 95*, 883–890.

Vaidya, C.J., & Gabrieli, J.D.E. (2000). Picture superiority in conceptual memory: Dissociative effects of encoding and retrieval tasks. *Memory and Cognition, 28*, 1165–1172.

Vecchi, T., & Cornoldi, C. (1999). Passive storage and active manipulation in visuospatial working memory: Further evidence from the study of age differences. *European Journal of Cognitive Psychology, 11*, 391–406.

Vogel, E.K., Woodman, G.F., & Luck, S.J. (2001). Storage of features, conjunctions and objects in visual working memory. *Journal of Experimental Pychology: Human Perception and Performance, 27*, 92–114.

Vogt, S., & Magnussen, S. (2006). *Long-term memory for 400 pictures on a common theme*. Manuscript submitted for publication.

Vuontela, V., Rämä, P., Raninen, A., Aronen, H., & Carlson, S. (1999). Selective interference reveals dissociation between memory for location and color. *Neuroreport, 10*, 2235–2240.

Wager, T.D., & Smith, E.E. (2003). Neuroimaging studies of working memory: A meta-analysis. *Cognitive, Affective, and Behavioral Neurosciences, 3*, 255–274.

Walker, P., Hitch, G.J., & Duroe, S. (1993). The effect of visual similarity on short-term memory for spatial location: Implications for the capacity of visual short-term memory. *Acta Psychologica, 83*, 203–224.

Wang, R.F., & Spelke, E.S. (2002). Human spatial representation: Insights from animals. *Trends in Cognitive Sciences, 6*, 376–382.

Wechsler, D. (1955). *The Wechsler Adult Intelligence Scale (WAIS)*. New York: The Psychological Corporation.

Weldon, M.S., & Bellinger, K.D. (1997). Collective memory: Collaborative and individual processes in remembering. *Journal of Experimental Psychology: Learning, Memory and Cognition, 23*, 1160–1175.

Weldon, M.S., & Coyote, K.C. (1996). Failure to find the picture superiority effect in implicit conceptual memory tests. *Journal of Experimental Psychology: Learning, Memory, and Cognition, 22*, 670–686.

Wheeler, M.E., & Treisman, A.M. (2002). Binding in short-term visual memory. *Journal of Experimental Psychology: General, 131*, 48–64.

Wichman, F.A., Sharpe, L.T., & Gegenfurtner, K.R. (2002). The contributions of color to recognition memory for natural scenes. *Journal of Experimental Psychology: Learning, Memory and Cognition, 28*, 509–520.

Wilson, M., Bettger, J., Niculae, I., & Klima, E. (1997). Modality of language shapes working memory. *Journal of Deaf Studies and Deaf Education, 2*, 150–160.

Wilson, M., & Emmorey, K. (1997a). A visuospatial "phonological loop" in working memory: Evidence from American Sign Language. *Memory and Cognition, 25*, 313–320.

Wilson, M., & Emmorey, K. (1997b). Working memory for sign language: A window into the architecture of the working memory system. *Journal of Deaf Studies and Deaf Education, 2*, 121–130.

Wilson, M., & Emmorey, K. (2003). The effect of irrelevant visual input on working memory for sign language. *Journal of Deaf Studies and Deaf Education, 8*, 97–103.

Xu, J. (2002). Encoding color and shape from different parts of an object in visual short-term memory. *Perception and Psychophysics, 64*, 1260–1280.

Yesavage, J.A., Rose, T.L., & Bower, G.H. (1983). Interactive imagery and affective judgments improve face-name learning in the elderly. *Journal of Gerontology, 38*, 197–203.

Zimmer, H.D. (1995). Size and orientation of objects in explicit and implicit memory: A reversal of the dissociation between perceptual similarity and type of test. *Psychological Research, 57*, 260–273.

Zimmer, H.D. (1996). Mentale Repräsentation visueller Zeichen: Informationsspezifische Verarbeitungsmodule. *Zeitschrift für Semiotik, 18*, 191–211.

Zimmer, H.D., & Engelkamp, J. (2003). Signing enhances memory like performing actions. *Psychonomic Bulletin and Review, 10*, 450–454.

Zimmer, H.D., & Speiser, H. (2001). The irrelevant picture effect in visuospatial working-memory: Fact or fiction? *Psychologische Beiträge, 44*, 223–247.

Zimmer, H.D., Speiser, H.R., & Seidler, B. (2003). Spatiotemporal working-memory and short-term object-location tasks use different memory mechanisms. *Acta Psychologica, 114*, 41–65.

Zimmer, H.D., & Steiner, A. (2003). Colour specificity in episodic and in object recognition with enhanced color impact. *European Journal of Cognitive Psychology, 15*, 349–370.

3 Action events in everyday life and their remembering

Hubert D. Zimmer, Tore Helstrup and Lars-Göran Nilsson

We are continuously performing actions. We are doing it now while writing this article, but we also did it when we walked to the office, when we prepared breakfast this morning and when we recently made a hotel reservation for the forthcoming vacation. We also remember actions. These may be important things such as our wedding or what happened when we witnessed a car accident. However, less important things – or let us say only temporarily relevant things – also need to be remembered; for example, that we locked the door when we left home. Finally, we plan actions (e.g., to buy tickets for the exhibition this afternoon), and we hope to remember our intention when we pass the shop. Obviously, everyday life is a continuous stream of actions and everyday memory is thus largely a memory for actions. In this chapter we report what we know about actions and memory for actions from laboratory research and relate it to everyday memory tasks and witnessing. However, before doing so we first illustrate the perspectives from which actions are studied in psychology, and which aspects of actions are investigated.

ACTIONS IN EVERYDAY LIFE: SOME ILLUSTRATIVE EXAMPLES

Our first example is a summer event. Try to imagine the following situation. It is a warm summer evening, and you have invited guests for a party. You have planned a barbecue, and you have prepared it well. You have bought the charcoal and the meat and have cleaned the grill. You lit the charcoal and, after a while, when you had a good glow, you prepared the meat. You seasoned the steak, put it on the grill, roasted it, turned it several times and, when it was medium rare, you served it. The next day you discussed this pleasant evening with your friends. This series of events represents typical everyday actions, and we shall use it here to highlight certain important aspects of actions.

Actions appear in two forms in this example. On the one hand, there is *knowledge of actions* used while they are being performed, and on the other hand there is *memory for a specific episode of action as personally experienced.*

Although both tasks need memory, they tap different types of memory. The first type provides information about how to make a barbecue correctly. It specifies the kind of supplies needed, the sequence of part actions that have to be carried out, etc. It even partly comprises implicit knowledge that can scarcely be verbalized, such as knowledge of the appearance of a steak and its consistency if it is medium rare. This is a different kind of memory to the one that we have the day after the party. The latter is memory of specific actions and our experiences during the barbecue on a summer evening. It includes memory for specific aspects of the action (e.g., how we prepared the food on this occasion), and perhaps a specific event (e.g., that someone burned his fingers).

In the scientific context this is the distinction between semantic memory and episodic memory (Tulving, 1972). Semantic memory is decontextualized memory (i.e., a generic knowledge of events) whereas episodic memory is memory for specific, spatiotemporally defined events and specific aspects of events. This distinction is important because the two types of memory are independent and they are probably provided or supported by different neural structures (Eichenbaum, 2005). For this reason,we discuss them separately.

Now we want to give a second example. It is the weekend; you are sitting at home and planning what has to be done on Monday. You intend making a short detour in order to pick up the package for which you were alerted by the postman. You may also plan to call your doctor in the afternoon to make an appointment for an overdue check-up, and you might add some notes to the to-do list of your Palm Pilot in order to be sure to remember important actions when you arrive at the office.

This is a different kind of memory from the previous ones. It is *prospective memory* (Brandimonte, Einstein, & McDaniel, 1996); memory for actions that one plans to perform in the future. More specifically, there are three types of it. The first is *event-based prospective* memory. We have to remember the plan of picking up the package as we approach the intersection where our route has to be changed in order to get to the post office. If the intended action does not pop up into consciousness at the right moment, we follow our normal habit and will arrive at the office without the package. This type of intended action is a different type of prospective memory from the intended phone call, which is *time-based prospective memory*. There is no external event that reminds someone to make the call. Finally, the last example (the to-do list) demonstrates *externalized memory*. We use external memory aids to avoid forgetting important things. In the laboratory, such situations are simulated. Event-based prospective memory, for example, is investigated by instructing a participant to stop an ongoing action and to push a button when a specific event occurs in the stream of the task being performed (e.g., Guynn, McDaniel, & Einstein, 2001).

Our third example has to do with the above-mentioned episodic memory. You visit a friend who is in his garden, cutting back bushes and planting flowers. You talk to him and watch him while he is doing his gardening. When you see that he is having difficulties cutting a thick branch, you spontaneously help him. Together you are successful, but unfortunately your friend injures himself. Some days later, you get a phone call. The customer representative of the health insurance company asks you what happened when you visited your friend and how the accident came about. This is a typical episodic memory task concerning a witnessed event. You have to remember actions. What aspects of the visit might you remember? What did your friend do? What did you do?

This is memory for *perceived actions* versus *self-performed actions*. In this regard, the efficiency of memory for the different input modalities was of interest. Researchers wanted to know whether performing actions contributes to memory, too. In the laboratory this situation is investigated as memory for lists of very simple actions such as "cutting bread", "knocking at the door", etc. If the participant only watched the action, this is commonly called an experimenter-performed task (EPT), while when performed by the participant it is called a subject-performed task (SPT).

GENERIC KNOWLEDGE OF ACTIONS

Action schemata, scripts and motor schemata

Let us first take a look at semantic memory for actions. This is generic knowledge of actions. At an abstract level we can describe actions as a hierarchy of action goals, each representing an interim goal that must be reached before the next part of the action can be performed. Such structures exist not only for sequences of movements (Oesterreich & Köddig, 1995) but also for social events such as going to a restaurant. In the latter case psychologists speak of scripts (Abelson, 1981). However, we also have personal routines that are not shared by others. Such routines are based on stable personal and decontextualized knowledge, which is (individual) semantic memory, and are often referred to as personal habits.

Because the hierarchy defines a meaningful sequence of the segments, actions are segmented into smaller pieces following a stable and sensible order. If someone loses this information, some of the part-actions are performed in an inappropriate order, as in apraxia (De Renzi & Faglioni, 1999). A somewhat similar irritation occurs when we are in a foreign culture where we do not know the scripts. Our actions may appear strange, or even impolite, although we are only naïve. In such situations we personally feel uncomfortable because we can neither predict the actions of our partners nor what we are expected to do next. The personal feeling of well-being therefore seems to rely to a considerable extent on the availability of stable (action) knowledge and thus on the ability to predict and to control the environment in everyday interactions.

Structured action representations exist not only at the level of abstract plans, but also at the different levels of movement representations. These structures, for example, allow the coordinated sequential innervations of fingers in complex hand movements. A consequence of this is a relatively fixed timing of individual movements. For instance, the time between strokes of fingers can be predicted by the hierarchical levels that have to be traversed between two moves (Rosenbaum, Kenny, & Derr, 1983). In an everyday context such patterns can be observed in skilled typewriting (Gentner, Larochelle, & Grudin, 1988). Interestingly, the individual patterns are so stable that the timing of typing has been suggested as an additional biometric feature to control access to a computer.

Within these hierarchies of action components a number of different levels can be distinguished, each of which has specific characteristics. For example, at superordinate levels, they describe abstract knowledge about movements. This conceptual knowledge, sometimes also called declarative knowledge, can be verbalized, but it cannot directly be used to perform a movement. For example, one might know perfectly well how one should move while performing a golf swing, but what one actually does might look very different. The latter knowledge is located at a subordinate level, which we wish to call a *sensory-motor level*. This information is movement knowledge proper, because it causes an overt performance of an action to happen. These pieces of information were therefore sometimes called motor programmes (Engelkamp & Zimmer, 1995).

Knowledge at the sensory motor level exists relatively independently of conceptual action-knowledge. Some information is only represented within this motor knowledge proper. It is implicit knowledge that is available if the action is performed. If we ask you, the reader, to describe where in your car the reverse gear is located and how it is reached, you are probably now mentally changing gears. In order to have access to such information one must perform the action either mentally or overtly (Engelkamp & Zimmer, 1984). This motor information is sometimes called a motor schema (Schmidt, 1975) to highlight the fact that it represents only a prototypical movement that does not represent the actual parameters specified by the concrete situation, such as the position of the hand when the movement is started or the size of the object to be grasped. In contrast, when a real action is performed, the parameters of the action have to be specified. This happens during action planning.

Acquiring action skills and the execution of actions

Most action knowledge is learned by observation and imitation followed by practising the movements (Blandin, 2002). Learning by observation was one of the basic learning principles acknowledged relatively early in psychology (Bandura, 1962), since then this hypothesis has acquired a neuropsychological foundation. It has been shown that primates have specific brain structures (mirror neurons) that are active if another primate is perceived performing a movement, and the existence of homologous structures in human beings has been discussed by Rizzolatti, Craighero, and Fadiga (2002). Even more so, imitation of actions is regarded as a central element not only of motor learning, but also of the development of social cognition and a theory of mind (Meltzoff, 2002). Furthermore, besides brain structures that guide motor actions and tool use, humans seem to have specific brain areas (parts of the superior temporal sulcus) that are dedicated to processing body movements (cf. Allison, Puce, & McCarthy, 2000), indicating that such movements define a specific subgroup of actions.

Performing or imitating actions are common ways of learning them. The knowledge necessary for movement control cannot be acquired by mere instruction; it has to be trained by actual performance. Our brain has to create a programme for the innervation of the muscles that reduce the discrepancies between the intended movement – or intended result – and the movement actually performed. Knowledge of results is therefore a central concept in movement learning (Adams, 1987). Most interesting, however, is the observation that mental practice also supports motor learning without any overt performance. Merely imagining performing the action enhances learning of the movement (Grouios, 1992a).

The effectiveness of mental practice might be less astonishing given our current knowledge of how the brain functions. Thanks to brain-imaging techniques, we know that central nervous system structures involved in motor control are also active in other tasks without an overt motor component, and in perception. Jeannerod (2001) summarized these tasks under the term "S-States", which are all mental states that simulate actions, and he reported a long series of data in support of his position. Such mental simulations are possible even for complex skills such as a golf swing, and the observation that neural activity is related to motor expertise (in the example, it was the golf handicap of the imagining participant) (Ross, Tkach, Ruggieri, Lieber, & Lapresto, 2003) suggests that S-States include motor representations in the narrower sense. However, not only well-known actions can be mentally simulated. Mental practice enhances the performance even of new actions if a basic motor ability is available (Mulder, Zijlstra, Zijlstra, & Hochstenbach, 2004), but not if it is unavailable. Mental practice obviously simulates actions, and in doing so it partly uses the same neural circuitries as are used in overt movements, thus contributing to the learning of actions. Like overt performance, an imagined performance causes a functional cerebral reorganization (Jackson, Lafleur, Malouin, Richardson, & Doyon, 2003). We therefore need to bear in mind that overt and mental performances of actions have much in common, a consequence of which is that such similarities might influence the accuracy of *memory* for actions, as will be shown later.

Once a set of actions has been learned, we have acquired abstract plans for more generalized extended actions. Motor schemata have been established for the movement parts of the whole complex motor movement such as a golf swing. These actions comprise one's repertoire of behaviours, the action knowledge that we mentioned in the introductory example. Let us now have a look at how this knowledge is used. We have already pointed out that there are hierarchies of actions, and the existence of such hierarchies has consequences for the control of behaviour. Actions can be controlled at a superordinate level, at which goals are specified, or at a subordinate level, at which action parameters are specified (Humphreys, Forde, & Riddoch, 2001). The two control structures coexist. Given that the level of control determines the content of conscious processing, the level that becomes activated might result in different memories.

One important consequence of this is that we consciously process only a small part of the information related to actions. We usually intend goals or effects, not movements (Prinz, 1997), and thus we tend to remember the goals. The importance of goals in action control can be seen even in imitation studies. While imitating the action of reaching, the movement performed is not a one-to-one copy of the perceived movements of the actor but is rather a movement aimed at the same goal as the perceived action (Bekkering, Wohlschläger, & Gattis, 2000). The same happens in everyday behaviour. As mentioned above, well-known everyday actions utilize a hierarchy of highly integrated action knowledge. It is assumed that actions are controlled by a sequence of activations within this network (Shallice & Burgess, 1996). Hence, when one intends to attain a specific action goal, the movement that is actually to be performed is more or less automatically selected depending on the level of activation. This activation is a joint effect of intent, of the existing action knowledge, and of the actually perceived environment. Perceived objects contribute to this selection by their "affordances" (Humphreys & Riddoch, 2001a, b), while action goals in turn influence what is perceived.

A corollary of this process is that after the initial selection, the final control of action is often accomplished by automatic processes, and these are, to a surprisingly large extent, independent of conscious decisions. It has been suggested that there are two independent neural routes: a ventral path from sensation to perception, and a dorsal path from sensation to action (Goodale & Humphrey, 1998). Usually both routes work in concert, but after specific brain injuries they can dissociate. For example, a patient might be able to use the size of an object to control the aperture of the fingers when grasping an object during action via the dorsal path, but be unable to use this information in a perceptual size judgment that uses the ventral path (Ungerleider & Mishkin, 1982). Note that this independence is not a specific effect of the brain damage. In healthy persons, too, a contribution of this direct specification of actions without consciousness has been confirmed (Neumann, 1988). Because we know that attention strongly influences memory, these differences between conscious and unconscious control of actions are of course also important for remembering. One might remember that one has done something (the effect), but not how one has done it.

The planning of a specific motor action is often described as parameter specification, which sets the values that specify the more abstract motor schema. In this process, sequences seem to be treated as units if they bind together a number of part-movements into one entity. If a unit exists, the individual elements are not separately specified in a sequence of planning-execution cycles of the constituent elements during execution. On the contrary, during motor control complete entities are "programmed" in advance. Speaking in favour of this position, for example, is the observation that the time needed to initiate such units is a function of their length (Sternberg, Mansell, Knoll, & Wright, 1978). The integration of part actions into higher units is also regarded as a central process within automatization of actions, often called chunking (J.R. Anderson, 1983). After a chunk has been created it is no longer necessary to consciously control the individual part actions, it being sufficient to address the abstract goal attached to the unit chunking the movement (e.g., intending a backhand drive). However, chunking also has "costs" for action control and perhaps for memory, too. A high degree of chunking reduces the control needed, but it does so at the expense of reducing the possibilities of adaptation to environmental changes, and vice versa.

Once actions have been learned, they are usually accurately performed. This is at least true in healthy persons, and for all actions over which we have adequate control because they do not make heavy demands of motor control. Most everyday actions are of this type. However, if a complex motor task or a task with a strong speed component is involved, the actual physical parameters may affect performance. This may be because the perceptual input differs (it has been getting dark), because the effectors have different biomechanical parameters (the tonicity of muscles differs due to being stressed by the tournament spectators) or because the environmental parameters are deviant (the grip of the golf club is unusual). All such influences cause a variability of the effects of motor actions, which prevent a perfect realization.

Sometimes, however, even everyday actions that are usually correct may fail. For example, although we intend to pour water into the water glass, we use the wine glass standing next to it. Such mistakes are called *slips of actions* (Norman, 1981). Why do people make such mistakes? It is assumed that the aims of the actions were underspecified, so that a wrong object (instrument, location, etc.) that also fits the goal of action could be used. We have mentioned that action planning can be modelled as an activation of goals within a more complex action plan. Usually, several goals exist in parallel, and the most strongly activated goal controls the action. It is easy to see how this can cause action slips. Other errors are caused by habits and by memory failures. We behave involuntarily in the usual way because the ordinary action tendency dominated the intended action, and actions are repeated because one has forgotten that they have already been carried out. In order to avoid the latter error, one must keep track in memory of which actions have already been performed and which have not.

Beside these occasional errors, the performance of actions can be persistently impaired. This can be severe, as in apraxia (for a recent review, see Koski, Iacoboni, & Mazziotta, 2002) and Alzheimer's disease, or in milder forms, as often claimed by elderly people, who report that they commit an increasing number of action slips as they get older. Because many cognitive capabilities such as processing speed, memory, etc. are reduced in older age (Nilsson & Larsson, chapter 12), such impairments are to be expected. Lindenberger brought this aspect to our attention in the cognitive permeation hypothesis. He pointed out that elderly people, particularly in very old age, undergo an increase in the cognitive control demands of sensory and sensorimotor aspects of behaviour at the same time as they experience a decrease in cognitive control capacity (Lindenberger & Baltes, 1994). To give an example, younger people control their balance during walking automatically, whereas the elderly need to do this consciously to a certain extent. The less efficient sensorimotor coordination has to be compensated for by conscious control. One demonstrated consequence of this is that the memory of elderly people was worse when they walked during encoding than when they were sitting still, while in younger people this made no difference (Lindenberger, Mariske, & Baltes, 2000). Furthermore, if environmental support for encoding was available elderly people used it less than did younger people, because for the elderly the control of walking took priority. In summary, for the elderly, action control usually means doing two (or more) things consciously at the same time and this impairs their performances. This "lack of resources", needed for control but not available, can partially explain action slips of elderly people and also their poorer memory for everyday actions.

VISUAL ENCODING OF ACTIONS

What is perceived?

This part of the chapter reviews what happens when actions by other persons are perceived. In the light of the above-mentioned results it is no wonder that perceiving actions to a great extent activates the same brain structures as performing actions (Buccino et al., 2001; Decety et al., 1997). Observing actions performed by others is an S-State according to Jeannerod (2001), and according to the direct matching hypothesis, understanding an action means mapping an observed action onto *motor representations* of that action (see also Flanagan & Johansson, 2003). This hypothesis can nicely explain the occurrence of ideomotor actions: Watching an action readies us to perform the same action. For example, watching a boxing match and observing punches being landed may induce a tendency to punch an imaginary adversary – sometimes up to the level of overt movement. This tendency is even more enhanced if the observer achieves the goal of the perceived action (intentional induction) (Knuf, Aschersleben, & Prinz, 2001). Intentions can thus modulate the way in which actions are perceived.

However, representations of actions are not only activated if actions are perceived (Grèzes & Decety, 2001). Even the perception of target objects or tools seems to activate movement-related neural structures. Perceiving isolated graspable objects without using them in actions may activate areas in premotor cortex (Mecklinger, Gruenewald, & Besson, 2002) – though the activation is modified by the task relevance of actions (Mecklinger, Gruenewald, & Weiskopf, 2004) – and in the middle temporal sulcus (Kellenbach, Brett, & Patterson, 2003). With monkeys it has been shown that within the ventral premotor cortex, cells that are active when a specific movement is performed are also activated if the corresponding action-related sound is heard (Kohler et al., 2002). Apparently, there is a close relationship between the input information that is processed when actions are perceived and the output information necessary to perform actions. More than this, some people assume that brain areas that are relevant for performing actions directly contribute to the representation of the semantic meaning of language, for example action verbs (Hauck & Pulvermüller, 2004).

All the above-mentioned examples come from laboratory research, where actions are characteristically isolated events that are clearly separated from each other by empty displays between the stimuli. In everyday contexts action perception is more complex. Actions are part of a continuous stream of events (Burt, Kemp, & Conway, 2003), and the objects are embedded in scene contexts. Therefore, perceiving actions nearly always leads to a need to cut events into segments (Zacks & Tversky, 2001). This has the consequence that the perceived content of actions (and consequentially the inferred reason of an action) depends to a considerable degree on the observer, and not solely on the stimulus. Hence, perception is the joint result of bottom-up (stimulus-driven) and top-down (observer-driven) processes, while furthermore, each event may be represented as a multitude within a partonomy of descriptions at different levels. This is the granularity problem (i.e., the decision of the size of an action unit). In order to solve this problem, one has to find an answer to the question: "Where is the beginning of an action and where is its end?"

Fortunately, observers are to a considerable extent in agreement as to where to set the breakpoints for segments, and this concordance is higher for familiar than for unfamiliar actions (Zacks, Tversky, & Iyer, 2001). However, the different granularities have consequences for memory, too. The preferred resolution of encoding varies with the level at which a coherent understanding of the event is possible (Zacks & Tversky, 2001) and at this level memory too varies. Inducing a more fine-grained segmentation brings about a better memory for physical characteristics and vice versa (Hanson & Hirst, 1989). Interestingly, it seems to be the case that the determination of high-level event boundaries is based on different cognitive operations than the determination of low-level boundaries. Patients with frontal lobe damage are specifically impaired at the higher level, at which larger clusters of events are considered (Zalla, Pradat-Diehl, & Sirigu, 2003). This indicates that the general level needs more inference processes than the lower level, which might represent action units more directly provided by perception. The lower units can be considered as goal-oriented actions on objects (accomplishments) (Zacks et al., 2001). This observation supports the assumption that even in perception, the cognitive processing of actions is oriented to goals. This tendency seems to be an inborn characteristic of the human cognitive system, because infants as early as 5 months old pay more attention to the target object of a perceived grasping movement than to the path of the moving arm (Woodward, 1998).

In summary, perceiving action events is a mapping of event segments onto a partonomy of action representations. At the lower level it represents actions related to an object, while at a higher level it represents general goals. The low-level actions refer to individual movement units, and a perceiver understands an action by mapping the perceived movement onto a representation used for performing the movement by him- or herself.

REMEMBERING PERCEIVED ACTION EVENTS

In this section we present what is known from laboratory studies about memory for perceived actions. We present only a selection of results and some of them are from research on the effect of so-called experimenter-performed tasks (EPT) (for memory of different types of perceived actions, see Engelkamp & Zimmer, 1994b). In an EPT task, the participant observes the experimenter performing a series of mini-tasks on command – often without real objects. All mini-tasks are located at the low level of the action partonomies discussed above. They can be regarded as the building blocks of more complex actions, and examples are lighting a candle, opening a bottle, etc. After the series of actions had been watched, participants were required to remember the commands, which they were either to recall or to recognize. This type of task was originally introduced as a contrast to the standard verbal task (VT) and to the subject-performed task (SPT), in which participants pretend to perform the action themselves. In these studies it was often observed that memory came out better for EPT than for VT (Cohen, 1983; Helstrup, 1984, 1986, 1987). If the observed actions were performed with real objects, memory was enhanced even further (Engelkamp & Zimmer, 1984, 1997; Nyberg, Nilsson, & Bäckman, 1991).

Hence, not only is memory for perceived actions good, it is even better than memory for their descriptions. Similarly, it was observed that memory for imagined actions was better than memory for their verbal descriptions (Helstrup, 1986). How can this result be explained? It is known from memory research that memory increases with an increase of the richness of features that are encoded to a to-be-remembered item (Craik & Tulving, 1975). In the preceding text, we have shown that action programmes are partially activated if actions are perceived. Additionally, it is assumed that not only verbal (i.e., conceptual information) is remembered, but also non-verbal information (Engelkamp & Zimmer, 1994a). In EPT, participants observe actions so that action-specific information is processed and the encoded features can become part of memory. Memory is thus enhanced in comparison with verbal encoding. However, perceiving or imagining the action does not completely activate the movement information. As we will see later, memory for perceived and imagined actions is therefore different from memory in SPT.

We do not know how detailed memory is for perceived actions. In laboratory studies of EPTs, memory for the category of the perceived action (i.e., what the experimenter was doing) has usually been investigated rather than memory for details of the movement (i.e., how the movement was performed). However, a recent field study compared memory for details of observed actions (a staged robbery) in a distance condition (watching a video) and in a presence condition (observing the action as a participant in the event) (Ihlebæk, Løve, Eilertsen, & Magnussen, 2003). It turned out that memory for details was reasonable in the distance condition but poor in the presence condition. These memory differences suggest that laboratory studies overestimate memory for perceived actions in everyday context. This is probably true, at least for conditions in which situational factors distract the observer's attention from the action.

This conclusion highlights an important issue in the everyday memory of actions. Episodic memory is only possible if the attention of the observer is directed to the to-be-remembered information. Importantly, attention can be very selective. For example, in one experiment a video was shown in which a group of persons were in a gymnasium playing with a ball. The relevant experimental condition is realized in the middle of this video sequence. A person dressed as a gorilla enters the room, walks through the group of players and leaves the room again. The participants in the experiment watched this video with the instruction to count how often the ball had moved between the players of one team. After the experiment, they were asked whether they had noticed any unusual event in the video. Most of the participants did not notice anything, although the "gorilla" was clearly visible in the video (Simons & Chabris, 1999). This demonstrates that attention can be strongly selective when solving a task. In terms of memory, a consequence is that information not attended to during perception will not be remembered. For perceived actions, the remembered information may therefore strongly depend on the task that was solved during perception. Additionally, thinking back at the control of actions, we doubt whether much information is remembered if it was automatically processed during performance, due to the abstract level of action control.

Poor memory due to selective attention can even be observed if the retention interval is very brief. Imagine that one is observing a video-recording of an action (e.g., two people are talking to each other). The camera changes the perspective briefly and then it switches back to the original view. However, it is not exactly the same scene, because now one of the actors is wearing a different piece of clothing (e.g., a different scarf, or a different picture is hanging on the wall). Would you notice this change because the new percept causes a mismatch with your memory? The answer: It is very likely that you would not (Levin & Simons, 1997). This effect is not restricted to vision. For example, even the change of the voice of a speaker was not detected by 40% of participants if their task was to repeat aloud each word from a heard list (Vitevitch, 2003), and this effect even occurs in real-life interactions. The unexpected substitution of a conversation partner was not noticed by about 50% of subjects (Levin, Simons, Angelone, & Chabris, 2002b; Simons & Levin, 1998). Phenomena like this are called change blindness (for a review, see Rensink, 2002). This is another demonstration of the fact that we have less memory than we believe. Consciously we perceive the world as stable, and we attribute this to our memory, so that most people have the wrong intuition that they would detect such changes (Levin, Drivdahl, Momen, & Beck, 2002a). In fact, much of this "memory" exists only in the persistence of objects in the world.

However, it is important to note that the necessity of attention for memory does not mean that intention is necessary for remembering. However information is processed, it contributes to memory independent of the intention of the person (Craik & Lockhart, 1972; Hyde & Jenkins, 1969). The intention to remember something may change the way of encoding or the selection of information, or it may induce specific strategies to memorize the information (mnemonic techniques). All these strategic operations will change memory (Helstrup, 1987, 1989a, c). However, according to our current knowledge, intention per se does not change the generation of memory. Neuropsychological results suggest that without any intention to remember, a memory entry is generated if neural activation caused by any kind of encoding makes contact with hippocampal structures (Paller & Wagner, 2002) and that a part of these representations is later consolidated in long-term memory (Paller, 2000). Which factors are critical for the generation, and in particular for the consolidation, of these entries is still unknown. Apparently, one factor is the significance or importance of the perceived event or action for the observer and his or her emotional reaction to the stimulus (Tucker & Luu, 2006). It could be shown that emotionally arousing stimuli cause a reaction of the amygdala, and that their activity influences the hippocampus and the medial temporal system (Paré, Collins, & Pelletier, 2002). As a consequence, memory is affected. Moreover, emotions directly influence attention and thereby the information that is processed and finally remembered. It has been observed that negative emotional stimuli focus attention on the central element of the event or action (e.g., the victim), with the result that context information is less well remembered than under neutral conditions. This phenomenon is called "tunnel memory" (Safer, Christianson, Autry, & Österlund, 1998). This brings us to the issue of the accuracy of memory for actions.

ACCURACY OF MEMORY FOR PERCEIVED AND IMAGINED ACTIONS

There are many factors that cause weak memory that is prone to errors. We are particularly unlikely to have an explicit memory for unnoticed aspects of an event. But what happens with those elements that are attended to? Are they veridically remembered? How does the rememberer experience those memories?

Psychology discusses two factors that induce the impression of having a memory for something. The first is recollection, and the second is familiarity (Mandler, 1980). Recollection is a kind of conscious retrieval or reinstatement of a previously experienced event and its spatiotemporal context. Familiarity is a feeling of having previously encountered an event, without being able to put it into the correct episodic context. Recollection is often investigated in so-called source memory tasks, in which participants have to decide in which episode an item was encoded (Johnson, Hashtroudi, & Lindsay, 1993). Recognition, in particular, can be based on familiarity. From a first-person point of view, familiarity-based recognition is experienced as knowing that something was there, whereas recollection is experienced as remembering having encountered that event thanks to the explicit retrieval of specific aspects of the episode (Gardiner & Java, 1993). Possibilities of empirically distinguishing these two factors (Yonelinas, 2002) and their neural realizations (Mecklinger, 2000) have been important issues in recent research (Zimmer, Mecklinger, & Lindenberger, 2006), and they are also important for the everyday memory of actions.

Recollection and familiarity are specifically relevant for an understanding of false memory (i.e., cases where people "remember" an event that never happened, cf. Schacter, 1996; see also Chapter 7). Two possibilities exist: False memory can be caused by an erroneous decision based on an eroded memory, or it uses an "intact" but distorted memory. During encoding or retention the memory entry might have been shaped in such a way that false features were integrated into the former episode. Given our previous discussion, one such condition immediately comes to mind. Separating perceived from imagined or performed actions might cause problems. If the same neural structures used during performing are partially activated by perceiving and imagining, it must be difficult to distinguish between memory traces of these two encodings. This task is referred to as "reality monitoring" (Johnson & Raye, 1981).

It is assumed that the presence of detailed sensory information is used for reality decisions (Johnson et al., 1993). An early study showed that imagining an action (drawing a geometric figure) can be confused with real performance (R.E. Anderson, 1984). In this study participants mentally or actually traced outlines of figures during encoding. In the following memory test, participants had great problems in deciding about the activity performed in response to a stimulus during study. A more recent study reveals that such effects might actually be based on memories of the former imagery process. In an EEG study (Gonsalves & Paller, 2000), words were presented with the instruction to visualize the named object. During the study of some of the words a real picture was also shown directly after imagination. Later, during testing, subjects had to decide whether or not a picture of that word had already been seen. Of interest are the false positives; items that subjects claimed to have seen a picture of, although it had not been presented. The EEG recorded during encoding revealed that the event-related potentials of electrodes at posterior sites of the scalp showed higher amplitudes for words that later became false positives than for subsequently correctly classified words. The topography of this effect suggests that the falsely classified words elicited more detailed images than the rejected ones, and as a consequence of this information these words might have been falsely recognized as already-perceived pictures during the following testing.

This false memory effect is not restricted to imagination of objects, but is also observed with imagination of actions. In order to investigate this effect a technique called "imagination inflation" was introduced. The technique was first used by Garry, Manning, Loftus, and Sherman (1996), who demonstrated that imagining childhood events inflated confidence that these imagined events had occurred. Later Goff and Roediger (1998) directly contrasted real events (i.e., actually performed actions) with imagining events. In a study phase, actions were encoded. Participants heard action phrases, imagined the denoted actions or actually performed the action. In a second session some time after the study phase, subjects were required to imagine actions. Some of the imagined actions were from the study phase while others were new ones. In a third session participants were asked to recognize old items in an exclusion condition, which means that only items from the first phase should be accepted. In Goff and Roediger's experiment, participants showed a strong tendency to falsely accept items imagined in phase 2 as having been performed in phase 1. However, imagining a formerly performed item did not change acceptance of those items that had actually been performed. Apparently, imagining performance made verbal commands more similar to really-performed items. Interestingly, imagination inflation is even observed with bizarre actions (e.g., kiss the magnifying glass); one might expect that their bizarreness would protect them against false confidence enhancement (Thomas & Loftus, 2002). Imagining events must therefore be considered as a possible reason for false memory (Hyman & Pentland, 1996).

The cause of this effect might be the same as was discussed in connection with the example of objects. Imagining performing an action adds action information to memory. Retrieving at testing the action information generated during imagining may lead subjects to make a false attribution of source. This view is supported by recent experimental results. In one study participants were forced to incorporate sensory details into their images of actions. This manipulation caused an increase of false memories compared to the standard imagination inflation condition (Thomas, Bulevich, & Loftus, 2003).

A second study by the same researchers showed that detailed items were more likely to be classified as recollected (remember category), whereas less detailed items were more likely judged as familiar when they were being remembered. Finally, in a third study, the content of the imagined action (i.e., the first-person versus third-person view) was crossed with the type of information judged during testing. The results showed that false positives were more likely if the previously visualized perspective matched the visual perspective used for the decision in the source memory task (Libby, 2003).

All these observations demonstrate that additional information that is self-generated after the study phase can distort memory. Importantly, such effects also occur without experimental manipulations. Hannigan and Reinitz (2001) presented slides depicting a sequence of actions in which either the cause of the action or its effects were not shown. During testing all pictures were presented, including the previously unshown slides depicting causes or effects. It turned out that participants often erroneously claimed to recognize plausible cause scenes as old (false positives), suggesting that they had already imagined the causes during study. Hence, although memory for perceived actions is good, it can nevertheless become mixed up with related information not belonging to the actual source. Given the expected frequency of mental simulations of actions (S-States), we should therefore be cautious regarding questions about the veridicality of memory for perceived actions.

INTENDING ACTIONS AND PROSPECTIVE MEMORY

After this look at memory for perceived actions, we now discuss studies that have investigated memory for performed actions. However, we first want to discuss what happens before an action is performed; that is, when it is intended. In the context of this chapter we always assume that the general decision in favour of the action has already been made. For this reason, we do not discuss action planning on a more general level, nor reasoning about action plans. The to-be-performed actions are therefore always given. But even then the control of an intended action is complex (Jeannerod, 2003).

When specific actions are performed in everyday situations they are usually parts of larger plans. At any given moment, usually more than one plan is relevant, out of several plans and actions that exist in parallel. We therefore need to schedule our different actions. Some actions are performed immediately if an action goal comes up, while others are delayed. This kind of temporal ordering is based on an evaluation of their importance (e.g., their benefits or costs, our liking or disliking of the actions, etc). We also mentally "simulate" some actions in order to test how they might be performed. This typically occurs when we face unfamiliar task situations. We may test whether the action will work, which we do without overt performance although with the help of action schemata. Finally we trigger the action, carry out the movement, monitor its realization, and update our plans.

In order to solve such tasks efficiently, a number of components must be available: a process of intention formation that marks actions as to-be-performed, a maintenance mechanism for the set of to-be-performed actions, an action planning and simulation status, a triggering operation that brings an action to overt performance, a monitoring device for action control, and a process of marking an action as done, which cancels the action from the set of to-be-performed actions.

Intending actions

What happens with intended actions? They seem to have a specific mental status. It is the persistence of intended actions that is remarkable. In the computational model of cognition, ACT-R plans are active nodes of activation (J.R. Anderson, 1993). Phenomenally, they are "hot spots" of cognition, and if the action is really important for me, it is spinning in my mind. This persistence guarantees that in time-based prospective memory tasks the goal will occasionally pop up into consciousness. There is empirical evidence in support of this kind of higher, sustained level of activation. Goal-related information is more accessible than out-of-goal information in many cognitive tasks (for a review, see Goschke & Kuhl, 1996).

In a recent study this persistence was related to SPTs and ageing (Freeman & Ellis, 2003). These authors required subjects to encode actions as verbal tasks (VT), as subject-performed tasks (SPT), and as to-be-performed actions (TBA). Both SPTs and TBAs enhanced accessibility compared to VTs, but the effects were non-additive. The authors therefore suggested that both effects partially rely on the same structures. From our point of view we assume that the effects depend on action schemata. Interestingly, the intention effect was of the same size in young and older adults, although older adults often complain that they forget intended actions. The assumption of similar structures for TBAs and SPTs is compatible with the conclusion drawn by Engelkamp (1997) from memory experiments. He observed a memory advantage of TBA over VT, which vanished in the context of SPT items. He explained this effect by interference caused by SPT. Another result in line with this thinking is the observation that planning actions partially activates the same neural structures as performing actions (Grossman & Blake, 2001).

In order to ensure that intended actions are really executed, the to-be-performed actions must be coordinated with ongoing actions. In event-based prospective memory tasks, participants have to perform an action if a specific cue is available. This cue has to be efficient in two ways. First, it has to foster retrieval of the to-be-performed action (Guynn et al., 2001), and second, the cue must reach conscious attention in competition with the ongoing task. Hence, the best overall performance will be obtained if selective attention is tuned in such a way that processing of information relevant for the ongoing task is maximal but information not relevant for that task is sufficiently processed, so that the execution of the postponed action is not omitted.

Prospective memory and its efficiency

It is easy to see that a reliable prospective memory is highly relevant for everyday performance of actions (e.g., in taking medication). As medication is particularly important in the elderly population, it is a problem that prospective memory deteriorates in ageing (Maylor, 1996; Smith, Della Sala, Logie, & Maylor, 2000). The prevalence of failure of prospective memory is high (Huppert, Johnson, & Nickson, 2000). However, in experimental studies age effects are not consistently found (Uttl, Graf, Miller, & Tuokko, 2001), and they are modulated by the type of prospective task concerned (Bastin & Meulemans, 2002; Vogels, Dekker, Brouwer, & de Jong 2002). The divergent findings may partly reflect individual differences and various environmental conditions.

Here we focus on two factors that cause and modulate this impairment. The first factor is an encoding deficit. Elderly people show less encoding activity than younger people, with the result that the to-be-performed task is less available (West, Herndon, & Covell, 2003). This is the retrospective memory component in prospective remembering. Improving encoding of the to-be-performed task would improve the chances of retrieval success of the intended action if the cue is perceived. The second factor is the less efficient self-initiated monitoring, which is attributed to impairments of attention with ageing. It is difficult to improve this component because it is probably associated with a deterioration of frontal lobe brain functions (Glisky, 1996).

If it is not possible to improve the monitoring process, the provision of external memory aids is recommended. Interestingly, external memory aids are frequently used by younger people whereas elderly people are less prone to use such devices (Zimmer, Herrmann, & Duppe, 1996). Asked for a reason for their behaviour, elderly people mention being afraid to lose memory efficiency if their memory is not used. This is a misattribution that should be changed. Elderly people are right in their assumption that memories can be trained (Verhaeghen, Marcoen, & Goossens, 1992), and they should not abstain from such training. However, this training is highly content-specific, so that memorizing actions to be performed is an inefficient training procedure. On the contrary, external memory aids support prospective memory (Vedhara et al., 2004), and they do this even in persons with mild dementia (Oriani et al., 2003), so that efficiency is unnecessarily lost if external memory aids are not used. Memory aids such as electronic devices may therefore help elderly people to overcome their problems in prospective memory.

MEMORY FOR PERFORMED ACTIONS

This section concerns the overt performance of actions and their memory. These are laboratory tasks that the participants perform themselves, and therefore this condition is called a subject-performed task (SPT). The tasks are usually the same mini-tasks as mentioned above for EPTs. They are presented as verbal commands and participants are required to perform or to pretend to perform the action. Memory is tested by a recall or recognition test, usually of the verbal commands. As with EPTs, therefore, in SPT tasks the memory test asks for verbal descriptions of what was done, not about how the action was actually carried out. It is an answer to the question: What did you do? This type of study was introduced in the 1980s in several laboratories. In the following years a large number of studies were performed using this paradigm. Since most of the results have been summarized in recent reviews (Engelkamp, 1997; Nilsson, 2000; Zimmer & Cohen, 2001), we are selective in this chapter.

Memory for subject-performed tasks

A robust effect obtained in this research is the high level of memory performance for performed actions. Memory for performed actions is much better than memory for actions that are only verbally encoded or perceived (for a wide-ranging review, see Engelkamp, 1997). Recognition memory of SPT is particularly good. There are exceptions (e.g., pair associate learning; Engelkamp, 1986) where SPT did not enhance memory, but it usually does so. From a first-person point of view, learning items by performing is an easy task. The good memory performance and the ease of learning inspired some authors to speak of effortless learning (Kausler, 1989) or of a non-strategic learning task (Cohen, 1981). Others pointed out that to abstain from elaboration can also be considered as a strategic choice (Helstrup, 1984, 1987). Like intending an action, performing an action also seems to improve the accessibility of information in memory. Items that were performed pop into mind if we think back to what we have done recently (Zimmer, Helstrup, & Engelkamp, 2000).

However, such memories seem to be based on a complex set of information. Performing an action on command elicits a cascade of cognitive processes. Figure 3.1 illustrates some of these elements. Many of these components probably contribute to the specific memory advantage of an SPT task. The memory advantage of SPT probably does not reflect a single homogeneous effect but rather a set of micro-effects that add up to a robust memory advantage. It is possible that different components or combinations of them contribute to specific memory effects obtained in the context of SPTs.

As a first step, the verbal command has to be understood, so that the actor knows what he or she has to do. This forces semantic processing of the command, independent of any additional orienting task given to the subjects. Some observations support a contribution of this component. Under SPT conditions, only small effects were observed if the depth of processing was manipulated (Nilsson & Craik, 1990; Zimmer & Engelkamp, 1999), and a secondary task during encoding impaired VT more than SPT (Bäckman, Nilsson, & Chalom, 1986; Engelkamp & Zimmer, 1996). The forced semantic

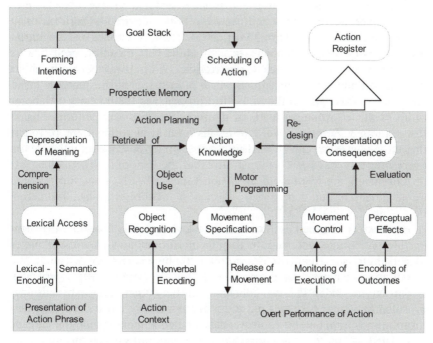

Figure 3.1 An illustration of the different subprocesses involved in intending, planning and executing actions in a subject-performed task in which participants act on verbal commands. (Adapted from Zimmer, 2001.)

processing might also work as environmental support for encoding, an aspect that we will discuss below.

The second step is action planning, which also contributes to memory. On the one hand, planning alone, without overt performance, led to better memory than verbal encoding alone. On the other hand, reducing planning in SPT decreased memory. The first effect was observed in a SPT no-go condition in which only one of two partners actually performed the instructed action (Zimmer & Engelkamp, 1984). Note, however, that overt performance did always cause better memory than the pure planning conditions. The second effect was obtained when actions were performed on imitation so that planning was much reduced. Now, memory performance was reduced in a condition that imitated STP, relative to the SPT-on-command condition (Zimmer & Engelkamp, 1996). However, elaborating on the actions analogous to deep-level processing did not further enhance SPT memory (Helstrup, 1987; Zimmer, 1984). An example of such an action is unpacking an object before it is used.

When actions are performed in everyday contexts, objects are usually involved. These objects always specify actions, and they deliver specific visual input (e.g., sensory information) as well as category-specific information (e.g., about the kind of object). Sensory features of the objects (e.g., their colour) are to some extent automatically encoded during enactment (Bäckman, Nilsson, & Kormi-Nouri, 1993). These components also contribute to memory. SPTs with objects brought about better memory performance than SPTs without objects (Nyberg et al., 1991). However, while object information adds to the enactment effect proper, it is not responsible for it. Experiments have shown the SPT effect proper (i.e., the memory advantage of an overt performance) to be of the same size with and without objects (Engelkamp & Zimmer, 1984, 1996). This result is plausible if one considers that motor schemata can be used employing prototypical object information. For example, it has been demonstrated that the temporal structures of sets of movements are identical if an action (open a bottle) is performed with an imaginary object, a perceived object or a real object (Weiss, Jeannerod, Paulignan, & Freund, 2000).

The next component is the most controversial one. Does a movement or "motor" component used for the execution of actions also contribute to SPT memory performances? This question has long been discussed and is still a matter of debate (Engelkamp, 2001; Helstrup, 1987, 2005; Nilsson & Kormi-Nouri, 2001). It is not controversial that specific information is only provided by actual performance and is therefore only memorized after performing an action, but it is controversial whether memory should therefore be considered as "motor" (Zimmer, 2001). We shall not go into any details of this discussion here but merely point out (1) that there is empirical evidence in support of this motor assumption and (2) that motor information exists at different levels that are differently close to the control of muscles. Today, due to brain-imaging techniques, it is widely accepted that the neural structures that represent memory include the perceptual processing areas. In analogy one can suggest that movement-specific neural structures that are only active in SPT tasks also contribute to memory and recent brain-imaging results seem to support this (Nilsson et al., 2000; Nyberg et al., 2001, Russ, Mack, Grama, Lanfermann, & Knopf, 2003). This demonstrates that memories of performed actions, like those of other types of information, are distributed representations comprising a net of components. Though consensus is not yet reached on what structures are relevant, all or many of these components probably contribute to the memory of performed actions.

Memory for movement-specific information of actions

We now turn to the question of whether and to what extent information on the specific movement can be remembered. Interestingly, this was not a central topic of the SPT research until recently, although some studies suggested that this information can be remembered. For example, it was shown that tracing a figure enhances memory for the shape of the figure (Hulme, 1979). Additonally, there is indirect evidence for such memory (e.g., changing the executing hand between study and test reduced recognition memory; Engelkamp, Zimmer, Mohr, & Sellen, 1994) and, particularly after SPT learning, the movement similarity of distractors influenced recognition similarity (Engelkamp & Zimmer, 1995).

A recent experiment (Zimmer, 2005) directly demonstrates that participants can use specific information about the action they had performed. During the study phase, participants viewed action phrases together with two pictures showing possible instruments for the action (e.g., "cutting bread"). For some actions, the instruments induced similar (e.g., two different keys) or dissimilar movements (e.g., a knife and a slicer). At encoding, subjects first were required to decide which instruments were adequate for the action. After the decision one object was marked by a frame around the picture, and subjects were required to associate this instrument with the action. In the VT condition no additional instruction was given. In the SPT condition each action was symbolically performed with the marked instrument. During testing each phrase was presented paired with each instrument and the subject's task was to decide whether this instrument was paired with that action or not. The results showed that if the two instruments induce the same action, SPT and VT had identical memory performances (70% correct). However, when the actions were different, the SPT group performed much better (90% correct) than the VT group (65% correct). This result suggests that movement information provided by enactment was remembered and used in recognition. Obviously, one can remember not only that one has done something. One can also remember that one has done something this way or that way. Sometimes we use memory of the "shape" of our own action as a retrieval aid. When searching in memory where the key is located, we may try to repeat *how* we placed the keys yesterday. However, whether we really use enactment information for that purpose is still an open question. In a relocation task, for example, actively putting objects at specific locations did not improve memory compared with a perceptual encoding condition (Zimmer, 1996). Interestingly, it has also been repeatedly observed that performance of movement patterns (e.g., sequences of steps forward, to the right, to the left, or backward, is remembered by both non-motor and motor cues; Helstrup, 1996a, 2000, 2001).

The question about remembering the "what" and "how" of actions apparently deals with somewhat different aspects of memory for actions. It has never been disputed, for example, that motor factors are important in skill acquisition (cf. procedural knowledge about how to carry out actions). When they are asked how an action was carried out (e.g., at the workplace or in court), people are clearly able to answer this question. The answer evidently must be based on retention of motor information. However, asking what actions a person performed is to ask for declarative knowledge about the action. It does not necessarily have to depend on memory of motor information (J.R. Anderson, 1980, 1996). In action memory research the distinction between "how" and "what" questions has not always been made. Perhaps they should not even be separated.

It seems that more sophisticated experiments on this topic are required, particularly in view of our present knowledge about action control. On the one hand, observations show that motor-related brain structures are activated in non-motor tasks, as we have described in earlier sections. The implication is that it may be impossible to observe separate motor effects of performance, because non-motor conditions also activate the same structures in similar ways (Helstrup, 2005). On the other hand, it was suggested that the critical component of movement knowledge of which we are aware is a forward model of actions representing the sensory consequences of actions (Blakemore & Frith, 2003). This means that we always think, and remember, in terms of effects. Hence, future research will have to disentangle the aspects of an overtly performed action, both when it comes to remembering what one actually did and how one did it.

Finally, there is the agency aspect of actions. Self-performed actions have the specific quality of the feeling of it-was-me-who-moved (cf. our discussion of action control). Such awareness of our own actions is an achievement of the cognitive and neural systems that cannot be taken for granted. It is possible to perform movements without this feeling, as has been shown in various forms of impaired action awareness (Blakemore, Wolpert, & Frith, 2002). It has recently been observed in schizophrenic patients who have difficulties in reality monitoring that, compared to EPT, they did not show the usual SPT effect in recognition (Daprati, Nico, Franck, & Sirigu, 2003). The authors suggest that such patients have no reliable first-person view, and that this reduces the SPT effect. If it is a reliable effect and the explanation is correct, it would add an interesting aspect to memory for actions. Healthy subjects remember very well whether or not they have performed particular actions, even after having studied as many as 200 items. Self-awareness of one's own actions might therefore have a specific status. This component might explain the high recognition performance in SPT tasks as well as subjects' confidence in performed/non-performed paradigms. We usually also have such confidence in our memories of everyday actions. An exception may be frequently repeated actions, where the problem may be that of remembering the specific action occurrence (its spatiotemporal context). The reason for this difficulty might be that for these items it has not to be decided *whether*, but *when*, an action was performed, and this decision is not directly supported by enactment.

The missed temporal information points to another aspect that would be considered in the context of memory for performed actions. The typical task in action memory is a list of separate actions. Performing these actions focuses cognitive processing on the individual action, and it enhances item-specific information (Nilsson, 2000; Zimmer & Engelkamp, 1989). Because the focus of processing in such tasks is on the individual item, the item-context association is not enhanced in SPT (Koriat, Ben-Zur, & Druch, 1991), and similarly, order information is not enhanced (Engelkamp & Dehn, 2000; Olofsson, 1996). SPT even hinders the association of actions that are semantically unrelated. An example is paired-associate learning (Engelkamp, Zimmer, & Denis, 1989). Only an active strategy that supports integration overrides this tendency and enables sufficient association performances to take place between unrelated pairs in SPT (Helstrup, 1989a, b).

The question of whether context supports action memory or not has been debated (Engelkamp, 1998; Helstrup, 1996b). There is research evidence suggesting that memory for subject-performed tasks does not profit from contextual support in the same way that memory for non-enacted material does. The explanation may lie in the difficulty of integrating motor and non-motor memory information. However, other experiments demonstrate equally good memory support under enactment and under non-enactment encoding conditions. When an integrative context is provided for a list of subject-performed tasks (e.g., when all action items are arranged as they occur naturally on a shopping trip), memory for performed tasks also displays temporal order and contextual integration (Cornoldi, Corti, & Helstrup, 1994; Helstrup, 1987, 1996b). Perhaps the conflicting observations reflect issues connected to the above-mentioned difference between "what" and "how" aspects of action memory. Context information may be more import-ant for remembering "what" than "how", and this difference may inadvertently have crept into the designs. Whether motor and non-motor cue integration takes place thus depends on several boundary conditions.

In summary, for everyday action one may often know whether an action has been performed or not without knowing where and when the action was performed. At other times, knowing that an action was performed at the same time gives access to information about where and when it was performed. However, subjective memory confidence may not be the most reliable information when it comes to deciding such questions of temporal and spatial contexts, especially if these were not action-relevant.

Performing as a memory aid

As we have seen, SPT implies a reliable memory increase compared to verbal and visual encoding conditions. In a large study with 1000 subjects ranging in age between 35 and 80 years, only 5% did not show an advantage as a result of performing actions (Nyberg, Persson, & Nilsson, 2002). Overt perform-ance, where conditions allow, can therefore be efficiently used as a memory aid. Even at the beginning of SPT research, it was shown that SPT is a very efficient type of learning instruction that can offset memory impairment. Cohen and Bean (1983) observed equal performances by mentally retarded persons and a standard control group in SPT. Enactment might be a good compensatory encoding condition when learning is impaired for some reason (Larsson & Rönnberg, 1987). Similarly, Alzheimer patients showed better memory performances in SPT and a reduced memory impairment than seen in normal subjects (Lekeu, Van der Linden, Moonen, & Salmon, 2002). Other groups for which the same outcome has been reported are Parkinson patients (Knopf, Mack, Lenel, & Ferrante, 2005) autistic children (Summers & Craik, 1994) and frontal lobe patients (Butters, Kaszniak, Glisky, & Eslinger, 1994, but see Knopf et al., 2005). Performing actions is thus an efficient alternative when other strategies are impaired.

Action performance has also been shown to overcome memory impairments due to ageing. Authors reported that ageing effects were reduced in SPTs compared to VTs (Brooks & Gardiner, 1994; Kausler, Lichty, & Freund, 1985; McDonald-Miszczak, Hubley, & Hultsch, 1996; Norris & West, 1993). However, other observations have shown equal decrements for SPT and VT (Knopf & Neidhardt, 1989; Rönnlund, Nyberg, Bäckman, & Nilsson, 2003). SPT was found to be efficient, but old and young adults showed comparable benefits from SPT so that the ageing decrement in memory was not compensated. It is therefore still an open question as to whether SPT may be able to level out ageing effects in memory and, if so, under what conditions.

Considering memory aids, recent research on the effects of signing on memory is also of interest. SPTs without objects resemble iconic signs as used in different sign languages used by deaf people. One might therefore ask whether signing is also memory-efficient in comparison with VT. This was tested by Von Essen and Nilsson (2003) and by Zimmer and Engelkamp (2003). Both research groups reported consistently that proficient signers recalled and recognized more signed than read items, and that the signing effect was of the same size as the SPT effect. The same effect was also observed for non-iconic signs, which were produced to nouns. Signing the noun for someone else caused the same memory advantage as generating a prototypical action to this noun. Therefore, for memory, signing was generally as efficient as performing actions, and hence it too might be used to enhance memory.

FINAL REMARKS

This chapter has tried to communicate a few basic principles about the processing of actions and their consequences for everyday memory. In closing we want to make a few final remarks about actions.

It should have become clear that actions are represented at various levels of abstraction, ranging from goals to motor schemata, and that they are organized in partonomies. This information is used for action planning and perception of actions. Actions are probably represented as a distributed network of individual components. These components are activated during perception, during execution, and during imagination or "simulation". However, this does not mean that there is a complete overlap of these components under all conditions. On the contrary, different brain regions are exclusively involved in processing specific input or output modalities. Furthermore, goals play an important role in processing of actions. A consequence of these observations is that at present, the separation between perception and action is less sharp than it used to be. Motor and non-motor conditions are less distinct than previously assumed. Furthermore, action information, like other sensory input information, is simultaneously processed at different levels of abstraction.

Because all components that are processed during encoding can in principle become parts of memories, memory is always based on sets of different components. In working memory research this principle was formulated as "memory of systems" instead of "systems of memory" (Fuster, 1997). Similarly, memory for performed actions is based on very different components, depending on the task situation, so that it is memory of several systems or types of information. This seems to explain the sometimes conflicting experimental results obtained. Performing actions elicits a cascade of processes that add up to a total positive effect on memory.

In closing, two more general aspects of the results presented here should be mentioned. These deal with memory of actions and eyewitness conditions. One aspect is attention and its influence on the reliability of memory. On the one hand attention is crucial for memory, while on the other it is highly selective, making only a part of the information available. The latter feature is optimal for the efficient control of behaviour – for which the brain evolved – but it is bad for the reliability of eyewitness memory. No wonder that eyewitness memory fails at times, even for self-performed actions. The second aspect is the level at which actions are controlled. The way in which actions are controlled influences consciously processed information and thus the memory of actions. This too has powerful consequences for the reliability of everyday memory of actions and for the memory of eyewitnesses.

REFERENCES

Abelson, R. (1981). Psychological status of the script. *American Psychologist, 36,* 715–729.

Adams, J.A. (1987). Historical review and appraisal of research on the learning, retention, and transfer of human motor skills. *Psychological Bulletin, 101,* 41–74.

Allison, T., Puce, A., & McCarthy, G. (2000). Social perception from visual cues: Role of the STS region. *Trends in Cognitive Sciences, 4,* 267–278.

Anderson, J.R. (1980). Concepts, propositions, and schemata: What are the cognitive units? *Nebraska Symposium on Motivation, 28,* 121–162.

Anderson, J.R. (1983). *The architecture of cognition.* Cambridge, MA: Harvard University Press.

Anderson, J.R. (1993). *Rules of the mind.* Hillsdale, NJ: Lawrence Erlbaum Associates, Inc.

Anderson, J.R. (1996). ACT: A simple theory of complex cognition. *American Psychologist, 51,* 355–365.

Anderson, R.E. (1984). Did I do it or did I only imagine doing it? *Journal of Experimental Psychology: General, 113,* 594–613.

Annett, J. (1995). Motor imagery: Perception or action? *Neuropsychologia, 33,* 1395–1417.

Bäckman, L., Nilsson, L.-G., & Chalom, D. (1986). New evidence on the nature of the encoding of action events. *Memory and Cognition, 14,* 339–346.

Bäckman, L., Nilsson, L.-G., & Kormi-Nouri, R.K. (1993). Attentional demands and recall of verbal and color information in action events. *Scandinavian Journal of Psychology, 34,* 246–254.

Bandura, A. (1962). Social learning through imitation. In M.R. Jones (Ed.), *Nebraska Symposium on Motivation* (pp. 211–269). Lincoln, NB: University of Nebraska Press.

Bastin, C., & Meulemans, T. (2002). Are time-based and event-based prospective memory affected by normal aging in the same way? *Current Psychology Letters: Behaviour, Brain & Cognition, 7,* 105–121.

Beauchamp, M.S., Lee, K.E., Haxby, J.V., & Martin, A. (2003). fMRI responses to video and point-light displays of moving humans and manipulable objects. *Journal of Cognitive Neuroscience, 15,* 991–1001.

Bekkering, H., Wohlschläger, A., & Gattis, M. (2000). Imitation of gestures in children is goal-directed. *Quarterly Journal of Experimental Psychology, 53,* 153–164.

Blakemore, S.-J., & Frith, C. (2003). Self-awareness and action. *Current Opinion in Neurobiology, 13,* 219–224.

Blakemore, S.-J., Wolpert, D.M., & Frith, C.D. (2002). Abnormalities in the awareness of action. *Trends in Cognitive Sciences, 6,* 237–242.

Blandin, Y. (2002). Observational learning: A tool for the acquisition of new motor skills. *Année Psychologique, 102,* 523–554.

Brandimonte, M., Einstein, G.O., & McDaniel, M.A. (1996). *Prospective memory: Theory and applications.* Mahwah, NJ: Lawrence Erlbaum Associates, Inc.

Brooks, B.M., & Gardiner, J.M. (1994). Age differences in memory for prospective compared with retrospective subject-performed tasks. *Memory and Cognition, 22,* 27–33.

Buccino, G., Binkofski, F., Fink, G.R., Fadiga, L., Fogassi, L., Gallese, V., Seitz, R.J., Zilles, K., Rizzolatti, G., & Freund, H.J. (2001). Action observation activates premotor and parietal areas in a somatotopic manner: An fMRI study. *European Journal of Neuroscience, 13,* 400–404.

Burt, C.D., Kemp, S., & Conway, M.A. (2003). Themes, events, and episodes in autobiographical memory. *Memory and Cognition, 31,* 317–325.

Butters, M.A., Kaszniak, A.W., Glisky, E.L., & Eslinger, P.J. (1994). Recency discrimination deficits in frontal lobe patients. *Neuropsychology, 8,* 343–354.

Chaminade, T., Meltzoff, A.N., & Decety, J. (2002). Does the end justify the means? A PET exploration of the mechanisms involved in human imitation. *NeuroImage, 15,* 318–328.

Cohen, R.L. (1981). On the generality of some memory laws. *Scandinavian Journal of Psychology, 22,* 267–281.

Cohen, R.L. (1983). The effect of encoding variables on the free recall of words and action events. *Memory and Cognition, 11,* 575–582.

Cohen, R.L., & Bean, G. (1983). Memory in educable mentally retarded adults: Deficit in subject or experimenter? *Intelligence, 7,* 287–298.

Cornoldi, C., Corti, M.T., & Helstrup, T. (1994). Do you remember what you imagined you would do in that place? The motor encoding cue-failure effect in sighted and blind people. *The Quarterly Journal of Experimental Psychology, 47A,* 311–329.

Craighero, L., Bello, A., Fadiga, L., & Rizzolatti, G. (2002). Hand action preparation influences the responses to hand pictures. *Neuropsychologia, 40,* 492–502.

Craik, F.I.M., & Anderson, N.D. (1999). Applying cognitive research to problems of aging. In D. Gopher & A. Koriat (Eds.), *Attention and performance XVII: Cognitive regulation of performance: Interaction of theory and application* (pp. 583–615). Cambridge, MA: MIT Press.

Craik, F.I.M., & Lockhart, R.S. (1972). Levels of processing: A framework for memory research. *Journal of Verbal Learning and Verbal Behavior, 11,* 671–684.

Craik, F.I.M., & Tulving, E. (1975). Depth of processing and the retention of words in episodic memory. *Journal of Experimental Psychology: General, 104,* 268–294.

Daprati, E., Nico, D., Franck, N., & Sirigu, A. (2003). Being the agent: Memory for action events. *Consciousness and Cognition, 12,* 670–683.

Decety, J., Grèzes, J., Costes, N., Perani, D., Jeannerod, M., Procyk, E., Grassi, F., & Fazio, F. (1997). Brain activity during observation of actions – influence of action content and subject's strategy. *Brain, 120,* 1763–1777.

De Renzi, E., & Faglioni, P. (1999). Apraxia. In G. Denes & L. Pizzamiglio (Eds.), *Handbook of clinical and experimental neuropsychologie* (pp. 421–440). Hove, UK: Psychology Press.

Eichenbaum, H. (2005). Memory binding by hippocampal relational networks. In H.D. Zimmer, A. Mecklinger, & U. Lindenberger (Eds.), *Binding in episodic memory: A neurocognitive approach.* Oxford, UK: Oxford University Press.

Einstein, G.O., & McDaniel, M.A. (1990). Normal aging and prospective memory. *Journal of Experimental Psychology: Learning, Memory, and Cognition, 16,* 717–726.

Engelkamp, J. (1986). Nouns and verbs in paired-associate learning: Instructional effects. *Psychological Research, 48,* 153–159.

Engelkamp, J. (1997). Memory for to-be-performed tasks versus memory for performed tasks. *Memory and Cognition, 25,* 117–124.

Engelkamp, J. (1998). *Memory for actions.* Hove, UK: Psychology Press.

Engelkamp, J. (2001). Action memory: A system-oriented approach. In H.D. Zimmer, R. Cohen, M.J. Guynn, J. Engelkamp, R. Kormi-Nouri, & M.A. Foley (Eds.), *Memory for action: A distinct form of episodic memory?* (pp. 49–96). New York: Oxford University Press.

Engelkamp, J., & Dehn, D. (1997). Strategy and consciousness in remembering subject-performed actions. *Sprache & Kognition, 16,* 94–109.

Engelkamp, J., & Dehn, D. (2000). Item and order information in subject-performed tasks and in experimenter-performed tasks. *Journal of Experimental Psychology: Learning, Memory, and Cognition, 26,* 671–682.

Engelkamp, J., & Krumnacker, H. (1980). Imaginale und motorische Prozesse beim Behalten verbalen Materials. *Zeitschrift für experimentelle und angewandte Psychologie, 27,* 511–533.

Engelkamp, J., & Perrig, W. (1986). Differential effects of imaginal and motor encoding on the recall of action phrases. *Archiv für Psychologie, 138,* 261–273.

Engelkamp, J., & Zimmer, H.D. (1983). Der Einfluß von Wahrnehmen und Tun auf das Behalten von Verb-Objekt-Phrasen. *Sprache & Kognition, 2,* 117–127.

Engelkamp, J., & Zimmer, H.D. (1984). Motor program information as a separable memory unit. *Psychological Research, 46,* 283–299.

Engelkamp, J., & Zimmer, H.D. (1994a). Motor similarity in subject-performed tasks. *Psychological Research/Psychologische Forschung, 57,* 47–53.

Engelkamp, J., & Zimmer, H.D. (1994b). *The human memory: A multimodal approach.* Seattle, WA: Hogrefe & Huber.

Engelkamp, J., & Zimmer, H.D. (1995). Similarity of movement in recognition of self-performed tasks and verbal tasks. *British Journal of Psychology, 86,* 241–252.

Engelkamp, J., & Zimmer, H.D. (1996). Organization and recall in verbal tasks and in subject-performed tasks. *European Journal of Cognitive Psychology, 8,* 257–273.

Engelkamp, J., & Zimmer, H.D. (1997). Sensory factors in memory for subject-performed tasks. *Acta Psychologica, 96,* 43–60.

Engelkamp, J., Zimmer, H., & Denis, M. (1989). Paired associate learning of action verbs with visual or motor imaginal encoding instructions. *Psychological Research, 50,* 257–263.

Engelkamp, J., Zimmer, H.D., Mohr, G., & Sellen, O. (1994). Memory of self-performed tasks: Self-performing during recognition. *Memory and Cognition, 22,* 34–39.

Flanagan, J.R., & Johansson, R.S. (2003). Action plans used in action observation. *Nature, 424,* 769–771.

Freeman, J.F., & Ellis, J.A. (2003). Aging and the accessibility of performed and to-be-performed actions. *Aging, Neuropsychology, and Cognition, 10,* 298–309.

Fuster, J.M. (1997). Network memory. *Trends in Neuroscience, 20,* 451–459.

Gardiner, J.M., & Java, R.I. (1993). Recognising and remembering. In A.F. Collins, S.E. Gathercole, M.A. Conway, & P.E. Morris (Eds.), *Theories of memory* (pp. 163–188). Hillsdale, NJ: Lawrence Erlbaum Associates, Inc.

Garry, M., Manning, C.G., Loftus, E.F., & Sherman, S.J. (1996). Imagination inflation: Imagining a childhood event inflates confidence that it occurred. *Psychological Bulletin and Review, 3,* 208–214.

Gentner, D.R., Larochelle, S., & Grudin, J. (1988). Lexical, sublexical, and peripheral effects in skilled typewriting. *Cognitive Psychology, 20,* 524–548.

Glisky, E.L. (1996). Prospective memory and the frontal lobes. In M. Brandimonte, G.O. Einstein, & M.A. McDaniel (Eds.), *Prospective memory: Theory and applications* (pp. 249–266). Mahwah, NJ: Lawrence Erlbaum Associates, Inc.

Goff, L.M., & Roediger, H.L. III (1998). Imagination inflation for action events: Repeated imaginings lead to illusory recollections. *Memory and Cognition, 26,* 20–33.

Gonsalves, B., & Paller, K.A. (2000). Neural events that underlie remembering something that never happened. *Nature Neuroscience, 3,* 1316–1321.

Goodale, M.A., & Humphrey, G.K. (1998). The objects of action and perception. *Cognition, 67,* 181–207.

Goodale, M.A., & Humphrey, G.K. (2001). Separate visual systems for action and perception. In E.B. Goldstein (Ed.), *Blackwell handbook of perception* (pp. 311–343). Malden, MA: Blackwell.

Goschke, T., & Kuhl, J. (1996). Remembering what to do: Explicit and implicit memory for intentions. In M. Brandimonte, G.O. Einstein, & M.A. McDaniel (Eds.), *Prospective memory: Theory and applications* (pp. 53–91). Mahwah, NJ: Lawrence Erlbaum Associates, Inc.

Grèzes, J., & Decety, J. (2001). Functional anatomy of execution, mental simulation, observation, and verb generation of actions: A meta-analysis. *Human Brain Mapping, 12,* 1–19.

Grossman, E.D., & Blake, R. (2001). Brain activity evoked by inverted and imagined biological motion. *Vision Research, 41,* 10–11.

Grouios, G. (1992a). Mental practice: A review. *Journal of Sport Behavior, 15,* 42–59.

Grouios, G. (1992b). On the reduction of reaction time with mental practice. *Journal of Sport Behavior, 15,* 141–157.

Guynn, M.J., McDaniel, M.A., & Einstein, G.O. (2001). Remembering to perform actions. A different type of memory? In H.D. Zimmer & R. Cohen (Eds.), *Memory for action: A distinct form of episodic memory?* (pp. 25–48). New York: Oxford University Press.

Hannigan, S.L., & Reinitz, M.T. (2001). A demonstration and comparison of two types of inference-based memory errors. *Journal of Experimental Psychology: Learning, Memory, and Cognition, 27,* 931–940.

Hanson, C., & Hirst, W. (1989). On the representation of events: A study of orientation, recall, and recognition. *Journal of Experimental Psychology, 118,* 136–147.

Hauk, O., & Pulvermüller, F. (2004). Neurophysiological distinction of action words in the fronto-central cortex. *Human Brain Mapping, 21,* 191–201.

Helstrup, T. (1984). Serial position phenomena: Memory for acts, contents and spatial position patterns. *Scandinavian Journal of Psychology, 25,* 131–146.

Helstrup, T. (1986). Separate memory laws for recall of performed acts? *Scandinavian Journal of Psychology, 27,* 1–29.

Helstrup, T. (1987). One, two, or three memories? A problem-solving approach to memory for performed acts. *Acta Psychologica, 66,* 37–68.

Helstrup, T. (1989a). Loci for act recall: Contextual influence on the processing of action events. *Psychological Research, 51,* 168–175.

Helstrup, T. (1989b). Memory for performed and imaged noun pairs and verb pairs. *Psychological Resarch, 50,* 237–240.

Helstrup, T. (1989c). Active and passive memory: States, attitudes, and strategies. *Scandinavian Journal of Psychology, 30,* 113–133.

Helstrup, T. (1996a). Recall of spatial movement patterns as a function of context and encoding. *Psychologische Beiträge, 38,* 393–403.

Helstrup, T. (1996b). What does it take for context to support action memory? *Scandinavian Journal of Psychology, 37,* 183–194.

Helstrup, T. (2000). The effect of strategies and contexts on memory for movement patterns. *Scandinavian Journal of Psychology, 41,* 209–215.

Helstrup, T. (2001). Concurrent and retroactive interference effects in memory of movement patterns. *Quarterly Journal of Experimental Psychology, 54A,* 547–560.

Helstrup, T. (2005). In search of a motor element in memory for enacted events. *European Journal of Cognitive Psychology, 17,* 389–403.

Hulme, C. (1979). The interaction of visual and motor memory for graphic forms following tracing. *Quarterly Journal of Experimental Psychology, 31,* 249–261.

Humphreys, G.W., Forde, E.M.E., & Riddoch, M.J. (2001). The planning and execution of everyday actions. In B. Rapp (Ed.), *The handbook of cognitive neuropsychology: What deficits reveal about the human mind* (pp. 565–589). New York: Psychology Press.

Humphreys, G.W., & Riddoch, M.J. (2001a). Detection by action: Neuropsychological evidence for action-defined templates in search. *Nature Neuroscience, 4,* 84–88.

Humphreys, G.W., & Riddoch, M.J. (2001b). Knowing what you need but not what you want: Affordances and action-defined templates in neglect. *Behavioural Neurology, 13,* 75–87.

Huppert, F.A., Johnson, T., & Nickson, J. (2000). High prevalence of prospective memory impairment in the elderly and in early-stage dementia: Findings from a population-based study. *Applied Cognitive Psychology, 14*, S63–S81.

Hyde, T.S., & Jenkins, J.J. (1969). The differential effects of incidental tasks on the organization of recall of a list of highly associated words. *Journal of Experimental Psychology, 82*, 472–481.

Hyman, I.E., & Pentland, J. (1996). Guided imagery and the creation of false childhood memories. *Journal of Memory and Language, 35*, 101–117.

Ihlebæk, C., Løve, T., Eilertsen, D.E., & Magnussen, S. (2003). Memory for a staged criminal event witnessed live and on video. *Memory, 11*, 319–327.

Jackson, P.L., Lafleur, M.F., Malouin, F., Richardson, C.L., & Doyon, J. (2003). Functional cerebral reorganization following motor sequence learning through mental practice with motor imagery. *Neuroimage, 20*, 1171–1180.

Jeannerod, M. (2001). Neural simulation of action: A unifying mechanism for motor cognition. *NeuroImage, 14*, S103–S109.

Jeannerod, M. (2003). The mechanism of self-recognition in humans. *Behavioural Brain Research, 142*, 1–15.

Johnson, M.K., Hashtroudi, S., & Lindsay, D.S. (1993). Source monitoring. *Psychological Bulletin, 114*, 3–28.

Johnson, M.K., & Raye, C.L. (1981). Reality monitoring. *Psychological Review, 88*, 67–85.

Kausler, D.H. (1989). Impairment in normal memory aging: Implications of laboratory evidence. In G.C. Gilmore, P.J. Whitehouse, & M.L. Wykle (Eds.), *Memory aging and dementia* (pp. 41–73). New York: Springer.

Kausler, D.H., Lichty, W., & Freund, J.S. (1985). Adult age differences in recognition memory and frequency judgments for planned activities. *Developmental Psychology, 21*, 647–654.

Kausler, D.H., & Wiley, J.G. (1990). Temporal memory and content memory for actions: Adult age differences in acquisition and retention. *Experimental Aging Research, 16*, 147–150.

Kausler, D.H., Wiley, J.G., & Phillips, P.L. (1990). Adult age differences in memory for massed and distributed repeated actions. *Psychology and Aging, 5*, 530–534.

Kellenbach, M.L., Brett, M., & Patterson, K. (2003). Actions speak louder than functions: The importance of manipulability and action in tool representation. *Journal of Cognitive Neuroscience, 15*, 30–46.

Kliegel, M., Martin, M., McDaniel, M.A., & Einstein, G.O. (2001). Varying the importance of a prospective memory task: Differential effects across time- and event-based prospective memory. *Memory, 9*, 1–11.

Knoblich, G., & Prinz, W. (2001). Recognition of self-generated actions from kinematic displays of drawing. *Journal of Experimental Psychology: Human Perception and Performance, 27*, 456–465.

Knoblich, G., Seigerschmidt, E., Flach, R., & Prinz, W. (2002). Authorship effects in the prediction of handwriting strokes: Evidence for action simulation during action perception. *Quarterly Journal of Experimental Psychology: Human Experimental Psychology, 55A*, 1027–1046.

Knopf, M., Mack, W., Lenel, A., & Ferrante, S. (2005). Memory for action events: Findings in neurological patients, *Scandinavian Journal of Psychology, 46*, 11–9.

Knopf, M., & Neidhardt, E. (1989). Aging and memory for action events: The role of familiarity. *Developmental Psychology, 25*, 780–786.

Knuf, L., Aschersleben, G., & Prinz, W. (2001). An analysis of ideomotor action. *Journal of Experimental Psychology, 130*, 779–798.

Kohler, E., Keysers, C., Umilta, M.A., Fogassi, L., Gallese, V., & Rizzolatti, G. (2002). Hearing sounds, understanding actions: Action representation in mirror neurons. *Science, 297*, 846–848.

Koriat, A., Ben-Zur, H., & Druch, A. (1991). The contextualisation of input and output events in memory. *Psychological Research, 53*, 260–270.

Kormi-Nouri, R. (1995). The nature of memory for action events: An episodic integration view. *European Journal of Cognitive Psychology, 7*, 337–363.

Kormi-Nouri, R., & Nilsson, L.G. (1999). Negative cueing effects with weak and strong intralist cues. *European Journal of Psychology, 11*, 199–218.

Koski, L., Iacoboni, M., & Mazziotta, J.C. (2002). Deconstructing apraxia: Understanding disorders of intentional movement after stroke. *Current Opinion in Neurology, 15*, 71–77.

Larsson, C., & Rönnberg, J. (1987). Memory disorders as a function of traumatic brain injury: Word completion, recall of words and actions. *Scandinavian Journal of Rehabilitation Medicine, 19*, 99–104.

Lekeu, F., Van der Linden, M., Moonen, G., & Salmon, E. (2002). Exploring the effect of action familiarity on SPTs recall performance in Alzheimer's disease. *Journal of Clinical and Experimental Neuropsychology, 24*, 1057–1069.

Levin, D.T., Drivdahl, S.B., Momen, N., & Beck, M.R. (2002a). False predictions about the detectability of visual changes: The role of beliefs about attention, memory, and the continuity of attended objects in causing change blindness. *Consciousness and Cognition, 11*, 507–527.

Levin, D.T., & Simons, D.J. (1997). Failure to detect changes to attended objects in motion pictures. *Psychonomic Bulletin and Review, 4*, 501–506.

Levin, D.T., Simons, D.J., Angelone, B.L., & Chabris, C.F. (2002b). Memory for centrally attended changing objects in an incidental real-world change detection paradigm. *British Journal of Psychology, 93*, 289–302.

Libby, L.K. (2003). Imagery perspective and source monitoring in imagination inflation. *Memory and Cognition, 31*, 1072–1081.

Lindenberger, U., & Baltes, P.B. (1994). Sensory functioning and intelligence in old age: A strong connection. *Psychology and Aging, 9*, 339–355.

Lindenberger, U., Mariske, M., & Baltes, P.B. (2000). Memorizing while walking: Increase in dual-task costs from young adulthood to old age. *Psychology and Aging, 15*, 417–436.

Ling, J., & Blades, M. (2002). Further evidence for automatic encoding of colour by children and adults. *British Journal of Developmental Psychology, 20*, 537–544.

Mandler, G. (1980). Recognizing: The judgement of previous occurrence. *Psychological Review, 87*, 252–271.

Maylor, E.A. (1996). Age-related impairment in an event-based prospective-memory task. *Psychology and Aging, 11*, 74–78.

McDaniel, M.A., Guynn, M.J., Einstein, G.O., & Breneiser, J. (2004). Cue-focused and reflexive-associative processes in prospective memory retrieval. *Journal of Experimental Psychology: Learning, Memory, and Cognition, 30*, 605–614.

McDonald-Miszczak, L., Hubley, A.M., & Hultsch, D.F. (1996). Age differences in recall and predicting recall of action events and words. *Journal of Gerontology: Series B: Psychological Sciences & Social Sciences, 51B*, P81–P90.

Mecklinger, A. (2000). Interfacing mind and brain: A neurocognitive model of recognition memory. *Psychophysiology, 37*, 1–18.

Mecklinger, A., Gruenewald, C., & Besson, M. (2002). Separable neuronal circuitries for manipulable and non-manipulable objects in working memory. *Cerebral Cortex, 12*, 1115–1123.

Mecklinger, A., Gruenewald, C., & Weiskopf, N. (2004). Motor affordance and its role for visual working memory: Evidence from fMRI studies. *Experimental Psychology, 51*, 258–269.

Meltzoff, A.N. (2002). Imitation as a mechanism of social cognition: Origins of empathy, theory of mind, and the representation of action. In U. Goswami (Ed.), *Blackwell handbook of childhood cognitive development* (pp. 6–25). Malden, MA: Blackwell.

Mulder, T., Zijlstra, S., Zijlstra, W., & Hochstenbach, J. (2004). The role of motor imagery in learning a totally novel movement. *Experimental Brain Research, 154*, 211–217.

Neumann, O. (1988). Kognitive Vermittlung und direkte Parameterspezifikation. Zum Problem mentaler Repräsentation in der Wahrnehmung. *Sprache & Kognition, 8*, 32–49.

Nilsson, L.G. (2000). Remembering actions and words. In F.I.M. Craig & E. Tulving (Eds.), *Oxford handbook of memory* (pp. 137–148). Oxford, UK: Oxford University Press.

Nilsson, L.-G., & Craik, F.I.M. (1990). Additive and interactive effects in memory for subject-performed tasks. *European Journal of Cognitive Psychology, 2*, 305–324.

Nilsson, L.-G., & Kormi-Nouri, R. (2001). What is the meaning of a memory-systems approach? Comments on Engelkamp. In H.D. Zimmer, R. Cohen, M.J. Guynn, J. Engelkamp., R. Kormi-Nouri, & M.A. Foley (Eds.), Memory for action: A distinct form of episodic memory? (pp. 136–143). New York: Oxford University Press.

Nilsson, L.-G., Nyberg, L., Klingberg, T., Åberg, C., Persson, J., & Roland, P. (2000). Activity in motor areas while remembering action events. *NeuroReport, 11*, 2199–2201.

Norman, D.A. (1981). Categorization of action slips. *Psychological Review, 88*, 1–15.

Norris, M.P., & West, R.L. (1993). Activity memory and aging: The role of motor retrieval and strategic processing. *Psychology and Aging, 8*, 81–86.

Nyberg, L., Nilsson, L.G., & Bäckman, L. (1991). A component analysis of action events. *Psychological Research, 53*, 219–225.

Nyberg, L., Persson, J., & Nilsson, L.-G. (2002). Individual differences in memory enhancement by encoding enactment: Relationships to adult age and biological factors. *Neuroscience and Biobehavioral Reviews, 26*, 835–839.

Nyberg, L., Petersson, K.M., Nilsson, L.-G., Sandblom, J., Aberg, C., & Ingvar, M. (2001). Reactivation of motor brain areas during explicit memory for actions. *NeuroImage*, 1–8.

Oesterreich, R., & Köddig, C. (1995). Das Generieren von Handlungsvorstellungen im Modell "Netz erinnerbaren Handelns" und der Tu-Effekt. *Zeitschrift für Experimentelle Psychologie, 42*, 280–301.

Olofsson, U. (1996). The effect of enactment on memory for order. *Psychological Research, 59*, 75–79.

Oriani, M., Moniz-Cook, E., Binetti, G., Zanieri, G., Frisoni, G.B., Geroldi, C., De Vreese, L.P., & Zanetti, O. (2003). An electronic memory aid to support prospective memory in patients in the early stages of Alzheimer's disease: A pilot study. *Aging and Mental Health, 7*, 22–27.

Paller, K.A. (2000). Neurocognitive foundations of human memory. In D.L. Mendin (Ed.), *The psychology of learning and motivation.* San Diego, CA: Academic Press.

Paller, K.A., & Wagner, A.D. (2002). Observing the transformation of experience into memory. *Trends in Cognitive Sciences, 6*, 93–102.

Paré, D., Collins, D.R., & Pelletier, J.G. (2002). Amygdala oscillations and the consolidation of emotional memories. *Trends in Cognitive Sciences, 6*, 306–314.

Prinz, W. (1997). Perception and action planning. *European Journal of Cognitive Psychology, 9*, 129–154.

Rensink, R.A. (2002). Change detection. *Annual Review of Psychology, 53*, 245–277.

Rizzolatti, G., Craighero, L., & Fadiga, L. (2002). The mirror system in humans. In M.I. Stamenov & V. Gallese (Eds.), *Mirror neurons and the evolution of brain and language* (pp. 37–59). Amsterdam: John Benjamins.

Rizzolatti, G., Fadiga, L., Fogassi, L., & Gallese, V. (1999). Resonance behaviors and mirror neurons. *Archives italiennes de biologie, 137*, 85–100.

Rönnlund, M., Nyberg, L., Bäckman, L., & Nilsson, L.-G. (2003). Recall of subject-performed tasks, verbal tasks, and cognitive activities across the adult life span: Parallel age-related deficits. *Aging, Neuropsychology, and Cognition, 10*, 182–201.

Rosenbaum, D.A., Kenny, S.B., & Derr, M.A. (1983). Hierarchical control of rapid movement sequences. *Journal of Experimental Psychology: Human Perception and Performance, 9*, 86–102.

Ross, J.S., Tkach, J., Ruggieri, P.M., Lieber, M., & Lapresto, E. (2003). The mind's eye: Functional MR imaging evaluation of golf motor imagery. *American Journal of Neuroradiology, 24*, 1036–1044.

Russ, M.O., Mack, W., Grama, C.R., Lanfermann, H., & Knopf, M. (2003). Enactment effect in memory: Evidence concerning the function of the supramarginal gyrus. *Experimental Brain Research, 149*, 497–504

Safer, M.A., Christianson, S.-A., Autry, M.W., & Österlund, K. (1998). Tunnel memory for traumatic events. *Applied Cognitive Psychology, 12*, 99–117.

Schacter, D.L. (1996). *Searching for memory: The brain, the mind, and the past.* New York: Basic Books.

Schmidt, R.A. (1975). A schema theory of discrete motor skill learning. *Psychological Review, 82*, 225–260.

Shallice, T., & Burgess, P. (1996). The domain of supervisory processes and temporal organisation of behaviour. *Philosophical Transactions of the Royal Society of London, B, 351*, 1405–1412.

Sherwood, D.E, & Lee, T.D. (2003). Schema theory: Critical review and implications for the role of cognition in a new theory of motor learning. *Research Quarterly for Exercise and Sport, 74*, 376–382.

Simons, D.J., & Chabris, C.F. (1999). Gorillas in our midst: Sustained inattentional blindness for dynamic events. *Perception, 28*, 1059–1074.

Simons, D.J., & Levin, D.T. (1998). Failure to detect changes to people during a real-world interaction. *Psychonomic Bulletin and Review, 5*, 644–649.

Smith, G., Della Sala, S., Logie, R.H., & Maylor, E.A. (2000). Prospective and retrospective memory in normal ageing and dementia: A questionnaire study. *Memory, 8*, 311–321.

Sternberg, S., Mansell, S., Knoll, R.L., & Wright, C.E. (1978). The latency and duration of rapid movement sequences: Comparison of speech and typewriting. In G.E. Stelmach (Ed.), *Information processing in motor control and learning* (pp. 118–152). New York: Academic Press.

Summers, J.A., & Craik, F.I.M. (1994). The effects of subject-performed tasks on the memory performance of verbal autistic children. *Journal of Autism and Developmental Disorders, 24*, 773–783.

Thomas, A.K., Bulevich, J.B., & Loftus, E.F. (2003). Exploring the role of repetition and sensory elaboration in the imagination inflation effect. *Memory and Cognition, 31*, 630–640.

Thomas, A.K., & Loftus, E.F. (2002). Creating bizarre false memories through imagination. *Memory and Cognition, 29*, 707–718.

Tucker, D.M., & Luu, P. (2006). Adaptive binding. In H.D. Zimmer, A. Mecklinger, & U. Lindenberger (Eds.), *Binding in episodic memory: A neurocognitive approach*. Oxford, UK: Oxford University Press.

Tulving, E. (1972). Episodic and semantic memory. In E. Tulving & W. Donaldson (Eds.), *Organization of memory* (pp. 381–403). New York: Academic Press.

Ungerleider, L.G., & Mishkin, M. (1982). Two cortical visual systems. In D.J. Ingle, M.A. Goodale, & R.J.W. Mansfield (Eds.), *Analysis of visual behavior* (pp. 549–586). Cambridge, MA: MIT Press.

Uttl, B., Graf, P., Miller, J., & Tuokko, H. (2001). Pro- and retrospective memory in late adulthood. *Consciousness and Cognition, 10*, 451–472.

Vedhara, K., Wadsworth, E., Norman, P., Searle, A., Mitchell, J., Macrae, N., O'Mahony, M., Kemple, T., & Memel, D. (2004). Habitual prospective memory in elderly patients with Type 2 diabetes: Implications for medication adherence. *Psychology, Health and Medicine, 9*, 17–27.

Verhaeghen, P., Marcoen, A., & Goossens, L. (1992). Improving memory performance in the aged through mnemonic traning: A meta-analytic study. *Psychology and Aging, 7*, 242–251.

Vitevitch, M.S. (2003). Change deafness: The inability to detect changes between two voices. *Journal of Experimental Psychology: Human Perception and Performance, 29*, 333–342.

Vogels, W.W., Dekker, M.R., Brouwer, W.H., & de Jong, R. (2002). Age-related changes in event-related prospective memory performance: A comparison of four prospective memory tasks. *Brain and Cognition, 49*, 341–362.

Von Essen, J.D., & Nilsson, L.-G. (2003). Memory effects of motor activation in subject-performed tasks and sign language. *Psychonomic Bulletin and Review, 10*, 445–449.

Weiss, P.H., Jeannerod, M., Paulignan, Y., & Freund, H.-J. (2000). Is the organisation of goal-directed action modality specific? A common temporal structure. *Neuropsychologia, 38*, 1136–1147.

West, R., Herndon, R.W., & Covell, E. (2003). Neural correlates of age-related declines in the formation and realization of delayed intentions. *Psychology and Aging, 18*, 461–473.

Woodward, A.L. (1998). Infants selectively encode the goal object of an actor's reach. *Cognition, 69*, 1–34.

Yonelinas, A.P. (2002). The nature of recollection and familiarity: A review of 30 years of research. *Journal of Memory and Language, 46*, 441–517.

Zacks, J.M., & Tversky, B. (2001). Event structure in perception and conception. *Psychological Bulletin, 127*, 3–21.

Zacks, J.M., Tversky, B., & Iyer, G. (2001). Perceiving, remembering, and communicating structure in events. *Journal of Experimental Psychology: General, 130*, 29–58.

Zalla, T., Pradat-Diehl, P., & Sirigu, A. (2003). Perception of action boundaries in patients with frontal lobe damage. *Neuropsychologia, 41*, 1619–1627.

Zimmer, H.D. (1984). Enkodierung, Rekodierung, Retrieval und die Aktivation motorischer Programme. In *Arbeiten der Fachrichtung Psychologie Nr. 91.* Saarbrücken, Germany: Universität des Saarlandes.

Zimmer, H.D. (1986). The memory trace of semantic or motor processing. In F. Klix & H. Hagendorf (Eds.), *Human memory and cognitive capabilities* (pp. 215–223). Amsterdam: North-Holland.

Zimmer, H.D. (1991). Memory after motoric encoding in a generation-recognition model. *Psychological Research, 53*, 226–231.

Zimmer, H.D. (1996). Memory for spatial location and enactment. *Psychologische Beiträge, 38*, 404–418.

Zimmer, H.D. (2001). Why do actions speak louder than words: Action memory as a variant of encoding manipulations or the result of a specific memory system? In H.D. Zimmer, R.L. Cohen, M.J. Guynn, J. Engelkamp, R. Kormi-Nouri, & M.A. Foley (Eds.), *Memory for action: A distinct form of episodic memory?* (pp. 151–198). New York: Oxford University Press.

Zimmer, H.D. (2005). *A contribution of action-specific information to recognition in SPT.* Paper presented at the 14th Conference of the European Society for Cognitive Psychology at Leiden (Netherlands).

Zimmer, H.D., & Cohen, R.L. (2001). Remembering actions: A specific type of memory? In H.D. Zimmer, R.L. Cohen, M.J. Guynn, J. Engelkamp, R. Kormi-Nouri, & M.A. Foley (Eds.), *Memory for action: A distinct form of episodic memory?* (pp. 3–24). New York: Oxford University Press.

Zimmer, H.D., Cohen, R.L., Guynn, M.J., Engelkamp, J., Kormi-Nouri, R., & Foley, M.A. (2001). *Memory for action: A distinct form of episodic memory?* London: Oxford University Press.

Zimmer, H.D., & Engelkamp, J. (1984). Planungs- und Ausführungsanteile motorischer Gedächtniskomponenten und ihre Wirkung auf das Behalten ihrer verbalen Bezeichnungen. *Zeitschrift für Psychologie, 192*, 379–402.

Zimmer, H.D., & Engelkamp, J. (1989). Does motor encoding enhance relational information? *Psychological Research, 51*, 158–167.

Zimmer, H.D., & Engelkamp, J. (1996). Routes to actions and their efficacy for remembering. *Memory, 4*, 59–78.

Zimmer, H.D., & Engelkamp, J. (1999). Levels-of-processing in subject-performed tasks. *Memory and Cognition, 27*, 907–914.

Zimmer, H.D., & Engelkamp, J. (2003). Signing enhances memory like performing actions. *Psychonomic Bulletin and Review, 10*, 450–454.

Zimmer, H.D., Helstrup, T., & Engelkamp, J. (2000). Pop-out into memory: A retrieval mechanism that is enhanced with the recall of subject-performed tasks. *Journal of Experimental Psychology: Human Learning, Memory and Cognition, 26*, 658–670.

Zimmer, H.D., Herrmann, M., & Duppe, E. (1996). Das Selbstbild des Gedächtnisses und die Gedächtnisleistung bei Teilnehmenden eines Gedächtniskurses und zweier Vergleichsgruppen. *Zeitschrift für Gerontopsychologie und -psychiatrie, 9*, 255–268.

Zimmer, H.D., Mecklinger, A., & Lindenberger, U. (Eds.) (2006). *Binding in human memory: A neurocognitive approach.* Oxford, UK: Oxford University Press.

4 Underestimated sensations: Everyday odour memory in clinical and forensic settings

Maria Larsson and Annika Melinder

A characteristic feature of research on everyday memory is its emphasis on how memory works in everyday life, on identifying its underlying processes and on exploring the functions it serves (Cohen, 1996). Everyday memory is typically context-bound and the events are embedded in a rich context of ongoing experiences. For example, you easily recognize the smell of mouldy bread and can recollect the view of your summer house. As recognized by a wealth of scientific findings, memory proficiency has been shown to be influenced by past experiences, by culture and demographics and by factors such as emotions, intelligence and personality. However, it is worthy of note that our current knowledge has primarily been obtained from research on our primary senses, vision and hearing, and evidence is scarce regarding the role played by one of our so-called minor senses – olfaction.

The sense of smell is important to human beings and is in constant use because environmental odours must be monitored on a continuous basis. While olfaction may have evolved as a mechanism for evaluating whether a particular food is edible (Engen, 1982), it also serves important social functions (Jacob, McClintock, Zelano, & Ober, 2002) and mediates psychological well-being (Blomqvist, Brämerson, Stjärne, & Nordin, 2004). As has been described in fiction and the scientific literature, olfactory sensations also have the ability to influence mood and behaviour and to evoke memories. This suggests that odours are highly associative and emotionally evocative (Chu & Downes, 2000; Herz, 2004; Proust, 1919). Although little scientific attention has been devoted to the sense of smell, interest in olfactory cognitive processing has increased gradually over the past decade. More knowledge regarding the neurological underpinnings (Davis, 2004; Savic, 2002), behavioural manifestations (Knasko, 1995) and experiential qualities (M. Larsson, Lövdén, & Nilsson, 2003) of higher-order olfactory processing has been gained. Unlike signals from all other sensory modalities, olfactory information is not sent to the thalamus and then relayed to a specialized region of the cortex (J.L. Price, 1987). Instead, olfactory information is directly projected to specific regions of the limbic system. The olfactory sensory system is thus unique in having direct contact with the neural substrates for emotion and memory. For example, only two synapses separate the olfactory nerve from the amygdala, a structure of critical importance for emotional signalling, and which maintains human emotional memory (Cahill, Babinsky, Markowitsch, & McGaugh, 1995). The bond between odours and emotions has long been recognized, and it is of interest to note that the limbic system was originally described as the rhinencephalon or the "smell brain" (Van Toller, 1988). The hippocampus, which is crucial for the integrity of declarative memory functions, is separated from the olfactory nerve by only three synapses (Eichenbaum, 1996).

The main aim of this chapter is to discuss how previous experiences and memory representations of olfactory information may come into play in everyday life. This will be illustrated by providing examples of various expressions of olfactory memory, ranging from conditioned olfactory responses to odour-evoked autobiographical memories. The latter part will be exemplified by an overview of olfactory cueing of memory representations.

We also highlight the olfactory sensory system (i.e., olfactory memory) from two neglected perspectives: forensic and clinical. To the best of our knowledge, no research has explicitly examined the potential use of probing for episodic olfactory information in a real forensic context. Here, we present a forensic case that illustrates the potential value of probing for episodic chemosensory information in forensic interviews. Emotionally conditioned behaviour is exemplified in a clinical perspective, in which an overview of olfaction in post-traumatic stress disorder (PTSD) is provided. This is further elaborated on by a PTSD case in which the individual was suffering from olfactory flashbacks and odour hallucinations.

ASPECTS OF HUMAN OLFACTORY MEMORY

As has been thoroughly documented, human memory is not a unitary faculty of the mind, but may instead be conceived of as a variety of dissociable processes and systems, which are supported by particular constellations of neural networks mediating different forms of learning (Gabrieli, Fleischman, Keane, Reminger, & Morrell, 1995; Tulving, 2002). An important distinction of human memory is that made between declarative and non-declarative expressions of memory (Graf & Schacter, 1985). Declarative memory is reflected by performance on tasks that demand conscious effort to recollect the past. It designates memory for facts and events, and is consciously accessible and expressible, which also makes this form of memory flexible and applicable to novel situations. Non-declarative memory is tapped when performance on a task is improved by past experiences, but in the absence of conscious recollection. This form of memory is inflexible, inexpressible and tied to the learning situation. Behavioural phenomena such as conditioning, priming, habits, and skills are supported by non-declarative information (Schacter, 1992).

Declarative memory systems are further characterized by different subsystems that reflect important everyday functions. One of these sub-systems is the episodic memory system. Episodic memory refers to memory for personally experienced events (Tulving, 1983, 2002) and provides infor-mation about the "what" and "when" of events (temporally dated experiences) and about "where" they happened (temporal-spatial relationships).

Few attempts have been made to construct a theoretical framework that might further our understanding of the various expressions of olfactory memory (M. Larsson, 2002; Stevenson & Boakes, 2003). This is probably due to the scarcity of empirical evidence capable of adequately addressing and identifying similarities and differences between the principles governing memory for odours as compared with other sensory representations. As noted by M. Larsson (2002), most research on human olfactory memory has been oriented towards declarative aspects of olfactory memory (e.g., episodic odour recognition, odour identification), with little attention paid to non-declarative (implicit) aspects of olfactory memory (e.g., odour aversions, conditioning).

Episodic recollection of olfactory information involves both memory for the odour itself and memories evoked by a specific odour. With regard to the former, recent research has called into question the often-held view that odours are encoded and stored as unique, non-linguistic whole percepts, yielding episodic olfactory representations that are resistant to interference and forgetting (Engen, 1987; M. Larsson, 1997). As is true for episodic recol-lection of verbal and visual information, research on episodic odour memory has demonstrated that this form of memory is also prone to be forgotten (M. Larsson, 1997; M. Larsson & Bäckman, 1997; Walk & Johns, 1984) and is not resistant to the passage of time (Engen & Ross, 1973). Likewise, epi-sodic recognition of olfactory information has been reported to involve a similar plasticity to memory representations acquired in other sensory modalities. For example, odour recognition performance is influenced by factors such as visual and verbal elaboration (Lyman & McDaniel, 1990), verbal suppression (Perkins & Cook, 1990), familiarity (Murphy, Cain, Gilmore, & Skinner, 1991) and identifiability (M. Larsson & Bäckman, 1993).

In contrast to declarative forms of olfactory memory, non-declarative odour representations are little influenced by the passage of time, which is reflected in the fact that we may experience conditional responses for stimuli that we may not have encountered for decades (Robin, Alaoui-Ismaïli, Dittmar, & Vernet-Maury, 1999). One illustration of this powerful learning mechanism is one of the most prominent features of the olfactory sensory system: the production of odour and taste aversions. The development of aversions may occur as a response to the ingestion of a sickness-provoking substance, which from an evolutionary perspective makes sense in that the aversion works as self-protection against food poisoning (Borison, 1989; Capaldi, Hunter, & Privitera, 2004). It is of interest to note that the ability to learn to avoid ingesting toxic substances is present in simple invertebrates, which implies that relatively primitive neural networks can mediate this form of learning (Sahley, Gelperin, & Rudy, 1981). This is supported by the notion that non-declarative forms of memory may have appeared early in evolution and is shared in various forms by most living organisms (Tulving, 1993). Conditioned odour/taste aversions may be difficult to extinguish because of the longevity of the association between the particular food and previous illness (Garcia, Laister, Bermudez-Rattoni, & Deems, 1985). Presumably, this observation is related to early findings that retroactive interference has a negligible impact on olfactory memory (Engen, 1982; Lawless & Cain, 1975). In a similar vein, recent evidence suggests that the principles governing acquisition of conditionalized emotional (fear) responses for auditory and visual information are also valid for olfactory information, although it is not clear whether odour-guided fear is acquired more rapidly or is more robust than other forms of fear conditioning (Otto, Cousens, & Rajewski, 1997; Robin et al., 1999).

Relatedly, olfactory research has indicated that evaluative (i.e., hedonic) reactions to olfactory stimuli are not innate, but rather are largely products of Pavlovian associative conditioning (e.g., Engen, 1982). Specifically, the acquisition of odour likes and dislikes has been shown to exhibit a remarkable plasticity not only in childhood but also during adulthood. Moreover, the acquisition of odour hedonics may occur outside of conscious awareness and, once acquired, the acquired odour connotation may exert an unconscious influence on behaviour (Hermans & Bayens, 2002). All in all, the available evidence suggests that the hedonic value of an odour is determined by its previous associational history, such that odours encountered in a positive atmosphere will be conceived of as pleasant, while odours experienced in a negative or distressful context will be associated with a congruent mood. In this regard, everyday olfactory memory is contextually dependent and embedded in ongoing activities in a similar way to visual memory representations.

Olfactory cueing of memory

Even though rarely thought of, all environmental spaces contain odour information. As a consequence, it is highly likely that olfactory information will become part of a memory representation that is linked to a specific event. The encoding specificity principle states that memory is enhanced when conditions present during retrieval match those that were present during encoding (Tulving & Thompson, 1973). Thus, in keeping with this principle, odours that are integrated with a specific event may serve as a potential cue or trigger for evoking all, or parts of, a specific target episode. This implies that odours have the potential to elicit emotional and cognitive associations originating from the contextual circumstance in which they were initially perceived.

Indeed, some evidence suggests that odours may serve as powerful reminders of past experiences. Two studies of olfactory cued autobiographical memories in older populations have indicated that odour-evoked memories are older and qualitatively different from verbally or visually evoked memories (Chu & Downes, 2000; Willander & Larsson, 2006). Specifically, odour-evoked memories have been shown to originate predominantly from childhood (< 10 years) rather than from the well-documented reminiscence bump period (10–30 years), which is the typical finding for verbally or visually evoked memory information (Rubin & Schulkind, 1997). Focusing on experiential qualities, memories evoked by olfactory information have been described as being more emotional than memories associated with cues perceived through other modalities (Herz, 2004). The direct synapsing from the olfactory area to the amygdala-hippocampal complex, the neural substrate of emotional memory, has been suggested as underlying these observations (Cahill et al., 1995; Herz, Eliassen, Beland, & Souza, 2004). In addition, odour-cued memories have been described as more vivid (Chu & Downes, 2000), and thought of but spoken of less often (Rubin, Groth, & Goldsmith, 1984; Willander & Larsson, 2006). The latter findings suggest that odour-associated information may not be spontaneously retrieved, but may benefit and gain accessibility from active probing or cueing.

Adopting an encoding specificity principle paradigm, two studies have reported that adults exposed to odours while working on a stressful task later experienced increased anxiety when they encountered these odours again (Kirk-Smith, Van Toller, & Dodd, 1983). In a similar vein, testing a group of children, Epple and Herz (1999) reported that an odour associated with failure had negative repercussions on a subsequent task that involved a cognitive challenge. Taken together, these results suggest that the meaning or experiential quality of an odour is linked to the circumstances in which it was originally perceived, which in turn affect subsequent emotional and cognitive behaviour.

HIGHLIGHTING OLFACTORY INFORMATION IN FORENSIC AND CLINICAL CONTEXTS

Given that all memory representations have the potential to carry olfactory information, it is of interest to consider tentatively some applied aspects of this knowledge. We do so here by highlighting the olfactory sensory system in forensic and clinical settings. As will be clear from the overview provided below, remarkably little research has focused on practical applications and the potential use of addressing olfactory information in these contexts. Even less research has been done on the possible strategic use of such information. Naturally, the lack of practical implementations is due to the scarcity of basic research on important questions such as the accuracy of olfactory memory reports as compared to reports that deal with other sensory modalities.

Olfaction set in a forensic perspective

In this section, we highlight the potential use of probing for olfactory information in a forensic context, offering first a brief overview pertaining to
memory performance following olfactory cueing and reinstatement techniques in forensics. This is followed by a description of a real forensic case,
illustrating how probing for olfactory information may result in better
memory recollection that ultimately accorded greater credibility to the
witness report.

Olfactory cueing in forensic practice

In the realm of forensic psychology, little attention has been paid to evaluating the potential value of integrating olfactory information as a tool for
enhancing memory recollection or evoking the emotional connotations of a
specific event. One laboratory study investigated whether physical reinstatement of sensations could enhance recall in a group of children. Specifically,
participants encoded a live event with a smell, a sound or a taste. At retrieval,
the same sensory stimuli as had been present during the live event were
reinstated. The results indicated that memory performance was not improved
by any physical reinstatement of the sensations (A. Larsson & Granhag,
2005). A recent study, employing a false memory design, also failed to show
any effect of the reinstatement of congruent olfactory cues on the total
memory recollection, source memory, or suggestibility scores of a group of
preschool children (Melinder & Larsson, 2006). On the other hand, preliminary data from another study suggest that olfactory cueing of an emotional
event encoded with a congruent odour (i.e., petrol and car accident) yielded
better memory for both event and circumstantial information than a control
condition in a group of adults (Willander, Christianson, Berndtsson, Schüler,
& Larsson, 2004). This finding suggests that reinstatement of olfactory
information present in a previous episode may result in better memory recollection for emotionally laden information, but may not affect recollection of
neutral events. The differences could also be explained by the age of the
sample, as the participants in the two former studies were children, whereas
the participants in the latter study were adults.

Reinstatement techniques and usage of contextual cues (e.g., physical
details from a crime scene) have recently been introduced as evidence-
gathering strategies in criminal cases (Hershkowitz, Orbach, Lamb, Sternberg,
& Horowitz, 2002; Salomon & Pipe, 2002). This work has partly been
inspired by laboratory studies showing that children as young as 3 years of
age retrieve more information about a target event when they are questioned
in the setting where the event occurred than they do in a neutral setting
(Pipe & Wilson, 1994; D.W.W. Price & Goodman, 1990). To the best of our
knowledge, no studies of forensic practice have specifically investigated the
potential positive value of probing for information processed by the chemical

senses. Likewise, no research has explicitly investigated the extent to which chemosensory information is reported spontaneously by witnesses, or how often this information is requested by the police in forensic interviews. It is noteworthy that the most widely utilized instruments for assessing the veracity of written statements (e.g., the Statement Validity Analysis, SVA, and the Content Based Criteria Analysis, CBCA) regard the amount of perceptual detail in a testimony as predictive of the reliability of testimony (Steller & Køhnken, 1989; Vrij, Akehurst, Soukara, & Bull, 2002). Thus, both methods hold the view that testimonies that include perceptual information are more indicative of truthfulness. This makes it all the more surprising that in a recent review of 120 records of children's testimonies in real forensic sexual and physical abuse cases, not a single reference was made to olfactory or taste information. Furthermore, when the interviewers' questions were analysed and categorized into types of questions (e.g., open-ended, direct, suggestive), no questions comprised olfactory or gustatory information or prompted for such information (Thoresen, Lønnum, Melinder, Stridbeck, & Magnussen, in press).

Given that perceptual information derived from our senses may be a reliable source of a statement's reliability, as opposed, for example, to cognitive operations, more research regarding the prevalence and the use of perceptual information in forensic interviews is needed. Of course, there are many important questions to answer before olfactory cueing can be introduced as a reliable evidence-gathering method in forensic cases. For example, and as noted above, one crucial question concerns the reliability and accuracy of olfactory reports as compared to memory reports processed by other sensory modalities.

Case report

In the case presented below, we report a section from a forensic interview, illustrating how prompting for chemosensory information may serve as an important and supportive tool in witness reports, ultimately increasing the credibility of a statement. It should be noted that the witness involved recalled the perceptual information when probed for it, and that in earlier interviews she had not communicated any information comprising chemosensory aspects of the target event.

Case LD

A 10-year-old girl (LD) was interviewed by the police after telling her mother and a friend of her mother about an abusive event that had taken place between her and her father some time ago. The particular event, according to the mother who reported the case to the police, concerned a well-defined sexual offence. After questioning LD for more details about the event, the mother claimed that the father had sexually abused the girl by letting her masturbate him while he was looking at pornography on television.

The parents had recently been divorced after a longer period of dispute and custody conflicts. Their conflicts had ended in court and the court's decision was that LD should continue to live with her mother, but the father was allowed to have extended contact with his daughter. The decision was unacceptable for the mother, who therefore appealed the decision to the court.

When the father was confronted by the mother's suspicion regarding the sexual activities, he initially denied every such contact. He claimed that LD might have seen pornography independently of him, and that LD's reports should be regarded as confabulations of such experience. However, after communication with his lawyer, the father claimed that the mother had implanted the stories in the child, creating false beliefs about the intra-familiar relationships. He argued that by doing so, the mother was using their daughter in the struggle for custody that she, in a way, had previously won.

In the forensic interview, the police initially posed questions regarding LD's daily life before going on to the issue of why she had come to the police officer for an interview. The police officer (PO) was a highly skilled professional, and recognized the importance of asking questions relating to all perceptual/sensory details. Ten minutes into the interview, when the interviewer was prompting the target event (i.e., the masturbation), the following dialogue occurred:

PO: Can you tell me why you are here today?
LD: I told my mother something . . . . . . but I don't want to talk about it right now . . . . . Because my father is also very kind to me.
PO: I see, hum, tell me about your father then!
LD: His name is Lars and . . . . is kind
PO: Anything more?
LD: He did that yucky thing with me, you know?
PO: I don't know really what you are thinking about. Could you try to tell me?
LD: I told mum . . . . and Ellen . . . (*Ellen is mother's friend*)
PO: What did you tell them?
LD: Don't you know?
PO: Children sometimes think that the police know everything, but we don't.
LD: I said that . . . he told me I had to hold around . . . here (points to her own genitals), and take it up and down (shows the movements with her hand).
PO: I see, like that (repeat the movements)
LD: (nods her head)
PO: What happened then?
LD: He peed, white pee came out of his . . . . . . yucky, yucky, yucky . . . . . (she frowns her nose and makes a grimace)*

* The PO subsequently explained that the girl's facial expression had led her to think of odours, which made her formulate the concluding questions.

PO: Do you remember if the thing that came out, the pee you said, if it smelled of something?

LD: It smelled sour.

PO: I see; it smelled sour.

LD: It tasted yucky.

PO: You tasted it?

LD: It was in my mouth, I had to spit it out in the sink. Then I cleaned my mouth with water. . . . .

As the above transcript shows, it is when the police officer asks LD "what happened then" that new information about the target event emerges. At this moment, LD wrinkles her nose, reflecting a chemosensory-induced emotional reaction. Research has indicated that odours are particularly potent in inducing facial expressions of emotional or hedonic experience (Soussignan & Schaal, 1996). In the present situation, the interviewer used the facial response to ask a follow-up question about the quality of the odour. Given LD's spontaneous and correct description of the chemosensory quality of sperm, the credibility of her witness testimony increased. For example, no additional questions were asked by the judges, the prosecutor, or the defence lawyer.

The present case illustrates how information processed by our chemical senses – smell and taste – may serve as useful and powerful supplements in forensic interviews. Specifically, case LD shows that explicit prompting for olfactory information has the potential to evoke more elaborate, event-specific information, that had not been previously documented. The prompting resulted in an extensive recollection, contributing to a more positive evaluation of the girl's credibility. Moreover, case LD also illustrates that children have an intact ability to adequately process and verbally describe chemosensory information, which is in congruence with previous findings (Jehl & Murphy, 1998).

Olfaction set in a clinical perspective

In the following section, we discuss the olfactory sensory system as a traumatic reminder of past experiences. Though clinical psychologists are aware of the potential of olfactory information to induce dramatic behavioural changes, little scientific evidence is available. We first provide a brief presentation of the clinical characteristics of post-traumatic stress disorder (PTSD), followed by an overview of olfaction in PTSD, with an emphasis on olfactory flashbacks. This review is exemplified and elaborated upon by the presentation of case SN, who was diagnosed with post-traumatic stress disorder (PTSD). Case SN illustrates specifically how trauma-related smells may serve as powerful cues of trauma-related memories capable of disabling the everyday life of the patient.

Clinical characteristics of PTSD

In everyday memory, positive and negative memory intrusions are fairly common (Brewin, Christodoulides, & Hutchinson, 1996a). At a certain point, however, intrusions negatively affect the general psychological functioning of the individual and result in psychopathology. PTSD is a well-documented cluster of emotional and psychophysiological reactions that can arise in the wake of exposure to an overwhelming life event (e.g., combat experiences, civil disasters, rape, fires). The main diagnostic features of PTSD include (1) re-experiencing symptoms (e.g., intrusive memories, nightmares), (2) protective reactions (e.g., emotional numbing, amnesia, cognitive avoidance), and (3) arousal symptoms (e.g., startle response and hypervigilance) (DSM-IV; American Psychiatric Association, 1994). Following exposure to a traumatic event, prevalence rates of PTSD average around 25–30% in the general population, and this figure decreases as time passes (Green, 1994). A typical behavioural feature in PTSD is an alternation between re-experiencing and avoidance of trauma-related memories. In principle, two types of memories are described in PTSD; intrusive memories, which appear rapidly and spontaneously, and more fragmentary memories without a corresponding recognizable event (Brewin, Dalgleish, & Joseph, 1996b). Although intrusive memories and thoughts are also common in non-clinical samples (Brewin et al., 1996a), the intrusive memories involved in PTSD often involve images accompanied by high levels of arousal. Such memories are experienced as re-enactments of the original trauma (flashbacks). In contrast, fragmentary memories typically carry information about isolated visual, auditory, olfactory or tactile events (Brewin et al., 1996a).

Smell as a traumatic reminder

As noted in the introduction, both behavioural and neuroanatomical observations indicate a potent connection between odour, emotion and memory (Davis, 2004). Olfactory projections synapse more directly to the amygdala-hippocampal complex than do afferents from other sensory systems. Olfactory information that is perceived during an intense emotional experience thus has the potential to be strongly engraved. It is of interest to note that neuropsychological research has indicated that PTSD is related to a dysfunction of the frontolimbic system (Vasterling, Brailey, & Sutker, 2000). However, using a task (i.e., odour identification) that targeted orbitofrontal integrity, Vasterling et al. reported that PTSD was associated with less proficient olfactory performance. Importantly, performance in tasks sensitive to prefrontal and mesial temporal structures was not impaired. These results suggest that PTSD also implicates dysfunction of the orbitofrontal region, one of the key structures that subserves olfactory processing (e.g., Davis, 2004; Savic, Gulyas, Larsson, & Roland, 2000).

Following exposure to a traumatic episode in which olfactory information was present, a patient may later re-experience the smell in a brief altered state of consciousness, a phenomenon that has been called "olfactory flashback" (Kline & Rausch, 1985). In some instances, the flashback is triggered by a similar odour, but in other cases there is no obvious olfactory cue evoking the memories. The latter form is an example of an olfactory hallucination or phantosmia that entails the discrete perception of an odour that is not object-ively there. Burstein (1987) describes the case of a man who was exposed to a large quantity of smoke in a fire. Some days after the traumatic event he claimed that he was experiencing the same smell as he had done during the fire, thus exhibiting olfactory hallucinations. Smell disorders, and in particular phantosmia, have received relatively little attention from the scien-tific community. However, olfactory hallucinations have been described in depression (Martin & Scharfetter, 1993), psychosis (Kwapil, Chapman, & Chapman, 1996) and epilepsy (Acharya, Acharya, & Luders, 1998). It is worth emphasizing that prevalence data on olfactory flashbacks and hal-lucinations are lacking and that there is no standardized procedure that captures potentially important trauma-related odour information in current diagnostic practice.

As noted above, clinical studies have showed that odours may serve as triggers of traumatic memories and symptoms in persons diagnosed with PTSD. Specific trauma-related smells such as diesel or burned and/or rotten flesh have been shown to work as precipitants of anxiety and fear-related memories in war veterans and patients with PTSD (Vermetten & Bremner, 2003).

Case report

Evidence is sparse regarding the role of olfaction in PTSD, and even less is known about how olfactory flashbacks and traumas evoked by smells could be treated. Case SN demonstrates that trauma-related pictures may evoke olfactory hallucinations that in turn serve as traumatic reminders of past experiences and also suggests that explicit re-directional instructions to avoid trauma-related information may improve psychological status.

Case SN

SN is a 35-year-old man who was deported as a refugee from the war in Afghanistan to Norway when he was 25 years old. SN sought psychiatric treatment for intrusive flashbacks, nightmares, food aversion and anxiety. Although he was married and had a university degree, SN was unable to work and function in his daily life for long periods of time.

During the anamnesis interview, SN explained that since the age of 6 he had witnessed several situations in which people had been killed. In particu-lar, SN had often served as a carrier of dead bodies when they were to be removed. As such, he remembered that the smell of rotten corpses made him sick and that in situations like these he often felt nauseated and had vomited. Furthermore, he had been involved in underground war-related activities involving executions, and in which he came into physical contact with dead bodies. Later, he was sent to prison and accused of counter-revolutionary activity. During a 3-year-long spell in a primitive prison, SN was seriously tortured, both physically and psychologically.

During his adolescence, SN experienced for the first time a meat-induced aversion that occurred after he had carried the dead body of a young man to his parent's house where the funeral was going to take place. Even though SN was not a vegetarian, he claimed that he consistently avoided meat, and then in particular the smell of meat. When asked about his reaction to the smell of meat, he said that the odour of meat evoked traumatic scenes and fears emanating from his childhood and the war in Afghanistan. SN therefore refused to participate in social occasions and also experienced difficulties in visiting the supermarket. He had thus developed various avoidance procedures to cope with and control the possibility that he would be exposed to an odour that might evoke a traumatic recollection. These procedures were still active when he arrived in Norway as a refugee and received psychiatric treatment.

However, concomitant with SN's avoidance behaviour, the therapist became aware that there were situations in which SN was deliberately exposing himself to scenes that activated his previous experiences. For example, when he watched television, he readily searched for channels that offered war films in which burned and dead bodies were being shown, along with other relevant destructive information. SN had adopted a re-experience behaviour, which is a commonly reported phenomenon in PTSD (DSM-IV; American Psychiatric Association, 1994). Typically, individuals suffering from PTSD are excessively focused on trauma-related information and involuntary seek out similarities between the present and their traumatic past that give them the opportunity to relive the traumatic event (Van der Kolk & Fisler, 1995). By doing this, SN falsely believed that reinstating the trauma yielded him better coping strategies for his upset feelings.

The sequence presented below illustrates how SN's re-experienced behaviour worsened his condition, induced olfactory hallucinations, and evoked traumatic passages of previous events. With regard to the dialogue reported below, SN is arriving at the therapist's (T) office in a significantly worse condition than in previous sessions. After a short notice about forthcoming appointments, the therapist comments:

T: I can see that something must have happened to you after our previous meeting, would you please tell me?

SN: I have been watching television for days. I found a new channel of documentary programmes. Lots of violent scenes and dead bodies. I could even perceive the smell of dead corpses in my nose.

T: You could perceive the smell? Tell me more about that.

SN: The smell of rotten, dead flesh. I got sick of it. I had to throw up. I have not eaten any meat of course, but the thing is that I cannot get rid of the stream of pictures from my own life. They are streaming in front of my eyes and I sense the smell from a long time ago. It is because of the smell, you know.

T: So, by looking at television, you got the sensation of that particular smell. Then, the smell made you think about the events that you experienced earlier.

SN: Umm. It is as if there was a smelling channel. I can smell it, it is everywhere in the room and it makes me sick. I cannot even sleep at night, and I have nightmares about things I have experienced.

T: Earlier you told me that you can not eat any meat after being in a supermarket, and that it is difficult to eat meat after seeing pictures of dead bodies and so on. Now, you are telling me that you actually perceive the smell of the bodies you see on television. But still, you are looking at programmes that specifically show scenes that evoke the most terrifying feelings. . . . .

The therapist then explained the importance of disrupting his destructive behaviour and pointed out that the olfactory associations emanating from the pictures and films were also triggering and fuelling his traumatic memories. By making explicit the connection between olfactory information and his traumatic experiences, the therapist was able to help SN to explore how his invaliding symptoms emerged. Thus, although SN thought that he had developed a higher degree of coping as a result of his re-experience behaviour, he gradually came to realize that this behavioural pattern was destructive in its production of intrusive traumatic memories of a ghastly war. Later in the treatment, the therapist was able to introduce techniques that supported distractibility processes and reinforced activity that focused on neutral themes, all in accordance with general trauma therapy (Gray & Litz, 2005). SN is still in treatment, although his ability to detect and monitor his unhealthy coping strategy is gradually improving. As an example, SN identified a smell in the therapist's waiting room that reminded him of the violent torture he had experienced. Instead of passively accepting the olfactory context, he asked the therapist to offer another entrance to the office. The smell was later identified as mould, which had probably been present on the walls in the torture room where he had been held as a prisoner.

Many therapists claim that olfactory cueing and olfactory sensations could be important tools in the treatment of severely disturbed and/or dysfunctional individuals. Olfactory information thus seems to provide a potentially valuable supplement in the diagnostic procedures of PTSD and anxiety disorders and in the treatment of such patients. The above-mentioned case illustrates that memory for smell is long-lasting, powerful, and sometimes an obstacle to health. The case also illustrates how, by making a patient conscious of destructive conditionalized olfactory behaviour, disconnected from awareness and voluntary control, the therapist may obtain significant improvement in this condition.

CONCLUDING REMARKS

The literature reviewed in this chapter illustrates how previous experiences and memory representations of olfactory experiences can come into play in everyday life. Olfactory representations, for example, may be expressed explicitly, as illustrated by episodic recollections of previous episodes triggered by olfactory cues. Non-declarative/implicit olfactory representations were exemplified by chemosensory derived aversions and emotionally conditioned behaviour, both of which show extremely slow forgetting. With regard to experiential qualities, olfactory memory has been described as being more emotional, more vivid but less often thought of and spoken of than verbal and visual memory. The latter findings suggest that odour-associated information may not be spontaneously retrieved, but may gain accessibility from active probing.

From a forensic perspective, it is our hope that our work will stimulate professionals in the domain of forensic investigation to actively address and probe for episodic chemosensory information in witness reports. As this chapter illustrates, active probing may provide valuable information that increases the credibility of a witness statement. Even though some guidance to forensic interviewing explicitly advocates questioning about all types of sensory information (e.g., the cognitive interview), our understanding is that very few practitioners actually do this. Of course, more experimental research is needed before practitioners will be able to reliably employ olfactory cueing techniques when questioning for forensically relevant information. However, to the extent to which this overview is valid, olfactory cueing may represent a valuable memory enhancement technique.

We have also wished to emphasize the extent to which traumatic experiences comprising olfactory information can disrupt the everyday life of individuals, and how such information may help the clinician in the diagnostic and therapeutic processes. Here, we have reported that making an individual aware of implicit olfactory representations as the generator for a dysfunctional behaviour pattern redirected his destructive behaviour and evolved as a fruitful treatment strategy.

REFERENCES

Acharya, V., Acharya, J., & Luders, H. (1998). Olfactory epileptic auras. *Neurology*, *51*, 56–61.

American Psychiatric Association. (1994). *Diagnostic and statistical manual of mental disorders – DSM-IV* (4th ed.). Washington, DC: Author.

Blomqvist, E.H., Brämerson, A., Stjärne, P., & Nordin, S. (2004). Consequences of olfactory loss and adopted coping strategies. *Rhinology, 42,* 189–194.

Borison, H.L. (1989). Area postrema: Chemoreceptor circumventricular organ of the medulla oblongata. *Progress in Neurobiology, 32,* 351–390.

Brewin, C.R., Christodoulides, J., & Hutchinson, G. (1996a). Intrusive thoughts and intrusive memories in a nonclinical sample. *Cognition and Emotion, 10,* 107–112.

Brewin, C.R., Dalgleish, T., & Joseph, S. (1996b). A dual representation theory of posttraumatic stress disorder. *Psychological Review, 103,* 670–686.

Burstein, A. (1987). Olfactory hallucinations. *Hospital and Community Psychiatry, 38,* 80.

Cahill, L., Babinsky, R., Markowitsch, H.J., & McGaugh, J.L. (1995). The amygdala and emotional memory. *Nature, 377,* 295–297.

Capaldi, E.D., Hunter, M.J., & Privitera, G.J. (2004). Odor of taste stimuli in conditioned "taste" aversion learning. *Behavioral Neuroscience, 118,* 1400–1408.

Chu, S., & Downes, J.J. (2000). Odour-evoked autobiographical memories: Psychological investigations of Proustian phenomena. *Chemical Senses, 25,* 111–116.

Cohen, G.C. (1996). *Memory in the real world.* Hove, UK: Psychology Press.

Davis, R.L. (2004). Olfactory learning. *Neuron, 44,* 31–48.

Eichenbaum, H. (1996). Olfactory perception and memory. In R. Llinas & P. Churchland (Eds.), *The mind-brain continuum* (pp. 173–202). Cambridge, MA: MIT Press.

Engen, T. (1982). *The perception of odors.* Toronto: Academic Press.

Engen, T. (1987). Remembering odors and their names. *American Scientist, 75,* 497–503.

Engen, T., & Ross, B.M. (1973). Long-term memory of odors with and without verbal descriptions. *Journal of Experimental Psychology, 100,* 221–227.

Epple, G., & Herz, R.S. (1999). Ambient odors associated to failure influence cognitive performance in children. *Developmental Psychobiology, 35,* 103–107.

Gabrieli, J.D.E., Fleischman, D.A., Keane, M.M., Reminger, S.L., & Morrell, F. (1995). Double dissociation between memory systems underlying explicit and implicit memory in the human brain. *Psychological Science, 6,* 76–82.

Garcia, J., Laister, P.S., Bermudez-Rattoni, F., & Deems, D.A. (1985). A general theory of aversion learning. *Annals of the NY Academy of Sciences, 443,* 8–21.

Graf, P., & Schacter, D.L. (1985). Implicit and explicit memory for new associations in normal and amnesic subjects. *Journal of Experimental Psychology: Learning, Memory, and Cognition, 11,* 501–518.

Gray, M.J. & Litz, B.T. (2005). Behavioral interventions for recent trauma: Empirically informed practice guidelines. *Behavior Modification, 29,* 189–215.

Green, B.L. (1994). Psychososcial research in traumatic stress: An update. *Journal of Traumatic Stress, 7,* 341–362.

Hermans, D., & Bayens, F. (2002). Acquisition and activation of odor hedonics in everyday situations: Conditioning and priming studies. In C. Rouby, B. Schaal, D. Dubois, R. Gervais, & A. Holley (Eds.), *Olfaction, taste, and cognition* (pp. 119–139). Cambridge, UK: Cambridge University Press.

Hershkowitz, I., Orbach, Y., Lamb, M.E., Sternberg, K.J., & Horowitz, D. (2002). A comparison of mental and physical context reinstatement in forensic interviews with alleged victims of sexual abuse. *Applied Cognitive Psychology, 16,* 429–441.

Herz, R.S. (2004). A naturalistic analysis of autobiographical memories triggered by olfactory, visual, and auditory stimuli. *Chemical Senses, 29,* 217–224.

Herz, R.S., Eliassen, J., Beland, S., & Souza, T. (2004). Neuroimaging evidence for the emotional potency of odor-evoked memory. *Neuropsychologia, 42*, 371–378.

Jacob, S., McClintock, M.K., Zelano, B., & Ober, C. (2002). Paternally inherited HLA alleles are associated with women's choice of male odor. *Nature Genetics, 30*, 175–179.

Jehl, C., & Murphy, C. (1998). Developmental effects on odor learning and memory in children: Olfaction and taste XII. *Annals of the New York Academy of Sciences, 855*, 632–634.

Kirk-Smith, M.D., Van Toller, C., & Dodd, G.H. (1983). Unconscious odor conditioning in human subjects. *Biological Psychology, 17*, 221–231.

Kline, N.A., & Rausch, J.L. (1985). Olfactory precipitants of flashbacks in post-traumatic stress disorder: Case reports. *Journal of Clinical Psychiatry, 46*, 383–384.

Knasko, S.C. (1995). Pleasant odors and congruency: Effects on approach behavior. *Chemical Senses, 20*, 479–87.

Kwapil, T.R., Chapman, J.P., & Chapman, L.J. (1996). Deviant olfactory experiences as indicators of risk for psychosis. *Schizophrenia Bulletin, 22*, 371–382.

Larsson, A., & Granhag, P.-A. (2005). Interviewing children with the cognitive interview: Assessing the reliability of statements based on observed and imagined events. *Scandinavian Journal of Psychology, 46*, 49–57.

Larsson, M. (1997). Semantic factors in episodic recognition of common odors in early and late adulthood: A review. *Chemical Senses, 22*, 623–633.

Larsson, M. (2002). Odour memory: A memory systems approach. In C. Rouby, B. Schaal, D. Dubois, R. Gervais, & A. Holley (Eds.), *Olfaction, taste, and cognition* (pp. 231–245). Cambridge, UK: Cambridge University Press.

Larsson, M., & Bäckman, L. (1993). Semantic activation and episodic odor recognition in young and older adults. *Psychology and Aging, 8*, 582–588.

Larsson, M., & Bäckman, L. (1997). Age-related differences in episodic odour recognition: The role of access to specific odour names. *Memory, 5*, 361–378.

Larsson, M., Lövdén, M., & Nilsson, L.-G. (2003). Sex differences in recollective experience for olfactory and verbal information. *Acta Psychologica, 112*, 89–103.

Lawless, H.T., & Cain, W.S. (1975). Recognition memory for odors. *Chemical Senses and Flavor, 1*, 331–337.

Lyman, B.J., & McDaniel, M.A. (1990). Memory for odors and odor names: Modalities of elaboration and imagery. *Journal of Experimental Psychology: Learning, Memory, and Cognition, 16*, 656–664.

Martin, P., & Sharfetter, C. (1993). Olfactory hallucinations in depression. *Fortschrift in Neurological Psychiatry, 61*, 293–300.

Melinder, A. (2004). *Perspectives on children as witnesses*. PhD thesis, Department of Psychology, University of Oslo.

Melinder, A., & Larsson, M. (2006). *I would have known which, if I had smelled the odor: Assisting childrens' source monitoring*. Unpublished manuscript.

Murphy, C., Cain, W.S., Gilmore, M.M., & Skinner, R.B. (1991). Sensory and semantic factors in recognition memory for odors and graphic stimuli: Elderly vs. young persons. *American Journal of Psychology, 104*, 161–192.

Otto, T., Cousens, G., & Rajewski, K. (1997). Odor-guided fear conditioning in rats: Acquisition, retention, and latent inhibition. *Behavioral Neuroscience, 111*, 1257–1264.

Perkins, J., & Cook, N. (1990). Recognition and recall of odours: The effects of suppressing visual and verbal encoding processes. *British Journal of Psychology*, *81*, 221–226.

Pipe, M.-E., & Wilson, J.C. (1994). Cues and secrets: Influences on children's event reports. *Developmental Psychology*, *30*, 515–525.

Price, J.L. (1987). The central and accessory olfactory systems. In T.E Finger & W.L. Silver (Eds.), *Neurobiology of taste and smell* (pp. 179–204). New York: Wiley.

Price, D.W.W., & Goodman, G.S. (1990). Visiting the wizard: Children's memory for a recurring event. *Child Development*, *61*, 664–680.

Proust, M. (1919). *Du coté de chez Swann*. Paris: Gallimard.

Robin, O., Alaoui-Ismaïli, O., Dittmar, A., & Vernet-Maury, E. (1999). Basic emotions evoked by eugenol odor differ according to the dental experience. A neurovegetative analysis. *Chemical Senses*, *24*, 327–335.

Rubin, D.C., Groth, E., & Goldsmith, D.J. (1984). Olfactory cuing of autobiographical memory. *American Journal of Psychology*, *97*, 493–507.

Rubin, D.C., & Schulkind, M.D. (1997). The distribution of autobiographical memories across the lifespan. *Memory and Cognition*, *25*, 859–66.

Sahley, C.L., Gelperin, A., & Rudy, J. (1981). One-trial associative learning modifies food odor preferences of a terrestrial mollusc. *Proceedings of the National Academy of Sciences*, *78*, 640–642.

Salomon, K., & Pipe, M.-E. (2002). Recalling an event 1 year later: The impact of props, drawing and a prior interview. *Applied Cognitive Psychology*, *14*, 99–120.

Savic, I. (2002). Imaging of brain activation by odorants in humans. *Current Opinion in Neurobiology*, *12*, 455–461.

Savic, I., Gulyas, B., Larsson, M., & Roland, P. (2000). Olfactory functions are mediated by parallel and hierarchical processing. *Neuron*, *26*, 735–745.

Schacter, D.L. (1992). Understanding implicit memory: A cognitive neuroscience approach. *American Psychologist*, *47*, 559–569.

Soussignan, R., & Schaal, B. (1996). Children's facial responsiveness to odors: Influences of hedonic valence of odor, gender, age, and social presence. *Developmental Psychology*, *32*, 367–379.

Steller, M., & Køhnken, G. (1989). Criteria-based content analysis. In D.C. Raskin, (Ed.), *Psychological methods in criminal investigation and evidence*. New York: Springer.

Stevenson, R.J., & Boakes, R.A. (2003). A mnemonic theory of odor perception. *Psychological Review*, *110*, 340–364.

Thoresen, C., Lønnum, K., Melinder, A., Stridbeck, U., & Magnussen, S. (in press). Theory and practice in interviewing young children: A study of Norwegian police interviews 1985–2002. *Psychology, Crime and Law*.

Tulving, E. (1983). *Elements of episodic memory*. Oxford, UK: Clarendon Press.

Tulving, E. (1993). Human memory. In P. Andersen, O. Hvalby, O. Paulsen, & B. Hökfelt (Eds.), *Memory concepts – 1993. Basic and clinical aspects* (pp. 27–45). Amsterdam: Elsevier Science Publishers.

Tulving, E. (2002). Episodic memory: From mind to brain. *Annual Review of Psychology*, *53*, 1–25.

Tulving, E., & Thompson, D.M. (1973). Encoding specificity and retrieval processes in episodic memory. *Psychological Review*, *80*, 352–373.

Van der Kolk, B.A., & Fisler, R.E. (1995). Dissociation and the fragmentary nature of traumatic memories: Overview and exploratory study. *Journal of Traumatic Stress*, *8*, 505–525.

Van Toller, S. (1988). Emotion and the brain. In S. Van Toller & G.H. Dodd (Eds.), *Perfumery: The psychology and biology of fragrance* (pp. 121–143). London: Chapman & Hall.

Vasterling, J.J., Brailey, K., & Sutker, P.B. (2000). Olfactory identification in combat-related posttraumatic stress disorder. *Journal of Traumatic Stress, 13*, 241–253.

Vermetten, E., & Bremner, J.D. (2003). Olfaction as a traumatic reminder in posttraumatic stress disorder: Case reports and review. *Journal of Clinical Psychiatry, 64*, 202–207.

Vrij, A., Akehurst, L., Soukara, S., & Bull, R. (2002). Will the truth come out? The effect of deception, age, status, coaching, and social skills on CBCA scores. *Law and Human Behavior, 26*, 261–283.

Walk, H.A., & Johns, E.E. (1984). Interference and facilitation in short-term memory for odors. *Perception and Psychophysics, 36*, 508–514.

Willander, J.M., Christianson, S., Berndtsson, J., Schüler, J., & Larsson, M. (2004). *Olfactory cuing of emotional events* (Abstract). Minneapolis, MN: Association for Chemoreception Sciences.

Willander, J.M., & Larsson, M. (2006). Smell your way back to childhood: Autobiographical odor memory. *Psychonomic Bulletin and Review, 13*, 240–244.

World Health Organization. (1993). *The ICD–10 classification of mental and behavioural disorders*. (1993). Geneva: Author.

5 The development of autobiographical memory: A new model

Gail S. Goodman and
Annika Melinder

Consider the following utterances:

> "He hit me and you were gone." (From a 3-year-old boy screaming to his mother when she got him from preschool after the event.)
> "Au, au, au (points to the fireplace and takes her own hand)." (From an 18-month-old girl when visiting her grandmother's house 3 months after she burned her hand badly in the fireplace.)

These quotations reflect everyday autobiographical memory in young children. The examples also illustrate children's memory for emotional events. For this chapter, both examples are of interest because we present a new model of autobiographical memory development that features the role of negative life experiences. The first quote is also relevant to the present chapter because, in the context of our model, we discuss children's everyday memory for attachment-related events.

The general thesis we attempt to develop, for the first time, is as follows: (1) A certain level of neurological development is a necessary prerequisite for autobiographical (and episodic) memory. Such neurological development is biologically programmed, but also influenced by environmental factors. (2) Children's early memories are likely to concern emotional (and other distinctive) events. In particular, negative experiences may play a special role. Children, like adults, often evince better memory for highly negative as opposed to positive or neutral experiences (e.g., Goodman, Hirschman, Hepps, & Rudy, 1991), and children are capable of showing more advanced cognitive processing of negative experiences (Lagattuta, 1999). Thus, early autobiographical memory may be supported by memory of negative incidents and, in fact, derive in part from the need to express negative experiences. (3) Many negative experiences for children are relevant to the attachment system. Children learn to look to their parents both for protection from negative events and for an understanding of negative (and other) experiences. The parents' own attachment orientation affects how parents discuss negative events with children (e.g., avoidant parents tend to avoid discussion of negative incidents with children), and discussion is known to affect children's autobiographical memory development (Nelson & Fivush, 2004). Children's own attachment orientation also influences how well they remember attachment-related and negative events (e.g., avoidant style is associated with worse autobiographical memory). Thus, important individual differences in autobiographical memory and its development may be related both to the parent's and the child's attachment orientation.

Our plan in this chapter is, first, to lay a foundation for discussing the development of autobiographical memory by addressing briefly such basic issues as the development of memory systems (i.e., explicit vs. implicit memory). We then describe several current models of the development of autobiographical memory.

After that, we consider whether there are characteristics of children's memory for distressing events that are in some way special, and therefore point to unique processing of negative information. There is evidence that negative emotional experiences are, to some extent, better remembered and as such have a specific status in the mind. We propose that negative events therefore play a special role in the development of autobiographical memory.

Because we believe it is important to incorporate everyday memory into a socioemotional context, we also focus on the role of parent–child attachment, and thus we discuss attachment theory as it relates to memory. Because the parents' interactions with the child are in part determined by the parents' own attachment history and orientation, we also discuss theory and research on adult attachment. Researchers have uncovered several important relations between attachment and memory, especially memory for negative life events, some of which may be relevant to the development of autobiographical memory. Overall, we postulate that attachment relations play a central role in the processing of many negative experiences during childhood, a role that has implications for individual differences in the development of autobiographical memory.

OVERVIEW OF MEMORY DEVELOPMENT

Episodic memory

Contemporary definitions of episodic memory refer to an explicit (consciously accessible) memory of events that took place at specific times and places in the individual's own personal history. Episodic memory in general, according to Tulving (1985), requires the ability to mentally travel back in time. The term "autonoetic" was introduced by him to refer to a special kind of consciousness that allows humans to be aware of the subjective time when an event took place. As such, autobiographical memory is part of the episodic memory system (Tulving, 1999) and is reflected in utterances like "I saw her because I was there" and "I know it happened then because I left right away". When people use their episodic memory, increased activity on both sides of the frontal lobes is observed using fMRI technology, in contrast to a single side when performing semantic memory tasks, a finding that implicates different neurological systems supporting episodic versus semantic memory (Tulving, 2002).

There has been considerable debate about when episodic memory is first available developmentally. According to Tulving, episodic memory is not present until about 4 or 5 years of age. He contends that what might appear to be episodic memory in younger children is actually semantic memory and does not involve "mental travel" back in time. Others assert that episodic memory is present much earlier in life, perhaps as early as the first year or two, as shown in elicited and delayed imitation tasks (e.g., Bauer, 1996; Bauer & Wewerka, 1995). Assuming that episodic memory development is a prerequisite for autobiographical memory development, this debate is relevant to the present chapter. However, autobiographical memory differs somewhat from more general episodic memory in that the former is said to be associated with a timeline of a person's life history *and* with life episodes that have personal significance, in addition to "mental time travel" phenomenology (Conway & Rubin, 1993).

Multiple systems view

Autobiographical memory development, as a part of episodic memory development, can be considered within broader conceptions of memory. Many scholars regard memory as a set of cognitive processes, which differentially contribute to our ability to store and recall information (Nadel, 1994; Schacter, 1996; Schacter & Tulving, 1994). These multiple interacting systems are related to each other, and information may often be stored in more than one system/subsystem. There is, however, considerable debate as to whether memory should be described in terms of multiple systems, or if it is more appropriate to talk about processes and functions (see Roediger, Buckner, & McDermott, 1999).

One multiple systems model holds that there are two major systems: a declarative and a non-declarative one (Cohen & Squire, 1980). Whereas the former refers to people's explicit knowledge and personal recollection, the latter captures implicit forms of memories, such as procedural and priming (perceptional representational system) functions.

Of specific relevance to the present discussion, the different systems underlying explicit and implicit memory are often assumed to have different developmental trajectories (C. Nelson, 1995, 1997, 2000; Perner, 2000). Of theoretical importance is whether such development proceeds as a continuous or discontinuous process. The discussion has direct implications for the understanding of infantile amnesia, the observation that individuals tend to be unable to remember anything before the age of about 3 years: If explicit memory is a late developing system (e.g., Pillemer & White, 1989; Schacter & Moscovitch, 1984), infantile amnesia may be the result of the operation of the earlier implicit memory system. As relevant to our thesis, we briefly outline some central aspects of the implicit and explicit memory-development debate, which sheds light also on the concept of infantile amnesia.

Discontinuous development view

In Charles Nelson's (1995) memory development model, the infant is presumed to start out with a "primitive" non-declarative memory system, usually without conscious awareness of an act of remembering. While in the uterus, the foetus can "learn" to recognize (and thus remember) specific rhythms, sounds and smells that later, after birth, may contribute to the infant's adaptation. For example, it is well documented that breastfed newborns prefer the auxiliary odour of their mother to that of a control woman (Cernoch & Porter, 1985). Nelson suggests that a neurological infrastructure, including the hippocampus, cerebellum and striatrum, functions as a hardwire pillar. Their function is primarily to support pre-existing (e.g., procedural) memory systems, which in turn are thought to underlie habituation and operant conditioning. This non-declarative memory system is distinguished from a declarative memory system, which develops over the first few years of life as a function primarily of neurological development (Greenough & Black, 1999; Johnson, 2000; C. Nelson, 1995). Reaching this next memory developmental plateau, permitting such functions as delayed imitation and recognition capacities, is dependent on structures in the medial temporal lobes and prefrontal cortex, which mature during the last part of the first year of life into the second year. Only later do children develop more mature declarative memory abilities. For example, evidence from event-related brain potential (ERP) scalp topography has uncovered that children as old as 9–10 years may lack sufficient inputs from frontal regions that are necessary for retrieval of episodic (source) information on some tasks (Cycowicz, Friedman, Snodgrass, & Duff, 2001; see Cycowicz, 2000, for a review). According to this multiple systems view, the declarative memory system would need to be sufficiently developed for children to be capable of autobiographical memory.

Unitary system view: continuous development

In contrast, Rovee-Collier (1997) has argued that if there are different memory systems, they are active from birth and do not develop hierarchically, but in parallel, and form a unitary, continuous process. Rovee-Collier has observed that implicit and explicit forgetting follow the same forgetting curve, which she takes as evidence for a unitary memory system. In place of a multiple system proposal, she claims that a single memory system exists with multiple routes of access (Rovee-Collier, Hayne, & Colombo, 2001). For example, the difference between implicit and explicit memory is, according to Rovee-Collier, the way in which memory is tested (the route of access; see also

Buchner & Brandt, 2003). Given the assumption of a continuous process in memory development, Rovee-Collier's ideas would lead to the conclusion that infantile amnesia does not reflect an abrupt mental event caused by the development of a new memory system, but is rather the result of problems with context reinstatement, retrieval cues and the like.

Conclusion

The models and debates reviewed so far have particular relevance for understanding the onset of infantile amnesia and thus to the beginnings of a consciously accessible autobiographical memory. In the present chapter, we are concerned less with debates about the reasons for the onset of infantile amnesia and more with memory development once it is possible to form an enduring autobiographical memory.

MODELS OF AUTOBIOGRAPHICAL MEMORY DEVELOPMENT

Previously, it was believed that infants lack memory (e.g., James, 1890). However, a wealth of developmental research now confirms memory even in young infants, albeit not likely of a form that is consciously accessible later (Fagan, 1970; Rovee-Collier, 1997). Freud (1916/1966) emphasized repression of early unacceptable memories and reconstruction of early memories into "screen memories" of a bland nature. However, because his ideas on this matter are largely considered passé, we discuss here two recent and more viable theoretical accounts.

Howe and Courage (1994a; Howe, 1997; Howe, Courage, & Peterson, 1995) proposed a model of autobiographical memory development that focuses in large part on the development of a sense of self, which in regard to memory, they term "the cognitive self". They propose that it is not the memory systems themselves that develop into a more mature stage, but rather that the emergence of a cognitive self makes it possible to organize information and experiences into an autobiographical form. The cognitive self appears around the age of 2 years, as indexed when the child understands that his/her picture in the mirror represents someone separate from his/her mother/others, and the child recognizes a "me". A self-schema can then develop around which autobiographical memory emerges. As such, the cognitive self may contribute to the demise of infantile amnesia. Importantly, even before the emergence of a cognitive self, the child will remember events; however, these experiences will not be recognized as events that happen to "me", and therefore a more elaborated and comprehensive synthesis of the personal past fails to exist at early phases of development.

If the cognitive self-schema underlies autobiographical memory, it is therefore logical to expect better memory skills for children who recognize themselves earlier in the mirror than for children who recognize themselves only later (Harley & Reese, 1999; Reese, 2002). Although evidence for such relations has been found in early childhood, these effects are overshadowed by maternal factors, specifically maternal reminiscing style (e.g., an elaborative style of maternal discussion; K. Nelson & Fivush, 2004), later in development. In addition, maternal elaboration predicts children's later memory reports, whereas being an early self-recognizer is uncorrelated with better memory when children grow older (Harley & Reese, 1999; Reese, 2002, in K. Nelson & Fivush, 2004). Maternal reminiscence style (e.g., maternal elaboration) is believed by K. Nelson and Fivush (2004) to play a particularly important role in the development of autobiographical memory. We turn to their model next.

According to K. Nelson and Fivush (2004), the emergence of autobiographical memory involves the development not only of memory per se but also of language and narrative skills, representation of self and others, and theory of mind. Moreover, all of these components are said to operate within cultural and social contexts, with one of the most important social contexts being the scaffolding for memory provided by maternal elaboration.

In their model of autobiographical memory development, K. Nelson and Fivush postulate that infants and toddlers start out with memory for events (routines and episodes) over hours, days, weeks and months. The system is social in nature, and thus the infant is born into a dialogue or a social interaction. At the time when the child develops a sense of self (the cognitive self; Howe, 1997; Howe & Courage, 1994a), this cognitive self is fused with the beginnings of language comprehension and expression, which for most children starts in the middle of the second year. Typically, the parents then start to talk to the child about their life: who the child played with, what the family is going to do later, and so forth. According to K. Nelson and Fivush (2004), this stage is especially important, because it fosters sequential thinking and temporal organization. Autobiographical memory is by definition time and space specific, and these interactions encourage such thinking.

In regard to relationships, this phase also helps with the psychological separation between the mother and the infant because it gives a new consciousness to the child of different states of mind that exist in self and others. The child's more developed theory of mind seems to be based on such a psychological separation (Gopnik & Astington, 1988; Perner, Leekam, & Wimmer, 1987; Perner & Wimmer, 1985).

K. Nelson and Fivush's (2004) model emphasizes two important milestones. The child learns to talk about events and experiences in a socially acceptable way and develops a form of narrative that aids recollection of information of whole episodes that are temporally and sequentially organized, rather than recounted as fragmented pieces. However, as a critique of Nelson and Fivush's ideas, in their model no attention is given to the importance of a safe and calm relationship for the development of autobiographical memory. They generally accept Howe and Courage's notions that a sense of self is important for autobiographical memory development, but neither group of theorists has sufficiently, in our view, related their work to how the development of a sense of self emerges from parent–child interactions.

Scholars from different traditions indicate that the emergence of the self is dependent on the relationship that exists between the primary caretaker and the infant (Bowlby, 1980; Mahler, Pine, & Bergman, 1975; Stern, 1985). Thus, to the extent that a cognitive self underlies autobiographical memory development, parent–child relationship factors need to be considered. Daniel Stern's idea of a "subjective self" relates to the infant's emerging understanding of the separate mind processes of others, which gives the child a new experience of subjectivity, that is, to be different and separate from others not only physically but also emotionally. Central in Stern's view is the regulation of affective states of the mind, which is thought to function as a bridge between the infant's internal emotional state and his/her actions. A sensitive caretaker, for Stern, is attuned to the infant's affective state as is reflected in the infant's external actions (Stern, 1985). During infancy, the main caretaker must support the infant's needs, which are communicated as a result of the infant's internal tensions, that is, negative states. If so, one would expect the sense of self to develop primarily from the experience of negative personal events that the caretaker seeks to ease (see also Mahler et al., 1975). The idea of sensitive caregiving is also featured prominently in Bowlby's Attachment Theory, about which we have more to say later.

NEGATIVE EVENTS: CHILDREN'S MEMORY, LANGUAGE AND COGNITIVE PROCESSING

We propose that young children often show more advanced processing of negative stimuli than of neutral stimuli, and even more than of many positive stimuli. For the sake of survival, children may be wired to give priority to survival-related information. This would include many negative situations, such as when a child is hurt or frightened. It would also include many attachment-related situations, because the attachment system is geared for infant survival and is likely to be activated when infants face or fear negative experiences.

Studies with both adults and children reveal that highly emotional, negative information tends to be remembered better than positive or neutral information (Berntsen, 2002; Canli, Zhao, Brewer, Gabrieli, & Cahill, 2000; Christianson, 1992; Goodman et al., 1991). Moreover, even at very young ages, children's accounts of negative personal experiences are particularly detailed. For instance, Howe, Courage, and Bryant-Brown (1994a) report that 2-year-old children were able to provide coherent and detailed recall of traumatic injuries and ensuing emergency room treatments that they had experienced several days previously. The children's recall (at least for the central details of the incidents) was still robust when tested 6 and 12 months later (Howe, Courage, & Peterson, 1994b). According to some, brain structures (e.g., the amygdala) and stress hormones (e.g., adrenalin) increase the distinctiveness and vividness of negative stimuli in memory, which facilitates later recall (LeDoux, 1992).

When adults try to recall their earliest memories from childhood, researchers often (although not always) find that adults recall negative events as their first autobiographical memory (e.g., going to the hospital; Cowan & Davidson, 1984; Howes, Siegel, & Brown, 1993; Usher & Neisser, 1993). For instance, Howes et al. asked 300 undergraduates to report the earliest memories in their lives. The study had the advantage of verification, if possible, from parents, other relatives and relevant others, of the undergraduates' accounts. There were more negative than positive or neutral earliest memories. However, in other studies, recall of positive and negative experiences is equal, and at times, there is even a slight advantage for positive information to be recalled as the earliest memory (e.g., Lindsay, Wade, Hunter, & Read, 2004; Usher & Neisser, 1993). According to our proposal here, one would predict either that the earliest memories would be of negative events relevant to survival and attachment or that early memories for negative events would be more accurate, vivid and/or detailed, all other things being equal. However, as will be explained later, individual differences in attachment are likely to affect adults', if not children's, recall of their earliest experiences. Thus, we would predict that if researchers do not take such individual differences into account in their studies, they may water down or even slightly reverse the advantage of negative information in early autobiographical memory.

Moreover, our proposal is that negative information provides an important platform for the development of autobiographical memory, but at this point we do not propose that it is the only platform for such development. Other factors such as distinctiveness may also play an important role. Furthermore, arousal in general may help support memory, including positive arousal. In their work on emotion, Lang and his colleagues (Lang, Bradley, & Cuthbert, 1997) differentiate the valence and arousal dimensions. However, arousal combined with negative personal relevance appears to be the most memorable (Block, Greenberg, & Goodman, 2004). (Note that there are also empirical studies indicating that negative emotion can impair memory, e.g., Merritt, Ornstein, & Spiker, 1994. Although such findings may derive from many possible sources, including methodological ones involving problems with measuring negative emotion and people's uneasiness or unwillingness to discuss negative events, we focus later on individual differences as moderators of the findings of better memory for negative life events.)

In any case, to the extent that negative events that evoke a high level of arousal are especially well retained and to the extent that memory underlies many other cognitive tasks, one would expect children to show more sophisticated cognition and language about negative than neutral or positive events. To bolster our case, we next review several lines of research indicating the superiority of negative information in children's language/communication and thought.

Once language is attained, children's earliest communications are almost entirely about negative events. Miller and Sperry (1988) found that over 80% of toddlers' earliest communications with parents are about being hurt (e.g., getting a "boo-boo") or other negative issues. Also consistent with our contention, in a longitudinal natural-language study of everyday parent–child conversations, with children between 2 and 5 years of age, Lagattuta (1999) discovered that the frequency of talk about past emotional experiences, causal explanations for emotions, and connections between emotions and mental states occurred at a significantly higher cognitive level when children and parents talked about negative in comparison to positive feelings. Note that there are more words generally in emotion lexicons for negative emotions than for positive emotions (Shaver, Schwarts, Kirson, & O'Connor, 1987), and also more facial expressions of negative than positive emotions (Ekman, 1992).

In several other studies of young children's theory of mind, Lagattuta (1999; Lagattuta & Wellman, 2002) reported that children evince more advanced theory of mind for negative emotional events. For example, in an experimental study, she investigated whether 3- to 7-year-olds and adults connect a person's current feelings to the past, especially to thinking about a prior experience. In one study, participants heard stories that featured a main character who felt sad, mad or happy after a particular event (e.g., sad to have lost a pet bunny), and who many days later felt that same emotion upon seeing a cue related to that prior incident (e.g., sad at returning to the location where the bunny was lost). For some story endings, the character's emotion upon seeing the cue was congruent with the current situation, whereas for others, the emotion mismatched the present circumstances. Participants were asked to explain the cause of the character's current feelings. As Lagattuta states, "Indeed, children 5 years and younger revealed strikingly cogent understanding of historical-mental influences . . . especially when they had to explain why a person, who had experienced a negative event in the past, was currently feeling sad or mad in a positive situation" (Lagattuta & Wellman, 2002, p. 82). And "Young children are more knowledgeable about historical-mental causes of negative emotions in comparison with positive emotions" (p. 100).

Finally, additional evidence of superior processing of negative events comes from studies of children's suggestibility. Children are *less* suggestible (although still subject to suggestive influence) about negative than neutral or positive events. This has been demonstrated in our own work on abuse-related suggestions (e.g., "He hit you, didn't he?"; Rudy & Goodman, 1991) and in our own work and that of others on false-memory formation ("Tell me about the time you fell off your tricycle and had to go to the hospital to get stitches," when in fact the parent reported to the researchers that the child had never experienced that event; e.g., Ceci, Loftus, Leichtman, & Bruck, 1994; Pezdek & Taylor, 2002; Schaaf, Alexander, & Goodman, 2005).

These mental processes (language/communication, theory of mind, resistance to suggestion) may be enhanced for negative information in part because of children's better memory for negative events, as is also found for adults (e.g., Christianson, 1992; Goodman et al., 1991). Memory supports many cognitive abilities and, by some accounts, cognitive development itself (e.g., Case, 1978). To the extent that children possess better memory, which supports more sophisticated cognitive and language processing of negative experiences, it is also likely that negative experiences play an especially important role in the development of autobiographical memory.

However, there are reliable differences in how individuals learn to process negative life experiences. To understand such individual differences, we turn to attachment theory.

ATTACHMENT THEORY: PARENT–CHILD ATTACHMENT

From an evolutionary perspective, the human species' long dependency as infants may have provided the possibility for developing interpersonal relationships that foster autobiographical memory development. Attachment Theory, as articulated by Bowlby (1980), is informed by evolutionary theory and deals explicitly with parent–child relationships. There is now strong evidence that attachment in infants is primarily the result of responsive parenting as opposed to infant temperament (e.g., Vaughn & Bost, 1999).

Parent–child attachment

In Bowlby's (1969, 1980) view, crucial elements in the child's and adult's personality depend on the quality of early caretaker–child relationships. Experiences with attachment figures are internalized in the form of "internal working models", which later are used to anticipate new situations and to channel behaviour.

Attachment behaviours (e.g., clinging, crying) permit the child to stay close to another person from whom the infant experiences support (Bowlby, 1982). In principle, there are two different categories of attachment behaviours: signal behaviours, such as facial expressions, gestures, smiles or bodily postures; and approach behaviours, such as crawling or clinging. These behaviours result in reduced tension if closeness to the secure base/attachment object (typically, but not necessarily, the mother) is successful, but separation anxiety develops if responsive closeness is impossible.

Activation of attachment behaviour

The attachment system is activated when the infant experiences stress, pain, fear or anxiety. Depending on the intensity of the child's emotions, the attachment behaviour will stop when appropriate action is taken by the caretaker. For example, if the child's arousal is quite low, it might be enough to see the caretaker, whereas if the child's arousal is high and the child is extremely upset, it might be necessarily for the caretaker to calm the child for a longer period of time. Attachment behaviour brings about emotional regulation, as also emphasized by Stern (1985). Absence of the attachment figure (the secure base) in aversive or overly novel situations results in anxiety and activation of the attachment system. Over time, the attachment figure's absence results in a specific pattern of reactions in the child (Bowlby, 1969). In studying children in orphanages and hospital settings, Bowlby observed that, first, the child cries and protests, but these expressions transform into despair and end with detachment from the attachment figure. Prolonged or multiple separations can result in difficulty in forming secure attachments to new individuals. Deprived children who have spent a long time without any secure base express no interest when the attachment figure returns (Spitz, 1945, 1946).

Relevant to this discussion is Bowlby's (1987) concept of "defensive exclusion". This is the idea that individuals may selectively attend to material that could activate the attachment system, or defensively not attend to such material. In observing parent–child reunions in children who had experienced prolonged separation from their attachment figures, Bowlby (1980) noted that such children frequently failed to display attachment behaviour, which he interpreted to mean that the children were selectively or defensively not attending to the attachment system-eliciting stimuli. Presumably, in this way, the children could regulate activation of the attachment system.

Individual differences in infant attachment

The "Strange Situation" is a test for older infants (e.g., 18 months of age) built from the assumptions that attachment and exploration are complementary systems, in which attachment behaviour can be elicited in the laboratory (Ainsworth, 1967). Briefly, the Strange Situation consists of attachment-related fear-evoking events, such as the mother (i.e., the attachment figure or the secure base) leaving the child, the entrance of a stranger, and the reunion of the child and the mother. Based primarily on the child's reaction when the attachment figure (e.g., the mother) returns, Ainsworth specified three attachment categories; insecure-avoidant (e.g., child does not pay attention to the mother when she comes back, and seeks help from the stranger), secure (e.g., the child seeks out the mother during the reunion and is easily calmed by the mother if upset), and insecure-ambivalent (also known as anxious-ambivalent: e.g., the child gets very upset when the mother leaves, and seeks both closeness and acts out rejection when she is back). Later scholars included a fourth category, insecure-disorganized (e.g., the child might approach the mother without looking at her, lacks emotional expressions, and seems depressed). Of importance, this categorization is said to reflect not an inherent personality trait, but rather the quality of the relationship between the attachment figure and the child at that point. In Ainsworth's original work, she noted that attachment could be conceived as involving two separable dimensions: anxiety and avoidance.

In Ainsworth's (1967) initial reports, children with a secure attachment were found to have more sensitive mothers than did children who were insecurely attached. However, in questioning these findings, researchers have shown that other aspects of the mothers' functioning (e.g., emotional support and degree of reciprocal relation) are as important (DeWolff & Van Ijzendoorn, 1997). Recently, children with disorganized attachment have been studied, and their behaviour has been correlated to abusive experiences and to parental unresolved grief (Barnett, Ganiban, & Cicchetti, 1999; Crittenden, 1992; Crockenberg & Leerkes, 2000).

Attachment theory: adult attachment

Derived from Bowlby's theory and Ainsworth's empirical studies, there is a growing body of research on adult attachment. Similar concepts are used in the adult and child attachment literatures. Mary Main and her colleagues (e.g., Main & Solomon, 1990) developed the Adult Attachment Interview (AAI), in which adults' autobiographical memories of childhood are probed specifically about relationships with the person's parents (e.g., "Tell me about a time in childhood when you did something fun with your father."). The goal is to uncover unconscious internal working models of parent–child attachment that follow the person into adulthood. The AAI predicts the attachment classification of the children, tested in the Strange Situation, of the adults given the AAI. The AAI test is, in effect, a test of adult autobiographical memory.

Taking a different approach, but one still deriving from attachment theory, Hazan and Shaver (1987; see also Mikulincer & Shaver, 2003; Shaver & Mikulincer, 2002) developed a model, and accompanying measure, of adult romantic attachment. Their work and measure have been especially useful in examining the relations between adult attachment and memory.

In Mikulincer and Shaver's (2003) current conceptualization, adult attachment, like infant attachment, can be described by the intersection of two orthogonal dimensions, avoidance and anxiety. Put into the language of adult attachment "styles", these dimensions can be used to create four cells: secure, preoccupied, dismissing avoidant, and fearful avoidant. These styles affect not only adult romantic relationships but also how adults relate to their children. Like secure babies, romantically secure adults find comfort in intimate relationships with others without being overly needy or avoidant. They tend to score low on both avoidance and anxiety dimensions. Securely attached adults talk to their children about both negative and positive life experiences, comfort their children during and after stressful events, and can take the listener's needs into account when describing life experiences (e.g., Edelstein et al., 2004; Quas et al., 1999). Preoccupied adults, who score high on the anxiety dimension and low on the avoidant dimension, are similar to anxiously attached infants: Such adults feel needy and rejected. During stressful events and later when discussing them, preoccupied adults tend to be overly anxious and intrusive, and have difficulty taking others' needs into account (e.g., Edelstein et al., 2004; Main, Kaplan, & Cassidy, 1985). Dismissing avoidant adults, who score high on the avoidant dimension and low on the anxious dimension, express the need to restrict intimate relationships with others and feel that in romantic relationships, their partner wants more of them than they can provide. They try to avoid discussion of negative experiences and are least likely to attempt to comfort their children when the children become stressed or after the children have experienced a stressful event (Edelstein et al., 2004; Quas et al., 1999). Finally, fearful avoidant adults, who score high on both anxiety and avoidance, are anxious and needy about intimate relationships, and fear rejection, but cope with such fears by being avoidant of such relationships. Like disorganized attachment in infants, fearful avoidant attachment in adults can result from abusive childrearing or childhood trauma. Although less is known about fearful avoidant individuals' relations with their children, in theory, they should appear frightened and helpless in stressful situations and possibly while discussing such situations with their children.

ATTACHMENT AND MEMORY

Recent research has examined attachment and memory in both children and adults. However, there are currently more published studies on adult attachment and memory than on children's attachment and memory.

In theory, attachment-related differences should be most evident for information that is likely to activate the attachment system (e.g., highly emotional or potentially threatening information; Bowlby, 1980). Avoidant people should limit their processing of potentially threatening information because they should be motivated to avoid activation of the attachment system (Edelstein & Shaver, 2004; Fraley, Davis, & Shaver, 1998). In contrast, anxious individuals should be hypervigilant to information that could result in activation of the attachment system. Such regulatory mechanisms on the part of the parents or their children may affect children's memory. As mentioned previously, for infants and young children, many types of negative situations will have the potential to activate the attachment system.

Children's memory and attachment

Surprisingly few studies have been published on children's attachment and memory. However, we know of a few that exist. For instance, Kirsch and Cassidy (1997) investigated relations among attachment categories, as assessed in infancy via the Strange Situation, and attention and memory in the same children once they became preschoolers. Children 3.5 to 4.2 years of age participated in two attention tasks and one memory task. In one of the attention tasks, for example, the preschoolers were shown drawings of different mother–child dyads engaged in positive, negative and neutral interactions. Consistent with the idea of defensive exclusion, insecure-avoidant children were especially likely to look away from the drawings. In the memory task, children were read six stories in which a mother responds to her child's bid for help (e.g., the mother responded sensitively to her child, to reflect parental behaviour associated with secure attachment; or the mother rejected her child, to reflect parental behaviour associated with avoidant attachment). Secure preschoolers recalled the responsive stories better than did the insecure-avoidant preschoolers and the rejecting stories better than did the insecure-ambivalent preschoolers. Although this pattern of results may reflect better memory generally, it may instead reflect the fact that secure children are able to successfully process both positive and negative information, rather than defensively avoiding negative information.

Belsky, Spritz, and Crnic (1996) examined whether 3-year-olds with secure attachment histories (measured at 12 months of age) would prove less distractible during positive than negative events (as displayed in a puppet show) and would remember positive events more accurately than negative events, with the reverse being true of children with insecure attachment histories. Support for this hypothesis emerged in the case of memory but not attention (for which no attachment effects emerged; but see Main et al., 1985), even when infants' temperament-emotionality and general verbal intelligence were taken into consideration. Thus, although developmental studies on these issues are sparse, the findings to date fit with the predictions of attachment theory.

Perhaps more surprising is that in several studies, researchers have found that *parents'* attachment classification, as indexed by Shaver's measures, predicts their *children's* memory errors in attachment-related situations. In more than four different studies of children's memory and suggestibility concerning their medical experiences or other negative events, Goodman and colleagues report that parental insecure attachment is associated with children's memory deficits (e.g., Alexander et al., 2002; Goodman, Quas, Batterman-Faunce, Riddlesberger, & Kuhn, 1997; Melinder, 2004; Quas, Goodman, Bidrose, Pipe, Craw, & Ablin, 1999). Moreover, the effects of stress on memory depended on parental avoidance (Alexander et al., 2002). That is, when children are highly stressed by the medical procedures, children of less avoidant parents evince better memory (consistent with the idea of better memory for negative experiences), whereas children of more avoidant parents evince worse memory. Such findings have been uncovered even when other individual-differences factors, such as parents' and children's personality and children's intelligence, are statistically controlled. Consistent with attachment theory, Goodman et al. (1997) reported that avoidant parents indicated that they had less time to deal with their children's emotions about the stressful medical events, talked less to their children about such events, comforted and prepared their children less, and so forth.

Thus, it is possible that children's own attachment orientation, as well as their parents' attachment orientation, are both important influences on children's memory. If so, one would predict that children who are avoidant themselves and/or who have avoidant parents would have less-developed autobiographical memories for negative events, in that they would engage in or be privy to less processing of negative experiences (e.g., avoidance of encoding negative, attachment-related information; less rehearsal due to less discussion) and perhaps poorer understanding of some negative events to start with (e.g., because of less parental preparation). Indeed, in a study of the relation of attachment status and emotional content of parent–child memory conversations, Farrar, Fasig, and Welch-Ross (1997) found that although mother–daughter dyads with insecurely attached girls engaged in relatively more negative memory talk than mother–daughter dyads with securely attached girls, mother–daughter dyads of secure girls *elaborated* more often on both positive and negative emotional themes than did the dyads of insecure girls, who primarily elaborated on positive themes. Given the key role of maternal elaboration in autobiographical memory development, the differences uncovered as a function of attachment style are of note.

Adult attachment and memory

Adult attachment researchers have uncovered a number of interesting relations concerning adult attachment and memory. The results of these studies are particularly consistent for avoidant individuals, and thus we focus here primarily on the avoidant dimension.

Mikulincer and Orbach (1995) asked adults to recall childhood memories associated with certain emotions, such as anxiety or happiness. They found that highly avoidant individuals recalled fewer emotional memories from childhood and took longer to recall them than did less avoidant individuals. These effects were particularly pronounced for childhood events associated with sadness or anxiety. Avoidant individuals also rated their emotions as less intense at the time of the event, and the events they recalled occurred at an older age in childhood. These findings suggest that avoidant individuals have less access to memories of early, highly emotional negative experiences. As mentioned previously, when the AAI is employed rather than Shaver's adult attachment measure, again it is found that avoidance is associated with restricted access to attachment-related and/or emotional memories from childhood (Main et al., 1985).

Fraley, Garner, and Shaver (2000) read a story about interpersonal loss to adult college students. In testing their immediate and delayed memory for the story, avoidance was negatively associated with recall of story details. Edelstein et al. (2005) examined memory for child sexual abuse in 102 victims 11 to 19 years after the assaults. Memory accuracy was predicted by an interaction of adult attachment-related avoidance and severity of the abuse. Specifically, victims who scored as highly avoidant on the Shaver measure demonstrated poor memory for particularly severe child sexual abuse, whereas less avoidant individuals were more accurate about severe cases. This pattern is similar to that reported by Alexander et al. (2002) in examining children's memory for inoculations. Thus, although the events (an inoculation vs. sexual abuse) and the ages (young children vs. older adolescents and adults) were quite different, a similar pattern of predicted results emerged. Moreover, in the Edelstein et al. study, memory accuracy was positively associated with maternal support and with the extent to which victims had talked about the abuse with others.

In conclusion, from a theoretical perspective, children's own attachment orientation would be expected to affect the encoding of or processing of attachment-related negative experiences, and thus the child's autobiographical memory, as would parents' attachment orientation as well. There is growing evidence that important and predictable relations exist between attachment and memory, especially for children and adults who score high on avoidant attachment.

PROPOSED MODEL

Our review of the empirical literature and psychological theory leads us to propose a new model of the development of autobiographical memory. Our model is still in its formative stage, and is in need of direct testing. Moreover, we acknowledge that our model may only account for part of autobiographical memory development. A diagram of important features of our model is presented in Figure 5.1. The model is meant to depict a *process* during early childhood but is not tightly connected to certain ages.

We propose, consistent with Tulving's (1999) formulation, that a certain degree of biological maturity is necessary before episodic and thus autobiographical memory is possible. To the extent that autobiographical memory is largely a form of episodic memory (although it may also have semantic components) and is influenced by cognitive developmental processes, it is likely to require a certain degree of brain development, perhaps even into the 2nd to 4th year of age. Thus, infantile amnesia effects as a universal human phenomenon are likely to be largely (although not completely) explained by brain maturation. However, it should be noted that the socioemotional and cognitive environment also affects brain development.

We also agree with K. Nelson and Fivush (2004) that autobiographical memory development should be considered within a social and cultural perspective, and not just from a cognitive developmental perspective. However, we add several novel and important additions to previous theories of autobiographical memory development.

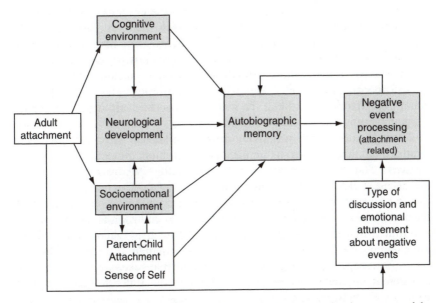

Figure 5.1 Important features of the autobiographical memory-development model.

First, our emphasis is on the fact that, from an evolutionary point of view, autobiographical memory is likely to have emerged in the context of human survival. That is, one reason to have an autobiographical memory system at all is to help humans survive. Autobiographical memory provides a means to reflect on one's past to avoid dangerous situations again. And it permits children to share their experiences with their parents to enhance their chances of survival.

Second, we propose that one important platform of autobiographical memory development concerns memory for highly negative experiences. We suspect that at virtually all ages, highly negative experiences are particularly well retained in memory (except perhaps when defending against such memories), again for survival reasons. If such events are particularly well retained in infancy and toddlerhood, then they should be among the first – if not the first – to enter into an autobiographical memory system, or at least to be most accurately or vividly retained in regard to central stressors. Of course, what is highly negative or stressful for an infant or toddler may be very different from what is highly negative or stressful for adults. As an example, for an infant or toddler, separation from one's main caretaker may be highly distressing, whereas for adults, it is less so. Negative experiences are not only particularly likely to be remembered; they are also particularly likely to be talked about by children during the age periods when autobiographical memory is first developing (toddlerhood). And they are discussed at a higher level of sophistication than are positive events.

If too many negative events are experienced, however, as in chronic trauma situations, this may have detrimental effects on the brain and autobiographical memory, consistent with the idea of chronic cortisol release and subsequent smaller hippocampal volume in individuals who have suffered abuse in childhood and who later develop post-traumatic stress disorder (PTSD; Bremner et al., 1995b). However, the data concerning such effects in humans are still contradictory (e.g., De Bellis, Hall, Boring, Frustaci, & Moritz, 2001; Gilbertson et al., 2002). In some ways, individuals with PTSD have particularly good memories of childhood trauma (Alexander et al., 2005).

Third, because many negative events in childhood are also attachment related, attachment theory is implicated in autobiographical memory development. Children's own attachment orientation may provide regulatory mechanisms that affect the processing of attachment-related experiences, including negative ones. Such regulatory processes that are associated with memory performance have been documented by at least the age of 3 years, and may exist during infancy as well (e.g., Belsky et al., 1996). And parental attachment affects if and how parents help children process attachment-related and negative experiences. To the extent that parental discussion with children is important for autobiographical memory development, as proposed by K. Nelson and Fivush (2004), then it is fairly clear from attachment theory and associated empirical findings that avoidant parents would be less likely to discuss highly negative events with their children. Such parents may be less elaborative, to use K. Nelson and Fivush's terminology. And parental elaborative discussion relates to narrative ability and autobiographical memory. Secure parents, who themselves have greater "coherence of mind", are likely to be better than insecure parents at discussing emotions, especially negative emotions, with their children, and thus to provide children with greater comfort and coherence of mind themselves (Main et al., 1985; Quas et al., 1999). Thus, individual differences in attachment should be related to individual differences in narrative and autobiographical memory development, as mediated by parental conversation and emotional attunement, as well as to mental health generally.

Fourth, attachment theory has important implications for the development of the self. According to Bowlby, parent–child attachment involves internal working models of the self in relation to others. To the extent that development of the self provides self-schemes around which autobiographical memory forms (Howe & Courage, 1997), attachment theory is also relevant. Children may be developing a more or less differentiated sense of self, as well as a sense of self as a worthwhile person who can deal with and coherently think about negative events, or as a less than worthwhile person who is threatened by parental rejection/hostility, loss, or lack of responsiveness, and who has more trouble dealing with and thinking about negative experiences.

Thus, in our model, adult attachment is hypothesized to influence socioemotional (e.g., parent–child attachment) and cognitive development, both of which influence neurological development. Neurological development establishes the human capacity for autobiographical memory. However, early autobiographical memory is then highly influenced by the processing of negative events, which is regulated by the child's own attachment system as well as that of the parents. Autobiographical memory in older childhood and adulthood is then also determined in part by these early interpersonal processes.

CONCLUSION

In conclusion, in this chapter, we provide a new model of autobiographical memory development. Our model is informed by previous models, such as that by K. Nelson and Fivush (2004), but ours adds important new dimensions. Of particular note, we propose an important and fundamental role for memory of negative experiences and for attachment-related processes that may well affect how children remember events of personal significance. The model also has implications for children's mental health.

ACKNOWLEDGEMENTS

We thank Asher Koriat, Robin Edelstein, and Phillip R. Shaver for helpful comments on an earlier draft.

REFERENCES

Ainsworth, M.D.S. (1967). *Infancy in Uganda: Infancy and the growth of love.* Baltimore, MD: Johns Hopkins University Press.

Alexander, K.W., Goodman, G.S., Schaaf, J.M., Edelstein, R.S., Quas, J.A., & Shaver, P.R. (2002). The role of attachment and cognitive inhibition in children's memory and suggestibility for a stressful event. *Journal of Experimental Child Psychology, 83*, 262–290.

Alexander, K., Quas, J.A., Goodman, G.S., Ghetti, S., Edelstein, R., Redlich, A., Cordon, I., & Jones, D.P.H. (2005). Traumatic impact predicts long-term memory for child sexual abuse. *Psychological Science, 16*, 33–40.

Barnett, D., Ganiban, J., & Cicchetti, D. (1999). Maltreatment, negative expressivity and the development of Type D attachments from 12 to 24 months of age. *Monographs for the Society for Research on Child Development, 64*, 97–118

Bauer, P. (1996). Development of memory in early childhood. In N. Cowan (Ed.), *The development of memory in childhood* (pp. 83–112). Hove, UK: Psychology Press.

Bauer, P., & Wewerka, S. (1995). One- to two-year olds' recall of events: The more expressed, the more impressed. *Journal of Experimental Child Psychology, 59*, 475–496.

Belsky, J., Spritz, B., & Crnic, K. (1996). Infant attachment security and affective-cognitive information processing at age three. *Psychological Science, 7*, 111–114.

Berntsen, D. (2001). Involuntary memories of emotional events. Do memories of traumas and extremely happy events differ? *Applied Cognitive Psychology, 15*, 135–158.

Berntsen, D. (2002). Tunnel memories for autobiographical events: Central details are remembered more frequently from shocking than from happy experiences. *Memory and Cognition, 30*, 1010–1020.

Block, S., Greenberg, S., & Goodman, G.S. (2004). *Remembrance of victim testimony: Emotional content, emotional tone, and personal relevance*. Paper presented at the American Psychological Society, Chicago, IL

Bowlby, J. (1969). *Attachment and loss. Vol. 1. Attachment*. New York: Basic Books.

Bowlby, J. (1980). *Attachment and loss. Vol. III: Loss, sadness and depression*. New York: Basic Books.

Bowlby, J. (1982). Attachment and loss: Retrospect and prospect. *American Journal of Orthopsychiatry, 52*, 664–678.

Bowlby, J. (1987). Defensive processes in the light of attachment theory. In J.L. Sacksteder, D. Schwartz, & Y. Akabane (Eds.), *Attachment and the therapeutic process: Essays in honor of Otto Allen Will, Jr.* (pp. 63–79). Madison, CT: International Universities Press.

Bremner, J.D., Krystal, J.H., Southwick, S.M., & Charney, D.S. (1995a). Functional neuroanatomical correlates of the effects of stress on memory. *Journal of Traumatic Stress, 8*, 527–553.

Bremner, J.D., Randall, P., Scott, T.M., Capelli, S., Delaney, R., McCarthy, G., & Charney, D.S. (1995b). Deficits in short-term memory in adult survivors of childhood abuse. *Psychiatry Research, 59*, 97–107.

Buchner, A., & Brandt, M. (2003). Further evidence for systematic reliability differences between explicit and implicit memory tests. *Quarterly Journal of Experimental Psychology: Human Experimental Psychology, 2*, 193–209.

Canli, T., Zhao, Z., Brewer, J., Gabrieli, J., & Cahill, L. (2000). Event-related activation in the human amygdala associates with later memory for individual emotional response. *Journal of Neuroscience, 20*, RC99.

Case, R. (1978). Intellectual development from birth to adulthood: A neo-Piagetian interpretation. In R.S. Siegler (Ed.), *Children's thinking: What develops?* (pp. 37–71). Hillsdale, NJ: Lawrence Erlbaum Associates, Inc.

Ceci, S.J., Loftus, E.F., Leichtman, M., & Bruck, M. (1994). The possible role of source misattributions in the creation of false beliefs among preschoolers. *International Journal of Clinical and Experimental Hypnosis, 42*, 304–320.

Cernoch, J.M. & Porter, R.H. (1985). Recognition of materal axillary odors by infants. *Child Development, 56*, 1593–1598.

Christianson, S.A. (1992). Emotional stress and eyewitness memory: A critical review. *Psychological Bulletin, 112*, 284–309.

Cohen, N.J., & Squire, L.R. (1980). Preserved learning and retention of pattern analyzing skill in amnesiacs: Dissociation of knowing how and knowing that. *Science, 210*, 207–210.

Conway, M.A., & Rubin, D.C. (1993). The structure of autobiographical memory. In A.F. Collins, S.E. Gathercole, M.A. Conway, & P.E. Morris (Eds.). *Theories of memory* (pp. 103–139). Hillsdale, NJ: Lawrence Erlbaum Associates, Inc.

Cowan, N., & Davidson, G. (1984). Salient childhood memories. *Journal of Genetic Psychology, 145*, 101–107.

Crittenden, P.M. (1992). Quality of attachment in the preschool years. *Development and Psychopathology, 4*, 209–241.

Crockenberg, S., &. Leerkes, E. (2000). Infant social and emotional development in family context. In C.H. Zeanah Jr. (Ed.), *Handbook of infant mental health* (2nd ed., pp. 60–90). New York: Guilford Press.

Cycowicz, Y.M. (2000). Memory development and event-related brain potentials in children. *Biological Psychology, 54*, 145–174.

Cycowicz, Y.M., Friedman, D., Snodgrass, J.G., & Duff, M. (2001). Recognition and source memory for pictures in children and adults. *Neuropsychologia, 39*, 255–267.

De Bellis, M.D., Hall, J., Boring, A.M., Frustaci, K., & Moritz, G. (2001). A pilot longitudinal study of hippocampal volumes in pediatric maltreatment-related posttraumatic stress disorder. *Biological Psychiatry, 50*, 305–309.

DeWolff, M., & Van Ijzendoorn, M.H. (1997). Sensitivity and attachment: A meta-analysis on parental antecedents of infant attachment. *Child Development, 68*, 571–591.

Edelstein, R.S., Alexander, K.W., Shaver, P.R., Schaaf, J.M., Quas, J.A., Lovas, G.S., & Goodman, G.S. (2004). Adult attachment style and parental responsiveness during a stressful event. *Attachment and Human Development, 6*, 31–52.

Edelstein, R.S., Ghetti, S., Quas, J.A., Goodman, G.S., Alexander, K., Redlich, A., & Cordon, I. (2005). Avoidant attachment and memory for child sexual abuse. *Social and Personality Psychology Bulletin, 31*, 1537–1548.

Edelstein, R.S., & Shaver, P.R. (2004). Avoidant attachment: Exploration of an oxymoron. In D. Mashek & A. Aron (Eds.), *Handbook of closeness and intimacy* (pp. 397–412). Mahwah, NJ: Lawrence Erlbaum Associates, Inc.

Ekman, P. (1992). Are there basic emotions? *Psychological Review, 99*, 550–553.

Fagan, J.F. (1970). Memory in the infant. *Journal of Experimental Child Psychology, 9*, 217–226.

Farrar, M.J., Fasig, L.G., & Welch-Ross, M.K. (1997). Attachment and emotion in autobiographical memory development. *Journal of Experimental Child Psychology, 67*, 389–408.

Fraley, R.C., Davis, K.E., & Shaver, P.R. (1998). Dismissing-avoidance and the defensive organization of emotion, cognition, and behavior. In J.A. Simpson & W.S. Rholes (Eds.), *Attachment theory and close relationships* (pp. 249–279). New York: Guilford Press.

Fraley, R.C., Garner, J.P., & Shaver, P.R. (2000). Adult attachment and the defensive regulation of attention and memory: Examining the role of preemptive and postemptive defensive processes. *Journal of Personality and Social Psychology, 79*, 816–826.

Freud, S. (1966). *Introductory lectures on psychoanalysis* (J. Strachey, Trans. and Ed.). [Original work published in 1916] New York: Norton.

Gilbertson, M.W., Shenton, M.E., Ciszewski, A., Kasai, K., Lasko, N., Orr, S., & Pitman, R. (2002). Smaller hippocampal volume predicts pathologic vulnerability to psychological trauma. *Nature Neuroscience, 5*, 1242–1247.

Goodman, G.S., Hirschman, J.E., Hepps, D., & Rudy, L. (1991). Children's memory for stressful events. *Merrill-Palmer Quarterly, 37*, 109–157.

Goodman, G.S., Quas, J.A., Batterman-Faunce, J.M., Riddlesberger, M.M., & Kuhn, J. (1997). Children's reactions to and memory for a stressful event: Influences of age, anatomical dolls, knowledge, and parental attachment. *Applied Developmental Science, 1*, 54–75.

Gopnik, A., & Astington, J.W. (1988). Children's understanding of representational change and its relation to the understanding of false belief and the appearance-reality distinction. *Child Development, 59*, 26–37.

Greenough, W.T., & Black, J.E. (1999). Experience, neural plasticity and psychological development. In N.A. Fox, L.A. Leavitt, & J.G. Warhol (Eds.). *The role of early experience in infant development* (pp. 29–40). Pompton Plains, NJ: Johnson & Johnson Pediatric Institute.

Harley, K., & Reese, E. (1999). Origins of autobiographical memory. *Developmental Psychology, 34,* 701–713.

Hazan, C., & Shaver, P. (1987). Romantic love conceptualized as an attachment process. *Journal of Personality and Social Psychology, 52,* 511–524.

Howe, M.L. (1997). Children's memory for traumatic experiences. *Learning and Individual Differences, 9,* 153–174.

Howe, M.L., Courage, M.L., & Bryant-Brown, L. (1994a). Reinstating preschoolers' memories. *Developmental Psychology, 29,* 854–869.

Howe, M.L., Courage, M.L., & Peterson, C. (1994b). How can I remember when "I" wasn't there? Long-term retention of traumatic memories and emergence of the cognitive self. *Consciousness and Cognition, 3,* 32–355.

Howe, M.L., & Courage, M.L. (1997). The emergence and early development of autobiographical memory. *Psychological Review, 104,* 499–523.

Howe, M.L., Courage, M.L., & Peterson, C. (1995). Intrusions in preschoolers' recall of traumatic childhood events. *Psychonomic Bulletin and Review, 2,* 130–134.

Howes, M., Siegel, M., & Brown, F. (1993). Early childhood memories: Accuracy and affect. *Cognition, 47,* 95–119.

James, W. (1890). *The principles of psychology.* New York: Dover.

Johnson, M.H. (2000). Functional brain development in infants. *Child Development, 71,* 75–81.

Kirsch, S., & Cassidy, J. (1997). Preschoolers' attention to and memory for attachment-relevant information. *Child Development, 68,* 1143–1153.

Lagattuta, K. (1999). The development of young children's understanding of the causes of emotions: Experimental and natural language studies. *Dissertation Abstracts International, 60* (5-B), 2386.

Lagattuta, K., & Wellman, H. (2002). Differences in early parent–child conversations about negative versus positive emotions: Implications for the development of psychological understanding. *Developmental Psychology, 38,* 564–580.

Lang, P.J., Bradley, M.M., & Cuthbert, M.M. (1997). Motivated attention: Affect, activation, and action. In P.J. Lang, R.F. Simons, & M. Balaban (Eds.), *Attention and orienting: Sensory and motivational processes* (pp. 97–135). Mahwah, NJ: Lawrence Erlbaum Associates, Inc.

LeDoux, J.E. (1992). Emotion as memory: Anatomical systems underlying indelible neural traces. In S.-Å. Christianson (Ed.). *The handbook of emotion and memory: Research and theory* (pp. 269–289). Hillsdale, NJ: Lawrence Erlbaum Associates, Inc.

Lindsay, D.S., Wade, K.A., Hunter, M.A., & Read, J.D. (2004). Adults' memories of childhood: Affect, knowing, and remembering. *Memory, 12,* 27–43.

Mahler, M., Pine, F., & Bergman, A. (1975). *Barnets psykiske fødsel: Symbiose og individuasjon.* Oslo: Gyldendal.

Main, M., Kaplan, N., & Cassidy, J. (1985). Security in infancy, childhood, and adulthood: A move to the level of representation. In I. Bretherton & E. Waters (Eds.), Growing points in attachment theory and research. *Monographs of the Society for Research in Child Development, 50* (1–2, Serial No. 209), 66–104.

Main, M., & Solomon, J. (1990). Procedures for identifying infants as disorganized/

disoriented during the Ainsworth Strange Situation. In M. Greenberg, D. Cicchetti, & E.M. Cummings (Eds.), *Attachment in the preschool years: Theory, research, and intervention* (pp. 121–160). Chicago, IL: University of Chicago Press.

McManis, M.H., Bradley, M.M., Berg, W., Cuthbert, B., & Lanf, P.J. (2001). Emotional reactions in children: Verbal, physiological, and behavioral responses to affective pictures *Psychophysiology*, *38*, 222–231.

Melinder, A. (2004). *Perspectives on children as witnesses.* Doctoral Dissertation, University of Oslo, Norway.

Merritt, K.A., Ornstein, P.A., & Spiker, B. (1994). Children's memory for a salient medical procedure: Implications for testimony. *Pediatrics*, *94*, 17–23.

Mikulincer, M., & Orbach, I. (1995). Attachment styles and repressive defensiveness: The accessibility and architecture of affective memories. *Journal of Personality and Social Psychology*, *68*, 917–925.

Mikulincer, M., & Shaver, P.R. (2003). The attachment behavioral system in adulthood: Activation, psychodynamics, and interpersonal processes. In M.P. Zanna (Ed.), *Advances in experimental social psychology, Vol. 35* (pp. 53–152). San Diego, CA: Elsevier Academic Press.

Miller, P.J., & Sperry, L.L. (1988). Early talk about the past: The origins of conversional stories of personal experience. *Journal of Child Language*, *15*, 293–315.

Nadel, L. (1994). Multiple memory systems: What and why, an update. In D.L. Schacter & E. Tulving (Eds.), *Memory systems 1994* (pp. 39–63). Cambridge, MA: MIT Press.

Nelson, C. (1995). The ontogeny of human memory: A cognitive neuroscience perspective. *Developmental Psychology*, *31*, 723–738.

Nelson, C. (1997). The neurobiological basis of early memory development. In N. Cowan (Ed.), *The development of memory in early childhood* (pp. 41–82). Hove, UK: Psychology Press.

Nelson, C. (2000). Neural plasticity in human development: The role of early experience in sculpting memory systems. *Developmental Science*, *3*, 115–130.

Nelson, K., & Fivush, R. (2004). The emergence of autobiographical memory: A social cultural developmental theory. *Psychological Review*, *2*, 486–511.

Pillemer, D.B., & White, S.H. (1989). Childhood events recalled by children and adults. In H.W. Reese (Ed.). *Advances in child development and behavior, Vol. 21* (pp. 297–340). New York: Academic Press.

Perner, J. (2000). Memory and theory of mind. In E. Tulving & F.I.M. Craik (Eds.), *Oxford handbook of memory* (pp. 297–312). New York: Oxford University Press.

Perner, J., Leekam, S.R., & Wimmer, H. (1987). Three-year-olds' difficulty with false belief: The case for a conceptual deficit. *British Journal of Developmental Psychology*, *5*, 125–137.

Perner, J., & Wimmer, H. (1985). John thinks that Mary thinks that: Attribution of second-order beliefs by 5- to 10-year-old children. *Journal of Experimental Child Psychology*, *39*, 437–471.

Pezdek, K., & Taylor, J. (2002). Memories of traumatic events. In M. Eisen, J.A. Quas, & G.S. Goodman (Eds.), *Memory and suggestibility in the forensic interview* (pp. 165–183). Mahwah, NJ: Lawrence Erlbaum Associates, Inc.

Pillemer, D.B., & White, S.H. (1989). Childhood events recalled by children and adults. In H.W. Reese (Ed.), *Advances in child development and behavior, Vol. 21* (pp. 297–340). New York: Academic Press.

Quas, J.A., Goodman, G.S., Bidrose, S., Pipe, M.E., Craw, S., & Ablin, D.S. (1999). Emotion and memory: Children's long-term remembering, forgetting, and suggestibility. *Journal of Experimental Child Psychology*, *72*, 235–270.

Reese, E. (2002). Social factors in the development of autobiographical memory: The state of the art. *Social Development*, *11*, 124–142.

Roediger, H.L. III, Buckner, R.L., & McDermott, K.B. (1999). Components of processing. In J.K. Foster & M. Jelicic (Eds.), *Memory: Systems, process, or function? Debates in psychology* (pp. 31–65). London: Oxford University Press.

Rovee-Collier, C. (1997). Dissociation in infant memory: Rethinking the development of implicit and explicit memory. *Psychological Review*, *104*, 467–498.

Rovee-Collier, C., Hayne, H., & Colombo, M. (2001). *The development of implicit and explicit memory*. Amsterdam: John Benjamins.

Rudy, L., & Goodman, G.S. (1991). Effects of participation on children's reports: Implications for children's testimony. *Developmental Psychology*, *27*, 1–26.

Schaaf, J., Alexander, K., & Goodman, G.S. (2005, April). *Individual differences in children's true and false memory*. Society for Research in Child Development, Atlanta, GA.

Schacter, D.T. (1996). *Searching for memory*. New York: Basic Books.

Schacter, D.L., & Moscovitch, M. (1984). Infants, amnesics, and dissociable memory system. In M. Moscovitch (Ed.), *Infant memory: Its relation to normal and pathological memory in humans and other animals* (pp. 173–216). New York: Plenum Press.

Schacter, D.L., & Tulving, E. (1994). What are the memory systems of 1994? In D.L. Schacter & E. Tulving (Eds.), *Memory systems* (pp. 1–38). Cambridge, MA: MIT Press.

Shaver, P.R., & Mikulincer, M. (2002). Dialogue on adult attachment: Diversity and integration. *Attachment and Human Development*, *4*, 243–257.

Shaver, P., Schwarts, J., Kirson, D., & O'Connor, C. (1987). Emotion knowledge: Further exploration of a prototype approach. *Journal of Personality and Social Psychology*, *52*, 1061–1086.

Spitz, R.A. (1945). Hospitalism: An enquiry into the genesis of psychiatric conditions in early childhood. *Psychoanalytic Study of the Child*, *1*, 53–74.

Spitz, R.A. (1946). Hospitalism: A follow-up report on an investigation described in volume 1, 1945. *Psychoanalytic Study of the Child*, *2*, 313–342.

Stern, D.N. (1985). *Spedbarnets interpersonligee verden*. Oslo: Gyldendal Akademisk.

Tulving, E. (1985). How many memory systems are there? *American Psychologist*, *40*, 385–398.

Tulving, E. (1999). On the uniqueness of episodic memory. In L.-G. Nilsson & H.J. Markowitsch (Eds.), *Cognitive neuroscience of memory* (pp. 11–42). Kirkland, WA: Hogrefe & Huber.

Tulving, E. (2002). Episodic memory: From mind to brain. *Annual Review of Psychology*, *53*, 1–25.

Usher, J.A., & Neisser, U. (1993). Childhood amnesia and the beginnings of memory for four early life events. *Journal of Experimental Psychology: General*, *122*, 155–165.

Vaughn, B.E., & Bost, K.K. (1999). Attachment and temperament: Redundant, independent, or interacting influences on interpersonal adaptation and personality development? In J. Cassidy & P. Shaver (Eds.), *Handbook of attachment: Theory, research, and clinical applications* (pp. 198–225). New York: Guilford Press.

6 Collaborative memory: How is our ability to remember affected by interaction with others?

Jan Andersson, Tore Helstrup and
Jerker Rönnberg

Socialization with relatives, friends and colleagues is often regarded as one of the main ingredients of life. Our thoughts, beliefs and ways of life are affected by socialization. The question to be discussed in this chapter is how social interaction affects our mental processes, especially our memory processes. The belief that group interaction facilitates performance has been questioned from a number of perspectives. The social loafing literature, for example, suggests that individuals do not invest the effort needed in groups that they would do if tested individually. The argument is based on (1) loss of motivation and (2) coordination problems (Brown, 1988; Steiner, 1972). Groups evidently do not seem to perform optimally. A similar pattern is obtained for cognitive tasks such as problem-solving (Faust, 1959) and brainstorming (Harkins & Jackson, 1985). The ways in which our memory is affected by social interaction has not been studied until relatively recently.

You have probably experienced the positive impact that a discussion between yourself and a friend has had on your ability to remember experiences that you would not have remembered on your own. Imagine, for example, that you and your friend discuss last night's activities in the nightclub. When she or he says (a), you remember (b), and she or he remembers (c), and so forth. It is amazing how well collaboration works, triggering both your memories to near perfection! However, is this positive effect of collaboration really true, or is it an illusion? Can you be certain that you would not have had remembered everything on your own? The straightforward answer to this rather simple question of facilitative effects is NO!

To our surprise, but in line with the statement above, the results from a Norwegian survey concur (Magnussen et al., 2006; see Chapter 1). In a large survey, 1000 Norwegians answered the following question: *Sometimes two or more persons are witnesses to the same event. A police investigator may interview the witnesses together or separately. When do you think he will obtain most information?* The majority answered *separate interviews* (70%) and a minority (18%) answered *joint interviews* (the remaining 12% was divided equally into uncertain and no difference). Thus, what was seen as a counterintuitive phenomenon by us (as memory researchers) was already known by the public. The bulk of empirical evidence reveals that individuals who collaborate during remembering outperform a single individual, but that at the same time they are inhibiting each other, so that we cannot therefore remember all the things that we would remember on our own. The problem for research is that we cannot assess the collaborative outcome without a good control condition. Such a control condition does not exist in everyday life, i.e., we do not know what we would have remembered on our own, or for that matter know what the other group member would have remembered on his or her own. The purpose of this chapter is to review the literature on this specific matter and to discuss how the effects obtained by collaboration are explained today.

Memory has traditionally been studied from an individual perspective. For some 150 years memory researchers have focused upon the processes and performances that we call memory proper. Everyday memory, on the other hand, is often used or embedded in social activities. We often discuss or rely on memories that one or both of us have experienced (even when we talk about the future and "things" to do), i.e., we use our memory when we solve problems and make decisions at work or at home. A major shortcoming of mainstream memory research has been the sad neglect of addressing memory functions from a social and communicative perspective.

Although this area is still relatively underexplored, the literature is growing. Collaborative memory research focuses especially on how the social situation affects people's *abilities* to remember, that is, how our memory performance is affected by the support provided by another person who is also involved in the memory task.

When two or more individuals come together and try to remember experiences they will recall more than one solitary individual would do (Andersson, 2001; Andersson & Rönnberg, 1996; N.K. Clark, Stephenson, & Kniveton, 1990; Dixon & Gould, 1998; Stephenson, Abrams, Wagner, & Wade, 1986). This has, not surprisingly, been demonstrated by most researchers and for most memory tasks. However, not only performance is affected by this interactive situation – other relevant aspects are clearly affected. For example, groups seem to show overconfidence in both true and untrue recollections, affecting testimonial validity (N.K. Clark et al., 1990; Stephenson et al., 1986). Social interaction effects on memory reliability will only be discussed briefly in this chapter, but will be elaborated on in more detail in the chapter on false memory (see Chapter 7).

The following part of this chapter will be devoted to collaborative memory (as defined above) and especially for the case when an *actual* group is compared to the *potential* of the same group. Thus, the purpose of this chapter is to present the scientific evidence on how our memory is affected by social interaction – a frequent and often forgotten aspect of memory in everyday life.

COLLABORATIVE MEMORY: PHENOMENON AND METHODS

With the aim of determining whether dyadic interaction during recall would enhance memory performance, Meudell, Hitch, and colleagues (Meudell, Hitch, & Boyle, 1995; Meudell, Hitch, & Kirby, 1992) performed a number of ingenious experiments. Their main purpose was to study whether pairs of people can cross-cue each other efficiently, i.e., can people cross-cue each other such that group recall reveals "new, emergent memories" – not available to either of the individuals recalling on their own. With the aim of studying cross-cueing, they needed to be able to distinguish "new" from "old" memories – i.e., new items that had not been remembered by the individual during an earlier recall session, from old memories remembered at an earlier recall session. They thus needed to know what each individual in a pair remembered on their own initially. Participants were therefore requested to recall twice: first individually, then by dyadic recall. Some participants recalled twice on their own and some recalled initially on their own and second in dyads. Consider the following example: Person A recalled items a, b, c and d (four items) and person B recalled items c, d, e and g (four items) at initial recall. Together they recalled items a, c, e, f, g, and h (six items) in their second, final recall. Their dyadic score would then be higher than their individual scores (6>4). Their nominal, non-redundant score would be a, b, c, d, e and g (six items). Their newly generated emergent memories would be (f) and (h), a total of two items. Their forgotten items would be (b) and (d), once again two items (Meudell et al., 1992, 1995, however, did not study forgotten items). The purpose of the control group, recalling twice on their own, was to control for reminiscence, i.e., to control for the effects of repeated recall sessions. The pairs recalled a small number of new memories, though no more than individual reminiscence controls. Meudell and co-workers concluded that the social interaction did not create a situation that enhanced memory performance. The pooled non-redundant score from two individuals is henceforth called the nominal score.

These experiments were followed up by Andersson and Rönnberg (1995, 1996, 1997). They also included forgotten items in their analysis. Their main objective was to determine how the dyads were affected from the perspective of total performance; i.e., pairs might not be able to cross-cue one another but rather to inhibit the process of forgetting previously recalled information. The straightforward result obtained was that dyads inhibited the recollection of previously recalled items. Overall, the social interaction revealed net negative effects: (1) no more "new" information was retrieved by the dyad than by the nominal group and (2) information that was recalled initially by an individual was forgotten in the dyadic setting (Andersson & Rönnberg, 1995).

At least two methodological perspectives exist in the literature when it comes to understanding the effects of collaboration on memory; one compares individual performances with performance for different kinds of group con-stellations (old vs. young groups; see, e.g., Dixon & Gould, 1998; Gould & Dixon, 1993). However, the approach discussed here is to compare a group's actual memory performance with the potential of the group. In order to conclude that a genuine positive effect of collaboration exists, the group should be able to produce memories that were not remembered by separate individuals. We therefore need to be able to trace what an individual would have recalled on his or her own.

The net negative effect of collaboration obtained by the chosen nominal group condition has been repeatedly obtained by a number of research groups (Basden, Basden, Bryner, & Thomas, 1997; Finlay, Hitch, & Meudell, 2000; Johansson, Andersson, & Rönnberg, 2005; Ross, Spencer, Linardatos, Lam, & Perunovic, 2004; Takahashi & Saito, 2004; Weldon, 2000; Weldon & Bellinger, 1997). Although all these groups conclude that dyads are negatively affected by collaboration, they also draw two more important conclusions. First, one individual is typically outperformed by two individuals working together. Second, the net negative effect is more evident during specific condi-tions, i.e., in explicit tasks compared with implicit and semantic tasks. Thus, the main overall finding is that net negative effects of collaboration exist for explicit and consciousness-demanding memory tasks.

EMPIRICAL FINDINGS RELATED TO NET EFFECTS OF SOCIAL INTERACTION

The size of the negative effect obtained varies due to a number of socially relevant factors (see Andersson, 2001; Weldon, 2000) such as friendship, age, gender and motivation. These factors are important from an applied, everyday-life perspective. Social interactions usually take place between people who know each other. With the argument that memory needs to be studied from an ecological perspective, collaborative memory performance also needs to be studied under circumstances that resemble everyday situ-ations. We therefore first turn to how friendship is involved in the effects of collaboration.

Friendship

A number of studies have studied friend dyads and non-friend dyads in comparison to the nominal group (Andersson, 1996, 2001; Andersson & Rönnberg, 1995, 1996, 1997; Johansson, Andersson, & Rönnberg, 2000, 2005; Takahashi, in press; Thompson, 2002). Friends were defined as having socialized in their free time for at least 1 year in these studies. Couples mar-ried for a very long time have also been studied (mean about 45 years of marriage). The overall conclusion is that friends and couples, compared to non-friends, can reduce the net negative effect of collaboration. They cannot, on the other hand, compensate to the extent that they perform better than baseline, i.e., the nominal group. Friends typically perform significantly less well than the nominal group, but significantly better than non-friends. However, Takahashi (in press) studied the effect of friendship in a false memory paradigm. He used words-lists as his to-be-remembered material and did not obtain a friendship effect. These data fit nicely with the results obtained by Andersson and Rönnberg (1995), who found that friends were only able to support each other in the story task (recalling a previously studied story). They argued that in order to gain from friendship the task has to be more complex, giving friends the opportunity to engage in less constrained ways of collaboration. A word-list task does not satisfy this criterion. Thus, the type of material seems to be important for the friendship effect to emerge.

Another interesting aspect of friendships was that the number of years that friend/couples had known the collaborating friend did not seem to matter (Johansson et al., 2000, 2005). The couples seemed to be as negatively affected by collaboration as friends. A final remark concerning the effects of friendship is that it might be the quality of the relationship that really matters. This was explicitly studied in one experiment (Johansson et al., 2005). The net negative effect of collaboration was found to vanish in some subgroups of couples, i.e., when these were characterized according to division of responsibility and agreement between the participating married couples about how to handle memory tasks in everyday life. Thus, the main point is that certain aspects of the quality of the relationship seem to matter, rather than the number of years spent together.

Gender effects

Attribute variables other than friendship that have been investigated within this area are age and gender. The net negative effect of gender on collaboration was studied by Weldon, Blair, and Huebsch (2000). They compared three-person groups (all female) with nominal female groups. The results showed that females suffered compared to their controls (e.g., the nominal group). Andersson (2001) investigated gender effects on two different types of memory task. Male groups were compared with female groups on spatial memory and verbal episodic memory tasks. First, net negative effects of collaboration were obtained in both genders. Second, this was found to be true for both types of task. Third, females, even though their performance suffered in collaboration, always outperformed males, replicating earlier findings of a gender superiority effect (Herlitz, Airaksinen, & Nordström, 1999; Hill et all., 1995). The Weldon et al. (2000) study did not focus on different gender constellations. However, when their data are inspected it can be seen that individual female recall and female group recall outperformed (or were as high as high cohesive groups) all the other groups (in four other experiments with exactly the same task material). The main finding was that net negative effects of collaboration exist for all types of gender group constellations, i.e., female, male and mixed groups. Second, female groups seem to outperform male groups in absolute terms.

Age effects

Age effects have been examined in a few studies. Johansson et al. (2000, 2005) studied whether old couples would reduce the net negative effects of collaboration. Even though the primary focus was not on investigating age, the finding was that older participants' memory performances were negatively affected by collaboration in the same way as those of college students. The old married couples (married for 45 years), however, were less affected than unacquainted couples (matched on age and gender), i.e., there was a "friendship effect". Another interesting result was obtained by post-hoc analyses in the Johansson et al. (2000) study and followed up by Johansson et al. (2005). On the basis of answers to a pre-posted questionnaire, all couples were categorized as high or low on two independent dimensions. Division of responsibility was one dimension and degree of agreement was the second. If responsibility was divided within the couple and the couple agreed upon the division of responsibility, they were classified as high on both dimensions. Johansson et al. (2005) compared the four subgroups on one episodic and one semantic memory task. The inhibiting effect of collaboration affected the categories very differently, but only in the episodic story recall task. Couples classified a priori as high on both dimensions had a non-significant positive effect of collaboration. At the same time, they were the worst performing couples from an absolute recall perspective, i.e., they performed better as a couple than with their own nominal score, but worse than the other couples. The most efficient couples were those who declared a division of responsibility but did not agree upon the declared division. This condition performed equally well as a couple as their nominal comparison and recalled more items than individuals in the other conditions. Thus, the conclusion by Johansson et al. (2005) was that the numbers of years spent as a couple was not important, but that the quality of the relationship was important for efficient memory collaboration.

Andersson (2001) compared different ages, i.e., dyads of 7-year-old and 15-year-old children. The data revealed that net negative effects of collaboration exist at both ages, with increased net negative effects in dyads of younger children. The conclusion was that younger children have not developed the cognitive abilities necessary to adopt another individual's perspective. This inability decreases the potential for perspective-taking (cf. Piaget, 1959). The consequence is that spoken words (cues) are insufficient for both members to a greater extent when they are unable to take the perspective of the other member (theory of mind; cf. Symons, 2004). Hence, larger net negative effects of collaboration would be expected. This is an interesting finding and will be discussed below.

Thompson (2002) studied age differences in various collaboration tasks.

She compared dyads of old friends and non-friend dyads with dyads of young friends and non-friend undergraduates, with nominal groups as the baseline, and found that older participants actually gained from collaboration in Experiment 1 in one of the tasks (semantic memory task). This finding is interesting and runs, at first glance, counter to previous findings. However, as has already been pointed out, net negative effects are dependent on specific circumstances. In the Thompson investigation, participants studied pictures of famous persons. Experiment 1 showed a positive effect of collaboration, but only in dyads of old friends (they recalled more new items).

Experiment 2 also used pictures of famous faces, but new information was integrated with each picture during an encoding phase. The episodic information that was requested later on was closely related to semantic face information (and in that sense was a good analogue to everyday memory). In this second experiment no net negative effects of collaboration were obtained. Andersson and Rönnberg (1997) obtained the same absence of negative collaboration effect when participants (students and military personnel) were to recall episodic information (word-lists) using cues produced by others. Cues produced by others were argued to be less distinctive than self-generated cues. When cues produced by others are used, negative effects of collaboration are not obtained. The concluding remark of Andersson and Rönnberg was that cues produced by others (in the Thompson study, names of famous faces) are more shared by both. Shared cues are less uniquely distinctive and dyadic retrieval is thus less negatively affected by collaboration per se. The positive effect of collaboration in Experiment 1 was not replicated. Instead, lower performances overall were obtained during dyadic recall (Thompson, 2002). This effect of collaboration was mainly due to a general decrease for all groups, but in elderly nominal dyads in particular. Thus, it is difficult to draw any straightforward conclusions from Experiment 2. Their findings from both experiments fit nicely with earlier findings on semantic and implicit tasks (discussed later). Nevertheless, this brilliant PhD thesis by Thompson (2002) reveals how tricky the matter of collaboration is; age and type of task interact in a complex fashion.

The evidence concerning friendship, age and gender shows a relatively clear pattern: First, friendship reduces the net negative effect of collaboration. Second, age matters – young dyads suffer more than older dyads. Third, both genders are affected in all kinds of constellations. Fourth, what counts is the quality of the relationship – not the numbers of years.

Motivational effects

Collaboration implies interaction among people. It is natural that cognitive psychologists turn to their theories to explain an observed memory phenomenon. It is not, however, obvious that these individually based theories offer the most promising account of socially determined cognition. Perhaps social psychology constructs might better explain the effects. The social psychology literature on group performance uses the concept of "social loafing" (Brown, 1988; Ringlemann, 1913, in Moede, 1927; Steiner, 1972, for some classical work on group processes) to explain similar negative effects of collaboration (e.g., shouting, rope pulling and clapping hands). In this area of research it is concluded that social loafing, i.e., people do not put in the effort they could due to collaboration, can be explained by losses of motivation and coordination. Thus, the net negative effects described above might be due to social aspects of the task. Weldon et al. (2000) accordingly performed five experiments to find out whether motivational aspects would affect collaborative memory performance. The motivational aspects were (1) personal accountability, (2) monetary incentives, (3) recall criterion, (4) group cohesion and (5) group gender. The results did not suggest that motivational aspects could explain the net negative effects of collaboration.

EMPIRICAL FINDINGS RELATED TO THEORETICAL EXPLANATIONS OF THE NET NEGATIVE EFFECTS OF COLLABORATION

Material effects

The obtained net negative effect of collaboration manifests itself in different types of material. Tasks such as word recall, story recall and videotaped lectures reveal the same effect. Pictures, spatial patterns and the combinations of pictures in spatial patterns all produce net negative effects (see Andersson, 1996, 2001; Andersson & Rönnberg, 1995). Thus, the negative effects of collaboration do not seem to be material-dependent. Task attributes (e.g., the complexity of the material) have been found to matter only in interaction with friendship, as discussed above. The important question is how the material to be remembered is mediated by organizational constraints of materials and cue support.

Retrieval organization

One aspect that affects the size of the negative effect of collaboration is retrieval organization. Basden et al. (1997) performed four experiments that varied material and retrieval organization. In their first experiment, with three-person groups and categorized word-lists, the results showed that net negative effects of collaboration were most pronounced for longer category lists (6 categories with 15 items compared to 15 categories with 6 items). This finding supports the assumed disruption of retrieval strategies. However, collaboration during recall also affected the number of categories retrieved. Net negative effects of collaboration were found for conditions with a large number of categories, but not for those with a small number of categories.

The conclusion was that when a group member provides an instance from a category, access to the remaining categories is inhibited.

A similar approach was taken by Basden et al. in their second experiment. Twenty-four categories with five instances were used as the material to be remembered (TBR). The groups (nominal and actual) received, or did not receive, the category names (cued vs. uncued conditions) at retrieval. The predicted interaction was confirmed. Net negative effects of collaboration were obtained for the cued but not the uncued conditions. This confirms that retrieval strategies were disrupted by the provision of category cues. The third experiment explicitly tested whether retrieval strategies are disrupted by collaboration. Some of the participants were requested to recall only parts of the whole TBR list. The prediction – that net negative effects would only occur during whole list recall – was supported. This means that negative effects vanish when members of a group have "their" own categories to remember. Evidently, the ways in which participants are allowed to organize their retrieval do in fact influence the amount of inhibition.

In a similar vein, but from a different approach, Finlay et al. (2000) conducted a number of experiments to scrutinize retrieval organization aspects. In the first experiment encoding was varied. Participants encoded on their own or in dyads. The aim of the experiment was to increase the similarity between the participants' organization of the TBR material. It should be noted that participants were requested to recall the material three times, since the purpose was to follow up the items that were recalled at recall 1 as well as at recall 2. The main finding of Experiment 1 was that collaborating dyads suffered as a result of collaboration, especially if participants were encoding on their own. This finding supports the notion of retrieval disruption. Manipulation checks revealed that individuals encoding on their own showed greater variability in the order in which the items were retrieved. Experiments 2 and 3 examined cued recall. The manipulations with cues were (1) cued versus non-cued conditions and (2) list presentation order, i.e., the dyad could be cued in the same order as they had been during encoding, or not. A resulting significant interaction revealed that actual dyads were negatively affected only by collaboration during free recall, especially if group members had encoded the TBR list in a different order. Again, checks revealed that requested order manipulations worked. The conclusion of these experiments by Finlay and collaborators (2000) is that subjective organization clearly determines whether negative collaboration effects will occur. Thus, inhibiting effects can vary depending on (1) how the material is organized and (2) how the retrieval situation restricts the possible ways in which the individual may solve the task. However, these experiments indicate that encoding factors might influence the outcome as well (cf. Finlay et al., 2000).

Encoding manipulations

Andersson and Rönnberg (1997) explicitly investigated the relative importance of encoding and retrieval in the light of net negative effects of collaboration. Using an encoding specificity paradigm (Tulving & Thompson, 1973; Wiseman & Tulving, 1976) and results from the self-generation superiority effect (Mäntylä & Nilsson, 1983), they predicted that encoding together as a couple would create fewer unique representations and consequently reduce the potential for correct recall under both individual recall and dyadic recall conditions. The task was to generate one association to each of 90 unrelated words. Participants did so individually or collaboratively. During recall, some participants were recalling by the cues generated initially by themself *or* generated by others, i.e., half of the subjects were to remember the same TBR list by associations/cues generated by others. Thus, encoding, retrieval and type of cue were orthogonally varied. First, recalling with cues generated by others revealed no differences between the four conditions that received these cues. Second, the main finding was that the uniqueness of cues diminished if they were generated together with someone else (encoded together), or if they were used together with another individual at retrieval. Overall, the most efficient condition was when an individual encoded alone and also recalled on his or her own. The conclusion was that the reduced cue distinctiveness hypothesis (RCD) was capable of explaining the net negative effects of collaboration obtained.

Another study by Weldon and Bellinger (1997) used a levels-of-processing paradigm. Deep encoding produced better recall than shallow encoding. However, there was no interaction effect with collaboration. Thus, even though the three-person groups studied in this experiment revealed inhibiting effects of collaboration, this was not affected by deep versus shallow encoding variations.

Memory task comparison

It has been argued that collaboration in general inhibits recall (Weldon & Bellinger, 1997). However, this has never been the case for semantic, implicit or knowledge questions (Andersson & Rönnberg, 1996, 1997; Johansson et al., 2005; Thompson, 2002). The inhibiting effects have only been shown for explicit/episodic and prospective memory tasks (Andersson, 2001; Basden, Basden, & Henry, 2000; Johansson et al., 2000; Weldon et al., 2000). The number of studies focusing on semantic memory tasks is much fewer. This is probably only one possible explanation for this less well-known empirical finding. Another explanation is that it is more difficult to substantiate claims for a null hypothesis. Nevertheless, the main finding is that collaborating dyads do not seem to suffer in terms of net negative effects when comparisons with semantic tasks are studied (Andersson & Rönnberg, 1996). Semantic memory represents our shared general knowledge of the world (Tulving,

1983, 1985). The semantic task used in collaborative investigations is often knowledge questions, i.e., questions about facts (information learned a long time ago). The findings are interesting and relevant in the light of theoretical explanations for the net negative effect. Spatial implicit memory tasks have also been used (Andersson & Rönnberg, 1996), as have pictures (Thompson, 2002). The general findings are the same as for verbal semantic tasks; no negative effects occur. As mentioned earlier, one might even obtain positive effects of collaboration if other conditions are fulfilled (cf. Thompson, 2002).

In order to pursue the explanations for obtained effects one must know what the crucial differences are between the episodic and semantic memory tasks used. The first difference from a practical perspective is that episodic tasks all include a controlled encoding phase. In a sense, episodic memory traces are explicit and vulnerable, whereas semantic memory traces are less vulnerable. One might speculate that net negative effects of collaboration might be obtained for memories that would be classified as "remember" answers, compared to no negative effects on "know" answers (Gardiner, Java, & Richardson-Klavehn, 1996); i.e., recollection would be inhibited but familiarity would not (cf. Jacoby, 1991).

Another distinguishing factor might be that all information represented in the same way among different individuals is less vulnerable to interference. The data presented above support this suggestion. A closer look at the semantic tasks used reveals that the tasks requested information that is shared among individuals. For example, if I asked a participant: "What happened on September 11?", I would predict that the answer would be the same, no matter whom I asked. The cue (September 11) would probably activate the same memory trace for most participants, i.e., the cue is shared. The participants would not even ask me what year I was asking about. Hence, if the memory task used in the investigations of collaboration contains information that is truly shared between dyad members, one can predict a true process gain. We argue that the condition used in the Thompson (2002) study (Experiment 1) fulfils this criterion, and further that the degree of reciprocity taps the quality of the dyadic relationship. This means that to really develop the reciprocity needed to overcome the superiority of individual uniqueness of cues (cf. Mäntylä, 1986a, b), a couple needs to develop a common understanding on how to solve memory issues (see Wegner, 1986, 1995; Wegner, Erber, & Raymond, 1991, on transactive memory). The study by Johansson et al. (2005) clearly points in that direction; couples who had developed a division of responsibility and a certain degree of agreement had in fact developed a social relation that influenced the effects of collaboration. The common denominator seems to be reciprocity in terms of the task itself and a common understanding in terms of how to solve the task. This suggestion is further supported by the fact that net negative effect size is greater for episodic tasks that are less complex (word-lists) than the more complex tasks such as story recall; see Andersson and Rönnberg (1995).

Other gains and losses due to collaboration

Two further consequences of collaboration are worthy of note. First, the main dependent variable in most studies of this topic has been the number of correctly retrieved items. However, the other side of the coin is represented by the number of errors. Basden, Basden, Thomas, and Souphasith (1998) and others (Ross et al., 2004) also focused upon how collaboration affects the number of errors made. Others (Andersson et al., 2006; Andersson & Rönnberg, 1995; Finlay et al., 2000; Johansson et al., 2005) have not found sufficient errors in their data to make such an analysis meaningful. Thus, the result seems to be that one of the benefits of collaboration is that it filters out wrong answers (Ross et al., 2004). However, there also exists evidence that points in a different direction (Basden et al., 1998).

Another aspect of the gains and losses question concerns whether, after a collaboration session, the members of a group might gain in subsequent memory recalls, due to the larger amount of information produced in the collaborative recall situation. As discussed earlier, collaborative recall always outperforms a solitary individual's performance. Thus, during the collaborative session the individual is exposed to more items at recall. This retrieval session could therefore be argued to be a more effective (second) encoding phase, enhancing subsequent performance. Two studies have examined this question in some detail. Weldon and Bellinger (1997) used three-person groups and actually found some effects of prior collaboration before individual recall. However, Finlay et al. (2000) did not replicate this observation. The conclusion drawn by Finlay was that the organization manipulations she used had probably disrupted retrieval and that groups need to be larger than the dyads she used. Thus, from a pedagogical, everyday learning perspective the conclusion concerning collaborative gains is problematic. Even if a collaborative recall session exposes the individual to more correct items, encoding is not optimal in other respects. As was shown in a study by Andersson and Rönnberg (1997), joint encoding inhibited performance in later recall sessions.

In sum, task material, encoding and retrieval conditions produce significant and systematic empirical effects that still demand better explanations.

TWO MAJOR HYPOTHESES

Two rival explanations for the effects of collaboration have been offered; one by Basden and colleagues (disruption of retrieval strategies, DRS) and the other by Andersson and colleagues (reduced cue distinctiveness, RCD). The DRS hypothesis suggests that individuals' unique ways of organizing information are disrupted when there is interaction with others at recall. The basic idea is that during recall, when one member is trying to retrieve requested information, the other member will implicitly or explicitly draw attention towards other items by cues used by him or her. When the other member talks the participant often listens to what is said. What is said is often related to the task at hand, and what is said is not presented in the way or order in which the participant had organized the information. Thus, the words do not only interfere with retrieval processes from a time perspective – i.e., you have to wait with your own response – it may also bring your thinking into other non-subjective retrieval routes. For example, if one member says *tomato* (a correct item), on hearing that word the other member remembers *knife* and reports this word. If the participant was recalling on her own she might have started with *car* and gone on to *shop* followed by *tomato* followed by *knife*: Car, shop, tomato, and knife being organized in her own unique way. The other member might have a completely different memory organization. Thus, during joint recall, hearing the words from others draws attention away from the personal and most efficient path to optimal recollection (Mäntylä & Nilsson, 1983), and thus produces net negative effects of collaboration (Basden et al., 1997; Finlay et al., 2000).

In a similar vein, the RCD hypothesis suggests that an individual's unique encoding demands unique retrieval cues to optimize recall performance (Mäntylä, 1986b). A cue provided by another group member at encoding is not the best cue to support optimal recall performance (cf. Mäntylä & Nilsson, 1983). The words reported during recall (by another group member) may not be the best triggers for your own retrieval of the target words. If, for example, participant A overtly starts to reflect upon "it was something that was related to pleasant dishes" (the member is trying to recall "tomato"), while participant B – who dislikes tomatoes – has quite different associations, the cues provided by A are insufficiently distinctive for B. If collaboration results in less unique or distinctive cue words for both members, net negative effects will occur for this group.

Explanations of existing data

How well do these hypotheses manage to explain the empirical findings obtained? How can the effects of friendship, gender, age, organization at recall, organization at encoding, and type of task on collaborative memory be explained?

Friendship

Friendship reduces the net negative effect. The reason for this reduction is that friends presumably have more detailed and elaborate knowledge about what the other party is saying than is the case for unacquainted pair members. For example, if your spouse says that your daughter is coming home at 8 o'clock in the evening, this probably means a lot to you because you and your spouse share a lot of information about your daughter. If a non-friend says the same thing you probably start to wonder why he is telling you that, instead of reflecting on what it actually means. The hypothesis that groups of friends actually can cue one another more efficiently than non-friends was explicitly tested by Andersson and Rönnberg (1997). The task was to generate three associations to each of 100 target words. Friends and non-friends later tried to recall (individually) the target words from the identical list (for them) or a new word-list. Instructions were also varied. Half of the participants were to generate associations for a friend and half were to generate associations for a non-friend (of the same academic background and age). Three main effects were obtained and there were no interactions. The results showed that (1) participants were more able to recall the original list by the use of cues produced by friends than by non-friends, (2) instructions at cue generation (generate cues for a friend or a non-friend) made it clear that a "friend instruction" improved recall performance, and (3) recall performance of the original list was of course better than the recall performance of a new list. The conclusion was that friends are more able to interpret the meaning of information given to each other than non-friends; i.e., cues provided by a friend are more distinctive and will reduce the net negative effects of collaboration. Thus, the RCD hypothesis can explain the effects of friendship. The DRS hypothesis can also explain to some extent the obtained effects of friendship (cf. Weldon et al., 2000). Friends' ways of organizing information, for instance, may be more similar to each other's than to those of non-friends. Hence, friends would disrupt one another's retrieval strategies less than non-friends. The friendship literature (Fleming & Darley, 1991; Fussell & Krauss, 1989) typically advances the argument that friends possess a common ground (cf. H.H. Clark, 1992) that makes them interpret and understand information in a similar fashion, and therefore each other, more easily.

Age

Age differences and collaboration effects can to some extent be explained by the RCD hypothesis. Dyads of younger pair members are more negatively affected by collaboration than are older pairs (cf. Andersson, 2001). It has been argued that younger participants are less able to understand the meaning of cues provided by another individual than more mature individuals are. Younger persons' difficulties in adopting another individual's perspective make them more vulnerable, which would make it more difficult for them to override the reduction in distinctiveness. However, the same argument might be based on the DRS hypothesis, i.e., a younger participant's organization of items might vary more than organizations by older participants. This, however, is a question that needs further examination.

Organization at recall and at encoding

How can manipulations of organization, and the results obtained by these manipulations, be understood by an RCD hypothesis? That the DRS hypothesis can explain these findings was made clear above. Finlay et al. (2000), in their Experiment 1, showed that the net negative effect is pronounced when dyads encode individually before dyadic retrieval. Their conclusion was that participants organized the material in a similar fashion if encoding was performed jointly. Perhaps the participants created shared cues that were sufficiently distinctive for both members, i.e., there was no loss of distinctiveness at retrieval. In their Experiment 2, two findings are important in this regard. First, the cued recall condition did not reveal net negative effects. Second, free recall with different list orders especially suffered from collaboration. The RCD hypothesis predicts that cued recall reduces cue distinctiveness for dyads. Thus, the best cue is a unique self-generated one. If such a cue is used at dyadic retrieval the unique cue for one member is not as distinctive for the other member. If a cue is shared, it is very often not as unique as a self-generated cue, and hence, absolute performance decreases for the dyad. However, in comparison with the nominal group, which is also supported by shared cues at retrieval, inhibition would be avoided, but the nominal and the actual dyad will perform less well. Collaboration would thus not be affected, since cues provided for individuals as well as dyads would work equally badly. This would be particularly true especially as the cues were provided by others and the relationship with the target word was weak (cf. Finlay et al., 2000). The significant effect in the free recall condition only for participants with different list orders might be accounted for by the RCD hypothesis in the following way. Words in a word-list are never encoded as independent items. This means that "independent" words will be uniquely related to each other by each participant. If, for example the words "cow", "hat" and "flower" were presented at encoding, they might be clustered together as a familiar cartoon picture. Thus, if list order varies at encoding between collaborating dyads, unique distinctiveness of the cues used to recall targets increases, relatively speaking. One consequence of this would be net negative effects of collaboration.

Another recent study looked at whether delayed memory testing can eliminate collaborative inhibition (Takahashi & Saito, 2004). Their results fit perfectly well with the RCD hypothesis. The task used was story recall. In Experiment 1 (immediate recall), net negative effects were obtained as predicted. In Experiment 2, using the same story and related questions again, but with a delay of 1 week between encoding and recall, no negative effects were obtained. However, absolute performance decreased. Thus, recalling 1 week later had reduced the unique cue distinctiveness, and performance decreased. But at the same time, cues used to support recall were as good (or bad) for both. Hence, negative effects of collaboration were also avoided after the delay of 1 week. This is difficult to account for with the DRS hypothesis.

Task effects

The size effect of collaboration is task-dependent. The RCD hypothesis explains the absence of difference between nominal and actual groups as being due to shared cues. If the memory task provides cues that are equally well understood and appreciated by both participants, no negative collaboration effects will occur. This implies that even if a task – classified as an episodic one – is supported by shared cues, negative effects will not be obtained. This conclusion is supported by the findings reported in a number of articles (Andersson & Rönnberg, 1997; Takahashi & Saito, 2004; Thompson, 2002). The word-list recall task, in the Andersson and Rönnberg study, was based on cues produced by others for half of the participants. Cues produced by others contain less distinctiveness (cf. Hunt & Einstein, 1981; Hunt & McDaniel, 1993; Hunt & Smith-Kelly, 1996; Mäntylä & Nilsson, 1983) and work equally well for both participants. However, from an absolute scoring criterion perspective, dyadic performance, of course, decreased to a great extent. However, net negative effects will vanish. The DRS hypothesis, on the other hand, would predict that dyads under these memory task conditions should suffer due to disruption at retrieval. If the cues produced by others were totally useless and neglected, ordinary net negative effects would occur, since the task would become exclusively episodic. If the cues produced by others were merely less sufficient, dyadic disruption of strategies would be predicted. Thus, it is difficult to explain the variation of collaboration effects due to task studied by the DRS hypothesis. The finding of positive effects for collaboration with semantic task materials (Thompson, 2002), reveals the same problem for the DRS hypothesis. In Experiment 1 (semantic face naming task) older participants even gained from collaboration. This is also difficult for the RCD hypothesis to completely explain on its own.

Andersson, Hitch, and Meudell (2006) completed a series of experiments, varying time and quality of cues, which might shed some light upon this problem. Their main finding was that cue distribution over time affects recall performance, and that the quality of the cue affects performance as well. The experiment was performed within a part-list paradigm and collaboration was only mimicked, i.e., individual recall was supported by an audio-tape that replayed words from the same word-list. The data should therefore be interpreted with caution in comparison to collaborative effects. However, organization of task materials and cue distinctiveness appear to work in parallel (time and quality of the information provided during dyadic recall). This means that to avoid net negative effects during collaboration, dyads need shared distinctive cues that are organized in similar ways for all participating group members.

These interpretations do not, however, explain other observed collaboration effects. According to Johansson et al. (2005), older dyads with specific relationship qualities (division of responsibility and degree of agreement) improved their memory performances in terms of reduced net negative effects of collaboration. The social dimension interacts with the cognitive dimension. To arrive at an optimal situation, a number of criteria must be fulfilled. Thus, the social and cognitive dimensions must be taken into account if a broader understanding of collaboration is to be attained.

EVALUATION OF HYPOTHESES DISCUSSED

This chapter has presented an overview of findings within the paradigm that uses nominal groups as the baseline for dyadic or triadic collaborative performance. In order to argue for group facilitation, collaboration should be able to produce unique materials that the individual could not produce on his or her own. Even though the nominal group does not exist in the real world we need this control group to enable us to interpret how, in our everyday life, we are affected by social interaction with relatives, friends and even non-friends. Recent research has accumulated partly unexpected evidence, and theoretical hypotheses to explain these findings have been suggested. The RCD (reduced cue distinctiveness) and the DRS (disrupted retrieval strategies) hypotheses are complementary in some respects, and in combination are capable of predicting a number of the phenomena observed. It is argued, however, that the RCD hypothesis better taps into the mechanism behind the negative effect. The RCD hypothesis clarifies the reason for the disruption of efficient retrieval and explains differences between friendship and task effects better than the DRS hypothesis. One of the arguments for the RCD hypothesis as against the DRS hypothesis is that it also brings the social aspects of collaboration into focus. The second argument for the RCD hypothesis is that it predicts the absence of negative collaboration effects obtained under semantic task conditions (Andersson & Rönnberg, 1997; Thompson, 2002) and with a delay of 1 week between encoding and test (Takahashi and Saito, 2004). However, recently published data also reveal that the cognitive explanation of these effects is not the whole story. The quality of the dyadic relationship seems to matter in an important way (Johansson et al., 2005).

The research discussed in this chapter reveals a complex but interesting pattern of findings. With the objective of understanding everyday memory, this paradigm is argued to be a fruitful and necessary step for memory researchers to take.

PRACTICAL APPLICATION OF EXPERIMENTAL FINDINGS

One obvious question that arises when we use the nominal baseline to understand how collaboration affects individual memory performance concerns how such empirical findings can be related to everyday life. From an overall perspective our memory processes are involved in most things we say or do. The collaboration experiments suggest how we can use our memory optimally under social task conditions. From a specifically applied perspective, a number of special situations can be discussed.

In the eyewitness literature, particularly that concerning child abuse, it is evident that a number of memory reliability problems exist (Goodman, 2005) especially so as far children are concerned (see Chapter 5). According to the data at hand, adults and children ought to give their testimony individually, without interaction with others. In many cases this is impossible, since there is a need for an interviewer to ask for information in order to get an answer. However we should be aware of possible inhibitory effects and conduct separate interviews to obtain the best results. This is exactly what the lay Norwegians answered on the survey conducted in Norway (Magnussen et al., 2006).

Meetings are a regular feature of job conditions. Entering a meeting with the aim of discussing more or less important work-related aspects, we are likely to have some ideas that we want to discuss. The meeting starts and runs as usual. A number of individuals talk and discuss the matters at hand, while we are normally engaged in what is going on. However, after the meeting we realize that we did not remember to bring up our own ideas. One of several probable reasons is that our memory became somewhat inhibited by listening to others. The cues needed to recall our own ideas were interfered with by the discussions.

However, the results reported also revealed that semantic memory tasks were unaffected by collaboration. In the meeting context, knowledge of work-related aspects is not inhibited by collaboration during the meeting. Thus, in an ecological setting such as a meeting, the discussion is driven by semantic knowledge and episodic memory, and it is difficult to disentangle the different kinds of memory. Another important aspect, which complicates the problem even further, is that both memories are supported by cues. The results reported here demonstrate that even the episodic memory task was unaffected by collaboration, as long as shared cues were used for retrieval. Hence, pinpointing how net negative effects of collaboration affect episodic memory in real-life is still problematic. The experimental data reveal a clear pattern, but more ecological settings will have to be studied before clear-cut conclusions can be drawn from reality.

The research evidence outlined here also reveals that joint encoding affects the retrieval process. The current educational system in Scandinavian countries has accepted a pedagogical approach that uses group discussions as a tool for learning. Do the memory collaboration findings suggest that group learning should be avoided? Not necessarily! Educational psychology has moved from traditional lectures to group discussions. In that respect encoding is less inhibited since pupils often tend to understand their friends better than their teachers. However, the question is rather how group conditions are utilized for the purpose of learning. Collaboration data suggest that pupils should start with individual engagement and thereafter discuss problematic aspects with friends, possibly followed by group discussions. Thus, the research evidence suggests that one should be aware of the inhibiting effects and organize learning accordingly. This knowledge should be taken into systematic consideration when planning practical educational situations.

Finally, in everyday life people act and perform collaboratively. Action memory research (see Chapter 3) clearly shows that actions are remembered more easily than memories that are not acted upon. Thus, episodic memories are located in time and place to a greater degree than semantic memories. When you recall what you had for breakfast this morning, you can probably see yourself performing specific actions. However, when you recall that Paris is the capital of France you hardly have such representations – you just know it. This means, speculatively, that the net negative effect of collaboration found in episodic memory tasks might be a consequence of an unrecalled action located in time and place. So far, to our knowledge, action memory has not been studied in the collaborative setting. Therefore, one obvious question that needs to be addressed is how joint actions influence collaborative recall. The collaborative approach might not only enhance our understanding of memory in everyday life; it might also advance our understanding of memory from a theoretical perspective.

REFERENCES

Andersson, J. (1996). *Two is one too many: Dyadic memory collaboration effects on encoding and retrieval of episodes.* PhD thesis, Linköping University, Sweden.

Andersson, J. (2001). Net effect of memory collaboration: How is collaboration affected by factors such as friendship, gender and age? *Scandinavian Journal of Psychology, 42,* 367–375.

Andersson, J., Hitch, G., & Meudell, P. (2006). Mimicking aspects of collaborative recall performance through the manipulation of timing and quality of part-list cues. *Memory, 14,* 94–103.

Andersson, J., & Rönnberg, J.R. (1995). Recall suffers from collaboration: Joint recall effects of friendship and task complexity. *Applied Cognitive Psychology, 9,* 199–211.

Andersson, J., & Rönnberg, J.R. (1996). Collaboration and memory: Effects off dyadic retrieval on different memory tasks. *Applied Cognitive Psychology, 10,* 171–181.

Andersson, J., & Rönnberg, J.R. (1997). Cued memory collaboration: Effects of friendship and type of retrieval cue. *European Journal of Cognitive Psychology, 9,* 273–287.

Asch, S.E., & Ebenholz, S.M. (1962). The process of free recall: Evidence for non-associative factors in acquisition and retention. *Journal of Psychology, 54,* 3–31

Basden, B.H., Basden, D.R., Bryner, S., & Thomas, R.L. III (1997). A comparison of group and individual remembering: Does group participation disrupt retrieval? *Journal of Experimental Psychology: Learning, Memory, and Cognition, 23,* 1176–1189.

Basden, B.H., Basden, D.R., & Henry, S. (2000). Costs and benefits of collaborative remembering. *Applied Cognitive Psychology, 14,* 497–507.

Basden, B.H., Basden, D.R., Thomas, R.L. III, & Souphasith, S. (1998). Memory distortion in group recall. *Current Psychology, 16,* 225–246.

Brown, R. (1988). *Group processes: Dynamics within and between groups.* Oxford, UK: Blackwell.

Clark, H.H. (1992). *Arenas of language use.* Chicago, IL: University of Chicago Press.

Clark, N.K., Stephenson, G.M., & Kniveton, B.H. (1990). Social remembering: Quantitative aspects of individual and collaborative remembering by police officers and students. *British Journal of Psychology*, *81*, 73–94.

Dixon, R.A., & Gould, O.N. (1998). Younger and older adults collaborating on retelling everyday stories. *Applied Developmental Science*, *2*, 160–171.

Faust, W.L. (1959). Group versus individual problem solving. *Journal of Abnormal and Social Psychology*, *59*, 68–72.

Finlay, F., Hitch, G.J., & Meudell, P.R. (2000). Mutual inhibition in collaborative recall: Evidence for a retrieval-based account. *Journal of Experimental Psychology: Learning, Memory and Cognition*, *26*, 1556–1567.

Fleming, J.H., & Darley, J.M. (1991). Mixed messages: The multiple audience problem and strategic communication. *Social Cognition*, *9*, 25–46.

Fussell, S.R., & Krauss, R.M. (1989). Understanding friends and strangers: The effects of audience design on message comprehension. *European Journal of Social Psychology*, *19*, 509–525.

Gardiner, J.M., Java, R.I., & Richardson-Klavehn, A. (1996). How level of processing really influences awareness in recognition memory. *Canadian Journal of Experimental Psychology*, *50*, 114–122.

Goodman, G.S. (2005). Wailing babies in her wake. *American Psychologist*, *60*, 872–881.

Gould, O.N., & Dixon, R.A. (1993). How we spent our vacation: Collaborative storytelling by young and old adults. *Psychology and Aging*, *8*, 10–17.

Harkins, S.G., & Jackson, J.M. (1985). The role of evaluation in eliminating social loafing. *Personality and Social Psychology Bulletin*, *11*, 457–465.

Herlitz, A., Airaksinen, E., & Nordström, E. (1999). Sex differences in episodic memory: The impact of verbal and visuospatial ability. *Neuropsychology*, *13*, 590–597.

Hill, R.D., Grut, M., Wahlin, Å., Herlitz, A., Winblad, B., & Bäckman, L. (1995). Predicting memory performance in optimally healthy very old adults. *Journal of Mental Health and Ageing*, *1*, 55–65.

Hunt, R.R., & Einstein, G.O. (1981). Relational and item-specific information in memory. *Journal of Verbal Learning and Verbal Behavior*, *20*, 497–514.

Hunt, R.R., & McDaniel, M.A. (1993). The enigma of organisation and distinctiveness. *Journal of Memory and Language*, *32*, 421–445.

Hunt, R.R., & Smith-Kelly, R.E. (1996). Accessing the particular from the general: The power of distinctiveness in the context of organisation. *Memory and Cognition*, *24*, 217–225.

Jacoby, L.L. (1991). A process dissociation framework: Separating automatic from intentional uses of memory. *Journal of Memory and Language*, *30*, 513–541.

Johansson, O., Andersson, J., & Rönnberg, J.R. (2000). Do elderly couples have a better prospective memory than other elderly people when they collaborate? *Applied Cognitive Psychology*, *14*, 121–133.

Johansson, O., Andersson, J., & Rönnberg, J. (2005). Compensating strategies in collaborative remembering in very old couples. *Scandinavian Journal of Psychology*, *46*, 349–359.

Magnussen, S., Andersson, J., Cornoldi, C., De Beni, R., Endestad, T., Goodman, G., Helstrup, T., Koriat, A., Larsson, M., Melinder, A., Nilsson, L.G., Rönnberg, S., & Zimmer, H. (2006). What people believe about memory. *Memory*, *14*, 595–613.

Mäntylä, T. (1986a). *How do you cue?* PhD thesis, University of Umeå, Sweden.

Mäntylä, T. (1986b). Optimizing cue effectiveness: Recall of 500 and 600 incidentally learned words. *Journal of Experimental Psychology: Learning, Memory and Cognition, 12*, 66–71.

Mäntylä, T., & Nilsson, L.-G. (1983). Are my cues better than your cues? *Scandinavian Journal of Psychology, 24*, 303–312.

Meudell, P.R., Hitch, G.J., & Boyle, M.M. (1995). Collaboration in recall: Do pairs of people cross-cue each other to produce new memories? *The Quarterly Journal of Experimental Psychology, 48A*, 141–152.

Meudell, P.R., Hitch, G.J., & Kirby, P. (1992). Are two heads better than one? Experimental investigations of the social facilitation of memory. *Applied Cognitive Psychology, 5*, 525–543.

Moede, W. (1927). Die Richtlinien der Leistungs-Psychologie. *Industrielle Psychotechnik, 4*, 193–207.

Piaget, J. (1959). *The language and thought of the child.* Thetford, UK: Lowe & Brydone.

Ross, M., Spencer, S.J., Linardatos, L., Lam, K.H.M., & Perunovic, M. (2004). Going shopping and identifying landmarks: Does collaboration improve older people's memory? *Applied Cognitive Psychology, 18*, 683–696.

Steiner, I.D. (1972). *Group process and productivity.* New York: Academic Press.

Stephenson, G.M., Abrams, D., Wagner, W., & Wade, G. (1986). Partners in recall: Collaborative order in the recall of a police interrogation. *British Journal of Social Psychology, 25*, 341–343.

Stephenson, G.M., Kniveton, B.H., & Wagner, W. (1991). Social influences on remembering: Intellectual, interpersonal and intergroup components. *European Journal of Social Psychology, 21*, 463–475.

Sternberg, R.J., & Tulving, E. (1977). The measurement of subjective organisation in free recall. *Psychological Bulletin, 84*, 539–556.

Symons, D.K. (2004). Mental state discourse, theory of mind, and the internalization of self-other understanding. *Developmental Review, 24*, 159–188.

Takahashi, M. (in press). Does collaborative remembering reduce false memories? *The British Journal of Psychology.*

Takahashi, M., & Saito, S. (2004). Does test delay eliminate collaborative inhibition? *Memory, 12(6)*, 722–731.

Thompson, R.G. (2002). *Collaborative memory in young and older adults.* Unpublished doctoral thesis, University of Bristol, UK.

Tulving, E. (1983). *Elements of episodic memory.* New York: Oxford University Press.

Tulving, E. (1985). How many memory systems are there? *American Psychologist, 40*, 385–398.

Tulving, E., & Thompson, D.M. (1973). Encoding specificity and retrieval processes in episodic memory. *Psychological Review, 80*, 1–52.

Wegner, D.M. (1986). Transactive memory: A contemporary analysis of the group mind. In G. Gullen & G. Goethals (Eds.), *Theories of group behaviour* (pp. 185–208). New York: Springer-Verlag.

Wegner, D.M. (1995). A computer network model of human transactive memory. *Social Cognition, 13*, 319–339.

Wegner, D.M., Erber, R., & Raymond, P. (1991). Transactive memory in close relationships. *Journal of Personality and Social Psychology, 61*, 923–929.

Weldon, M.S. (2000). Remembering as a social process. In D.L. Medin (Ed.), *Psychology of learning and motivation, Vol. 40* (pp. 67–120). San Diego, CA: Academic Press.

156 *Everyday memory*

Weldon, M.S., & Bellinger, K.D (1997). Collective memory: The nature of individual and collaborative recall. *Journal of Experimental Psychology: Learning, Memory, and Cognition, 23*, 1160–1175.

Weldon, M.S., Blair, S., & Huebsch, P.D. (2000). Group remembering: Does social loafing underlie collaborative inhibition? *Journal of Experimental Psychology: Learning, Memory, and Cognition, 26*, 1568–1577.

Wiseman, S., & Tulving, E. (1976). Encoding specificity: The relations between recall superiority and recognition failure. *Journal of Experimental Psychology: Human Learning and Memory, 2*, 349–361.

7 Memory illusions and false memories in the real world

*Gail S. Goodman, Svein Magnussen,
Jan Andersson, Tor Endestad, Lene
Løkken and Agnes Cathrine Moestue*

Miscarriage of justice is of concern to society as a whole. Therefore, memory must also be of concern to society as a whole, because certain miscarriages of justice are caused by problems with human memory. And certain problems in memory, including problems with substantial legal implications, may be more "everyday" than most people believe.

Fortunately, research psychologists can play a special role in preventing miscarriages of justice that involve memory errors. Memory errors can range from harmless misremembering of trivial details, to larger errors within a generally accurate memory representation, to, at the extreme, dangerous false memories of traumatic and criminal events that did not in fact occur. This latter type of memory error has become known as "false memory". The term "false memory" previously referred to a specific psychological phenomenon in which an individual reports entire events that she or he had not in fact experienced, but more recently the term has sometimes also been applied to other memory errors, such as those involving semantic associates or misinformation effects regarding details of an event (e.g., Porter, Spencer, & Birt, 2003; Roediger & McDermott, 1995). Although we discuss a variety of memory errors in this chapter, we focus primarily on false reports of entire events that did not occur but presumably have become incorporated as part of a person's autobiographical memories.

We all make memory errors at times. Many of these errors are inconsequential, but in recent years, research psychologists have been increasingly interested in distortions of eyewitness memory, which by their very nature are often quite consequential (Koriat, Goldsmith, & Pansky, 2000; Loftus, 1979). In particular, psychologists have recently paid special attention to false-memory phenomena (e.g., false memory of child sexual abuse). How, you might ask, could someone come to believe that entire events – including very traumatic ones, such as murder and rape – were experienced when in fact they were not? And how, you might also ask, can research psychologists study such a phenomenon? Our goal in this chapter is to illuminate the psychology of eyewitness memory errors, especially false-memory mistakes.

After a brief introduction, we describe several actual cases – some from Norway and some from the United States – that may involve false memory or other potentially consequential types of memory errors. Several of the examples involve legal cases. However, it should be kept firmly in mind that in many legal cases, it is impossible to know for certain the extent to which memory error is involved. Nevertheless, in some cases, we can be more confident than in others.

In this chapter, several of the cases we discuss involve adults' memory, whereas other cases involve children's recollections. After describing these cases in some detail, we then consider relevant laboratory research and psychological theory to explain how it is that a person's autobiographical memory may become distorted in various ways. We also discuss recent research on psychological mechanisms that guard against memory error – after all, often (perhaps most often) our memories are basically correct. We end with describing some implications of memory-error research.

MEMORY ERRORS IN EVERYDAY LIFE

Memory errors are probably part of everyone's recollections of their personal history. Most people acknowledge that their memory is not perfect. What is less obvious is that, at times, adults and children may have false memories of entire events, and that such false memories may be more common than has formerly been recognized.

Many of the false memories arising in everyday life seem to refer to childhood events, and laboratory inductions of false memories use fabricated stories from the participants' childhoods (Loftus & Pickrell, 1997; Wade, Garry, Read, & Lindsay, 2002). However, there is both anecdotal and other evidence that false memories may arise in adulthood and refer to alleged adult experiences (e.g., Bottoms, Shaver, & Goodman, 1996). Most of such memories may go undetected either because we normally do not bother to check the facts or because the facts are not available. However, sometimes it is possible to study the spontaneous development of memory illusions and false memories. Next, we provide examples of memory errors, including likely false memory, arising in adulthood, followed by examples of such memories arising in childhood.

Memory errors and false memories about experiences in adulthood

Spontaneous distorted memories in natural contexts: the Robinson Expedition

In this section, we first describe an example of distorted memories in adults about a dramatic situation that took place during the recording of the reality television show, "The Robinson Expedition". The event was recorded on videotape, and the participants were interviewed on two occasions, first when they returned from an island, and second after the series had been shown on television.

In the Robinson Expedition, 18 participants were "stranded" on a remote island in Asia. They were partly deprived of sustenance and had to hunt for food, in addition to performing several practical tasks and competitions. These all served the purpose of picking a winner in the end, who was awarded a substantial sum of money. The competition was set up so that the participants, after an introductory phase, select by secret vote a loser who is then sent home, and then the process begins again. The activities of the participants were constantly monitored by a number of cameras. The final version that was shown as a series of programmes on public television was an edited version of the events. Although the show superficially appeared to be a fun competition among young people on a fantasy island, a number of similar reality shows have revealed that the role-playing takes on the shape of reality during the shooting period and that sometimes strong, genuine interpersonal conflicts develop, conflicts that survive the shooting sessions.

In collaboration with the Norwegian production team, we had the opportunity to view some of the incidents captured on the original, unedited tapes and compare what really happened with participants' later recall. We have observed a number of instances of memory distortions and false memories that have spontaneously arisen among the participants for the various reality episodes. In this section, we describe a single event that took place early in the show, at a time when no one had been sent home; we were thus able to analyse each participant's memory for the event. The event was called the "cage" and was a competition between two teams, where some of the team members were "buried" in a small wooden box in the sand. Above them, one team member was locked inside a cage, and their task was to dig themselves out, and then use long sticks to pick up the keys, unlock, and "save" the captured member. The incident was filmed by six cameras on the ground, and by one infrared camera placed inside the wooden box. This allowed for detailed analysis of the actions and verbal utterances of every team member.

In the following, we only discuss the memories of participants on the winning team. John is locked up inside the cage. Underground his team members Tom, Bill, Alex, Janet, and Susan are waiting for their "go" signal to start digging their way from underground into the cage. It is completely dark. Before the game started, the team was informed about anxiety and claustrophobic reactions of one of the team members, Susan, and while they are waiting for a "go" signal, Susan is crying quietly, but she doesn't say anything. In the dark, someone says, "Think about tonight when we are going to relax and enjoy ourselves"; apart from this utterance there is no strategy planning or contact between the team members, and there is no encouragement or emotional support of Susan's claustrophobic tendencies. They are quietly waiting. When the "go" signal is given, Bill starts digging and tells the others, "We will soon be out now". Bill is the first one out of the hole in the ground. Second comes Tom, third is Janet, and the last one out is Susan.

Underground, Susan says to the others, "You guys go ahead," she digs a little bit, and she says she is afraid to get stuck. When Bill gets out of the hole in the ground and into the cave, John says, "Get Susan out as soon as possible."

When they are all out of the cave, they work efficiently on their tasks, collect the keys, and open the locks, thus freeing the final team member, and they win the competition. Susan doesn't look well, and she is waiting almost paralysed inside the cage. After the victory, Bill goes over to Susan and kisses her, and so does Tom. John says to Susan "Everything that doesn't kill you, makes you stronger".

The participants were interviewed about this incident 2–4 weeks after the shooting of the programme and a second time 6–7 months after the first interview. The following are spontaneous recollections of three male participants:

TOM: Yes I remember the episode well because it was great, because some of what impressed me most about it was Susan. She had super claustro-phobic anxiety, she cried, the only thing you could hear was her scream-ing. It was a small hole in the ground that we had to go into, about 2×1m, and we were seven or eight people in there. I remember that I was impressed with Susan going down there. And that it was great joy to actually win the competition. To be buried underground and having to dig yourself out was really cool, but there were many who got a little bit shaky down there. To be underground and have the feeling of losing control over the situation, and you get a bag over your head, makes you a little bit shaky. And I got shaky as well, but when you see the light from the sun you get very happy, so even though it was uncomfortable, it was a very cool experience. It is not something you experience everyday you know. The special thing was Susan who started crying and saying that "This is not working, I am going to pass out, I cannot finish this" etc.

It was Bill and I who started digging, and I sent him first up, because he is lighter than me. And I came ... no that can't be ... it wasn't Susan second. Well, I actually don't remember. It was Ann.

BILL: We were pushed down into a cage below the ground, and then they dug sand over us, and it was pitch dark. It was when Susan had claustro-phobia and did a major accomplishment. We were waiting for the "go" signal about three or four minutes, and Susan is crying. And that's when I am back to my "friendly" self and say, "This will work out" and tell her some stories. And Susan is laughing a little bit and then crying again, so I spent a lot of time trying to calm her down. When the game starts, Tom and I are digging and doing the whole job as usual. Somebody else took care of Susan while we were digging. I am first out of the hole in the ground. While I am digging and can see the light I shout at Susan "We will soon be out now." We did a really good job on this competition. We had made a perfect strategy; if we had done that on other competitions we would have won those as well. It was all very cool.

JOHN: It was Bill who came first up out of the hole and second was Susan I think because she had claustrophobia, and I think that Bill was digging really hard to get Susan out of there, but I am not 100% sure about it. And I think it was Bill who said "Get Susan out of there as soon as possible," and I think the whole thing took about three minutes, it was very quick.

All participants remembered that particular competition and agreed on some of the major features of the event, like who was on the winning team. Some of them remembered details from the event, but the majority of the participants had incomplete memories. However, the memories of the individual participants not only varied in the number of details they remembered, but their stories also varied in what had actually happened. For example, some of the male participants remembered being helpful and nice towards Susan, whom they knew was claustrophobic. Bill remembered that Susan was crying hysterically, so being a nice guy he sat down with her, comforted her, and told her stories that made her laugh and forget about the situation. But Bill did nothing of the sort. The footage from six different cameras on the scene shows us that they were all sitting quietly waiting, and nothing was said except "*Think about tonight when we are going to relax and enjoy ourselves,*" and there was no other comforting of Susan.

Why does Bill remember the event the way he does? Has the memory been edited to fit a self-image of a helping, caring person, a schema of how he would have liked to behave in such situations? It is after the competition that he goes up to Susan to give her a hug. So here we see a falsely added element – telling her stories – together with a misattribution (Schacter, 2001) of memory elements, by attributing the behaviour in one situation to a previous situation. Of interest, the self-image expressed by Bill must have been shared by some of the other team members. For example, John remembered that it was Bill who exclaimed, "Let us get Susan out," while in fact it was John himself who said it and who was the only person who tried to help her.

Another memory error was the recollection of getting Susan out as fast as possible. In fact, she was the last one out. Possibly the memories of the male members of the team were governed by a schema of how a man should behave. Such memory editing is well known (Schacter, 2001). Long ago, Bartlett (1932) pointed out that information that can be assimilated into an active schema is more likely to be recalled than schema-irrelevant information (see also Goodman, 1980). He showed that episodes are remembered in terms of generic schemata, and their representations are systematically shifted or changed to fit these schemata. It has also been shown that people systematically reconstruct their past to fit into their current self-image schema (Ross & Buehler, 1994). Also when an attempt is made to remember details that are not available in the schematic representation, people may try to reconstruct the missing details using schema-based inference processes at the time of remembering (Bartlett, 1932; Neisser, 1967). In fact, the only person remembering what happened correctly was Susan herself.

Another possible explanation of the erroneous memory of helping Susan by the male participants, and Bill in particular, is source misattribution, a blending of memories for different episodes. Schacter (2001) describes a case of source misattribution connected to the Oklahoma City bombing in 1995. For a long time the police looked for a second suspect, a man who supposedly had accompanied Timothy McVeigh to a car rental company. However, it turned out that the witness had seen the sought-after man, the completely innocent Private Todd Bunting, in the car rental company with his friend, Sergeant Michael Hertig – who resembled McVeigh – on another day during a completely unrelated visit. In the study of eyewitness memory, several such cases have been reported, indicating a certain risk of blending components from different events into a coherent memory episode. In the Robinson series, Bill did comfort Susan but that was later that day in another context, and he also attended to her in other situations on different days. Thus he probably mixed times and events. Tom must likewise have mixed episodes (or at least confused names) when he remembered that Ann comforted Susan underground, because Ann did not participate in this competition at all. She was in fact not even present.

The participants' memory for the event changed over time. At the first interview their memories differed regarding how they behaved on the occasion. At a second interview, some months later, they all remembered the situation more coherently. Still they remembered erroneously that they had helped Susan and that she was one of the first out of the box, but now new components of the episode had entered their stories. First, they all remembered a lot of planning and strategic activity that was not captured by the cameras. For example, they all remembered that Bill had been a strong leader. This is interesting, because Bill hardly could be regarded as having a leading role at all. He was first out of the hole, but in no way attempted to organize or coordinate the others in the team. The only person who attempted to instruct the team, calling out for the others to help Susan, was John. Perhaps the team, looking back, had problems explaining how and why they won. Typical schemata for group success involve proper planning and leadership. Thus, over time, the memory of the team members was apparently modified in accordance with this schema.

How is it possible that they all produced accounts of the events altered in the same direction? The cage episode was one of the more dramatic events of the series, and it is likely that it became a conversation piece among the participants. And when one of the team members fills in memory blanks by telling the others that he or she did a certain thing, it might become difficult to discriminate genuine memories of the events from the tales of other participants. Strong social pressure towards group coherence adds a certain pressure towards remembering the same things after the event. However, it should also be kept in mind that people who volunteer for reality television shows may be somewhat of a special breed (e.g., overly dramatic, attention seekers), and not representative of people in general.

Adult cases of recovered memories in psychotherapy: claims of Satanic ritual abuse

The Robinson Expedition case involves distortions of memory for an event that actually occurred. And much of what the participants recounted was correct. However, there are other situations in which what appear to be false memories of entire events have been documented, including highly traumatic events that are likely never to have occurred.

In the 1900s, a rash of cases involving alleged repressed memory came to public attention. Some of the cases involved allegations of Satanic ritual abuse. The extreme end of these allegations derived mainly from adults who came forward to claim that, as children, they had been raised in Satanic cults by people who had become demonically possessed and were no longer human. The allegations included that hundreds, if not thousands, of babies had been murdered by the cult members. The adults making the claims would often include that they themselves had been involved in the torture of the babies. Not all of the recovered, formerly "repressed memories" of such horrific crimes arose in the course of psychotherapy, but many did. Other claims, sometimes in part emanating from children involved in forensic interviews, were that Satanists had infiltrated American preschools so as to sexually abuse the children there, because Satanists, being evil, particularly like to prey on those who are most innocent and pure. Members of the FBI and local governments were also said to be involved in Satanic ritual abuse. However, when research was conducted to investigate these claims, no hard evidence of such cult activity, including the hundreds if not thousands of disappearing babies, could be found (e.g., Bottoms et al., 1996).

Some of those making the allegations later recanted their claims, and in some cases, they pointed to highly inappropriate techniques that were used by clinicians to induce false reports. These techniques included hypnosis and psychotropic drugs. In a fair number of cases, the person had sought psychotherapy because of depression or other symptoms of psychopathology. Some of the therapists, apparently believing in Satanic abuse, then would hospitalize the person who had sought treatment. During the hospitalization, hypnosis and psychotropic drugs were at times used to, in effect, induce false reports. Such cases have been documented in research by Bottoms et al. (1996), who conducted a large-scale nationwide survey in the United States of all county level prosecutor and child protection offices, as well as law enforcement agencies, and a large subset of American clinicians. The lack of hard evidence, in cases where such evidence should reasonably exist, led Bottoms et al. to conclude that false memory lay behind most if not all allegations of Satanic ritual abuse (see also Loftus, 1996; Qin, Goodman, Bottoms, & Shaver, 1998).

This is not to say that there are no people who self-identify as Satanists. In fact, there are such people. But allegations that Satanists who are no longer human in large organized groups have infiltrated preschools and the FBI to sexually abuse children are likely to involve false memory. It is possible that those making the claims have been victimized in other ways, and therefore that there is some core truth to part of their allegations. However, the specific claims made are likely to be false, with serious implications for innocent people. And such false memories can arise in adulthood.

The case of the murdered jogger

A recent court trial in Norway also suggests that false memories of rape and murder can arise in adulthood. In a series of articles published in 2000–2002, the Norwegian newspaper *Verdens Gang* (VG) covered a case of false memories for ritual abuse and murder. The case was brought to trial by the then 70-year-old architect, Torbjørn Fjeldstad, who sued a psychotherapist for creating false memories in female patients. The unusual feature of this trial was that several patients of the same therapist identified the same persons as perpetrators, including Fjeldstad, his brother, and several acquaintances. The psychotherapist was a male nurse, with no formal training in psychotherapy except for courses in gestalt therapy, and who practised age regression, where patients were brought back to the "land of childhood" to meet repressed memories. This is a type of therapy that is associated with a high risk of creating false childhood memories (Schooler & Eich, 2000). Many of his patients "remembered" horrible crimes committed by people they knew, and common to all was that they had no previous recollections of the crimes. On two occasions, the Asker and Bærum police investigated allegations of criminal activity that emanated from the therapeutic sessions conducted by this therapist. One of the cases also involved first-degree murder.

The case started when a young teenage boy was referred to the therapist for behaviour problems. At that time there were no suspicions of criminal activity. The therapist soon started to treat adults in the family. Then a wave of grotesque stories surfaced, where a total of eight persons were identified as victims and nine persons as perpetrators, with the core members supposedly forming a gang that committed ritual crimes against children and adults, and who practised gang rapes and "Ritual séances where a gang of four emptied slimy intestines from animals on victims. Bizarre abuse practices in a torture chamber, located at Lillehammer. Sexual abuse of children below one year of age" (VG, February 26, 2002). The key female witness in the trial remembered being abused from the time she was a baby and claimed to have been raped the last time at the age of 38 in 1994. The police interviewed this witness on 12 occasions, in parallel with the therapeutic sessions that uncovered new stories. "It was like a curtain that was slowly removed and behind the curtain the patient 'saw' the most grotesque scenes from early childhood up to adult age" (VG, February 26, 2002).

The key event of the trial dated back to 1972 when the witness was a young adult. She remembered that the Fjeldstad brothers tied her hands and feet and drove her off to a parking lot in the woods of Asker, near Oslo, where they raped her. When surprised by a jogger, the two men were said to have stoned the jogger to death and covered the body with leaves and branches; they then continued abusing the girl. Later the girl was forced to help them get rid of the body, and a young boy, then 13 years of age, was forced to assist in wrapping the body in a green cover and dumping it in the lake of Lyseren at Asker. The witness gave a detailed description of the dead jogger.

In police interviews, the psychotherapist expressed beliefs in the patient stories, and strongly rejected the idea that he had produced false memories. The key female witness was (in 2000) still convinced about the reality of her memories. However, the boy who was alleged to have assisted in hiding the body categorically denied any participation. In 1999, the police picked up Thorbjørn Fjeldstad at work in his architectural office. However, the police were unable to discover any evidence of murder or other criminal activities, there was no record of a jogger reported missing in Asker around that time, and further thorough investigations disclosed no other evidence for satanic practices of Fjeldstad and his friends (VG, September 1, 2000 and October 22, 2000). Thus, all charges were dropped. However, Thorbjørn Fjeldstad, who felt that the accusations still tainted his reputation, sued the psychotherapist. In the trial, research psychologists testified. Fjeldstad won, and on March 15, 2002, he was awarded a large sum of money by the Asker and Bærum District court (Case No. 01–977A).

Adult case implications

These extreme examples (and there are others, such as space alien abductions; Clancy, 2005) may reflect part of more normal cognitive processes by which autobiographical memories can be contaminated by false suggestions. Later in this chapter we will delve further into the findings of scientific research, but it is worth noting here that although it had been known for many years that memory can be distorted by schema-related processes (Bartlett, 1932) and post-event misinformation (Loftus, 1979), it was not until Elizabeth Loftus conducted her "Lost in the Mall" experiment that psychologists had a paradigm for experimental investigation of false-memory formation for entire autobiographical events. Such research indicates that a certain percentage of people are particularly subject to false memory. In the real world, there are undoubtedly other sources of false-memory formation, including false suggestions by authorities (such as psychotherapists) to emotionally vulnerable clients, self-generated false memories, and group-generated false memories. Before turning to the research base, we consider several examples of memory errors and possible false memories in childhood.

Memory errors and false memories in childhood

It is typically difficult to know, in actual cases, if reports are totally false, partly false and partly true, or actually true. This is the situation in the child cases we report next. According to some theories of false memory (e.g., Loftus & Pickrell, 1995), false information combines with true information to form a false memory. Thus, it would not be surprising if there is some truth to certain claims. In some cases involving children, as in the cases involving adults, it is impossible to know if the event really never occurred, or if the children are just partially wrong.

A case of domestic violence

The young woman's body was found, badly decomposed, in the shower; she had a noose around her neck. At first, the coroner thought it was suicide, but as the investigation proceeded, it appeared to be murder. The woman had been married to a man with a history of domestic violence, and at the trial, two of his former female partners testified to how he had tried to strangle them. The two children of the deceased woman's and the man's union had witnessed their parents' domestic violence in the past. The question was if they had witnessed murder as well. When they were first questioned about the death, it was about 4 months later. The older child, then only 4 years old, knew that his mother had died. He claimed that the father had given her a black eye (the child had witnessed the father giving the mother a black eye a few weeks previous to the death, as reported at the time to authorities) and then shot her with a gun. The woman had not been shot, but the child's statement may have reflected the child's idea of how someone is typically killed. The younger child, only 2.5 years old, could not report anything of relevance. Neither child testified at trial. The man was convicted, but 8 years later, the conviction was overturned on appeal due to a technicality concerning the judge's instructions to the jury. The children, now 12 and 10 years old, were re-interviewed. They now stated that they had witnessed the murder, and both children provided considerable detail. Specifically, they claimed to have witnessed the murder while hiding under the kitchen table, from which they said they could look down the hall into the bedroom, where, they alleged, their mother had been strangled by a man. (Poignantly, they did not remember that the man was their father, despite the older child having said it was the father 8 years previously.) However, police investigation revealed that it was not possible to view the bedroom from under the kitchen table, and the grandmother admitted talking to the children about her version of her daughter's unfortunate death. Although it is very likely that the father murdered the mother (a new jury convicted him again, despite the children's statements not being presented, and there was strong circumstantial evidence linking him to the crime), were the boys accurate or did they suffer from false memory of actually witnessing her death? As discussed in later sections, empirical research by psychologists is relevant to answering these questions.

California case

Back in the 1970s, allegedly, there were several rings of paedophiles sexually abusing children in Bakersfield. When suspicions of the alleged crimes were reported to authorities, some of the interviews of the children were quite leading, as documented on videotape. Several of the videotapes were then lost: One videotaped interview was found years later in the garage of a law enforcement official who, quite shockingly, had been murdered by one of the attorneys! For other children, the exact nature of the interviews remains unknown, since no recordings were made, as far as anyone now knows. The prosecutions of the alleged sex ring members led to many jail sentences.

As the psychological research on children's suggestibility rediscovered situations in which children could be demonstrated to make false reports (e.g., Ceci & Bruck, 1993; Garvin, Malpass, & Wood, 1998), and as it became apparent that some of the techniques likely employed in the Bakersfield interviews arguably could have led to false reports, many of the convictions were overturned. However, one man in particular, John Stohl, remained in prison for nearly 19 years.

A group of attorneys, based in California, who were part of a larger group of advocates calling their work the "Innocence Project", decided to file a habeas corpus petition on John Stohl's behalf. They had sent investigators out to interview the children (all males and now adults) who had testified against Stohl. Four of these five males immediately confessed that they had lied on the stand and that they had been coerced by the Bakersfield authorities into making false statements. They said they always knew their testimony was a lie, and that they had not had false memories of abuse. However, the remaining child – again, now an adult – still claimed to have been sexually abused by John Stohl, and wanted Mr Stohl to remain in jail even longer. This one boy was John Stohl's son. He was the youngest of the boys at the time of the arrests (6 years old at that time), and perhaps therefore the one most susceptible to false memory.

Nevertheless, the story is more complicated than it first might sound. Of potential importance, before the allegations were made, John Stohl had rented part of his property to a known sexual offender, who had a long history of paedophilia. The original claims made by John Stohl's son were against this paedophile, who had access to the boys when they all played at Stohl's house. It is possible that there was truth to the allegations of sexual abuse, but that through overly suggestive interviewing of the children, the allegations spread to Mr Stohl. However, one might wonder why Mr Stohl, the recently divorced father of a 6-year-old boy, would rent part of his property to a paedophile.

In any case, at the habeas corpus hearing, the four former child witnesses testified as to Mr Stohl's innocence. The young Mr Stohl testified to his father's guilt. A psychologist testifying for the court, rather than for any one side (a highly unusual situation in American criminal courts), provided relevant scientific findings, not only on child suggestibility but also on recantation of abuse. In the end, the court decided to release Mr Stohl.

Regarding false memory, we will never know whether Mr Stohl's son developed a false memory about abuse by his own father. If indeed he did, this would be a form of child emotional abuse in itself, an emotional abuse that deprived him of a loving father. It is also possible that Mr Stohl sexually abused his son but not the other boys. On the other hand, is it possible that the other four boys had a false memory of not having been abused? Research indicates that males are more likely than females to categorize acts of sexual abuse as non-abusive (Widom & Morris, 1997), and thus there is the potential for them to redefine sexual acts as non-crimes. Moreover, there is a suggestion in the literature that males, on average, may have more difficulty than females in retrieving early emotional events from memory (Davis, 1999) and to be somewhat less accurate in long-term memory of childhood sexual abuse, perhaps due to avoidance of thinking about or discussing humiliating incidents (Alexander et al., 2005). Certainly, if children and adults can have false memories of traumatic events such as torture and murder, there is also the likelihood that they can have false memories of having not been abused when in fact they were. In the Stohl case, like so many others, we may never know the truth.

RESEARCH ON AND PSYCHOLOGICAL MECHANISMS UNDERLYING FALSE MEMORY

If it is possible to have a false memory, even for traumatic events such as those just described, how do such memories arise? As mentioned earlier, scientists gained an important tool in the study of false memory when Loftus and Pickrell (1995) published their "Lost in the mall" research. In the original study, the researchers contacted parents of college students, asking the parents to describe true events that had happened to their children around the age of 4 or 5 years, as well as asking the parents if the children had ever been lost in a mall in childhood (the false event). The parents who indicated their child had never been lost in a mall in early childhood were then recruited to help the researchers construct a credible story of a lost-in-the-mall experience.

The college students were then interviewed about the true events but also, interspersed among the true events, about the one false event. Loftus and Pickrell reported that approximately 25% of the college students affirmed, in part or in whole, the false event. Some participants elaborated on the false event over time and rated the event as quite memorable. However, overall, the false memories were rated as less detailed and less vivid compared to memories of the true childhood events.

Of note, the rate of false memory is substantially lower when only full false memories are considered. In the Loftus and Pickrell study, partial false memories included when participants indicated that they did not believe they had ever experienced the childhood lost-in-the-mall event. But if the participant then provided hypothesized information (e.g., "Although I do not believe this ever happened, if it did happen, probably X, Y and Z occurred"), this was scored as a partial false memory. Arguably, it is not false memory at all, and one would doubt that such statements would pass muster from a legal perspective.

In any case, some adults do provide full false memories, including that of a childhood hospital stay, spilling a punch bowl at a wedding, and an animal attack (e.g., Hyman & Billings, 1998; Porter, Birt, Yuille, & Lehman, 2000). However, Pezdek has argued that when an event is implausible – and more like child sexual abuse – it is much more difficult to induce false memory in adults. In their important research, Pezdek, Finger, and Hodge (1997) used the "Lost in the mall" methodology but asked additionally about receiving an enema in childhood. Although about 20% of the adults affirmed the lost-in-the-mall scenario, none of the adults affirmed receiving an enema in childhood when they had, in fact, not received one. Thus, there was not a single false memory about the enema. Although the Pezdek et al. work does not indicate that false memory about traumatic events is impossible, it does serve as appropriate warning to researchers, as well as legal professionals, not to overgeneralize previous findings.

What psychological mechanisms underlie false memory? Loftus and her associates (e.g., Hyman & Loftus, 2002), as well as others, have pointed to source monitoring errors, as, for example, when perceptual detail is added to an imagined event and then the source of the vivid imagination is confused with reality, as well as pointing to familiarity misattributions. Loftus explains that the mere mention of the false event lays down a memory trace. As the person thinks about the event, memories of other similar events are activated. Over time, the "tag" that indicated that the false information was based on suggestion begins to fade. Components of the true memories then become combined with the false information to form a false memory. Moreover, if events are made more plausible, such that inferences from semantic memory better support false recollection, false-memory acceptance may be enhanced (Mazzoni, Loftus, & Kirsch, 2001; Pezdek & Hodge, 1999).

Imagery and false memory

For false memories to exist, information from external sources or self-imagined events must be incorrectly identified as personal, real-life experience. Exactly how this comes about we do not fully know, but mental imagery has been identified as a factor that facilitates the development of false memories, and the results of several lines of research suggest that imagery may be a core factor in false-memory generation. Several studies show that when people are encouraged to visualize or imagine a suggested event, the likelihood of mistaking implanted stories for real ones increases (Garry, Manning, Loftus, & Sherman, 1996; Hyman & Pentland, 1996; Mazzoni & Memon, 2003; Thomas & Loftus, 2002). Most people report that event memory is accompanied by, or even consists of, spontaneous visual memory images, but visual imagery is not just reproductive in the sense that previously perceived scenes and events are generated to the inner eye. Novel images may also be generated from verbal descriptions of non-experienced events (Kosslyn, 1994). It is quite likely that stories told or read may lead to mental images of the described event, and when this process is repeated, the memory of imaged events is strengthened and is at some later time misidentified as the memory of a real event. Experiments with modern brain-imaging techniques, such as PET and fMRI, have shown that real and imagined perceptual experiences activate overlapping brain areas within the auditory (Halpern, Zatorre, Bouffard, & Johnson, 2004; Yoo, Lee & Choi, 2001), tactile (Yoo, Freeman, McCarthy, & Jolesz, 2003) and visual (Cabeza & Nyberg, 2000; Knauff, Kassubek, Mulack, & Greenlee, 2000; Mellet, Petit, Mazoyer, Denis, & Tzourio, 1998) modalities. In the visual domain, the overlap is substantial in perceptual processing areas, at least beyond visual area 1 (V1). A recent study by Ganis, Thompson, and Kosslyn (2004) indicates some degree of overlap in all brain regions activated during on-line perception, and that the degree of overlap increases towards higher processing areas in the frontal and parietal cortex. Such results strongly suggest that visual perception and visual memory, in the form of imagery, draw on the same neural circuits. It is therefore not surprising that memories of verbally or conceptually constructed visual images and memories of real events, stored and retrieved by the same neural processes, are sometimes confused. Moreover, a recent study by Gonsalves et al. (2004) provides neural evidence from an fMRI study that imagining is associated with false memories, at least of visualized objects. Perhaps fMRI studies of the future will be able to identify brain regions associated with imagery involved in false memories of entire events.

Social influences on false memory

From an everyday memory perspective, memories are often reconstructed in the context of and in discussions with other people, as the examples reported in this chapter show. We interact with other people frequently, and this has been proven to affect, in a complex way, our abilities to remember (see Chapter 5). The examples of real-life false memories we described earlier reveal reports of entire events that did not occur: some of these false memories may have been formed through social interaction. The concept of false memories has also been applied to other memory errors, as stated in the introduction. Laboratory research on social influences on memory errors can enhance our understanding of false memories of real-life events that in fact have not occurred.

It is important here, however, to differentiate between two different types of social influence. One type of social influence is where a person has a specific agenda to provide false information. In regard to research studies, this can be referred to as a "social contagion paradigm". It may mimic some legal situations where an interviewer is so biased as to present forceful misinformation to a witness. The other type of social influence is when people recall information together, with each presumably trying to be as accurate as possible. In discussing relevant research, we refer to the latter as "collaborative memory".

In a study of social contagion, Meade and Roediger (2002) investigated whether memory errors could be transmitted between people (see also Roediger, Meade, & Bergman, 2001; Walther, Bless, Strack, Rackstraw, Wagner, & Werth, 2002). Their general approach was to use a confederate and an "actual" participant at encoding and recall. The procedure included the viewing of six scenes, followed by dyadic recall – that is, recall by two people. In the dyadic recall setting, the confederate generated false memories in specific ways (the task was always to recall items from the scenes). The dyadic task was followed by individual recall and finally a (individual) recognition test. Thus, the purpose was to explore if memory errors were incorporated into the "actual" participants' individual memory recall (the session after dyadic recall). The results clearly indicated that participants incorporated errors into their own individual recall even if they were warned that the confederates might have made "mistakes". The memory-error social contagion effect was, however, decreased by this warning. It was also shown that the confederate had to be an actual individual since contagion protocols (the participant was given a protocol from an earlier experiment, i.e., a proto- col from a simulated confederate) did not result in the same contagion effect as did misinformation from living confederates. Thus, the main conclusion was that memory errors could be mediated by social influences.

The social contagion effect obtained reveals how easy it is to implant errors into the memories of a group member. However, the study did not concern self-experienced events, and thus generalization of the results of this study to everyday memory may be hazardous. But speculatively, the social contagion effect might reflect how easy it is for a biased interviewer who presents mis- information to a witness to replace or reconstruct the memories of interest even though the intention is to avoid such contamination.

Basden, Basden, Thomas, and Souphasith (1998) focused upon how collaboration, as opposed to social contagion, affects memory errors. These researchers used a false-memory task that is quite different from the types of false-memory situations referred to earlier in this chapter concern- ing actual legal cases. The false-memory task used is often called the Deese–Roediger–McDermott (DRM) task. It involves presenting people with lists of semantically related words, such as pin, thread, cloth, sewing, and then determining if the false memory of hearing "needle" occurs (a non-presented critical word). This type of false memory is in fact a highly robust psychological phenomenon. It is arguably quite different from false memory for entire events that did not occur, such as murder and torture, but it is nevertheless of great interest. To the extent that both types of false memories may result from changes in the criteria used to evaluate what is a memory and what is not, there may be some similarities.

Basden et al. used the DRM task to study effects of collaboration on false-memory formation. The data revealed negative effects of collaboration on memory. Basden et al. therefore showed that false-memory effects could be extended to collaborative recall. Overall intrusions were also shown to be greater for the collaborative group's recall compared to individual recall.

However, two articles provide the opposite picture (Ross, Spencer, Linardatos, Lam, & Perunovic, 2004; Takahashi, in press), and even suggest that one of the benefits of collaboration is that the group filters out wrong answers. Takahashi argues for a reality monitoring process that is accentuated by collaboration. The consequence of an enhanced reality monitoring process is a stricter criterion (i.e., a decrease in the production of false memories).

Principe and Ceci (2002) "combined" the two approaches discussed above in a novel way. Preschoolers' reports of an archaeological dig were studied. The preschoolers were divided into three groups. One-third witnessed the dig including two target activities; one-third consisted of classmates who witnessed the dig excluding the two target activities; and one control group did not witness the event and were not classmates. Second, the preschoolers were interviewed in two different ways; one neutral and one suggestive. The classmates who did not see the two target events nevertheless reported that they saw the target activities, especially in the suggestive interview condition. Thus, this study reveals that memory errors about the event were clearly affected by (1) peer conversation and (2) interview "style" (a social contagion effect).

From an experimental perspective, false memories and other memory errors can be transferred by a confederate (i.e., evidenced in the social contagion paradigm); enhanced by collaboration regarding semantically related material (e.g., in the DRM task); reduced due to a collaborative "filter out" process; and increased by peer conversation of non-experienced events. However, collaborative memory experiments with more complex material in a more "ecological" setting have not necessarily shown these effects.

Do these empirical findings tell us something about the false memory examples we reported earlier? They might if we also consider how members reflect upon the false recall that they have produced. First, in some studies even when groups are more accurate than individuals about events the participants witnessed (Clark, Stephenson, & Kniveton, 1990; Stephenson, Abrams, Wagner, & Wade, 1986), groups were also more overconfident in inaccurate answers. Thus, groups were overall more confident that a group answer was correct even if it was incorrect. Warnick and Sanders (1990) and Yarmey (1992) did not, however, find this overconfidence: When the group discussion was followed by individual recall (Yarmey, 1992), more false recalls were produced via individual recall compared to group recall. Yarmey and Morris (1995) even concluded that group recall minimizes the number of false recalls.

Relevant to legal cases, but from the perspective of jurors rather than eyewitnesses, in a study by Pritchard and Keenan (2002), it was shown that confidence in memories before a deliberation affected whether jurors changed their verdict, rather than the deliberation per se. They showed that deliberation only slightly improved memory (e.g., corrected errors), and did not produce more false memories. If a verdict changed as a consequence of the deliberation, it was not due to the accuracy of memories before the deliberation – it was due to the low confidence in memories. Furthermore, Allwood, Granhag, and Johansson (2003) showed that if individual recall and confidence ratings preceded group recall and confidence ratings, lower overconfidence was obtained compared to that in the individual recall session. They showed that items with different answers from group members at individual recall were given lower confidence ratings at a dyadic recall. Taken together, degree of confidence in specific memories seems to determine, at least in part, if social influence will affect the individual (i.e., if the individual will stick to the initially believed memory trace or will incorporate a new memory).

Thus, these experimental data suggest how memories, especially memories with low confidence, are reconstructed by social influence and might become the memories that are in fact believed to have occurred. The Robinson case presented earlier reveals that the three male participants made memory errors about the event. Speculatively, this special event was probably discussed among the participants, and their memory for details (items) within the cave experience about which they were uncertain (low confidence) might easily have been reconstructed in discussions to fit their schemata.

Individual differences in false-memory susceptibility

Researchers have uncovered several individual-difference variables that make people more prone to false-memory formation. One of them is age, with young children being more susceptible than older children or adults. Another concerns forms of psychopathology and relational problems. It is possible that, at least in part, such vulnerability derives from lack of confidence in one's memory, as just discussed regarding collaborative recall. There may be other factors at play as well.

Age differences in false-memory susceptibility

It is perhaps not surprising that, if adults are subject to false-memory formation, children would be, too. In one of the first studies of false memory with children, Ceci and colleagues (Ceci, Crotteau, Smith, & Loftus, 1993) asked 3- and 5-year-olds if the children had ever experienced a set of true and false events. The children were told that their parents had been consulted about the list. Approximately 30–40% of the 3-year-olds affirmed the false events, and some provided elaborate detail. In a second study, when the instructions were made even more strongly suggestive, such as telling children that their parents said all the events had been experienced by the children, telling the children to make pictures in their heads of the events, and telling them it was a game and to pretend the events occurred, the effects were strengthened and increased over repeated interviews. Schaaf, Alexander, and Goodman (2005) found that when children were repeatedly questioned, within the same interview session, about true and false events, 3-year-olds compared to 5-year-olds more quickly assented to the false events, and at times provided false detail.

However, of forensic significance, research indicates that children are less prone to false memory when the false information concerns negative events (Ceci et al., 1993; Schaaf et al., 2005), which are of most concern in typical forensic situations. Moreover, Quas et al. (1999) found that when American and New Zealand children were questioned about a false event (i.e., a fictitious nose surgery), although many young children at first affirmed the false event, when the specifics of the surgery were described, almost all of the children then accurately denied that they had experienced the event. Cultural differences were also uncovered: Virtually all the children who continued to affirm the false event were from New Zealand. This suggests social factors at play. Quas et al. hypothesized that the New Zealand children, in contrast to their American agemates, had been trained to be more polite and not to disagree with adults.

Why are young children likely, on average, to be more susceptible to false-memory effects? There are probably multiple factors at work. Developmental theory would predict that young children have greater difficulty coordinating two representations (e.g., Case, 1992; Fischer, 1980; Piaget, 1954), one representation being of the reality of their experiences and the other of false suggestions by adults. Younger children are also more intimidated when questioned by adults, which can make them more susceptible to suggestion, perhaps by having less confidence in their memories (e.g., Carter, Bottoms, & Levine, 1996; Goodman, Bottoms, Schwartz-Kenney, & Rudy, 1991). Moreover, young children are more likely to think that events are plausible, including bizarre events (note their belief in the Tooth Fairy!). In a recent study by Schaaf et al. (2005), it was found that young children at times answer false event questions based on a true experience in their lives. For example, if the researcher asked about a trip to Disneyland (when the parent reported to the researcher that the child had never been there), some children affirmed the trip and then described their trip to the Disney store, which they had visited. It appeared that the children interpreted the words (Disneyland) to fit their experience (Disney store). Finally, as explained later, many young children may lack the metacognitive skills needed to counter false-memory formation.

Mental health and relational predictors

Not everyone is equally susceptible to false memory. Early in the scientific study of this phenomenon, Hyman and Billings (1998) reported that adults who score high on dissociative tendencies were more likely to fall for false-memory manipulations. Dissociation is the term used for the mental process of removing oneself psychologically from trauma or pain. Although people normally have "dissociative moments", more extreme tendencies toward dissociation, which become, in effect, personality traits, are believed to result from chronic trauma in childhood (Eisen & Goodman, 1999; Putnam, 1997). Dissociation as a personality trait is associated with gaps in autobiographical memory (e.g., Goodman et al., 2003), as well as with other symptoms (e.g., feelings that experiences are not real, inattention to ongoing events).

Given the fact that many Satanic ritual abuse cases uncovered in the Bottoms et al. (1996) survey involved individuals who initially suffered from depression or other mental health problems, we suspect that such problems may increase susceptibility to false memory, as well as placing such individuals at particular risk if certain clinical or forensic techniques are used.

However, when Qin and Goodman (1999) examined predictors of false-memory formation in adults, they found that parental adult attachment (Hazan & Shaver, 1990) predicted false memory better than did scores on the standard dissociation measure, the Dissociative Experiences Scale (DES). Parental adult attachment, which derives from Bowlby's Attachment Theory (Bowlby, 1980), refers to the types of interpersonal relationship styles that adults (in this case, the adult participants' parents) have adopted. For instance, dismissing avoidant individuals tend to express less need for others and downplay negative emotions associated with loved ones. Anxious individuals tend to express high need for others and anxiety about social relationships with loved ones. In the Qin and Goodman study, adults whose parents scored high on insecure attachment (specifically fearful avoidance) were more susceptible to false memory.

What could underlie these findings of mental health and relational predictors of false-memory susceptibility? One hint comes from Qin and Goodman's (1999) study. People who have less stringent criteria for what they are willing to call a true memory may be more susceptible. Qin and Goodman found that there was a correlation between false memory on the DRM task and false memory in the lost-in-the-mall paradigm in terms of the criterion used in both tasks to indicate that a false memory was a true memory. People who have mental health or relational issues may use a less stringent criterion because of factors such as more memory gaps, less confidence in their memories, and/or greater nervousness and desire to please in social situations (but see Wilkinson & Hyman, 1998). Further research is needed on these possibilities.

Guarding against false memories

Although there has been considerable research on false memory, there has been much less on the psychological mechanisms that guard against false-memory formation. However, recent theorizing and research of false-memory rejection provide enlightenment. Some theorists propose that there are automatic mental processes that help protect against false memory. Specifically, based on fuzzy trace theory, Brainerd and Reyna (2002) propose that a mechanism termed "recollection rejection" allows the suppression of false reports that are gist consistent with events that did occur. According to their view, a verbatim memory trace of a true event is compared to the gist of the false event, and (hopefully) the verbatim memory then supports accurate reporting. This is viewed as an automatic process requiring little cognitive control. In contrast, Koriat, Goldsmith, Schneider, and Nakash-Dura (2001) discuss conscious control processes related to metamemory that have potential to explain false-memory rejection. Specifically, they propose that there is a trade-off between accuracy and completeness of reporting that can be modified using conscious control processes, although this trade-off is not always successfully accomplished by young children.

Providing a somewhat different twist on the control processes approach, Ghetti (2004; Ghetti & Alexander, 2004) has argued that there are certain metacognitive mechanisms that can help guard against false memories. In particular, use of certain memorability heuristics, specifically the "memorability-based strategy", is one such mechanism. Put simply, this is the principle that "If that had happened, I would remember it. Thus, if I do not remember it, it did not occur". However, young children do not appear to utilize this strategy successfully on their own.

To investigate the memorability-based strategy, in a recent false-memory study that included 5-, 7-, and 9-year-olds and adults, Ghetti and Alexander (2004) manipulated event salience, plausibility, and recency. An example of a highly salient false event was as follows: "Once you took a trip to the Grand Canyon with your family. You drove through the desert, which you thought was very cool. But what you really liked was that the Grand Canyon was so deep. You kept saying that it was so deep". A low salient false event was, for example, a summer craft class. An example of a high-plausible false event from the study was, for instance, the above-mentioned trip to the Grand Canyon, whereas a low-plausible event was being attacked by a big black bird that landed on the person's head. Recency was manipulated by telling participants that the events happened when they were 3 years old versus 1 year before to the interview (e.g., age 6 years for 7-year-olds, age 8 years for 9-year-olds; although for adults, age 8 years was indicated).

Results of the study showed that, overall, the 5-year-olds were significantly more likely to affirm false memories than were the older age groups: No significant differences in false-memory acceptance were found among the other ages. Moreover, relevant to mechanisms underlying developmental differences in false memory, Ghetti and Alexander also demonstrated that older children and adults were more likely to reject false events based on event salience than were younger children (e.g., 5-year-olds). That is, events that had been judged by an independent sample as highly salient (e.g., the Grand Canyon trip) were less likely to be affirmed than events that had been judged of low salience (e.g., the summer craft class) by all age groups except the youngest children. Ghetti and Alexander further found that high-recency false events were more likely to be rejected than low-recency false events. Consistent with prediction, recency moderated the effect of salience. That is, generally speaking, regardless of age, high-salient and low-salient false events were rejected at about the same rates when the events were described as having occurred early in childhood, but high-salient events were rejected at higher rates than low-salient events when the false event was said to have occurred more recently. Thus, even the 5-year-olds showed some appreciation for the fact that it is hard to remember even salient events from early childhood. Given the emphasis others have placed on plausibility in regard to false-memory acceptance, it is of interest that no significant effect of plausibility emerged. However, plausibility did affect confidence levels, such that low-plausibility/high-salient events were rejected with the greatest confidence by all age groups.

What can explain these developmental findings? Ghetti and Alexander (2004) argue that young children are less likely than older children and adults to use the memorability-based strategy, consistent with the fact that young children are unlikely to successfully utilize other sophisticated memory strategies (Bjorklund, 1997). Instead, young children only reject false events under favourable conditions (i.e., conditions that would lead to high levels of true memory). In contrast, older children can often successfully rely on the memorability-based strategy, as do adults (Strack & Bless, 1994).

There are, however, certain beliefs, sometimes encouraged in clinical practice or elsewhere, that can surely dampen the use of such heuristics. One is likely to be the belief that memories of trauma can be repressed. If one believes that trauma memory can be repressed such that an individual cannot readily access their recollection of trauma experiences, clearly this belief could counter the memorability heuristic. Also, if one suffers from gaps in autobiographical memory, as reported by some individuals with self-reported childhood trauma histories, these gaps may diminish reliance on the memorability heuristic. Another relevant issue concerns what is plausible to an individual. For example, in the case of Satanic ritual abuse claims, false memory may be more likely in those who believe in the devil and that all bad things that happen in the world are due to evil. Such individuals may therefore feel that the devil must be behind child sexual abuse, and that anyone who would do such acts to a child has to be Satanic. In this case, the idea that organized cults of Satanists are sexually abusing children, and perhaps had abused the adult him- or herself, becomes more plausible.

CONCLUSIONS AND IMPLICATIONS

Our review of the false-memory research literature, and our description of several actual cases, leads us to assert several applied and theoretical implications.

First, we believe there are several different routes to false-memory formation. Some routes may be self-generated. Other routes involve highly suggestive or coercive techniques. In any case, important contributors to false-memory formation include that the individual accepts that the event was plausible, that the individual develops a mental image of the event, and that the individual does not apply optimal source monitoring to the "memory". These factors may contribute to other types of autobiographical memory errors as well.

Second, our review of research on social influence reveals how false memories might be constructed, or rather reconstructed, by conversation. The social contagion and the collaboration paradigms are useful for studying how interviewers or confederates can affect memories. These paradigms have also shown that conversations between friends and group members, who have no explicit intentions to contaminate memories, adversely affect people's recollections. However, collaboration data also suggest that social interactions can filter out wrong answers, and thus decrease memory errors. These contradictory findings might be explained by the different settings studied, but also by people's confidence in their specific memories. Social influence appears to be most potent for memories that are held with lower confidence. Memories about which one is sure are not as easily affected by social influence (Bless & Strack, 1998).

Third, there are important individual differences in tendencies toward memory errors, including false-memory errors. Age is an important individual-difference factor, but additionally, there is typically substantial variation within any one age group. Researchers have begun to identify some of these individual-difference factors. Dissociative tendencies (which can be heightened by childhood trauma experiences), lack of confidence in one's memory, relational patterns, and gaps in autobiographical memory have been identified as predictors of false-memory susceptibility.

Fourth, there are mechanisms that guard against false memory. For instance, metacognitive strategies can be used to resist false-memory formation. Understanding the psychological mechanisms that underlie false-memory rejection is crucial for both theory and application. For example, regarding the latter, to the extent that such strategies can be taught to children, forensic interviewers and others might help children guard against false memories.

Finally, we end with a comment relevant to our introduction. Specifically, based on scientific research, we can not only learn fascinating and important things about the human mind, but we can also hopefully reduce miscarriages of justice.

ACKNOWLEDGEMENTS

We thank the Center for Advanced Study, Norwegian National Academy of Letters and Science for their support. Thanks also go to Kenneth Gnoss of the Sonoma County District Attorneys Office in California. We are also grateful to Dr James Ost for helpful comments on an earlier draft of this chapter.

REFERENCES

Alexander, K., Quas, J., Goodman, G.S., Ghetti, S., Edelstein, R., Redlich, A., Cordon, I., & Jones, D.P.H. (2005). Traumatic impact predicts long-term memory of documented child sexual abuse. *Psychological Science, 16*, 33–40.

Allwood, C.M., Granhag, P.A., & Johansson, M. (2003). Increased realism in eyewitness confidence judgments: The effect of dyadic collaboration. *Applied Cognitive Psychology, 17*, 545–561.

Bartlett, F.C. (1932). *Remembering: An experimental and social study*. Cambridge, UK: Cambridge University Press.

Basden, B.H., Basden, D.R., Thomas, R.L. III, & Souphasith, S. (1998). Memory distortion in group recall. *Current Psychology, 16*, 225–246.

Bjorklund, D. (1997). The development of memory strategies. In N. Cowan (Ed.), *The development of memory in childhood* (pp. 201–247). Hove, UK: Psychology Press.

Bless, H., & Strack, F. (1998). Social influence on memory: Evidence and speculations. In V. Yzerbyt, G. Lories, & B. Dardenne (Eds.), *Metacognition: Cognitive and social dimensions* (pp. 90–106). New York: Sage.

Bottoms, B.L., Shaver, P.R., & Goodman, G.S. (1996). Allegations of ritualistic and religion-related child abuse. *Law and Human Behavior, 20*, 1–34.

Bowlby, J. (1980). *Attachment and loss*. New York: Basic Books.

Brainerd, C., & Reyna, V. (2002). Recollection rejection: How children edit their false memories. *Developmental Psychology, 38*, 156–172.

Cabeza, R., & Nyberg, L. (2000). Imaging cognition II: An empirical review of 275 PET and fMRI studies. *Journal of Cognitive Neuroscience, 12*, 1–47.

Carter, C., Bottoms, B.L., & Levine, M. (1996). Linguistic and socioemotional influences on the accuracy of children's reports. *Law and Human Behavior, 20*, 335–358.

Case, R. (1992). Neo-Piagetian theories of child development. In R. Sternberg & C. Berg (Eds.), *Intellectual development* (pp. 161–196). New York: Cambridge University Press.

Ceci, S.J., & Bruck, M. (1993). Suggestibility of the child witness: A historical review and synthesis. *Psychological Bulletin, 113*, 403–439.

Ceci, S.J., Crotteau, M., Smith, E., & Loftus, E.F. (1993). Repeatedly thinking about non-events. *Consciousness and Cognition, 3*, 388–407.

Clancy, S. (2005). *Abducted: How people come to believe they were kidnapped by aliens*. Cambridge, MA: Harvard University Press.

Clark, N.K., Stephenson, G.M., & Kniveton, B.H. (1990). Social remembering: Quantitative aspects of individual and collaborative remembering by police officers and students. *British Journal of Psychology, 81*, 73–94.

Davis, P. (1999). Gender differences in autobiographical memory for childhood emotional experiences. *Journal of Personality and Social Psychology, 76*, 498–510.

Deese, J. (1959). On the prediction of occurrence of particular verbal intrusions in immediate recall. *Journal of Experimental Psychology, 58*, 17–22.

Eisen, M., & Goodman, G.S. (1999). Trauma, memory, and suggestibility in children. *Development and Psychopathology, 10*, 717–738.

Fischer, K.W. (1980). A theory of cognitive development: The control and construction of hierarchies of skills. *Psychological Review, 87*, 477–531.

Ganis, G., Thompson, W.L., & Kosslyn, S.M. (2004). Brain areas underlying visual mental imagery and visual perception: An fMRI study. *Cognitive Brain Research, 20*, 226–241.

Garry, M., Manning, C.G., Loftus, E.F., & Sherman, S.J. (1996). Imagination inflation: Imagining a childhood event inflates confidence that it occurred. *Psychonomic Bulletin and Review, 3*, 208–214.

Garvin, S., Malpass, R., & Wood, J. (1998). More than suggestion: Effect of interviewing techniques from the McMartin Preschool case. *Journal of Applied Psychology, 83*, 347–359.

Ghetti, S. (2004). Memory for nonoccurrences: The role of metacognition. *Journal of Memory and Language, 48*, 722–739.

Ghetti, S., & Alexander, K. (2004). "If it happened, I would remember it": Strategic use of event memorability in rejection of false autobiographical events. *Child Development, 75*, 542–561.

Gonsalves, B., Reber, P., Gitelman, D., Parrish, T., Mesulam, M., & Paller, K. (2004). Neural evidence that vivid imagining can lead to false remembering. *Psychological Science, 15*, 655–660.

Goodman, G.S. (1980). Picture memory: How the action schema affects retention. *Cognitive Psychology, 12*, 473–495.

Goodman, G.S., Bottoms, B.L., Schwartz-Kenney, B., & Rudy, L. (1991). Children's memory for a stressful event: Improving children's reports. *Journal of Narrative and Life History, 1*, 69–99.

Goodman, G.S., Ghetti, S., Quas, J.A., Edelstein, R., Alexander, K., Cordon, I., & Jones, D.P.H. (2003). A prospective study of memory for child sexual abuse: New findings relevant to the repressed memory controversy. *Psychological Science, 14*, 113–118.

Halpern, A.R., Zatorre, R.J., Bouffard, M., & Johnson, J.A. (2004). Behavioral and neural correlates of perceived and imagined musical timbre. *Neuropsychologia, 42*, 1281–1292.

Hazan, C., & Shaver, P.R. (1990). Love and work: An attachment-theoretical perspective. *Journal of Personality and Social Psychology, 59*, 270–280.

Hyman, I., & Billings, F.J. (1998). Individual differences in the creation of false childhood memories, *Memory, 6*, 1–20.

Hyman, I., & Loftus, E.F. (2002). False childhood memories and eyewitness memory errors. In M. Eisen, J. Quas, & G.S. Goodman (Eds.), *Memory and suggestibility in the forensic interview* (pp. 63–84). Mahwah, NJ: Lawrence Erlbaum Associates, Inc.

Hyman, I.E. Jr, & Pentland, J. (1996). The role of mental imagery in the creation of false childhood memories. *Journal of Memory and Language, 35*, 101–117.

Knauff, M., Kassubek, J., Mulack, T., & Greenlee, M.W. (2000). Cortical activation evoked by visual mental imagery as measured by fMRI. *NeuroReport, 11*, 3957–3962.

Koriat, A., Goldsmith, M., & Pansky, A. (2000). Toward a psychology of memory accuracy. *Annual Review of Psychology*, *51*, 481–537.

Koriat, A., Goldsmith, M., Schneider, W., & Nakash-Dura, M. (2001). The credibility of children's testimony: Can children control the accuracy of their memory reports? *Journal of Experimental Child Psychology*, *79*, 405–437.

Kosslyn, S.M. (1994). *Image and brain*. Cambridge, MA: MIT Press.

Loftus, E.F. (1979). *Eyewitness memory*. Cambridge, MA: Harvard University Press.

Loftus, E.F. (1996). Memory distortion and false memory creation. *Bulletin of the American Academy of Psychology and Law*, *24*, 281–295.

Loftus, E.F., & Pickrell, J.E. (1995). The formation of false memories. *Psychiatric Annals*, *25*, 720–725.

Mazzoni, G., Loftus, E.F., & Kirsch, I. (2001). Changing beliefs about implausible autobiographical events: A little plausibility goes a long way. *Journal of Experimental Psychology: Applied*, *7*, 51–59.

Mazzoni, G., & Memon, A. (2003). Imagination can create false autobiographical memories. *Psychological Science*, *14*, 186–188.

Meade, L.M., & Roediger, H.L. III (2002). Explorations in the social contagion of memory. *Memory and Cognition*, *30*, 995–1009.

Mellet, E., Petit, L., Mazoyer, B., Denis, M., & Tzourio, N. (1998). Reopening the mental imagery debate: Lessons from functional anatomy. *Neuroimage*, *8*, 129–139.

Neisser, U. (1967). *Cognitive psychology*. East Norwalk, CT: Appleton-Century-Crofts.

Pezdek, K., Finger, K., & Hodge, D. (1997). Planting false childhood memories. *Psychological Science*, *8*, 437–441.

Pezdek, K., & Hodge, D. (1999). Planting false childhood memories in children: The role of event plausibility. *Child Development*, *70*, 887–895.

Piaget, J. (1954) *The construction of reality in the child*. New York: Ballantine.

Porter, S., Birt, A.R., Yuille, J.C., & Lehman, D.R. (2000). Negotiating false memories: Interviewer and rememberer characteristics relate to memory distortion. *Psychological Science*, *11*, 507–510.

Porter, S., Spencer, L., & Birt, A. (2003). Blinded by emotion? Effect of the emotionality of a scene on susceptibility to false memories. *Canadian Journal of Behavioural Science*, *35*, 165–175.

Principe, G., & Ceci, S.J. (2002). "I saw it with my own ears": The effects of peer conversation on preschoolers' reports of nonexperienced events. *Journal of Experimental Child Psychology*, *83*, 1–25

Pritchard, M.E., & Keenan, J.M. (2002). Does jury deliberation really improve jurors' memories? *Applied Cognitive Psychology*, *16*, 589–601.

Putnam, F. (1997). *Dissociation in children and adolescents: A developmental perspective*. New York: Guilford Press.

Qin, J.J., & Goodman, G.S. (1999, November). *Individual differences and characteristics of false memory*. Psychonomics Society Convention, Los Angeles, CA.

Qin, J.J., Goodman, G.S., Bottoms, B.L., & Shaver, P.R. (1998). Repressed memories of ritualistic and religion-related abuse. In S. Lynn & K. McConkey (Eds.), *Truth in memory* (pp. 260–283). New York: Guilford Press.

Quas, J., Goodman, G.S., Bidrose, S., Pipe, M.-E., Craw, S., & Ablin, D. (1999). Emotion and memory: Children's remembering, forgetting, and suggestibility. *Journal of Experimental Child Psychology*, *72*, 235–270.

Roediger, H.L. III, & McDermott, K.B. (1995). Creating false memories:

Remembering words not presented in lists. *Journal of Experimental Psychology: Learning, Memory, and Cognition, 21*, 803–814.

Roediger, H.L. III, Meade, M.L., & Bergman, E.T. (2001). The social contagion of memory. *Psychonomic Bulletin and Review, 8*, 365–371.

Ross, M., & Buehler, R. (1994). Creative remembering. In U. Neisser & R. Fivush (Eds.), The remembering self: Construction and accuracy in self narrative. *Emory Symposium on Cognition, Vol. 6* (pp. 205–235). New York: Cambridge University Press.

Ross, M., Spencer, S.J., Linardatos, L., Lam, K.H.M., & Perunovic, M. (2004). Going shopping and identifying landmarks: Does collaboration improve older people's memory? *Applied Cognitive Psychology, 18*, 683–696.

Schaaf, J., Alexander, K., & Goodman, G.S. (2005). *Predictors of children's true and false memory*. Paper presented at the Society for Research on Child Development Meetings, Atlanta, GA.

Schacter, D. (2001). *The seven sins of memory: How the mind forgets and remembers*. Boston, MA: Houghton-Mifflin.

Schooler, J.W., & Eich, E.E. (2000). Memory for emotional events. In E. Tulving & F.I.M. Craik (Eds.), *Oxford handbook of memory* (pp. 379–394). New York: Oxford University Press.

Stephenson, G.M., Abrams, D., Wagner, W., & Wade, G. (1986). Partners in recall: Collaborative order in the recall of a police interrogation. *British Journal of Social Psychology, 25*, 341–343.

Takahashi, M., (in press). Does collaborative remembering reduce false memories? *The British Journal of Psychology*.

Thomas, A.K., & Loftus, E.F. (2002). Creating bizarre false memories through imagination. *Memory and Cognition, 30*, 423–431.

Wade, K., Garry, M., Read, J.D., & Lindsay, S. (2002). A picture is worth a thousand lies: Using false photographs to create false childhood memories. *Psychonomic Bulletin and Review, 9*, 596–603.

Walther, E., Bless, H., Strack, F., Rackstraw, P., Wagner, D., & Werth, L. (2002). Conformity effects in memory as a function of group size, dissenters and uncertainty. *Applied Cognitive Psychology, 16*, 793–810.

Warnick, D.H., & Sanders, G.S. (1990). The effect of group discussion on eyewitness accuracy. *Journal of Applied Social Psychology, 10*, 249–259.

Widom, K., & Morris, S. (1997). Accuracy of adult recollection of childhood victimization, Part 2: Childhood sexual abuse. *Psychological Assessment, 9*, 34–46.

Wilkinson, C.L., & Hyman, I.E. Jr (1998). Individual differences related to two types of memory errors: Word lists may not generalize to autobiographical memory. *Applied Cognitive Psychology, 12*, S29–S46.

Yarmey, A.D. (1992). The effect of dyadic discussion on earwitness recall. *Basic and Applied Social Psychology, 13*, 251–263.

Yarmey, A.D., & Morris, S. (1995). The effects of discussion on eyewitness memory. *Journal of Applied Social Psychology, 28*, 1637–1648.

Yoo, S.-S., Freeman, D.K., McCarthy, J.J., & Jolesz, F.A. (2003). Neural substrates of tactile memory: A functional MRI study. *NeuroReport, 14*, 581–585.

Yoo, S.-S., Lee, C.U., & Choi, B.G. (2001). Human brain mapping of auditory imagery: An event-related functional MRI study. *NeuroReport, 12*, 3045–3049.

8 Memory sensitivity in autobiographical memory

Cesare Cornoldi, Rossana De Beni and Tore Helstrup

In an everyday memory social context, autobiographical memory has a series of important functions related to how a person remembers his or her life and uses it in the present. However, both the intensity with which people engage in and enjoy reminiscing about their past, and the extent to which they rely on it, varies in different individuals. In this chapter we review some basic aspects of autobiographical memory (cf. Conway, 1990) and reminiscence (cf. Webster & Haight, 1995), focusing on what we have termed "memory sensitivity".

Memory sensitivity (MS) is a new construct (Cornoldi & De Beni, 2003) that refers to the tendency of some individuals to pay particular attention and accord particular value to their autobiographical memory, i.e., their memories of life events.

Everyday experience shows that people vary in MS. Some "memory sensitive" people like to think back to events in their life and collect elements very carefully (Habermas & Paha, 2002) that can help them to do this. Others very efficiently use their semantic memory but are opaque with respect to their autobiographical memory and, in general, do not like to re-establish details of events they have experienced.

In the first part of this chapter we examine the issues related to memory sensitivity, its role in autobiographical memory and its relationship with other functions.

In the second part, we present a research programme that explored some characteristics and implications of MS, drawing on studies carried out with the collaboration of Doctors Federica Fumagalli, Alessia Forina and Marta Malanchin. In a first study of this programme, we drew up a provisional questionnaire for finding differences in MS and we examined its relationship to autobiographical memory. On the basis of a psychometric analysis of the properties of the provisional MS Questionnaire, we then developed a second version (presented here, with slight modifications, in the Appendix) and we used it in two further studies. In particular, in the second study we tested the hypothesis that MS is affected by gender and by lifespan. In the third study we explored the relationship of MS with other cognitive systems. In this chapter we briefly review the main results of our research project without adhering strictly to the chronology of our studies.

FUNCTIONS OF REMINISCENCE AND AUTOBIOGRAPHICAL MEMORY

Autobiographical memory and reminiscence have been the object of a growing number of studies (see Conway & Pleydell-Pearce, 2000), some of which have focused not only on the functioning of autobiographical memory but also on memory functions in other psychological domains such as decision making, reasoning, problem solving, the construction of self-schemata, etc.

Autobiographical memory has traditionally been studied within a general psychological perspective. The reviewing of one's own past (here called "reminiscence") has mainly been studied among the elderly, often with a more clinical orientation. The two research traditions complement rather than contrast each other, as pointed out by Bluck and Alea (2002) and by Webster (2003). Our memory sensitivity concept may readily be conceived of as referring to a special kind of reminiscing disposition that is not related to age. In this chapter we discuss MS as a general autobiographical memory factor.

Wilson and Ross (2003), in particular, have described how autobiographical memory plays an important role in the construction of personal identity. Individuals' current self-views, beliefs, and goals influence their recollections and appraisals of former selves. In turn, people's current self-views are influenced by what they remember about their personal past, as well as how they recall earlier selves and episodes. People's reconstructed evaluations of memories, their perceived distance from past experiences, and the point of view of their recollections have implications for how the past affects the present. Nelson (2003) pointed out that this type of function is biologically and culturally rooted in human beings. Personal autobiographical memory is functionally and structurally related to the use of cultural myths and social narratives, and the relative emphasis put on the self in various cultural and social contexts influences the form and function of autobiographical memory and the need to develop a uniquely personal life narrative in those contexts. Libby and Eibach (2002) showed that a change in self-concept affects visual perspective in autobiographical memory. They showed that participants tended to use a third-person observer perspective when visualizing memories of actions that conflicted with their current self-concept. The use of autobiographical memory is also socially and contextually situated (Middleton & Brown, 2005). Pasupathi (2001) described conversational recounting of experiences as a potential mechanism by which people socially construct themselves and their worlds over their lifespan and the resulting implications for understanding adult development. Pasupathi (2001) proposed two principles that govern the conversational recounting of past events: co-construction (the joint influences of speakers and contexts on conversational reconstructions of past events) and consistency (the influence of a conversational reconstruction on subsequent memory).

The literature reviewed above has extended the consideration from autobiographical memory per se to its use and functions (e.g., Bluck & Habermas,

2000). However, the privilege given to memory with respect to other psychological functions, as happens in MS, has not been a direct object of systematic study. Research has occasionally commented on specific issues. For example, Walker, Skowronski, and Thompson (2003) observed that recollecting past events can be a source of pleasure. People's recollections of the past are often positively biased. In fact, people perceive events in their lives to be more often pleasant than unpleasant. Furthermore, the affect associated with unpleasant events fades faster than the affect associated with pleasant events. This could also be due to the fact that a negative event is no longer negative once its consequences have been overcome. The authors conclude that "autobiographical memory represents an important exception to the theoretical claim that bad is stronger than good". The affect linked to autobiographical recollection may be one, although not the sole, source of the human tendency to cultivate past memories.

MEMORY SENSITIVITY

The construct of memory sensitivity (MS), as we mentioned above, refers to the tendency of some individuals to pay particular attention and accord particular value to their autobiographical memory, i.e. to their memories of life events. Some people enjoy reminiscing about their own or shared pasts, whereas others spend little time on such activities. "To live in the past" is a commonly used catch-phrase referring to people who apparently see their lives predominantly in the perspective of their past. However, those who appear to lack a time perspective are often considered as being "shallow". A person sensitive only to his or her own private memories tends to be seen as somewhat "egocentric". A person with a proper combination of sensitivity for private *and* shared memories, on the other hand, is characterized as having "obtained life wisdom".

Memory sensitivity reflects a preference, more stable than situation-dependent memory strategies, but probably less stable than other styles, abilities or personality traits (cf. Sternberg, 1987; Zelniker & Globerson, 1989). Like other cognitive styles, MS has a developmental history, where parental MS styles probably have a heavy influence. MS styles are presumably acquired also because they are of functional importance in relation to self and social relationships and in providing relevant information in contexts of problem solving (Bluck & Alea, 2002; Pillemer, 1998; Webster, 2003).

To settle them down to sleep, most small children are told bed-time stories, and many parents also talk about forthcoming events, relating these to experiences of the recent past. This may relate to the frequently observed bedtime monologues of children, who reminiscence aloud about recent and ongoing events. Parents' ways of communicating with the child about its past will certainly be among the main determinants of individual differences in MS.

Parentally induced reminiscing contributes to the formation of the child's developing self-image. Later self-induced reminiscing activities probably help to keep one's established self-image and eventually to transform it in desirable directions. Many self-related memories are private, but several are shared with other persons. Joint reminiscence over a shared past serves important social functions, especially for communicative and group cohesion purposes.

Successful problem solving depends on efficient use of past experience, for instance in transforming unknown task elements so that the problem-solver can come to recognize the familiar aspects of the task situation (Helstrup, 2006; Raaheim, 1988). Reminiscing is a useful way of gaining access to relevant past experiences.

Since one's past encounters will certainly have met with various degrees of success, reflections upon them will have variable emotional tones. Some reminiscences re-awake unpleasant feelings; others re-awake more pleasant ones. Overall emotional tones of reminiscences are likely to be important in determining MS styles. Highly memory-sensitive people presumably enjoy reminiscing. Their past is likely to be generally in harmony with their established selves. Furthermore, opening of their pasts for renewed reflection tends to bring them closer to other persons.

Reminiscence is a kind of storytelling. With repetition, one's past acquires a schematic outline. Repeated retrievals of private and shared pasts consolidate the "stories" told by the reminiscences. Cherished stories are kept, and "retold". According to this reasoning, we might expect similar standardizations or schematizations of reminisced autobiographical memories as is observed for memories of stories in general (Alba & Hasher, 1983; Bartlett, 1932; Schank & Abelson, 1977).

Taken together, the comments in this chapter make it highly likely that there are marked individual differences as regards reminiscing engagements. We have termed this difference factor "memory sensitivity" (MS). Memory sensitivity is not purely situationally dependent, but has developed in the course of time into persistent cognitive styles with different kinds of functional importance, as pointed out above.

THE CONSTRUCTION OF A QUESTIONNAIRE TO ASSESS MS

Our study of MS started with attempts to create a tool that would be capable of capturing individual differences in MS. In this effort, we considered all the main aspects of MS. Through interviews and clinical observations we selected a set of behaviours and beliefs that typically describe the memory-sensitive individual. In the first version of the MS Questionnaire we listed 43 items, which were later reduced to 34 items with a 4-point rating scale (total score ranging between 34 and 136) in the final version. This final version, the MS Questionnaire, is presented in the Appendix.

The items of the MS Questionnaire describe the following aspects (numbers of items refer to the final version).

a   Behaviours devoted to saving memories of our life: 1, 2, 9, 21, 22, 25, 26, 30, 31, 32
b   Habits of thinking back to our past events: 3, 4, 5, 13, 29
c   Frequency and appreciation of spontaneous recollection of past events: 6, 7, 10
d   Tendency to reconsider recent life events: 8, 11
e   Intensity of memories of life events: 12, 14, 18, 27
f   Affective implications of memories: 15, 17, 20, 23
g   Autobiographical memory as a reference point: 16, 33, 34
h   Fear of forgetting life events: 19
i   Appreciation of the role of external aids in maintaining memories of past events: 24, 28

The choice of items reflects our assumption that memory sensitivity defines a coherent dimension focused on memories central to the person. Such memories should be desired to be kept in store (a,h,i), should be rehearsed and appreciated when called forth (b,c), should have consequences for one's self-image (d,e), and should refer to important episodes in the person's life (f,g).

The Questionnaire has high internal consistency (Cronbach alpha = .81 in the first study and = .86 in the second study) and high split-half reliability (Guttman's correlation = .85, n = 119). Based on a second administration after 7 months to the 90 participants of the first study, the Questionnaire also revealed good test–retest reliability (Pearson's r = .92). The high internal consistency suggests that the MS Questionnaire is actually measuring something unitary. In the following we report some results obtained using this Questionnaire.

Is MS related to memory behaviour?

Why have people developed a high MS and how is it related to memory ability? One possibility is that people high in MS have good memory and for this reason tend to use it to a larger extent. However, people with a high MS present more behaviours devoted to saving memories of their life; for this reason, another possibility is that they developed such an attention for memory and behave in such a way to preserve their memory, because they have discovered that their memory ability is poor and their memories rapidly become very weak.

In order to examine the relationship between MS and memory ability, we administered some memory tests 2 months after the administration of the MS Questionnaire to 90 senior high school students, 47 girls and 43 boys, aged between 17 and 20 (mean age = 17.76).

One multiple memory test ("Memory for recent events") tested the young-sters' memory for three shared events that had happened during the previous year: Memory test-a – the preceding *Visit* of the experimenter (2 months earlier) for the administration of the MS Questionnaire, Memory test-b – the *"Autogestione"* i.e., the week when the school was run by the students them-selves, 6 months earlier, and Memory test-c – a school *Trip* 1 year before. These events were tested by means of 23 open-ended questions, which were scored by two independent judges on a 0–3 scale.

The other memory test, the "Autobiographical Agenda", tested the vivid-ness of remote personal memories. Participants were invited to give vividness ratings on a 7-point Likert scale on 19 aspects of their life (e.g., life in the kindergarten, their first day with their bicycle, their best friend at primary school, etc.: examples are given in the Appendix).

We found significant positive correlations between the MS total score and the following two scores: memory for the *Visit* of the experimenter (Memory test-a) (Pearson's $r = .421$, $p < .001$) and the vividness ratings of remote memories in the Autobiographical Agenda ($r = .474$, $p < .001$). However, memory sensitivity did not correlate with the accuracy of the recall of the other two events, i.e. *"Autogestione"* ($r = .023$) and *Trip* ($r = -.141$). The results clearly show that people who pay great attention to memory do not do so because they have a poor memory, but because they assign high import-ance to their memories. Their memory may be as good as the memory of other people or even better for an event that was particularly relevant for them, like the visit of the experimenter.

Memory test-a, on the *Visit* of the experimenter, included six questions concerning memory of the series of the events associated with the adminis-tration, 2 months earlier, of the MS Questionnaire, i.e., it asked about the organization of the MS Questionnaire itself (e.g., how many items), how it was administered and the experimenter's visit. Since the experience involved high MS students in an aspect they considered particularly relevant, it is not surprising that they had a better memory of it.

Furthermore, at the subjective level taken into consideration by the Auto-biographical Agenda, participants with a high MS rated their remote memor-ies as being more vivid. This result cannot be interpreted with certainty in the sense that participants with high MS really had better memories of these events (evidence concerning the inter-subject comparisons between vividness ratings and accuracy of memories is still ambiguous; see Koriat, Goldsmith, & Pansky, 2000), but clearly shows that the subjective feelings associated with those memories include the impression that they are more vivid. In other words, people with a high MS also maintain a vivid memory of past relevant events and are presumably readier to give a rich description of them, irrespective of their factual accuracy.

These results were replicated in a subsequent study, in which we adminis-tered to 130 university students (86 females and 44 males; age range = 19–27, mean age = 20.95 years) a slightly modified version of the Autobiographical

Agenda, already used in the preceding study. Students were invited to fill out the MS Questionnaire and the Autobiographical Agenda, in which they had to rate on a 6-point scale the vividness of a series of very remote or more recent events. The Agenda has good psychometric properties (Cronbach's alpha was .82) and turned out to correlate significantly with the MS score ($r = .44$).

Age and gender differences in MS

Gender notoriously affects autobiographical memory. For example, Thorne and McLean (2002) found that some gendered reminiscence practices found in prior studies of children are reflected in late adolescents' self-defining reminiscences. Janssen, Chessa, and Murre (2005) found that the reminiscence bump has its peak earlier in women (at about 13–14 years) than in men (15–18 years).

In our first study we had also found that gender affected the level of MS. By dividing the group of participants on the basis of the median score, we found that 36 girls and only 9 boys were above the median, whereas 11 girls and 34 boys were below the median. The result is coherent with the observation that there are gender effects related to the use of memory souvenirs, more frequent in the girls than in the boys (Habermas & Paha, 2002). Obviously, this fact raises a doubt as to whether memory differences could at least be partially attributed to a gender effect rather than to a specific effect of MS. At the same time it shows the importance of examining the relationship between gender and MS. However, this particular aspect should be considered specific to the particular context we studied, as it is possible that in other sociocultural contexts other patterns could be observed. Notice that the boys, although they tended to have lower scores, had higher scores for specific items (e.g., those concerning the use of a camera). Furthermore, gender effects might also be dependent on the subject's age, as it has been shown that attitude towards memory changes during life. For example, Bluck and Habermas (2000) reported a growing tendency from young to middle-aged and then to older adults to evaluate the present in relation to the remembered past, suggesting that MS is not only a gerontological issue but also a lifespan developmental one.

Concerning gender, De Vries and Watt (1996) examined memory for life events in the context of an individual's life story in 60 participants aged 18–86 years. Women identified a greater number of life events and reported a younger age at which their first event took place than did men; this was especially true for older women. Pillemer, Wink, DiDonato, and Sanborn (2003) studied memory styles of older adults and found that women's memory styles were markedly more specific or episodic than were men's styles. Participants' ratings of the ways that they use memory in daily life suggested that women place a greater value on purposeful reminiscence than men do. However, these results overshadow the fact that elderly men, especially when they retire, also tend progressively to rediscover the importance of memory. It is typical of both female and male elderly people to enjoy going back into their past and telling stories about their life.

In order to examine these issues, in a study we administered the MS Questionnaire to 130 college students (86 females and 44 males), 61 mature adults (aged between 50 and 63; 40 females and 21 males), and 78 elderly people (aged between 65 and 89; 51 females and 27 males). The three groups were matched for schooling and socioeconomic status. We found significant effects due to age and to the interaction between gender and age. The results also replicated the gender effect found in the first study for youngsters and extended it to the adult group. For the youngsters group the mean score of the females on the MS Questionnaire was 104.93 (SD = 10.34), as opposed to a mean score of 94.91 (SD = 12.66) for the males. A similar difference of 10 points was also found in the adult group (who had, in general, a slightly lower MS): the female group had a mean score of 97.83 and the male group 87.00. On the contrary, in the elderly group, gender did not produce a significant difference, as the females maintained the preceding high levels of MS (mean score = 99.88) and also the males – differently from the younger male groups – obtained high MS scores (mean score = 97.80). (These results, however, cannot be applied to all elderly communities, as further observations showed that the pattern of responses can vary depending on the specific characteristics of the tested community.)

These results give a better insight into the observations in the literature as they show the specificity of MS. In fact, the time course in MS does not exactly reflect the time course observed by Bluck and Habermas (2000) for the use of the past in the interpretation of the present. In our case, in fact, the group lowest in MS was the middle-aged one rather than the youngest. Furthermore our elderly males turned out to have high MS, comparable to the female MS, once again showing that MS can be different from a simple reference to one's past life, as studied by De Vries and Watt (1996).

MS and the belief system

Memory, especially autobiographical memory, has been shown to be related to memory beliefs. For example, Rubin, Schrauf, and Greenberg (2003) found that vividly experienced memories almost always had strong visual images and that remember/know judgements made on autobiographical memories were more closely related to belief than to actual recollection.

In particular, MS can be considered as a part of human metacognitive knowledge (Cornoldi, 1995), i.e., of the naive theories people have about mind in general, and about memory in particular (cf. Chapter 1). This type of knowledge has a specific status as it is only partially conscious and/or declarative, is less organized and coherent than other forms of knowledge, is more directly connected with the self-image and emotional feelings, and may have an influence on cognitive behaviour. Knowledge of memory has been the subject of a series of studies that have considered different age groups. For example, the literature has distinguished between different types of knowledge related to strategies, the self, memory functioning, tasks, effects due to the material, forgetting, etc.

More generally, we can assume that an individual's knowledge of memory is not isolated but is connected with his or her knowledge of the mind and psychological functioning. For example, people may recognize that memory is related to other cognitive functions like attention, perception, language, intelligence and so on, but also that it is related to emotional components of the mind and of memory itself. A particular aspect of knowledge of memory that seems more directly related with MS is the degree of positive appreciation of memory. People may think that memory is not particularly relevant in psychological functioning or that it is crucial for a series of activities and decisions. Memory may be regarded as a mechanical low-level function, based on the principle of repetition, or a high-level function involving a series of intelligent and salient processes. Memory may be seen as the source of the elements that produce self-identity and self-guidance, or as heavy luggage that slows down human activity. These different appreciations of the value of memory can be found not only in the reflections of normal people, but also in the history of ideas. One of us has reviewed some of these ideas in an earlier work (Cornoldi, 1995), illustrating some significant examples. For example, memory has been considered differently in the educational field, as some traditions have put memory at the centre of the educational focus. Other people have assumed that memory is less relevant; for example, some teachers exalt thinking with respect to memorizing, as they consider the latter a form of scarcely intelligent passive assimilation of information.

In the particular context represented by the study of memory sensitivity, we were especially interested in the appreciation given to autobiographical memory. People who write their autobiographies think that it is important, sometimes an internal necessity, to recover the events of their lives and that doing so may also help other people. Other people think that the retrieval of autobiographical memories overloads memory and does not exercise it. These aspects seem strictly related to the MS construct. For this reason, we can predict that MS is related to, affects, and is affected by aspects of metacognitive knowledge concerning memory.

In order to examine this issue we drew up a metacognitive questionnaire, which concerned "Naive theories of memory" and included 14 questions with a 5-point Likert scale expressing agreement with the content of the question. Items explored what people think abut memory, whether they think memory is a central part of our life and/or is related to intelligence, whether a good memory of our past may help in everyday life, and whether negative memories must be removed or re-elaborated. We compared the scores on the MS Questionnaire with the specific responses to this metacognitive questionnaire and we found that a high MS is primarily related to some of the metacognitive beliefs. In particular people high in MS strongly believe that memory of the past help to guide their life. This result is not surprising, as this possibility was already implicitly suggested in the MS Questionnaire itself. Yet it clearly illustrates the role of the value assigned to memory. By summing the scores concerning the nine metacognitive questions expressing a positive evaluation of memory we found a positive overall correlation of the sum with the MS total score ($r = .50$).

Components of MS and the personality of the MS individual

The high internal consistency of the MS Questionnaire suggests that MS can be regarded as an unitary concept. However, different aspects are obviously involved in MS, as already mentioned in the description of the items. In particular we observed, within the group of individuals with a high MS, two subtypes that we called "internalizing memory-sensitive" and "pragmatic memory-sensitive". The internalizing individuals seem to focus mainly on cultivating their past memories. For these people, memories are always present and intense and represent a critical part of their life. They like to think back on their past, reconstruct specific episodes, experience again the same sensations and the same emotions. The internalizing component of MS may be associated with other internalizing personality aspects. The pragmatic individuals share with the internalizers the importance given to memory, but they are more actively involved in behaviours devoted to saving memories, to have cues helping the retrieval of evanescent information. These aspects may also be associated with other personality characteristics, in this case not only internalizing, but also externalizing. For example, a tendency to collectionism could enhance the habit of collecting, organizing and looking back at pictures of trips, important events and so on. On the contrary, internalizers are expected to be more apt to engage in private re-experiencing, e.g., in terms of visual imagery. Involuntary memories (cf. Berntsen, 1996) will presumably be efficient triggers for reminiscing activities for internalizers, whereas pragmatic externalizers are more likely to produce their own cues for reminiscing.

Despite the possible specifications within the MS dimension, until now our research was focused on the general dimension, including the study of its relationship with other aspects of human personality. Among the many personality characteristics that can be associated with MS, we decided to focus our project on "time perspective" (TP), a dimension that was first introduced by Zimbardo and collaborators. In particular, Zimbardo and Boyd (1999, p. 1271) described time perspective as "the often nonconscious process whereby the continuous flows of personal and social experiences are assigned to temporal categories, or time frames that help to give order, coherence, and meaning to those events". Zimbardo and Boyd developed a measure for assessing TP (the TP Inventory), which requires participants to respond on a 5-point rating scale (1= *very uncharacteristic*, 5 = *very characteristic*) to 56 items and grouped the items into five main TPs – the past negative, the present hedonistic, the future, the past positive and the present fatalist. Research has showed that people who differ in TP are also different in other aspects of personality and behaviour.

Specifications of the five TPs and examples of items proposed by Zimbardo and Boyd (1999) are as follows.

1   Past negative (reflects a generally negative, aversive view of the past): "I think about the bad things that have happened to me in the past", "I often think of what I should have done differently in my life".

2   Present hedonistic factor (reflects a hedonistic risk-taking "devil-may-care" attitude to time and life): "Taking risks keeps my life from becoming boring", "I often follow my heart more than my head".

3   Future factor (reflects a general future orientation): "I am able to resist temptations when I know that there is work to be done", "It upsets me to be late for appointments".

4   Past positive factor (reflects an attitude towards the past that is very different from that captured from the past negative as it reflects warm sentimental attitude towards the past): "It gives me pleasure to think about the past", "I like family rituals and traditions that are regularly repeated".

5   Present fatalist factor (reveals a fatalistic helpless and hopeless attitude towards present and life): "My life path is controlled by forces I cannot influence", "Often luck pays off better than hard work".

We administered both the MS Questionnaire and the TP Inventory to a group of 110 university students. It was reasonable to expect that people high in MS would also have presented a high score in the past positive dimension, and this is what we found. However, less trivial predictions could be made with respect to the other dimensions. In fact, one could have predicted that people high in MS, being focused on their past life, would have low scores in the other TPs. But the opposite prediction could also be made. In fact, people high in MS are not simply nostalgically oriented towards their past, but seem to use their memories in a rich and positive way, developing a general and complete schema for the analysis and enjoyment of present and future events, on the basis of the re-elaboration of their past experiences. For example, the following item of the TP Inventory loading on the present-hedonistic factor, "When listening to my favourite music I often lose all track of time", describes the enjoyment found in the present by re-experiencing a past emotion. The result also ties in with the observation of Bluck and Habermas (2000), who found that remembered past evaluations were related to current evaluations of life: Even after personality, current affect, and life satisfaction had been controlled for, evaluations of the remembered past and present life evaluations were significantly and positively associated. Similarly, Pillemer (2003) suggested that vivid memories of personal experiences provide models for present activities and contribute to successful problem solving and adaptation. The memories serve important directive functions: they inform, guide, motivate and inspire. This is especially interesting since an accepting attitude towards oneself, combined with a will to take control over one's life, is closely connected to positive health expectancies in later life (Oakley, 2004).

For similar reasons, items describing a future TP reflect a pattern of behaviour, reviewing elements of one's life, present in the memory-sensitive individual: In fact, she or he not only enjoys reviewing in the evening what happened during the day, but also what could happen during the day to come, as is mentioned by item 6 of the TP Inventory "I believe that a person's day should be planned ahead each morning". We thus predicted that people high in MS have also a better present and future perspective. In fact we found that our participants who were high in MS had significantly higher scores than participants low in MS in the present-hedonistic factor and in the future factor.

These results show that there is no overlap between MS and past-positive TP, but rather that MS describes a broader attitude towards personal memories related to the way people consider the events of their life and their attitude towards them.

CONCLUSIONS

Memory sensitivity (MS) appears to be a new construct related to the positive appreciation people give to the use of memory for retrieving the events of their past life. This dimension appears to be deeply rooted in human individuals as it seems to affect their lives in different ways, and it appears to be connected with their ideas and behaviours. In this chapter we present an assessment procedure that revealed good psychometric properties and good discriminative power. In fact, the MS Questionnaire showed high internal consistency, high reliability and good construct validity, as it was able to discriminate between groups assumed to have different memory sensitivity and appeared to be related to other cognitive and personality aspects.

On the basis of the results obtained with the use of the MS Questionnaire, we can conclude that memory sensitivity (MS) is related to, but independent of, other functions and characteristics of autobiographical memory, as is demonstrated by the specific gender and age differences we found. In particular, females are more sensitive than males, but this difference tends to disappear in elderly people. Age has also an impact on MS, but this impact is not linearly related to the course of time, as the lowest MS score was, in some cases, observed in middle-aged adults who had lower scores than either youngsters or elderly people.

The relationship between MS and memory ability seems to have specific implications. As MS includes a main feature that concerns the attention devoted to saving memories of the past, it could be argued that MS is particularly well developed in people who know they have poor memory. Results show that, in general, memory-sensitive persons do not have a poorer autobiographical memory than people with a low MS score. On the contrary, they sometimes have a better memory, as happened in one of our studies, for the event (for them particularly relevant) represented by the visit of the experimenter who introduced them to the problem.

Furthermore, individuals high in MS maintain very vivid memories of past events, giving high vividness ratings to the events included in an autobiographical agenda.

MS can be studied within wider contexts. For example, MS is related to the metacognitive ideas that people have about memory. In particular it is related to the emphasis given to memory within cognitive functioning. With respect to personality, MS is an important and partially specific component that has relationships with the time perspective. However, MS does not simply represent a positive perspective towards the past, as people high in MS also have a better attitude than people low in MS towards the present and the future. This suggests that MS may have a more general adaptive function in helping people to have a well-organized representation of the whole time course of their lives. (Recent results, still in elaboration, suggest that a high MS score is one of the best predictors of life satisfaction.)

In conclusion, one might ask why people vary in memory sensitivity. Why do some people engage more in reminiscing their past than others? We can only offer some suggestions. Of several possible reasons two seem to be likely candidates. On the one hand, those who have discovered the functional adaptive utility of reminiscing will presumably be more prone to engage in MS activities. Obviously rewarding also are the social benefits obtained by reminiscing over shared memories. Our guess is that children raised by parents who engage in small talk about their personal pasts, their own as well as their children's, have a greater likelihood of developing long-lasting MS styles.

On the other hand, reminiscing activity is often experienced as highly rewarding in itself when it succeeds in recovering the past in fuller flavour than that routinely obtained by schematized reminiscing. Full-fleshed reminisced autobiographical memories are akin to the experience of some involuntary memories so thoroughly described by Marcel Proust (1913) in his multivolume novel describing a search for lost personal time.

The recovery of one's own lost past (in Proustian sense) represents a way of overcoming time. The experience of overcoming time bears a resemblance to certain ecstatic conditions of consciousness, and is of importance for self-functioning in that it offers a broadened perspective on one's life here and now.

Having experienced positive and rewarding effects of searching one's past, one is more likely to engage in new attempts. Reminiscing develops into a cognitive style that can be backed up by knowledge about different pathways to one's own episodic memories (see Chapter 13).

REFERENCES

Alba, J.W., & Hasher, L. (1983). Is memory schematic? *Psychological Bulletin, 93*, 203–231.

Bartlett, F.C. (1932). *Remembering: A study in experimental and social psychology.* Cambridge, UK: Cambridge University Press.

Berntsen, D. (1996). Involuntary autobiographical memories. *Applied Cognitive Psychology, 10*, 435–454.

Bluck, S., & Alea, N. (2002). Exploring the functions of autobiographical memory: Why do I remember the autumn? In J.D. Webster & B.K. Haight (Eds.), *Critical advances in reminiscence work: From theory to application* (pp. 61–75). New York: Springer.

Bluck, S., & Habermas, T. (2000). The life story schema. *Motivation and Emotion, 24*, 121–147.

Conway, M.A. (1990). *Autobiographical memory: An introduction.* Buckingham, UK: Open University Press.

Conway, M.A., & Pleydell-Pearce, C. (2000). The construction of autobiographical memories in the self-memory system. *Psychological Review, 107*, 261–288.

Cornoldi, C. (1995). *Metacognizione e apprendimento* (Metacognition and learning). Bologna, Italy: Il Mulino.

Cornoldi, C., & De Beni, R. (2003). Leopardisti: Gli amanti della memoria (Leopardists: The memory lovers). *Psicologia Contemporanea, 1*, 4–11.

De Vries, B., & Watt, D.(1996). A lifetime of events: Age and gender variations in the life story. *International Journal of Aging and Human-Development, 42*, 81–102.

Habermas, T., & Paha, C. (2002). Souvenirs and other personal objects: Reminding of past events and significant others in the transition to university. In J.D. Webster & B.K. Haight (Eds.), *Critical advances in reminiscence work: From theory to application* (pp. 123–139). New York: Springer.

Helstrup, T. (2006). *Problem solving: How modular, how creative, how veridical?* Manuscript in preparation.

Janssen, S.M.J., Chessa, A.G., & Murre, J.M.J. (2005). The reminiscence bump in autobiographical memory: Effects of age, gender, education, and culture. *Memory, 13*, 658–668.

Koriat, A., Goldsmith, M., & Pansky, A. (2000). Toward a psychology of memory accuracy. *Annual Review of Psychology, 51*, 481–537.

Libby, L., & Eibach, R. (2002). Looking back in time: Self-concept change affects visual perspective in autobiographical memory. *Journal of Personality and Social Psychology, 82*, 167–179.

Middleton, D., & Brown, S.D. (2005). *The social psychology of remembering.* Thousand Oaks, CA: Sage.

Nelson, K. (2003). Self and social functions: Individual autobiographical memory and collective narrative. *Memory, 11*, 125–135.

Oakley, R. (2004). How the mind hurts and heals the body. *American Psychologist, 59*, 29–40.

Pasupathi, M. (2001). The social construction of the personal past and its implications for adult development. *Psychological Bulletin, 127*, 651–672.

Pillemer, D.B. (1998). *Momentous events, vivid memories: How unforgettable moments help us understand the meaning of our lives.* Cambridge, MA: Harvard University Press.

Pillemer, D. (2003). Directive functions of autobiographical memory: The guiding power of the specific episode. *Memory, 11,* 193–202.

Pillemer, D., Wink, P., DiDonato, T. & Sanborn, R. (2003). Gender differences in autobiographical memory styles of older adults. *Memory, 11,* 525–532.

Proust, M. (1913). *À la recherche du temps perdu: Du côté de chez Swann.* Paris: Gallimard.

Raaheim, K. (1988). Intelligence and task novelty. In R.J. Sternberg (Ed.), *Advances in the study of intelligence, Vol. 4.* (pp. 73–98). Hillsdale, NJ: Lawrence Erlbaum Associates, Inc.

Rubin, D., Schrauf, R., & Greenberg, D. (2003). Belief and recollection of auto-biographical memories. *Memory and Cognition, 31,* 887–901.

Schank, R.C., & Abelson, R. (1977). *Scripts, plans, goals, and understanding.* Hillsdale, NJ: Lawrence Erlbaum Associates, Inc.

Sternberg, R.J. (1987). Intelligence and cognitive style. In R.E. Snow & M.J. Farr (Eds.), *Aptitude, learning and instruction, Vol 3. Conative and affective process analyses* (pp. 77–97). Hillsdale, NJ: Lawrence Erlbaum Associates, Inc.

Thorne, A., & McLean, K. (2002). Gendered reminiscence practices and self-definition in late adolescence. *Sex-Roles, 46,* 267–277.

Walker, W.R., Skowronski, J. & Thompson, C. (2003). Life is pleasant – and memory helps to keep it that way! *Review of General Psychology, 7,* 203–210.

Webster, J.D. (2003). The reminiscence circumplex and autobiographical memory functions. *Memory, 11,* 203–215.

Webster, J.D., & Haight, B.K. (1995). Memory lane milestones: Progress in reminiscence definition and classification. In B.K. Haight & J.D. Webster (Eds.), *The art and science of reminiscing: Theory, research, methods, and applications.* Washington, DC: Taylor & Francis.

Wilson, A., & Ross, M. (2003). The identity function of autobiographical memory: Time is on our side. *Memory, 11,* 137–149.

Zelniker, T., & Globerson, T. (Eds.) (1989). *Cognitive style and cognitive development.* Norwood, NJ: Ablex.

Zimbardo, P.G., & Boyd, J.N. (1999). Putting time in perspective: A valid, reliable individual differences metric. *Journal of Personality and Social Psychology, 77,* 1271–1288.

APPENDIX

The MS questionnaire

The present questionnaire intends to explore the attitude people have towards their memories. Please read it carefully and fill it sincerely. For each question you will have to give a rating on a 4-point rating scale according to the frequency and/or the intensity of your position.

- often, yes (4)
- sometimes, enough (3)
- rarely, a little (2)
- never, absolutely no (1)

Do not leave out any question.

1 You take notes of what happens to you
2 You note the experience of meaningful emotions
3 You reread old notes (in a diary, agenda, etc.) that give you the possibility to re-establish what happened
4 You think again to events of your past
5 You reconstruct, in detail, facts of your life
6 A smell evokes a memory (of a fact, a person, an emotion . . .)
7 A song brings back to life past memories
8 During the week you like to think what you did in your leisure time
9 If you had a meaningful experience (a concert or others) you save related material, like the ticket of the concert, or the train or a shop
10 You enjoy it when memories of the day pop out spontaneously to your memory
11 During the evening you like to think again of the facts that happened in the same day
12 Many memories are still present for you as if you had camera pictures available
13 You like to think of your past experiences
14 When you think again of episodes of your life you feel again the same emotions you felt when the episodes really happened
15 You are sentimentally attached to contexts you have experienced
16 When you have to take decisions you think back to similar situations you already met
17 You like to recall your past events
18 You have an intense memory of a particular occasion, like the Christmas day of 4 years ago
19 You are sorry if you discover that you have forgotten aspects of important past events of your life
20 You feel tied to your past
21 You like to have pictures fixating images of people you have known
22 You hold pictures of places that are important for you
23 You are attached to places where you have been
24 Pictures, a diary, etc. may help you to maintain clear memories of specific events, like a trip or a feast
25 You are used to collecting and ordering pictures
26 You add written comments to the pictures you have
27 Memories of episodes of your life may be very clear without the need for external supports
28 You think pictures may protect your memory from forgetting due to time
29 You like to reconstruct when you first met people you now see very often
30 When you have to remember something specific, e.g., an appointment, you prefer to take precautions

31 If you fear you could forget something, you use specific strategies or memory techniques
32 You use an agenda
33 You think that memories of your life can help you to understand yourself better
34 It may be useful to stop and think what happens

Autobiographical agenda

Examples of items (to be rated on a 6-point vividness scale) (NO = I could not have that experience)

PRIMI RICORDI (Early memories)

La prima volta che sei andato in bicicletta.   (No) 0 1 2 3 4 5
(Your first time on a bike)
Il primo giorno di scuola elementare.   (No) 0 1 2 3 4 5
(Your first day at the primary school)

RICORDI PIU' RECENTI (More recent memories)

Il primo bacio.   (No) 0 1 2 3 4 5
(The first kiss)
Il diciottesimo compleanno.   (No) 0 1 2 3 4 5
(The eighteenth birthday)

9 Memory experts: Visual learning, wine tasting, orienteering and speech-reading

*Rossana De Beni, Cesare Cornoldi,
Maria Larsson, Svein Magnussen and
Jerker Rönnberg*

THE STUDY OF EXPERTISE

In a large-scale memory survey of people's beliefs about human memory, one of the questions asked was whether memory capacity could be improved by training, like the strengthening of muscles by physical exercise (Magnussen et al., 2006; Chapter 1). More than 90% of the respondents believed that memory can be trained. What does memory research tell us?

The closest answer to the question comes from the study of memory expertise. Expert performance refers to a consistently superior performance on a specified set of representative tasks for a given knowledge domain (Ericsson & Lehmann, 1996). High expertise is typically associated with prolonged and maintained practice, lasting many years, and involving daily exercises. For example, by the age of 20, top-class violinists will have practised for a total of around 10,000 hours, starting very early, around 5 years of age, with approximately 4 hours of concentrated practice per day (Ericsson & Charness, 1994).

The field is vast, involving expertise in a wide range of areas such as sports (e.g., skating), games (e.g., bridge), cognitive processes (e.g., problem-solving, memory), academic areas (e.g., physics), professions (e.g., medical diagnosis) or motor abilities (e.g., juggling) (Ericsson & Lehmann, 1996). The model of expertise research is the chess player (Binet, 1894; De Groot, 1946/1978), as chess offers a series of advantages: in chess, the experts can reach very high levels of competence, the expertise of all participants studied is related to the same well-defined ability, this ability is measurable, and the implications of expertise can be tested as the materials and tasks are easily adapted to laboratory needs. However, too narrow a focus on chess expertise may cause us to lose sight of some important pieces of information, with the risk that data and models based on chess expertise cannot be generalized to other areas.

In this chapter we discuss some areas of research relevant to the question of memory expertise that have not been widely discussed within this context. The research selected reflects the interests of the authors, and illustrates that expertise involves modifications at several levels of information processing, from the very specific superiority of basic perceptual discriminations to higher level visuospatial expertise of a more general nature, or permanent perceptual and cognitive skills that involve language and semantic knowledge. This will give us a broader perspective on expertise, and enable us both to examine how different domains of expertise produce specific outcomes and to answer some general questions.

In the first part of the paper we introduce some important questions in the field. These represent some of the critical issues that have emerged from the expertise literature (Ericsson & Lehmann, 1996), which we believe can be effectively elucidated from the areas of expertise examined in this chapter. We then present data related to these research areas. Finally, we examine some general points emerging from a comparative analysis of the data presented. It may be worth remembering at this point that in a sense we are all memory experts in more or less specific fields of knowledge. A general principle, in the study of information acquisition and memory, is that it is easier to encode into long-term memory information that fits with previous knowledge, and the more elaborate the existing knowledge structure, the more easily will new long-term memories be formed (Chi, Glaser, & Rees, 1982). Thus people remember better information from their own areas of interest than from other fields; for example, the football fan's memory for all players in this year's top league is the result of a combination of frequent self-exposure to relevant information and the facility of long-term memory encoding of this information.

SOME BASIC QUESTIONS

One basic question in the field of expertise concerns the *expert's memory*. In fact, it is well known that experts have a better memory for materials related to their domain of expertise, mainly for material with which they are already familiar. For example, chess experts have a better memory for chess positions (Chase & Simon, 1973) and experts in bridge have a better incidental memory for original bridge hands (Engle & Bukstel, 1978). However, it is not clear to what extent experts also have a better memory of less familiar material or of completely new material in their domain. A widely debated issue concerns whether chess players are also better at remembering random position arrays, as it was traditionally considered that this was not the case (Charness, 1991). It has been repeatedly shown that expert chess players are actually signifi-cantly better than non-experts in this case too, although the difference between the two groups becomes smaller. However, expert memory has been traditionally considered within a framework in which experts have better memory because they exploit their existing knowledge and patterns (Chase & Ericsson, 1982).

The possibility of extending memory superiority to material different from the one in which the individual became expert is related to a more general second question concerning *transfer effects in expertise.* The literature on transfer has oscillated between a strict negative position, coming back to Thorndike's (1913) theory of identical elements, and a more optimistic position, for example represented by metacognitive theory (Lucangeli, Galderisi, & Cornoldi, 1995), according to which some general abilities transferable to other fields can be learnt. The comparison between different areas of expertise seems crucial for examining the transfer issue. Furthermore, research on perceptual learning represents an ideal area for studying the effects of transfer, as very specific well-measurable competences can be trained and it is possible to examine how these competences can be extended to other related ones.

A third question concerns the role of *initial ability* and practice in contributing to the development of expertise. The traditional view (e.g., Galton, 1869/1979) assumed that all the most important individual differences reflected innate basic capacities. Very expert performance is viewed as the result of "natural" talent, where instruction and practice are necessary, but not sufficient, to attain high levels of performance. This view has been largely criticized on the basis of the assumption that expert knowledge and expert task-specific reactions must have been acquired through experience. However the question is still controversial; despite the fact that experts have generally developed their competence through an impressive amount of practice, a dissociation between amount of experience, even when this has been deliberate and goal-oriented, and level of performance has been demonstrated in various areas, including expert decision-making and judgement, computer use, etc. (Ericsson & Lehmann, 1996). Obviously, different levels of performance that are not predicted by amount of practice in the domain cannot necessarily be attributed to different/innate abilities, as they could be attributed to the learning of certain types of operations that are not particularly frequent during practice. From this perspective, the practice view comes back to the traditional behaviourist's view (Watson, 1924), according to which anyone, via appropriate experience, could become a good lawyer, etc. This strongly contrasts with emerging neuroscientific approaches that insist on biologically innate bases of talent. However, neurobiological differences between experts and novices (as in the case of London taxi drivers; Maguire, Frackowiak, & Frith, 1997) may also be interpreted as the consequence, rather than the cause, of expertise. In fact, a study by Maguire and co-authors (Maguire, Valentine, Wilding, & Kapur, 2003) failed to find systematic differences in brain anatomy between people with exceptional memory and controls; different patterns of brain activation during memorization were directly attributable to the different encoding strategies used by the two groups and not to original neurological differences.

A fourth question concerns how the development of expertise within a specific domain may have a *retroactive effect* on more general cognitive ability. In other words, even assuming that the initial underlying abilities were equal, does the practice associated with the development of expertise have an effect in increasing the underlying ability? For example, do people involved in a specific verbal or spatial domain develop general better verbal and spatial abilities respectively? Typically, responses to this question are negative. The fact that differences in levels of expertise are not correlated with either IQ or other basic cognitive abilities such as perception and reaction time (Ericsson & Lehmann, 1996) should suggest not only that expertise is not influenced by basic abilities, but also vice versa, that these are not affected by increased expertise. However, evidence concerning people with particularly high skills (Rönnberg, 1993) seems to show that the opposite may also be true.

A fifth question concerns *sociomotivational factors*, i.e., the extent to which social context (parental support, interactions with friends, cultural models, etc.) and motivation can affect the development of expertise. These factors could contribute together with basic abilities to the development of expertise; for example, a person with a highly developed spatial ability should more easily engage in rewarding spatial tasks. However, the contributions of motivation and ability should be dissociable. Furthermore, motivation is typically considered as an alternative to ability as a factor producing increased effort to attain expertise, as this passage suggests:

> Reviews of adult expert performance show that individual differences in basic capacity and abilities are surprisingly poor predictors of performance . . . These negative findings, together with strong evidence for adaptive changes through extended practice, suggest that the influence of innate, domain-specific basic capacities (talent) on expert performance is small, possibly even negligible. We believe that the motivational factors that predispose children and adults to engage in deliberate practice are more likely to predict individual differences in levels of attained expert performance.
>
> (Ericsson & Lehman, 1996, p. 281)

EXPERTISE IN PERCEPTUAL DISCRIMINATION AND MEMORY

An extraordinary visual memory

In spite of the fact that very high-level memory abilities in the perceptual domain can be the consequence of practice, there are large individual differences in certain types of memory performance. Starting with Sir Francis Galton's famous survey of people's memory of their breakfast tables, memory researchers have been aware of the large individual differences in the richness of visual memories. While most people are able to generate memory images of previously viewed visual scenes, a small minority are able to generate images with an astonishing clarity and detail, almost bordering on the richness of the on-line perceptual image (Haber & Haber, 1988). This natural visual expertise of eidetic imagery does not correlate with other cognitive or memory abilities (Paivio & Cohen, 1979), and appears to be a special talent that persists over the years (Haber, 1979). Stromeyer and Psotka (1970) described an example of extraordinary eidetic imagery – a 23-year-old woman, a skilled artist, who claimed to be able to hallucinate at will a beard on a beardless man, leaves on a barren tree, or a page of poetry in a known foreign language that she could copy from bottom to top as fast as her handwritng permitted. These hallucinations might even obscure the real object. However, even more remarkable were the formal tests carried out by Stromeyer and Psotka. In contrast to most studies of eidetic subjects, which probe the memory for naturalistic pictures, they presented their subject with random-dot stereo images. In a random-dot stereogram each picture consists of an apparently random matrix of black-and-white tiny squares or dots; however, some of the squares are systematically shifted in position to stimulate disparate points on the two retinae, so when the two pictures are viewed in a stereoscope, subjects with normal stereoscopic vision perceive a three-dimensional (3-D) shape rising out of the randomly patterned background.

Figure 9.1 shows two examples of the random-dot stereograms used by Stromeyer and Psotka (1970). In the upper pair a T rises out of the background when the patterns are fused in binocular vision, while in the lower pair a square emerges from the background. The eidetic subject, who had no knowledge of random-dot stereograms and was given no information before the experiment, viewed the right pattern with the right eye for 2 minutes, and rested for 10 minutes before being presented with the left pattern to the left eye. She spontaneously reported the T, which was as clear and distinct as when the pair was later viewed simultaneously. In a subsequent experiment with the lower stereo pair, the subject scanned the right pattern with the right eye for four 3-minute periods, and 24 hours after was presented with the left pattern to the left eye. Within 10 seconds she reported the 3-D square shape appearing from the background and was able to accurately trace it on a screen with an optical pointer. Thus, the complex, random-dot pattern she viewed on the previous day must have been perfectly stored in visual memory and fused with the on-line image to produce the 3-D object. In subsequent experiments the authors obtained a similar performance with patterns containing 10,000 elements for as long as 3 days, and million-dot patterns with delays of 4 hours.

While this memory performance may rely on low-level mechanisms of visual memory closely tied to the perceptual process (Magnussen, 2000), the remarkable imagery performance of this subject may also have involved high-level mechanisms of visual memory. However, such performance is limited to the visual perceptual domain, and does not transfer, for example, to the auditory domain. Moreover, it is not the result of specific training, although the eidetic skill may perhaps be reinforced by experience. It is a special talent, only slightly modifiable by practice. The study of eidetic persons, although

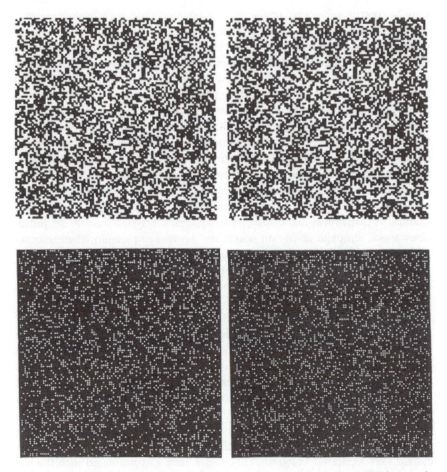

Figure 9.1 Random-dot stereograms used by Stromeyer and Psotka (1970) in a study
of the visual memory of an eidetic subject. In the upper pair, a square in
front of the background is seen in the stereoscopy, in the lower stereopair,
a T pops out of the background.

they exhibit very advanced memory expertise, may therefore be of limited
interest to the study of expertise in general.

EXPERTISE AND PRACTICE IN VISUAL DISCRIMINATION AND MEMORY

When listening to sports commentators on radio and television, we are
often impressed by their acute observations and comments on details of the
athlete's performance. Particularly impressive are commentators of downhill
skiing who, well beyond levels of chance, are able to identify minute misses

in a turn or in a jump that cost the runner a few hundredths of a second, details of performance that most of us are quite unable to detect. A number of studies have shown that this sort of visual expertise can be trained by directing the attention of the observers to relevant information in the visual array, and by training them to look for this sort of information (Gibson, 1951). Several studies have also shown that certain kinds of visual discriminations can be trained so that the fidelity of the sensory discriminations improves during training, and the resulting expertise may be highly specific.

In two classical papers, Fiorentini and Berardi (1980, 1981) showed that the fidelity of spatial discrimination improved with practice over many sessions, and that this improvement was highly specific to the spatial characteristics of the practised patterns. The type of stimuli they used were complex gratings, which are composed of a set of simple stripe patterns that vary in spatial luminance waveform, contrast and spatial frequency or stripe width. They found that the ability to detect the presence of certain grating components, and to discriminate their spatial phase and contrast, increased with practice across a large number of trials. This sort of practice effect has since been replicated in a number of studies of various types of visual tasks, such as the discrimination of vernier displacement or vernier acuity (Fahle, 1997; Fahle & Edelman, 1993), the discrimination of orientation and curvature (Fahle, 1997), luminance contrast detection (Snowden, Rose, & Davies, 2002), and the discrimination of direction and speed of moving targets (Lieu & Weinshall, 2000; Saffell & Matthews, 2003). The practice effects may develop in the course of several thousand trials and the expertise that has been established can be tracked for months (Snowden et al., 2002) or even years (Sagi & Tanne, 1994), although it is likely that without topping-up practice it will eventually be lost.

An important feature of this sort of expertise is that it is highly specific; it cannot be transferred between tasks. For example, practice on direction of motion discrimination does not carry over to speed discrimination (Lieu & Weinshall, 2000), and there is no carry-over between vernier acuity, curvature and orientation tasks (Fahle, 1997). Fiorentini and Berardi (1981) also found that the effect of practice on spatial frequency discriminations did not carry over from one orientation to another; thus, practice with vertical gratings improved spatial discriminations for these gratings but not for horizontal gratings, and vice versa. These results suggest that the expertise acquired during training is very specific and involves modifications of low-level visual mechanisms, and these findings are usually regarded as an example of adult cortical plasticity. Karni and Bertini (1997) argued that the learning changes involved modifications of representations at the earliest levels at which the stimulus features trained were represented; hence the high specificity of some of the practice effects. However, there is also some evidence for more general learning effects (Lieu & Weinshall, 2000).

Sireteneau and Rettenbach (2000) argued that if the neural modifications that take place in perceptual learning involved the very same structures as are primarily responsible for processing this function, perceptual learning may take place at many locations in the human brain, depending on the task that is trained. Training more complex or higher-order visual tasks may therefore not show the same specificity as training of low-level feature discriminations. They provided evidence for this hypothesis using a visual search task, in which the subject looks for one target element among a number of distractors. Sireteneau and Rettenbach found that practice produced an overall decrease in search time and a change towards parallel searching, and that the effect of practice transferred between features and was independent of location. Thus, practice produced more efficient search strategies. However, practice with simple features did not carry over to feature conjunction search, and although extensive practice with feature conjunction search resulted in an overall decrease in search time, it did not change the serial character of the search.

Studies of perceptual learning of more ecologically relevant tasks were carried out by Snowden, Davies, and Roling (2000), who recorded the development of novices' detection of low-contrast features in X-ray images. They showed that expert X-ray film readers were better at detecting low-contrast features in X-ray images than were novices, and that the performance of novice film readers improved with practice with both artificial and real medical X-ray images. In these and many other studies of improvement of basic feature discrimination skills, the practice effects developed quite rapidly, but some studies have shown that they may develop in the course of weeks or months, and are retained for many years. Karni and Bertini (1997) identified rapid and slow learning processes, which may or may not correspond to general and specific learning effects. Most of their experiments tracked the changes across fairly short practice periods and probably recorded only immediate, rapid learning processes.

The development of expertise observed in these studies is highly specific, does not carry over to perceptual discriminations in general, and probably involves modifications of low-level mechanisms of visual information processing. It is an open question whether the expertise in visual discrimination aquired through learning also involves superior perceptual memory for such perceptual attributes (Magnussen, 2000; Magnussen, Greenleee, Aslaksen, & Kildebo, 2003).

Wine expertise

The enhancement of sensory discriminations may not be limited to the visual modality. One group of professionals who are thought to excel in discrimination and memory for chemosensory information are professional wine tasters. Few well-controlled experiments have examined the processes that underlie the perceptual learning of olfactory information. One way of studying this topic is to focus on groups of persons with extensive experience with odours, such as wine experts. The study of wine expertise may offer additional insights into the general nature of expertise, and elucidate whether the principles governing odour expertise are similar to those that have been localized for other domains. In general, wine expertise refers to a superior ability to discriminate between, recognize and describe different wines. At first glance, wine expertise may be thought of as an expertise domain that primarily depends on perceptual proficiency. However, the available evidence suggests that various cognitive processes play an important role in wine expertise (Hughson & Boakes, 2001).

Wine experts differ from novices in a number of perceptual and cognitive dimensions, ranging from absolute thresholds for chemosensory stimuli through discrimination to proficiency in verbal identification of chemosensory information. It has been suggested that wine experts excel in perceptual judgements because they start off with a superior basic sensory capacity compared to novices. Thus, one important question concerns whether experts have more sensitive noses than novices. An early study examined detection thresholds for two wine-related elements, tannin and alcohol, in a group of experts and novices, and found no difference (Berg, Filipello, Hinreiner, & Webb, 1955). Addressing a similar question, Bende and Nordin (1997) assessed experts and controls in absolute thresholds for n-butanol, an odour unrelated to wine, and found equal sensitivity in both groups to the odour. Hence, it appears that the better performance of experts is not driven by an innate sensory superiority as determined by tests of olfactory sensitivity for different odorous compounds, nor have they aquired such enhanced sensitivity in the process of becoming experts.

As noted above, it is widely accepted that expert superiority usually relies on domain-specific knowledge (Ericsson & Kintsch, 1995). This is illustrated by the phenomenon that experts have a better memory for information related to their domain of expertise. The available evidence suggests that a wine expert's perceptual judgements are largely determined by an experience-derived vocabulary (i.e., semantic knowledge) that influences the perception and description of a given wine sample. For example, wine experts consistently perform better in tasks assessing wine discrimination. This is true for tasks that employ a "triangle test" paradigm in which the odd wine of a group of three has to be identified (Solomon, 1990), as well as in tasks using matching procedures (Melcher & Schooler, 1996). One explanation for the expert superiority in discrimination tasks may be related to the fact that experts have access to a larger set of verbal descriptors and that they make more consistent use of them (Solomon, 1990). Likewise, research on the nature of wine descriptions has consistently shown that experts provide more detailed descriptions of a wine than do novices (Lawless, 1984; Solomon, 1990). Experts generate a greater number of odour terms (e.g., sensory dimensions) and use more concrete associations to describe flavours (Lawless, 1984). Moreover, analyses of responses to different wines show that experts typically group wines according to grape variety, whereas novices describe wines using more basic perceptual features such as sweetness. Basic research on the principles governing olfactory memory has indicated that learning to attach labels to unfamiliar odours increases a person's ability to discriminate between them (Rabin & Cain, 1984), and that verbal factors and labelling facilitate odour recognition (Larsson, 1997). All in all, the evidence suggests that a key component of wine expertise is the availability of a vocabulary that experts can use in order to efficiently discriminate between odours. The use of a similar vocabulary among experts also presumably underlies the observation that experts are able to match a wine to a description provided by other experts, whereas novices are unable to perform this task (Solomon, 1990).

In a related vein, Gawel (1997) proposed that knowledge of a specific wine variety drives the search for a relevant verbal label and creates an expectation of its typical characteristics that ultimately increases the likelihood of identification. Support for this hypothesis was provided by Pangborn, Berg, and Hansen (1963), who showed that adding colouring to a white wine to make it look like a rosé resulted in experts judging the wine as sweeter, whereas novices did not.

Little is known about potential transfer effects of perceptual olfactory learning. Research shows that experience with certain odours improves the ability to detect them, to discriminate them from others and to identify them (Larsson & Bäckman, 1998; Rabin, 1988; Rabin & Cain, 1986). However, it is not yet clear whether experience with specific odors will improve the detection, discrimination and identification of *other* odours as well. Rabin (1988) reported improved discrimination for odours with which subjects were specifically trained. However, the study failed to demonstrate improved discrimination for other odours, implying that perceptual learning of specific olfactory information does not generalize to an increased sensitivity to other odours.

To summarize, the available knowledge suggests that superior wine expertise generally relies on domain-specific knowledge (Ericsson & Kintsch, 1995). It develops gradually from experience and training with wine compounds rather than from a general sensory superiority in experts. The evidence also suggests that olfactory perceptual learning is tied to specific odour information, with no evidence of transfer effects. Furthermore, wine expertise that is typically conceived of as relying primarily on perceptual ability is similar to other domains of expertise in that it actually relies heavily on conceptual knowledge (Hughson & Boakes, 2002).

Thus, results on wine expertise show that the superior memory of experts is the result of a higher-level cognitive skill that does not depend on a higher sensitivity for chemosensory stimuli in general.

HIGHER-LEVEL PERCEPTUAL LEARNING AND MEMORY

What we remember depends on what we perceive. Studies of perceptual learning of visual discriminations indicate that we may be able to distinguish and identify finer nuances of the perceptual image, and hence retain a more detailed memory of visual scenes. A recent study by Vogt (1999; Vogt & Magnussen, in press) indicates that it is possible to train the way we look at the world, and that such training also affects memory. In this study, the eye movements of professional painters and non-professional control subjects with no special interest in art were recorded while they inspected naturalistic and abstract pictures; their memory for the pictures was subsequently recorded in free recall. The idea that artists may have a different way of looking at pictures than novices comes from one aspect of art training, namely that, in order to be able to represent the world, painters have to break down their natural perceptual constancy and observe the distributions of light and colour across the image; in the words of Gibson (1951), artists as artists need to adopt a "visual field" rather than a "visual world" attitude to perception. The results of these experiments also showed that the eye movement patterns of professional artists were qualitatively different from those of naïve observers.

Figure 9.2 is an example of typical eye movement patterns shown by artists and naïve viewers. The eye movements of the latter group tended to cluster on points of significance and meaning such as objects and human figures, confirming the classic experiments of Yarbus (1967), whereas the artists exhibited a wider pattern of movements, scanning the whole picture completely

Figure 9.2 Original picture (top) and eye-movement scanning patterns of a professional artist (left) and a naïve viewer (right). Unpublished picture by S. Vogt (2004; see Vogt & Magnussen, in press).

independently of its pictorial content. In subsequent memory tests, the artists remembered many more pictorial details in free recall than did a matched control group of novices. Artistic training thus affected subsequent visual memory. It is perhaps not surprising that the way we look at the world determines our memory of it.

Expertise in orientation skills

The study of expertise in orientation skills is interesting because it offers the possibility of extending the expertise framework into a particularly important everyday area, but also because it enables us to examine the role of specific issues that are also related to some of the basic questions mentioned in the introduction.

One important issue concerns the question of the expert's memory and, in particular, the generality of the assumption that experts have a better memory in their domain; this issue has been largely studied in other areas. However, in many of these cases there was confusion between expertise in the field and familiarity with the domain: for example, chess masters are not only more expert in chess playing but they also know the chess configurations. Data showing that chess players are also better at remembering random chess configurations suggest that familiarity with specific configurations is not essential. However, stimuli remain the same and random chessboard patterns rely on familiar meaningful patterns. On the other hand, in space orientation, new environments may introduce more elements of novelty. Therefore, we may ask whether, in the memory of a new map, experts are also better than novices.

Second, the study of orientation can offer information concerning basic questions regarding the roles of ability and practice. Orientation skills are clearly associated with one of the most important basic skills, i.e., spatial ability, illustrating the interaction between initial ability and development of expertise. In this respect, given that spatial ability is typically associated with gender differences, we can also look at whether ability differences interact with gender differences. The study of orientation ability, which seems to be the combination of a series of subskills, could thus extend the study of expertise beyond the limits of areas of expertise in which competence appears to be highly specific and cannot be generalized to more general abilities.

The study of orientation skills may also illlustrate the specific characteristics assumed by a particular type of expertise. Spatial expertise seems to represent an important element of everyday life and for this reason it is important to discover the types of representations, strategies, and processes that characterize the expert. A study of expertise in the treatment of spatial environmental information was run by Gilhooly, Wood, Kinnear, and Green (1988), who compared subjects able and poor in map reading and found that skilled readers were more able to use organized schemata, made less use of literal information (names of the places) and had a better memory of the maps. However, the two groups were similar in the times required to scan a map.

The specific case of orienteering appears to be of particular interest, as this aspect not only involves cognition, but also action. Orienteering is a sport requiring the use of a map to find as rapidly as possible a series of specific landmarks within a new spatial environment such as a forest, a complex natural environment, etc. Orienteering has not been deeply studied thus far. Malinowski and Gillespie (2001), studying a group of 978 military college students, found that previous experience was a good predictor of wayfinding performance (in a task that required them to find at least 8 out of 10 points in a 4-hour time period, while covering about 6 km of woodland terrain). They also found that typical predictors of laboratory spatial performance (such as gender, mathematical ability and map-use skills) were also significant predictors of spatial behaviour in large-scale tasks. The same author (Malinowski, 2001) also studied the effects of an orienteering task in a group of people without expertise, finding a significant correlation between mental rotation skills and wayfinding performance. He also found that males had higher mental rotation scores than females but not always better wayfinding skills. Ottosson (1997) found with adults that the motivation for orienteering is based on two main elements: a social-recreational one and the search for internal stimulation. Age and gender appeared to affect the motivational pattern.

A few studies have focused more directly on people expert in orienteering. Eccles, Walsh, and Ingledew (2002) studied 17 adults (mean age = 30) in the UK orienteering team. Subjects appeared to be particularly good at adapting to the constraints of the task, using anticipation and simplification. In particular they anticipated the environment from the map and simplified the information required to navigate. In this way they could circumvent processing limitations, leaving them resources available for meeting unexpected task requests. In fact it has been shown that, also in experts in orienteering, fatigue can reduce the ability to perceive checkpoints presented in slides (Hancock & McNaughton, 1986).

Cornoldi, De Beni, Pazzaglia, and Favaretto (2003) tested 72 participants, aged between 21 and 33, divided into three groups of 24 participants (12 males and 12 females). The groups were: experts in orienteering who had been practising the sport for many years, mainly members of the Italian National team; novices in the practice and competition of orienteering (having participated in no more than five competitions); and naïve individuals without any orienteering experience. Cornoldi et al. used map material (see an example in Figure 9.3) taken from an atypical context, i.e., a town like Venice (which was not known by the participants) characterized by the unpredictable organization of its streets and canals, rather than the most typical natural contexts with which experts have presumably developed a high degree of familiarity and competence.

The experimental session was divided into two phases. In the first, participants were administered a self-evaluation Questionnaire (QOS; Pazzaglia,

Figure 9.3 Example of a map used in the orienteering study. Participants had to learn the locations of the nine landmarks indicated in the map and the corresponding pathway.

Cornoldi, & De Beni, 2000, which has proved to be a good predictor of actual performance) and a Mental Rotation test (Vanderberg & Kuse, 1978). In the second phase participants were invited to learn two pathways on a map of Venice, each of them containing three critical landmarks. One was learnt under interference due to a concurrent spatial tapping and the other without interference (the order was also balanced between subjects). After studying the pathways participants were given a "blank" map and were invited to indicate the critical landmarks.

The results showed that experts were significantly better than novices and naïve subjects in remembering the critical landmarks: The two latter groups displayed similar performances. No gender effects were found. In this case, only expertise produced by long practice, rather than initial ability or interest (presumably different in novices and naïve subjects and in males and females), influenced the memory for maps. As the maps were obviously new, data confirm that the experts' memory superiority is not limited to already known material.

The experts made also higher scores in the spatial ability task than the beginners, who were slightly better than the naïve group. This suggests that there is a causal relationship between practice and mental rotation skills. In fact, both experts and novices probably had a better spatial ability and this could have affected their decision to practise this sport; however, only experts had a good mental rotation skill. This could be due to the fact that experience in orienteering produces a habitual way of representing environments, possibly starting from the canonical point of view (North at the top) but also in the absence of any correspondence between the representational direction and the direction of the path. This should create the ability to make mental rotations in all the cases when there is no correspondence. In spatial rotation, too, a slight difference between novices and controls and a strong gender effect was found. The gender difference was also found in the group of experts: If we assume that females had the same degree of practice as the males (but this is difficult to demonstrate), practice did not compensate for unequal abilities. The result could also be interpreted with reference to the observation by Malinowski (2001) that, at equal levels of wayfinding skills, females have lower mental rotation scores. Altogether, the data suggest that practice, to a large extent, but also initial differences (obviously not necessarily innate) contribute to the differences that can be found in a general ability (in this case mental rotation ability) associated with the domain of expertise. Differences in the basic ability could be better predictors of wayfinding in beginners than in expert individuals.

This study also offered a series of specifications of the characteristics of the types of competence acquired by the expert orienteering group. On the self-rated orientation skills that emerged from the responses to the Pazzaglia et al. (2000) questionnaire, experts showed significantly higher scores than the other two groups. In one particular case (knowledge and use of North and South), female participants expert in orienteering produced slightly higher scores than males, whereas there was a strong opposite effect for the controls. This result is particularly interesting because it suggests that the use of a very effective spatial cue (the cardinal points) is affected both by initial preferences and by the development of expertise. Expertise may strengthen the use of a strategy, in this case the reference to the cardinal points, which is already present in some competent, mainly male, naïve persons.

As it has been shown that self-ratings are highly correlated with actual performance, data obtained in this study with the QOS suggest that experts had developed general better orientation skills, had a better survey representation of the space, a better representation of routes and made more use of the cardinal points when they described pathways. Furthermore, as the ratings also reflect the confidence people have in their orientation skills, experts appeared to have a higher perception of spatial self-efficacy.

Speech-reading expertise in the deaf

Sometimes expertise develops as a result of a primary sensory or cognitive deficiency, as for example speech-reading in deaf persons. Expertise in speech understanding tasks seems to be connected to a high working memory capacity. Three extremely skilled visual speech-readers have been assessed on their communicative habits and cognitive profiles: Case GS (Rönnberg, 1993), who communicates by means of tactile and visual information about speech, Case MM (Rönnberg et al., 1999), who is a native bilingual, and Case SJ (Lyxell, 1994), who is a pure visual speech-reader. GS and SJ suffered post-lingual onsets of deafness (at 8 and 13 years of age, respectively), while MM has a congenital moderate hearing impairment.

One of the cases, GS, will be focused on here because he illustrates in several interesting ways how expertise can be developed with a new kind of speech communication mode: tactiling. Tactiling denotes that GS uses his hand to pick up vibrations from the collar-bone and neck of the speaker, which he combines with what he can visually extract from lip movements and facial expression. When GS became deaf (after having meningitis at the age of 8), he spontaneously learnt that when he held his hand on the throat of his mother, he suddenly understood her lip movements when she read stories to him. At first, this sounded like a mystery, and it was not well documented. However, GS was able to offer a high cognitive performance: He went on to main-stream school, and today he has a Master's degree in microbiology from Uppsala University in Sweden. After the first couple of months following his discovery, he shifted his "throat-strategy" to a socially more acceptable form of tactiling, namely touching the shoulder, or some-times the collarbone, of the speaker. He has used his tactiling method for half a century; he has learnt to speak English in an intelligible way by relying on visual (from a mirror) and tactile feedback – despite the fact that he has never heard a word of English.

First and foremost, however, GS excels in tests of speech tracking (repeating back read words) by communicating at a rate of 80 words per minute (wpm). Normal rates are around 80–120, which makes him almost function-ally hearing. Like the other two cases, his phonological processing and lexical access speed (Pichora-Fuller, 2003) are at a normal level, i.e., his automatic (implicit) language processing skills are normal and thus not sufficient for expertise to occur. Since visual-tactile speech information is still poorly specified compared to clear speech and normal hearing, Rönnberg (2003a) suggested that explicit working memory resources help to resolve ambiguities retrospectively, in addition to supporting predictions for the rest of the dia-logue. To be able to do that efficiently, a large simultaneous processing and storage capacity is required. GS is extremely well equipped in this respect. Tests of listening span, which measure the capacity of working memory to simultaneously make semantic judgements while processing sentences for later recall, show that he performs at ceiling in the test used, getting about twice as many items correct as the control group (Rönnberg, 1993). This test is not targeted at a particular component of working memory such as the phono-logical loop, but rather estimates general processing and storage capacity (Daneman & Merikle, 1996). GS shares this explicit processing ability with the other two cases. Thus, the cognitive profiles of GS and of the other two cases are very similar and seem to transcend the boundaries of communication mode and linguistic experience. However, while explicit working memory capacity is characteristic of GS and the other cases, there are several levels of description and explanation concerning his particular method. GS would never have succeeded in understanding stories when he was a child if it had not been the case that what he could pick up with his hands easily combined with what he could decode from lip movements.

Experimentally, we know that phonemes that can be visually perceived are hard to detect as heard speech in noise, and phonemes that de facto can be heard in noise are more difficult to perceive visually (Summerfield, 1987). Thus, there is an interesting audiovisual complementarity, which in itself is an argument for studying speech perception audiovisually. The key point here, however, is that tactiling plays a similar role: Those phonemes and phonetic contrasts that are easier to detect tactilely are harder to detect visually and vice versa (Öhngren, Rönnberg, & Lyxell, 1992). There are even neurophysiological data that suggest similarities in activation between heard and tactilely perceived information about speech (Levänen, 1998). In other words, GS happened to discover a perceptual method by which he could optimize the perceptual qualities for speech understanding.However, the perceptual level of description and explanation is obviously not sufficient. Combined with GS's high working memory capacity, spoken elements that are hard to perceive can be disambiguated more effectively. Even so, this explanation is not sufficient to grasp the way GS communicates via tactiling.

At a social level of explanation, it is easy to observe that GS has a well-developed strategy of approaching the talker and starting to communicate with him or her, while rather unobtrusively placing his hand on the speaker's shoulder. People typically do not realize that GS is deaf. His way of behaving demands social competence, otherwise he risks being misunderstood. Again, it may be that he is saved by also having a high general working memory capacity, enabling him to be communicatively strategic, minimizing the number of repetitions and clarifications needed, and perhaps also minimizing what is needed in terms of "hands-on". There are thus several levels of description and explanation of the tactiling method used by GS. At the heart of his skill lies a tremendous general working memory capacity that has the potential to integrate perceptual and social levels of explanation.

The skills demonstrated by GS are truly remarkable and shed light on several issues related to acquisition of expertise. The first general point that can be made is about the generality of his memory skills. It is clear that it is a complex working memory function that is selectively developed in GS's repertoire. This can be understood on the basis of the inherent communicative demands he constantly faces as a deaf person: When the contents of what is said are poorly specified in the speech signal, and when inference-making supported by cues held in working memory is necessary to continue a conversation, success or failure seem to critically depend on a high capacity to predict (at topic and sentence level) what is to come in the conversation, while keeping contextual and linguistic information alive in working memory. GS is relatively normal in other memory domains such as simple span or short-term memory tasks, as well as in semantic or lexical long-term memory access tasks (Rönnberg, 1993).

Pertinent to the issue of acquisition of expertise is the issue of initial ability vs. practice. What GS has in common with SJ is that they have had many thousands of hours of visual speech-reading practice over a period of 35–40 years. This has presumably provoked a radical development of cognitive competences relevant for speech-reading.

Until recently, few studies had revealed practice effects in working memory per se. However, Klingberg, Forssberg, and Westerberg (2002) demonstrated that not only did intense visuospatial working memory training in children with ADHD result in significant practice effects of similar visuospatial working memory tasks, but there were also interesting transfer effects, e.g., to the ability to solve Raven's matrices. It is thus possible that many years of everyday practice with the intricacies of speech understanding have contributed to the development of a complex, material-independent working memory capacity, rather than the other way round. Nevertheless, it should be noted that very high early estimates of GS's nonverbal IQ and the fact that MM is a native bilingual in signed and spoken Swedish point to the possibility that relatively general cognitive-linguistic abilities may also be part and parcel of the development process underlying speech-reading skill. As we are dealing with case studies, we cannot be certain which factor is the most crucial one, but it seems likely that there is a very qualitatively specific interaction between initial abilities and relevant communicative demands. The lack of either basic abilities/skills or the appropriate communicative demands will result in no improvement in complex working memory or in speech-reading expertise.

Recent data from sign language research also suggest that native sign language users in general become better at spatial, attention and certain visual memory tasks. Likewise, early use of high-powered hearing aids, or early dependence on visual speech, cause improvements in visual speech understanding (Rönnberg, 2003b). These general conditions will lead to cognitive and communicative compensations for individuals in general but, again, expertise is only acquired in a few cases. GS, MM and SJ represent the few cases who really excel in visual speech-reading in a database of around 1000 individuals.

Finally, with respect to the motivational issue, it is clear that GS was highly motivated to continue practising his tactiling skill, as it gave such a direct and natural improvement in his understanding of his mother when she read stories to him. Without such formative episodes in his early years he would presumably not have pursued the development of the skill in the ways he actually did.

QUESTIONS ON EXPERTISE

With respect to the models of expert memory, data reported here show that different mechanisms can explain why expertise is associated with high memory capacity. Expert memory may refer both to cases of people who have developed special skills in memory and to people who have developed expertise in a particular domain and, as a consequence, have a particularly good memory for material concerning that domain.

With particular reference to the case of chess expertise, Gobet (1998) described four different models of expert memory. The chunking theory (Chase & Simon, 1973) assumes that the expert, e.g., the chess player, is advantaged by the possibility of reducing the quantity of to-be-processed information. Another example of chunking can be found in short-term memory tasks, where the capacity of memory – defined in number of chunks – being equal, people who chunk together more items have a better span.

Two theories, the skilled-memory and long-term working memory theories (Ericsson & Kintsch, 1995), mostly using data from memory tasks and from the mnemonic field, explain the high memory capacities of experts in terms of encoding processes that are more rapid, make a better use of prior organized knowledge and include retrieval pathways. These aspects, already described in an earlier phase of the development of the approach, were shown to interact with efficient use of working memory. In fact, the expert maintains efficient cues in a temporary store; these include either retrieval structures or knowledge structures that are associated with long-term memory information. This theory was applied not only to digit span memory, but also to other cases such as memory for menu orders, mental calculation and medical expertise.

The knowledge-based paradigm (Chi et al., 1982) assumes that the knowledge of experts has a better qualitative organization, including schemata, and hierarchic organization, which means that it can be more easily and more flexibly retrieved and used. The paradigm was used, for example, for experts in physics, whose problems are organized at a more abstract level than those tackled by novices.

Expertise models have been developed specifically with reference to particular contexts and there is no clear evidence that they can easily fit into different contexts. In particular, studies of chess expertise, which provided the basis for the above-mentioned models, cannot be directly applied to contexts that involve complex and different cognitive abilities, or social interaction, action, coordination processes and personality dimensions. Furthermore, the four models described by Gobet (1998) seem to describe complementary mechanisms rather than contradictory options. For example, the data presented in this chapter can be interpreted with reference to all the four models. In fact experts are more efficient in processing information (as is obvious in perceptual learning), probably better in chunking information, but also characterized by better knowledge of the domain (as happens in spatial orienteering) and largely rely on efficient interaction between short- and long-term memory (as for example happens in the case of expert speech-reading). Furthermore, what seems to be a common denominator among all four kinds of models is that the interaction between long-term and short-term or working memory is facilitated for a particular knowledge domain or stimulus materials, exact in its representation (e.g., representation of orientation of lines) or more abstract (e.g., orientation skills). The exact terms used for this interaction may be chunking, verbal labelling (e.g., wine-tasting expertise), schema-driven processing (e.g., expert speech-reading) or the like, all intended to describe the interface between cognitive operations in working memory and the mental operations that facilitate processing of the task at hand.

It is also interesting to note that basic cognitive abilities like mental rotation may be developed as a function of expertise in radically different domains serving quite different purposes. Orienteering skills are a case in point, in that mental rotation obviously simplifies map reading. But the acquisition of a new communicative skill such as sign language also contributes to improved mental rotation, but for quite a different reason: When you communicate with sign language, you typically rotate the scene that you are describing to your partner – as a service to better understand what is intended in terms of the topographical aspects of what is being signed (Emmorey, Klima, & Hickok, 1998). Thus, a limited number of basic cognitive abilities presumably mediate the acquisition of more domain-specific cognitive representations, which in turn are important for the development of knowledge structuring and expertise in different domains. At this point we can only start to be explicit about such occurrences, that await further theoretical precision.

Reverting to our initial questions, we observe that the data we presented here can offer some important insights for the study of expertise. Concerning our first two questions, related to the degree of transfer of expert memory and, more generally, expertise, the observations here presented offer important insights. In particular, the generalizability of expertise seems to depend upon the level of cognitive processing involved, being difficult or even impossible for basic low-level skills, but subject to substantial training for complex high-level skills. In fact, in perceptual discriminations following training, expertise is very specific and does not even transfer to parallel tasks, but in other cases experts can also extend their advantages to new material. For example, with reference to expert memory associated with an expert skill, an advantage was observed in people used to practising orienteering, who were better at recalling a new map. The advantage was also evident in other experts described in this chapter, who tended to demonstrate good performance with new material. It must be observed that this effect can be sometimes overshadowed by the fact that the improvement is not as extraordinary and immediate as in the case for which memory was trained. For example, chess players are not spectacular in their memory for random positions, although they are better than lay people. Similarly, in the field of perceptual learning, people trained in processing a specific direction are not better in processing orthogonal directions; however, the learning curve for the second direction is steeper.

Concerning the transfer of expertise in a particular skill to other skills, the data seem to show both the absence and the presence of transfer effects. On one side, impressive data exist that show that the practice developed in processing a particular perceptual feature cannot improve the ability to process another feature. However, when the ability becomes more complex, transfer effects seem possible. This can also be shown at the perceptual level, as was found, for example, by Sireteanu and Rettenbach (2000) using a visual search task. Moving from the perceptual field to cognitive superior processes, it is possible that more general transfer effects can also be identified. For example, Lucangeli, Galderisi, and Cornoldi (1995) found that children trained in the use of memory strategies were more able to use a new unknown strategy than children who had not received this type of training.

Concerning the third question, data seem constantly to show that there is a continuous interaction between initial individual characteristics and experience. Obviously, deaf speech-readers were able to develop their skills thanks to prolonged exposure to this type of stimuli. However, only some of them (actually 3 out of 1000) were able to reach a particularly high level of competence. An even more impressive case is the eidetic subject studied by Stromeyer and Psotka (1970), who showed a very rare ability to retain specific sensory information for long periods of time. The case is reminiscent of other cases of exceptional memory, like the Russian journalist S. studied by Luria (1968), who combined high visual memory and synaesthesias with long practice in the use of memory strategies. These extraordinary cases show the role of initial basic abilities, but they also raise the risk of offering a particular, unrepresentative view of the nature of expertise. In fact, it appears that in general, practice, even in the absence of particular initial abilities, can produce extraordinary levels of performance. The study on orienteering presented here showed how people trained in this sport were able to develop very advanced spatial skills. Although we cannot exclude the possibility that in this case initial abilities and/or interests were also affecting the performance, the general pattern of data offered by research on expertise has offered sufficient evidence on the role of practice. Thus, while practice appears to be important, the degree of practice necessary for developing expertise in a field depends on the complexity of the ability involved. Studies of perceptual learning have shown that even simple training can make people very expert in a particular area. However, when the area is more general, very long constant practice is necessary in order to become expert.

Concerning the fourth question, there is evidence that the expertise developed in a particular area can have general retroactive effects on the basic ability that is involved in the expert's domain. For example, training in how we look at the world (Vogt & Magnussen, in press), in the use of memory strategies with elderly, adults or children (Cornoldi & De Beni, 1996; De Beni & Moe, 2003; Lucangeli et al., 1995), or in the use of visuospatial working memory (Klingberg et al., 2002) not only improved the ability in the specific trained skill but also had a general effect on memory ability. Furthermore, data on sign language showed that native sign-language users increase their general spatial and visual memory abilities.

Finally, spread but coherent observations confirm that the development of expertise is strictly interconnected with motivational and personality characteristics. For example, the compensatory effects found in sensory handicapped people seem to be affected by the strong motivation of such people to overcome and compensate for their difficulties. The study of cases of exceptional memories offers another example of how people, poor in other cognitive abilities, try to find a personal and social reward from the demonstration of very good memory performance. De Beni and Piccione (1995) studied the case of a totally blind, mildly retarded young man who had trained his cognitive skills, especially rote memory and calendar calculation, in order to gain the social appreciation he was not able to obtain in other ways. His emotional attitude to memory was impressively confirmed by the way he used to introduce himself to other people. In fact, he did not say "I have a good memory", but "I *am* a good memory".

CONCLUDING POINTS

It is noteworthy that the present chapter addresses expertise across all the different sensory modalities: vision, olfaction and taste, audition, taction, but also, in the case of orienteering, kinaesthetic information. In some instances, the examples of expertise discussed here illustrate cross-modal learning (e.g., combining visual-tactile information about speech when tactiling), while others exemplify highly modality- and stimulus-specific learning (e.g., visual eidetic memory). Based on this review of the various domains of expertise, a few points that highlight some of the principles governing expert performance may be put forward.

First, we can note that potential transfer effects may occur as a function of the degree of specificity of expertise. Transfer is typically low or nonexistent in tasks that pose high domain-specific demands (e.g., wine tasting), whereas transfer effects are more likely to occur when the expertise domain is supported by a set of multiple skills (e.g., speech understanding).

Furthermore, the development of more complex expertise skills may be viewed as a function of the efficiency of the interaction between working memory and long-term memory. For instance, it is highly likely that this interface is facilitated by verbal processes (e.g., labelling) and/or by schema-driven structures of knowledge. A further interesting observation is that when more complex knowledge structures are involved in the interaction between working memory and long-term memory, there is more room for a potential transfer effect.

Finally, more complex and flexible ways of utilizing knowledge and cognitive representations presumably require the orchestration of several basic cognitive abilities (e.g., in orienteering and speech-reading skills), which in turn demand many years of practice.

As a concluding speculation, motivational and social factors may well come into play in a relatively more pronounced way in expertise that depends on several subskills than in more specific examples of expertise. Stimulus- and modality-specific expertise may depend relatively more on genetic contributions to the skill, whereas expertise in complex skills may be the combined result of genetic, experiential, motivational and sociocultural factors.

REFERENCES

Bende, M., & Nordin, S. (1997). Perceptual learning in olfaction: Professional wine tasters versus controls. *Physiology and Behavior*, *62*, 1065–1070.

Berg, H., Filipello, F., Hinreiner, E., & Webb, A. (1955). Evaluation of thresholds and minimum difference concentrations for various constituents of wine. *Food Technology*, *9*, 23–26.

Binet, A. (1894). *Psychologie des Grands Calculateurs et Joueurs d'Échecs*. Paris: Hachette. [Re-edited by Slatkine Resources, Paris, 1981.]

Charness, N. (1991). Expertise in chess: The balance between knowledge and search. In K.A., Ericsson & J. Smith (Eds.), *Toward a general theory of expertise: Prospects and limits* (pp. 39–63). Cambridge, UK: Cambridge University Press.

Chase, W.G., & Ericsson, K.A. (1982). Skill and working memory. In G.H. Bower (Ed.), *The psychology of learning and motivation, Vol. 16* (pp. 1–58). New York: Academic Press.

Chase, W.G., & Simon, H.A. (1973). Perception in chess. *Cognitive Psychology*, *4*, 55–81.

Chi, M.T.H., Glaser, R., & Rees, E. (1982). Expertise in problem solving. In R. Sternberg (Ed.), *Advances in the psychology of human intelligence, Vol. 1*. Hillsdale, NJ: Lawrence Erlbaum Associates, Inc.

Cornoldi, C., & De Beni, R. (1996). Mnemonics and metacognition. In D. Herrmann, C. McEvoy, C. Hertzog, P. Hertel, & M. Johnson (Eds.), *Basic and applied memory research. Practical applications*, 2 (pp. 237–253). Mahwah, NJ: Lawrence Erlbaum Associates, Inc.

Cornoldi, C., De Beni, R., Pazzaglia, F., & Favaretto, S. (2003). Abilità spaziali e senso dell'orientamento in persone che praticano l'orienteering. [Spatial abilities and orientation in individuals practising orienteering.] In R. Baroni & S. Falchero (Eds.), *In memoria di M. Peron*. Padova, Italy: Cleup.

Daneman, M., & Merikle, P. M. (1996). Working memory and language comprehension: A meta-analysis. *Psychonomic Bulletin and Review*, *3*, 422–433.

De Beni, R., & Moe, A. (2003). Presentation modality effects in studying passages. Are mental images always effective? *Applied Cognitive Psychology*, *17*, 309–324.

De Beni, R., & Piccione, G. (1995). Abilita eccezionali di memoria e di calcolo: Capacita innate o acquisite? [Exceptional memory and exceptional calculation ability: Innate or acquired abilities?] *Giornale Italiano di Psicologia*, *22*, 175–199.

De Groot, A.D. (1978). *Thought and choice and chess*. [First published in 1946] The Hague, Netherlands: Mouton.

Eccles, D.W, Walsh, S.E., & Ingledew, D.K. (2002). A grounded theory of expert cognition in orienteering. *Journal of Sport and Exercise Psychology, 24*, 68–88.

Emmorey, K., Klima, E., & Hickok, G. (1998). Mental rotation within linguistic and non-linguistic domains in users of American sign language. *Cognition, 68*, 221–246.

Engle, R.W., & Bukstel, L.H. (1978). Memory processes among bridge players of differing expertise. *American Journal of Psychology, 91*, 673–689.

Ericsson, K.A., & Charness, N. (1994). Expert performance: Its structure and acquisition. *American Psychologist, 49*, 725–747.

Ericsson, K.A., & Kintsch, W. (1995). Long-term working memory. *Psychological Review, 102*, 211–245.

Ericsson, K.A., & Lehmann, A.C. (1996). Expert and exceptional performance: Evidence of maximal adaptation to task constraints. *Annual Review of Psychology, 47*, 273–305.

Ericsson, K.A., & Polson, P.G. (1988). A cognitive analysis of exceptional memory for restaurant orders. In M.T.H. Chi, R. Glaser, & M.J. Farr (Eds.), *The nature of expertise* (pp. 23–70). Hillsdale, NJ: Lawrence, Erlbaum Associates, Inc.

Ericsson, K.A., & Smith, J. (Eds.) (1991). *Toward a general theory of expertise: Prospects and limits*. Cambridge, UK: Cambridge University Press.

Fahle, M. (1997). Specificity of learning curvature, orientation and vernier discriminations. *Vision Research, 37*, 1885–1895.

Fahle, M., & Edelman, S. (1993). Long-term learning in vernier acuity: Effects of stimulus orientation, range and of feedback. *Vision Research, 33*, 397–412.

Fiorentini, A., & Berardi, N. (1980). Perceptual learning specific for orientation and spatial frequency. *Nature, 287*, 43–44.

Fiorentini, A., & Berardi, N. (1981). Learning in grating waveform discrimination: Specificity for orientation and spatial frequency. *Vision Research, 21*, 1149–1158.

Galton, F. (1979). *Hereditary genius: An inquiry into its laws and consequences*. [First published in 1869] London: Friedman.

Gawel, R. (1997). The use of language by trained and untrained experienced wine tasters. *Journal of Sensory Studies, 12*, 267–284.

Gibson, J.J. (1951). *The perception of the visual world*. Boston, MA: Houghton-Mifflin.

Gilhooly, K.J., Wood, M., Kinnear, P.R., & Green, C. (1988). Skill in map reading and memory for maps. *Quarterly Journal of Experimental Psychology: Human Experimental Psychology, 40*, 87–107.

Gobet, F. (1998). Expert memory: A comparison of four theories. *Cognition, 66*, 115–152.

Gobet, F., & Simon, H.A (1996). Recall of random and distorted positions: Implications for the theory of expertise. *Memory and Cognition, 24*, 493–503.

Gobet, F., & Simon, H.A. (1998). Expert chess memory: Revisiting the chunking hypothesis. *Memory, 6*, 225–255.

Haber, R.N. (1979). Twenty years of haunting eidetic imagery: Where is the ghost? *Behavioral and Brain Sciences, 2*, 583–629.

Haber, R.N., & Haber, L.R. (1988). The characteristics of eidetic imagery. In L.K. Obler & D. Fein (Eds.), *The exceptional brain: Neuropsychology of talent and special abilities* (pp. 218–241). New York: Guilford Press.

Hancock, S., & McNaughton, L. (1986). Effects of fatigue on ability to process visual information by experienced orienteers. *Perceptual and Motor Skills, 62*, 491–498.

Hughson, A.L., & Boakes, R.A. (2001). Perceptual and cognitive aspects of wine expertise. *Australian Journal of Psychology, 53*, 103–108.

Hughson, A.L. & Boakes, R.A. (2002). The knowing nose: The role of knowledge in wine expertise. *Food Quality and Preference, 13*, 463–472.

Karni, A., & Bertini, G. (1997). Learning perceptual skills: Behavioural probes into adult cortical plasticity. *Current Opinion in Neurobiology, 7*, 530–535.

Klingberg, T., Forssberg, H., & Westerberg, H. (2002). Training of working memory in children with ADHD. *Journal of Clinical and Experimental Neuropsychology, 24*, 781–791.

Larsson, M. (1997). The influence of semantic factors in episodic recognition of common odors: A review. *Chemical Senses, 22*, 623–633.

Larsson, M., & Bäckman, L. (1998). Modality memory across the adult life span: Evidence for selective age-related of factory deficits. *Experimental Ageing Research, 24*, 63–82.

Lawless, H. (1984). Flavour description of white wine by "expert" and nonexpert wine consumers. *Journal of Food Science, 49*, 120–123.

Levänen, S. (1998). Neuromagnetic studies of human auditory cortex function and reorganization. *Scandinavian Audiology, 27* (Suppl 49), 1–6.

Lieu, Z., & Weinshall, D. (2000). Mechansims of generalization in perceptual learning. *Vision Research, 40*, 97–109.

Lucangeli, D., Galderisi, D., & Cornoldi, C. (1995). Specific and general transfer effects following metamemory training. *Learning Disabilities Research, & Practice, 10*, 11–21.

Lunner, T. (2003). Cognitive function and hearing aid use. *International Journal of Audiology, 42*, S49–S58.

Luria, A.R. (1968). *The mind of the mnemonist*. Oxford, UK: Basic Books.

Lyxell, B. (1994). Skilled speechreading: A single case study. *Scandinavian Journal of Psychology, 35*, 212–219.

Magnussen, S. (2000). Low-level memory processes in vision. *Trends in Neurosciences, 23*, 247–251.

Magnussen, S., Andersson, J., Cornoldi, C., De Beni, R., Endestad, T., Goodman, G., Helstrup, T., Koriat, A., Larsson, M., Melinder, A., Nilsson, L.G., Rönnberg, S., & Zimmer, H. (2006). What people believe about memory. *Memory, 14*, 595–613.

Magnussen, S., Greenlee, M.W., Aslaksen, P.M., & Kildebo, O.\. (2003). High-fidelity long-term memory for spatial frequency revisited – and confirmed. *Psychological Science, 14*, 74–76.

Maguire, E.A, Frackowiak, R.S.J., & Frith, C.D. (1997). Recalling routes around London: Activation of the right hippocampus in taxi drivers. *Journal of Neuroscience, 17*, 7103–7110.

Maguire, E.A., Valentine, E.R., Wilding, J.M., & Kapur, N. (2003). Routes to remembering: The brains behind superior memory. *Nature Neuroscience, 6*, 90–95.

Malinowski, J.C. (2001). Mental rotation and real-world wayfinding. *Perceptual and Motor Skills, 92*, 19–30.

Malinowski, J.C., & Gillespie, W.T. (2001). Individual differences in performance on a large-scale, real-world wayfinding task. *Journal of Environmental Psychology, 21*, 73–82.

Melcher, J.M., & Schooler, J.W. (1996). The misremembrance of wines past: Verbal and perceptual expertise differentially mediate verbal overshadowing of taste memory. *Journal of Memory and Language*, *35*, 231–245.

Öhngren, G., Rönnberg, J., & Lyxell, B. (1992). Tactiling: A usable support system for speechreading? *British Journal of Audiology*, *26*, 167–173.

Ottosson, T. (1997). Motivation for orienteering: An exploratory analysis using confirmatory factor analytic techniques. *Scandinavian Journal of Psychology*, *38*, 111–120.

Paivio, A., & Cohen, M. (1979). Eidetic imagery and cognitive abilities. *Journal of Mental Imagery*, *3*, 53–64.

Pangborn, R., Berg, H., & Hansen, B. (1963). The influence of color on discrimination of sweetness in dry table-wine. *American Journal of Psychology*, *76*, 492–495.

Pazzaglia, F., Cornoldi, C., & De Beni, R. (2000). Differenze individuali nella rappresentazione dello spazio e nell'abilità di orientamento: Presentazione di un Questionario autovalutativo. *Giornale Italiano di Psicologia*, *27*, 627–650.

Pichora-Fuller, K. (2003). Processing speed and timing in aging adults: Psychoacoustics, speech perception, and comprehension. *International Journal of Audiology*, *42*, 68–76.

Rabin, M.D. (1988). Experience facilitates olfactory quality discrimination. *Perception and Psychophysics*, *44*, 532–540.

Rabin, M.D., & Cain, W.S. (1984). Odor recognition: Familiarity, identifiability, and encoding consistency. *Journal of Experimental Psychology: Learning, Memory, and Cognition*, *10*, 316–325.

Rabin, M.D., & Cain, W.S. (1986). Determinants of measured olfactory sensitivity. *Perception and Psychophysics*, *39*, 281–286.

Rönnberg, J. (1993). Cognitive characteristics of skilled tactiling: The case of GS. *European Journal of Cognitive Psychology*, *5*, 19–33.

Rönnberg, J. (2003a). Cognition in the hearing-impaired and deaf as a bridge between signal and dialogue: A framework and a model. *International Journal of Audiology*, *42*, 68–76.

Rönnberg, J. (2003b). Working memory, neuroscience and language: Evidence from deaf and hard of hearing individuals. In M. Marschark & P. Spencer (Eds.), *The handbook of deaf studies, language, and education* (pp. 478–489). Oxford, UK: Oxford University Press.

Rönnberg, J., Andersson, J., Samuelsson, S., Söderfeldt, B., Lyxell, B., & Risberg, J. (1999). A speechreading expert: The case of MM. *Journal of Speech, Language and Hearing Research*, *42*, 5–20.

Saffell, T., & Matthews, N. (2003). Task-specific perceptual learning on speed and direction discrimination. *Vision Research*, *43*, 1365–1374.

Sagi, D., & Tanne, D. (1994). Perceptual learning: Learning to see. *Current Opinion in Neurobiology*, *4*, 195–199.

Sireteanu, R., & Rettenbach, R. (2000). Perceptual learning in visual search generalizes over tasks, locations and eyes. *Vision Research*, *40*, 2925–2949.

Snowden, P.T., Davies, I.R.L., & Roling, P. (2000). Perceptual learning of the detection of features in X-ray images: A functional role for improvements in adults' visual sensitivity. *Journal of Experimental Psychology: Human Perception and Performance*, *26*, 379–390.

Snowden, P.T., Rose, D., & Davies, I.R.L. (2002). Perceptual learning of luminance contrast detection: Specific for spatial frequency and retinal location but not orientation. *Vision Research, 42,* 1249–1258.

Solomon, G. (1990). Psychology of novice and expert wine talk. *American Journal of Psychology, 105,* 495–517.

Stromeyer, C.F., & Psotka, J. (1970). The detailed texture of eidetic images. *Nature, 225,* 346–349.

Summerfield, Q. (1987). Some preliminaries to a comprehensive account of audio-visual speech perception. In B. Dodd & R. Campbell (Eds.), *Hearing by eye: The psychology of lipreading* (pp. 3–51). Hillsdale, NJ: Lawrence Erlbaum Associates, Inc.

Thorndike, E.L. (1913). *Educational psychology.* New York: Teachers College Press.

Vanderberg, S.G., & Kuse, A.R. (1978). Mental rotation: A group test of three-dimentional spatial visualization. *Perceptual and Motor Skills, 47,* 599–604.

Vogt, S. (1999). Looking at paintings: Patterns of eye movements in artistically naïve and sophisticated subjects. *Leonardo, 32,* 325.

Vogt, S., & Magnussen, S. (in press). Expertise in pictorial perception: Eye movement patterns and visual memory in artists and laymen. *Perception.*

Watson, J. (1924). *Behaviorism.* Chicago, IL: University of Chicago Press.

Yarbus, A. (1967). *Eye movements and vision.* New York: Plenum Press.

10 Compensatory changes in everyday memory and communication: Disabilities, abilities and social context

Jerker Rönnberg and Annika Melinder

In this chapter, we discuss the concept of psychological compensation. We focus on communicatively disabled persons who depend on technical and/or alternative support systems in their everyday communication with others. Thus, after defining central distinctions in the compensation literature, we review in detail the effects of spontaneous compensation on memory functions and strategies in congenitally deaf and blind persons, in special populations such as those with Williams syndrome and autism, and in elderly collaborating couples. The concepts of episodic, working and collaborative memory are used to link up the overall patterns of effects seen across forms of communication, disability and social context.

COMPENSATION RESEARCH: THE NOTION AND SOME CONSTRAINTS

When everyday environmental demands on memory and communication are too taxing, a perceived need for compensation may arise within the individual. For example, elderly hearing-impaired persons may have problems understanding what is being said in a dialogue. This is due not only to their physical impairment, but perhaps also to their less capacious working memory. Cognitive ageing reduces the capacity of working memory to maintain a sufficient amount of perceived linguistic elements in mind (Rönnberg, 2003a). This dual deficit has a potentially dramatic effect on elderly hearing-impaired persons. For example, their speech understanding capabilities may be reduced, as the role of working memory in this example is to support guessing of what is to come in a dialogue, partially based on the ability to retrospectively disambiguate what has been said.

Technical compensation is about fitting a hearing aid. The main function of the psychological compensation in this example, however, is to improve working memory capacity or guessing ability. But this matter is even more complicated. To achieve optimal technical compensation, the cognitive prerequisites of the individual must be taken into account (Lunner, 2003).

Origins, means and criteria of compensation

According to Bäckman and Dixon (1992), the origins of compensation are to be found in a mismatch between the current skills or abilities of an individual and the environmental demands that he or she faces. It is important that the gap between skills and demands should be neither too large nor too small to motivate compensatory behaviour. The process of compensation aims to close the gap between expected performance in a certain task or social setting and a subject's actual, suboptimal performance. Given that the individual accepts that the skills themselves have deteriorated or that they are no longer amenable to practice, several potential compensatory mechanisms exist. In principle, the individual either attempts to maintain or substitute skills already in his or her own repertoire, or develops new means of compensation. However, the individual's awareness of the compensatory mechanisms is not always high, and the consequences of compensation may be either negative or positive (Dixon & Bäckman, 1995).

In line with Bäckman and Dixon's analysis (1992) and Dixon and Bäckman's conceptual analysis (1995), we adopt a rather strict criterion when we define compensation. To be labelled as compensation, the compensatory behaviour in question must be significantly superior to that of a matched control group. Substituting one kind of information for another, thereby capitalizing on previously elaborated perceptual mechanisms, may lead to improvement over the alternative of no substitution at all, although it does not necessarily lead to compensation (Rönnberg, 1995a). When the strict criterion is employed, the distinction between the development of new skills and the use of intact skills becomes less important. When compensation in the strict sense is achieved, there will always be an element of "newness" to it. That is because the same "old" skills have developed significantly and beyond the level of what is considered normal – and thus become "new" in that sense – or alternatively, previously "new" skills have become successively "older" as they have become integrated into the repertoire of the individual. For this reason, our further analysis will not be based on the distinction of intact old vs. new cognitive skills.

Disability and ability

Compensation research on communicative competence has shown that high performance is not necessarily caused or mediated by a compensatory change in those abilities that are specifically related only to the impairment in question. It is equally important to address ability-based compensation, independent of the impairment or disability (Rönnberg et al., 1998). Ability-based compensation is more intimately linked to the actual cognitive abilities that have generally proved to be important for success in certain tasks and situations, and hence, by implication, includes both persons with and without impairment. Bäckman and Dixon (1992) focused on the current skills or abilities of the learner by advocating an individual differences approach to spontaneous compensatory processes in memory and communication. The general reason for such a focus is that individual variability – and sometimes very special forms of ability or disability – will reveal much more about human potential in a compensatory context than would otherwise be the case.

In this chapter, we focus on the various forms of interplay between different kinds of communicative disabilities and different kinds of cognitive abilities.

Spontaneous compensation

The possibilities of compensation in everyday life better illustrate the ecologically relevant circumstances that stimulate compensatory change. In this vein, it is also important to view memory abilities in relation to communicative and social competence. Charting these kinds of conditions can then be a point of departure in rehabilitation or training programmes. As such they open possibilities, at the same time setting constraints on potential intervention regimes. Thus, research on spontaneous compensation can be relevant for everyday learning, memory and communication, and this represents an important first step in the overall endeavour to induce compensatory change. One hypothesis that may be nurtured is that episodic memory may be particularly amenable to compensation in this context; episodic memory is a complex and late developing system in the ontogeny of the individual, which may enable it to be plastic and sensitive to environmental pressures for longer periods of time. The general pattern of evidence for this may be cited from the literature on the selective effects of various kinds of brain damage on different memory systems. Here episodic memory, in comparison with semantic and procedural memory, for example, is more sensitive to such circumstances as a rule of thumb.

SENSORY IMPAIRMENT AND SPONTANEOUS EPISODIC MEMORY COMPENSATION

Two general aspects of spontaneous compensation should be noted when sensory impairment is being discussed. First, congenital impairments (or sensory deprivation) have a more profound compensatory impact on information processing than adventitious impairments. Second, compensation seems to emerge at a cognitive rather than a sensory or even perceptual level (Rönnberg, 1995a). This general pattern, of course, gives credence to the possibility that actual episodic memory compensation can be seen in relation to sensory impairment.

Congenital deafness

Congenital deafness, combined with early use of sign language and the natural passing of the milestones of language development, brings about substantial consequences for a variety of cognitive functions. These functions include peripheral visual attention, visuospatial cognition (e.g., mental rotation, visual imagery) and episodic memory for faces (see Rönnberg, 2003b, for a review). These compensatory changes are also mirrored to some extent by right-hemisphere language processing areas active only in native signers (see Rönnberg, Söderfeldt, & Risberg, 2000, for a review) – in particular, in those persons who have acquired sign language before puberty (Newman, Bavelier, Corina, Jezzard, & Neville, 2002).

What these compensatory changes have in common is that they are examples of a tentative generalization that can be formulated about one of the mechanisms underlying compensation. When cognitive or mnemonic compensation occurs, the corresponding functions develop because they play a mediating or supporting role in the ways in which a person communicates; otherwise, compensatory pressure is less likely to arise. For example, the development of peripheral visual attention, i.e., an expansion of the visual field, certainly compensates for the fact that persons with deafness cannot rely on auditory cues when they meet with persons approaching from the side or from behind (Neville & Lawson, 1987). Furthermore, mental rotation and image generation of objects are better in congenitally deaf persons (Emmorey, Klima, & Hickok, 1998; Emmorey & Kosslyn, 1996) – mental rotation abilities are at the root of the perspective taking (and transversal of scenes) necessary for communicating by sign, and imagery supports topographical functions and descriptions via signing.

Therefore, we should not be surprised when compensatory changes in face recognition are very specific to those local features of faces that have a communicative relevance for signing as such; that is, for nose and eyes, which typically carry grammatical information in addition to signing. When those features are manipulated in episodic face recognition experiments, deaf participants perform better than controls (McCullough & Emmorey, 1997). Thus, episodic memory compensation can be demonstrated, as long as it plays a communicative role.

Congenital blindness

Compensatory processes and mechanisms in blind persons have frequently been suggested. Recent research has also shown that there are distinct neural, cortical reorganization effects of being congenitally blind. Reading Braille in late-blind subjects activates certain areas of the visual cortex to a larger extent than in early blind readers. These areas include both primary and higher visual areas (Burton, Snyder, Diamond, & Raichle, 2002). It is even the case that tonotopic areas in the auditory cortex of the blind expand compared to those of sighted individuals (Elbert et al., 2002), a finding that may also be related to compensatory decoding of speech (Rönnberg, 1995b).

Lessard, Pare, Lepore, and Lassonde (1998) studied how an ecologically critical function, three-dimensional spatial mapping, was carried out by early-blind individuals with or without residual vision. The authors found that early-blind subjects could map the auditory environment with equal or better accuracy than sighted subjects. Furthermore, unlike sighted subjects, they could correctly localize sounds monaurally. Blind individuals with residual peripheral vision localized sounds less accurately than sighted or totally blind subjects, confirming that compensation varies according to the aetiology and extent of blindness. Research using the dichotic listening procedure shows that congenitally deaf individuals, just like congenitally or early-blind individuals, show enhanced attention sensitivity (Hugdahl et al., 2003). Thus, compensation occurs when specific communicative demands are sufficiently well articulated for a particular group of impaired persons.

Similarly, Tinti, Galati, Vecchio, De Beni, and Cornoldi (1999) found that appropriate manipulation of auditory information supports visual imagery in blind persons. However, in mental imagery tasks requiring the manipulation of visuospatial information, blind persons can perform as well as the sighted (for a review, see Cornoldi & Vecchi, 2000). In a recent study, Tinti and Cornoldi (2004) found that totally congenitally blind persons may perform even better than the sighted, in a task in which participants are required to develop a spatial representation of an explored pathway.

More crucial to the present argument is the fact that several recent studies also show compensatory episodic memory functions. This may be viewed as an expression of the basic theme that compensation only occurs when there is a clear communicative mechanism involved. Thus, (1) early visual cortex activation correlates with superior verbal memory performance in the blind (Amedi, Raz, Pianka. Malach, & Zohary, 2003), and (2) episodic recognition of previously sentence-embedded words is superior in blind participants, and is mirrored by more pronounced late potentials in event-related brain recordings in the blind participants (Roder, Rosler, & Neville, 2001). Furthermore, (3) it has been demonstrated that blind participants are – after either physical or semantic encoding – better at episodic recognition of environmental sounds than matched controls (Roder & Rösler, 2003). Finally, (4) learning to recognize the odour of everyday substances is better in blind persons (Murphy & Cain, 1986), and (5) deaf-blind individuals compensate by demonstrating enhanced tactile encoding in a matching-pairs game, but reveal normal storage and retrieval operations (Arnold & Heiron, 2002).

Thus, the effect of congenital sensory impairments seems to be pervasive at the neurophysiological and cognitive levels, and both qualitative and quantitative aspects suggest the existence of compensatory episodic memory mechanisms that play a central role in communication and interaction with the social and physical environment.

As we have argued so far, there may be a general memory system-specific explanation of compensatory memory functions. However, although this may hold true for the patterns of data seen in congenitally deaf and blind persons, there seems to be a broader spectrum of effects that may be understood on the basis of other types of everyday learning and communication. As will be seen, procedural memory development and learning of "new" skills are also commonplace, as is compensation by means of working memory-related functions.

SPONTANEOUS COMPENSATORY LEARNING UNDER SPECIAL EVERYDAY CIRCUMSTANCES

If a focus on disability or some other special person-related reason for compensatory change shifts to long-term exposure to everyday environments, it is important to study those special, everyday tasks that actually have the potential to modify memory, as well as the functional and structural anatomy of the brain. The study of this thought-provoking possibility has begun to shed light on the causes of brain plasticity.

The example noted in Chapter 9 regarding taxi drivers' navigational skills and episodic memory (Maguire, Valentine, Wilding, & Kapur, 2003) is rather dramatic and leads to the more general question of whether the brain – as a function of learning new skills in everyday life – is always functionally/ structurally modifiable.

Learning in several other skill domains seems to provide further support for the claim that our mind is modifiable in particular tasks as a function of longer periods of practice. Abacus experts, for example, are extremely proficient in mental calculation and recent studies make it clear that they use mental images to remember and manipulate numbers (Hanakawa, Honda, Okada, Fukuyama, & Shibasaki, 2003). In particular, these authors documented an increased involvement of neural correlates of visuospatial processing (e.g., right premotor and parietal areas) in expert abacus users compared to non-experts, especially when the size of the numerals was large. Professional violinists' long-term training and acquisition of equilibristic movements of the little finger produce more intense signals from motor cortex, as well as bringing about the development of larger motor cortices than in non-violinists (Lotze, Tan, Braun, & Birbaumer, 2003). Other attempts to localize morphological differences between world-class memory experts and novices have not been successful (Maguire et al., 2003). However, neural activation patterns revealed that spatial memory strategies characterized skilled persons, and that these strategies were related to hippocampal brain regions.

Whereas a close connection between brain morphology, psychological function, and specific everyday learning environments can be demonstrated at least in some cases, a general understanding of *why* these cases appear is still lacking. Nevertheless, two general observations apply to the collective data presented so far: to achieve substantial compensatory effects, (1) very long-term and systematic *training* is needed (see de Beni et al., Chapter 9, on expertise), and (2) the effects are shaped and stimulated by *specific social* constraints, contexts, and tasks.

WORKING MEMORY ABILITIES SUPPORT INDIVIDUAL COMPENSATION FOR COMMUNICATIVE DISABILITY

As we have shown, brain plasticity – and thus the compensatory potential – of cortical function and structure is possible in ways not previously envisaged within the field of neuroscience. One remarkable aspect of the data is the task specificity with which changes occur, and another is that the changes can be structural and/or functional. This is in keeping with the rule of task specificity in the general literature of memory training and transfer of learning (Gobet, 1998; Magnussen et al., 2006; Vincente & Wang, 1998; see also Chapter 1). The neurofunctional data can provide hints about which subsystems are typically engaged in memory compensation.

However, the other side of the coin is that compensation need not be task specific, given that the focus is on general cognitive mechanisms. As a consequence, general cognitive memory abilities may play a general mediating role in the build-up of several communicative skills involved in reading and speech and sign understanding. We now focus on working memory and its components, and how working memory mediates communicative skill.

Reading script

It is well known that phonological capacities in working memory predict the ease with which children acquire the alphabetic code through reading and writing (Hulme, 2002). When phonological problems are manifest, they are related to difficulties with word decoding, which in turn is assumed to be the cardinal symptom of dyslexia. Word decoding ability can be measured by tests that assess the segmentation of words into constituent phonemes, with reading and repeating nonsense words, and with Spoonerism tasks (Griffith & Frith, 2002).

Orthographic skills involved in building up the visual input lexicon also contribute to reading ability (Samuelsson, 2000). In beginning readers (8 years), evidence has been found of both phonological and orthographic contributions to reading ability, whereas as early as the age of 10, only orthographic contributions are significant predictors of reading (Samuelsson, Gustafsson, & Rönnberg, 1996). Phonological processing deficits are more pervasive in relation to some types of dyslexia than are orthographic skills. However, the genetic contribution to both orthographic and phonological processing skills is significant and independent of each other, suggesting subtypes of dyslexia (Gayan & Olson, 2003). Nevertheless, surface dyslexia seems to be more dependent on cultural reading practices and "how many books there are at home" than the phonological subtype (Gustafson, 2002).

As evidenced by priming tasks (Samuelsson, Gustafsson, & Rönnberg, 1998), phonological and orthographic representations are dissociable and represented in long-term memory. The efficiency with which these representations are accessed from long-term memory suggests a basis for cognitive individual differences of dyslexia. Although well-known attempts have been made to relate dyslexia to visual sensory processing deficits (Stein, 2003) and auditory temporal processing skills (Tallal, Merzenich, Miller, & Jenkins, 1998), the dominant view advocates a cognitive, phonological source of individual differences in script decipherment (Stanovich, Siegel, & Gottardo, 1997).

Individual cognitive compensation can be related to high performance in orthographic and phonological tasks (e.g., Muter & Diethelm, 2001) that in turn mediate lexical access, combined with "top-down" compensation, by means of using script-related information in working memory (cf. the interactive compensatory model advocated by Stanovitch, 1980; Sovik, Samuelstuen, & Flem, 2000). Top-down, working memory-based compensation may be reflected in a change in the cortical network serving the reading process in reading disabled individuals. A heightened reliance on inferior frontal and right-hemisphere regions has been suggested as compensating for the subnormal activity in left-hemisphere posterior difficulties (Pugh et al., 2001).

The concept of working memory represents a general mechanism that can serve to integrate sensory with stored long-term information about what is read, and how skills in particular functional components can play compensatory roles.

Speech and sign reading

In a similar vein, skills – and hence compensatory potential – in visual, audiovisual and visual-tactile speech-reading tasks (i.e., where the sensory input is poorly specified) are mainly predicted on the basis of certain "bottom-up" (i.e., phonology and lexical access speed) and "top-down" (i.e., inference-making) cognitive skills (Lyxell, 1989; Rönnberg, 2003c). The bottom-up predictors account for most of the variance in sentence-based speech understanding, but in the case of more extreme compensations for poorly specified speech input, a high general working memory capacity interwoven with good verbal inference-making abilities is the rule. The cases of GS (see Chapter 9; Rönnberg, 1993), MM (Rönnberg et al., 1999), and SJ (Lyxell, 1994) all show extreme speech-reading skill, but different habits of communication (Rönnberg, 1995b). GS uses tactiling, i.e., tactile and visual information about speech; MM is a native bilingual (sign and speech) and is a very skilled speech-reader; and finally, SJ is a skilled (visual only) speech-reader, with a mimicking dialogue strategy. Despite these differences in habits, extremely high-complex working memory storage and processing capacity, as assessed by reading span (Daneman & Carpenter, 1980), is what binds these experts together. Bottom-up working memory functions such as lexical access speed and phonological representations are within the normal range, while complex processing and storage capacities in working memory are at least twice as well developed (e.g., Rönnberg, 1993).

Wilson and Emmorey (1997a, b, 1998) have demonstrated in a series of studies that classical manipulations of working memory performance, such as word length and phonological similarity, may also be accomplished with signs as stimuli. Parameters in sign that can be manipulated are "phono-logical" similarities in movement type, hand shape, and position in space. A working memory-based account of sign language understanding has been proposed, which assumes that the input to the lexical access system is at the syllable level, a level of phonological representation that has also proved to be critical for speech-reading and understanding (Rönnberg, 2003a).

Thus, while there are differences between reading and speech-reading in the particular units of phonological processing that are crucial for lexical access (i.e., phonemes – Hulme, 2002 – vs. syllables – Rönnberg, 2003a), the similar-ities in compensatory top-down potential is apparent in working memory and script-related inference-making skills. Unexpected similarities may prove to be the case between working memory for sign and speech at the phonological and articulatory levels of representation in a working memory task (Bellugi, Bihrle, Neville, Jernigan, & Doherty, 1992), while on the other hand, explicit storage and processing capacity may prove to be language modality specific (Rönnberg, Rudner, & Ingvar, 2004).

All in all, a comparative perspective on speech, script and sign reading and understanding is therefore important for potential generalization about communication modes, language modality and the level of abstraction at which compensatory mechanisms in working memory are most appropriate.

WORKING MEMORY, FACE PROCESSING AND "THEORY OF MIND" IN SPECIAL POPULATIONS WITH PROBLEMS OF COMMUNICATION

Working memory has been studied in a number of other disabling conditions (e.g., Tourette's syndrome, multiple sclerosis (MS), cerebral paresis (CP), attention deficit hyperactivity disorder (ADHD), central auditory processing deficit (CAPD) and Parkinson's disease (PD), and some general features can be discerned. In some of the conditions, the general problem in working memory is inhibition of responses (e.g., Tourette's, ADHD), whereas in others the opposite problem of slowness and loss of integrative executive functions appears to be the case to some extent (e.g., PD and MS) (Rönnberg, 1999). However, systematic hypotheses about the relationships between cognitive prerequisites on the one hand and communicative skills on the other have been less developed than the above-mentioned research. Nevertheless, some other special populations have attracted both extensive theorizing and research.

William's syndrome

William's syndrome (WS) is a disorder characterized by mild mental retard-ation, a specific cognitive profile, and unique personality characteristics (extremely sociable and overfriendly). The cognitive profile is generally strong in the auditory working memory and verbal language areas, with pronounced weaknesses in the visuospatial domain. In a particularly illuminating study by Robinson, Mervis, and Robinson (2003), it was found that verbal working memory indices such as backward digit span were correlated with grammat-ical ability, suggesting that persons with William's syndrome rely more on working memory capacity than normal children matched for grammatical ability. Thus, children with good grammatical competence seemed to acquire this competence by means of individual differences in compensatory working memory functions, as indexed by backward digit span.

Furthermore, other research has shown that the working memory of people with William's syndrome may be selectively impaired for spatial span, but not for visual span (Vicari, Belluci, & Carlesimo, 2003). Although the overall cognitive level is in the range of mental retardation, within the visual-spatial domain face recognition skills appear to be relatively well preserved in William's syndrome. Recent research has shown that people with WS have an intact ventral processing stream (Paul, Stiles, Passarotti, Bavar, & Bellugi, 2002). This further attests to the importance of understanding the role of the face in a communicative context for William's children. As a matter of fact, Tager-Flusberg, Plesa-Skwerer, Faja, and Joseph (2003) found evidence that people with William's syndrome encoded and recognized faces holistically and in the same way as normal controls (i.e., using the same underlying neurocognitive mechanisms).

Taken together, these data demonstrate a rather straightforward relation-ship between individual cognitive prerequisites and particular compensatory and communicative performances. Once again, the working memory concept serves to integrate knowledge across several disabilities, conditions and forms of communication. It is also important to note that the integration of facial and auditory information may be accomplished in a working memory system that is geared to social exchange and communication.

Autism spectrum disorders

A key concept related to working memory and communication is the concept of "Theory of Mind" (ToM). Following interwoven cognitive, neurological, language and social trajectories the child gradually develops an understand-ing of other people's minds and actions, which has been called ToM since the first comparative studies of animal cognition were carried out (Premack & Woodruff, 1978).

Individuals with autism and Asperger syndrome have an impaired ability to "read" other people's minds, or reduced ToM capability. This disability constitutes two (out of three) of the main diagnostic features of autism, which include a lack of imaginary thinking (pretend-play activities) and communicative impairment (American Psychiatric Association, 1994; World Health Organization, 1993). Others have debated whether the deficit is an extreme value of the normal quantitative variation in any sample (e.g., the male pattern) (Baron-Cohen, 2000a, b; Baron-Cohen & Wheelwright, 2003; Keysar, Lin, & Barr, 2003).

However, individuals with autistic and Asperger spectrum disorders demonstrate a pattern of brain activity during face discrimination that is consistent with feature-based strategies that are more typical of non-face object perception (Schultz et al., 2000). The primary difference involved (when estimated by functional magnetic resonance imaging: fMRI) increased activity in the inferior temporal gyrus (ITG) in both groups of patients. Among the controls, the ITG was the area most strongly associated with object-specific perceptual discrimination. Furthermore, and consistent with all earlier studies on face perception, the control group showed focal areas of activation in the right fusiform gyrus during face discrimination, while the autistic group did not (Schultz et al., 2000).

There are also findings that indicate inverted but improved performance on some cognitive tasks by autistic children compared to controls. For example, children with autism showed a holistic processing advantage when face recognition depended on mouths, but were significantly impaired compared to matched controls in recognizing the eye region of the face (Joseph & Tanaka, 2003). Children with autism have also proved to be as good as controls in labelling inverted photographs of expressions, but less successful than controls at labelling upright facial expressions (Tantam, Monagham, Nicholson, & Stirling, 1989). Finally, Teunisse and Gelder (2003) showed that autistic children were less prone to use the contextual information of the face in a visual-search task. Instead, they used a feature-based processing style.

Compensation strategies for the social and communicative disability in autistic individuals has paralleled clinical observations of certain strengths in visual-spatial and perceptual areas, in many of which autistic individuals become highly skilled. For example, case files revealed that a 3-year-old autistic child successfully performed an upside-down 1000-piece jigsaw puzzle; an 8-year-old autistic child wrote down and named intricate connections in a plumbing system, and a 7-year-old autistic boy identified and even named details in a car engine. All of these demonstrate a special competence, significantly better than in normal individuals of same age (second author's files). It is of interest that autistic children tend to learn and appreciate signed Norwegian very quickly. It might be that this visual language reduces the amount of social interaction that demands ToM capabilities, and at the same time provides access to their compensatory possibilities (e.g., use of spatial and feature-based information). If so, autistic individuals may improve not only their special skills in certain areas, but also their communication, by making more efficient use of their semantic memory.

More recent research has shown that other groups of disabled persons, such as those with cerebral palsy and deafness, also suffer from less effective perspective-taking abilities (Peterson & Siegal, 1999). The consequence of a comparative perspective has resulted in other kinds of explanations as to the origins of ToM deficits. For example, in deaf people conversational opportunities in sign language are an important prerequisite for competence in ToM tasks (Marschark, Green, Hindmarsh, & Walker, 2000), and given optimal conditions this may even lead to genuine compensatory developments in deaf children (Courtin, 2000). It has also been claimed that frontal lobe structures associated with executive functions play an important role in the development of theory of mind (Dahlgren, 2002; Wellman, Cross, & Watson, 2001). As a matter of fact, mental rotation abilities inherent in sign language may require a certain kind of visuospatial working memory capacity – and individual differences in working memory capacity may thus contribute to individual compensation (Reed, 2002). However, the rule seems to be that autistic children as a group demonstrate less neural activity in spatial working memory-related executive components (Luna et al., 2002), but the opposite may well be true for children with cerebral palsy and deafness. This is not in conflict with the observation that autistic children can capitalize on signed Norwegian, as this kind of communication is still speech-based and therefore does not demand the kinds of mental rotation and working memory abilities inherent in genuine sign language.

Auditory and visuospatial working memory thus play selective but important roles for persons with William's syndrome or an autism spectrum disorder. Individual differences in working memory capacities relate to kinds of face processing, abilities to comprehend communicative intent – and thus to compensatory possibilities. Neural correlates corroborate the cognitive and communicative profiles of the syndromes discussed. The complexities of selective cognitive and perceptual abilities/disabilities are obviously tightly interwoven with social compensations as well as with lack of social capacities.

SOCIAL MEMORY COMPENSATION: THE CASE OF COLLABORATION IN ELDERLY COUPLES

While William's syndrome and autism may be said to represent the extremes of a cognitively based social continuum, research in many other areas has not primarily been preoccupied with social cognition. Many of the original examples of compensation research stem from the area of cognitive ageing (Bäckman & Dixon, 1992; Dixon & Bäckman, 1995, 1999) and from the area of rehabilitation of brain-injured persons (Prigatano & Klime, 2003; Wilson,

2002), and have not always fully acknowledged the roles played by cognitive abilities in the social and communicative context (Dixon & Cohen, 2001).

Here, we focus on a relatively new area in everyday memory and cognitive ageing, viz. collaborative remembering. The issues discussed are related to the role of cognition (here episodic and semantic memory) in communication, and to the possibilities of compensation (Dixon, 1996). Effective collaborative remembering presupposes that the two persons involved share general knowledge of the memory task and materials involved, as well as specific knowledge about the strengths and weaknesses of each other's memory (that is, they possess a *theory of another person's mind*), and that they are willing – as a consequence of that knowledge – to divide and manage some of the workload involved.

Previous research has shown that when dyads collaborate in episodic memory tasks they tend to perform less well together than would be expected on the basis of their pooled individual performances (Andersson & Rönnberg, 1995). This so-called negative net effect of collaboration is confined to episodic and explicit memory tasks, whereas semantic and implicit memory tasks are less affected by collaboration losses. The net effect is also independent of gender, and is reduced by friendship and long-lasting relationships in elderly couples (Andersson & Rönnberg, 1995, 1996, 1997; Johansson, Andersson, & Rönnberg, 2000; see also Chapter 6).

Although the search for conditions that actually optimize partner cueing in episodic tasks remains active, Johansson et al. (2000) found that an ad hoc subgroup of elderly couples who claimed that they used a *transactive* memory strategy (Wegner, Raymond, & Erber, 1991), i.e., a memory system that is shared by both members of the dyad, actually did not reveal any negative net effect. Thus, transactive memories may not only transcend the capacities of the individual but also help to compensate for cognitive ageing effects by means of social support from the partner(s).

Following up this transactive lead, Johansson, Andersson, and Rönnberg (2005) postulated two a priori dimensions – that purported to measure transactivity – on the basis of which the subjects rated themselves: *division of responsibility* and *agreement*. A dyad high on *division of responsibility* was assumed to be more successful when it collaborated in episodic memory tasks, and the degree to which division of responsibility *is agreed on* further determines performance. A certain level of disagreement was shown to stimulate dyadic discussion in such a way that compensation was obtained. In short, the results demonstrate that an optimal social memory compensatory strategy is most likely to emerge from couples who are highly responsible for the memory task. The interesting aspect of the data, however, is that the couples do not necessarily have to be high on agreement – if they agree, collaboration is less required or stimulated. Therefore, dyadic collaboration benefits the most when agreement is only moderate for responsible couples, and when the memory tasks are complex, unfamiliar, and demand explicit processing. Compensation is here taken to mean that there is a positive net effect of collaboration, as compared to the typically obtained negative net effect (for theoretical explanations, see Andersson, Helstrup, and Rönnberg, Chapter 6).

Here we thus have a case of social episodic memory compensation that does not focus on the compensatory improvement in individual brain structure or cognitive function per se, but which rather addresses social cognition and communication under everyday collaborative circumstances.

GENERAL DISCUSSION

In this chapter we have focused on spontaneous memory compensation from a disability and an ability perspective. We have seen that there do indeed exist systematic signs of cognitive and memory compensation such that when compensation occurs, it is very often intertwined with communicative and social demands. It appears that, when compensatory pressure brings about compensatory changes in everyday memory function, it is specific to particular cognitive mechanisms or perceptual details that either enable, or at least are relevant to, efficient communication with others. It is thus hard to find examples of memory compensation in a social vacuum, but many questions remain regarding the *why* of certain compensatory behaviours. One tentative generalization that can be made at this point is that the effects of compensatory memory are tied to particular tasks, social situations or contexts, or to general memory mechanisms (e.g., working memory) rather than selectively to one memory system that is prioritized over another. Currently, it is also true that although compensation can be demonstrated for all major memory systems currently debated, episodic memory seems in many instances to be the main subject of compensatory change. However, it is difficult to determine whether this actually reflects the true nature of the field or merely greater research interest in that particular memory system.

Although many of the observed compensatory effects can be ascribed to general adaptations to special environmental/communicative demands and/ or to the cognitive-perceptual make-up of special populations, there is also a growing consensus in the communicative disability literature that certain cognitive concepts possess the ability to tie different levels of description together by proposing mechanisms that operate vertically over levels of scientific explanation. We have presented data pertinent to the concepts of *working memory* and *theory of mind*, and we have seen that the concepts allow for the testing of competing hypotheses about representation and function at the neural level. We have also presented data about how the concepts may link the processing of social objects such as faces with abilities and inabilities to use social constraints in communication and collaboration.

The integration of vertical knowledge is one means of proceeding in compensation research. Horizontal knowledge integration – across disabilities, social contexts or everyday memory tasks – is another means of testing the generality/precision of concepts. We have given some examples of how complex working memory capacity is a central resource on which individuals can capitalize when communicative forms and languages are compared. The details of such a theoretical development concern several questions, some of which are not specific to compensation research. First, are working memory and its putative components specific to the communication mode or language used, or can modality-free models of working memory be framed? Second, what are the necessary components of a general working memory system for on-line understanding of script, speech or sign? Third, how does working memory capacity relate to capacity for theory of mind – and is that interaction also constrained by language modality?

Another central issue in compensation research is how and why skill development occurs. In this review we have offered a variety of examples of skilled people, such as abacus experts, taxi drivers, and tactiling experts (see also Chapter 9 on expertise). Common denominators for the successful development of skills may be length of practice, type of practice, and degree of social/communicative relevance, mediated by some core cognitive concept. Comparative research in this field is very rare. However, interventions that target certain key concepts of importance for social interaction will take compensation research one step beyond the issues of spontaneous compensation, towards generating more causal hypotheses about skill development. Research on explicit training and spontaneous compensation may need to be carried out in parallel in order to determine the boundaries of task dependence and issues of causality and generalization.

In a set of recent studies, Klingberg and colleagues have demonstrated that computerized multimodal and intensive (>20 days during 5–6 weeks) training of working memory in children with ADHD produces significant and substantial positive effects (Klingberg, Forssberg, & Westerberg, 2002). This holds true for the working memory tasks on which the children were trained but also for non-trained working memory tasks, as well as for other cognitive tasks such as Raven's progressive matrices. The effects have been replicated in a larger sample of children with ADHD paralleled by significant reductions in ratings of symptoms of inattention and hyperactivity (Klingberg et al., 2006). Working memory training is also manifest at the neural level of description and explanation, as an increase in activity was observed in inferior parietal and prefrontal cortices, suggesting neural plasticity in a prefrontal-parietal cortical network (Olesen, Westerberg, & Klingberg, 2003). The conclusion that can be drawn is that a central cognitive ability such as working memory does not have a fixed capacity. It can be trained and the effects are not as task-dependent as in many cases of skill development. Working memory training has a more general compensatory potential. It remains to be seen exactly *which mechanisms were trained* in the studies by Klingberg et al., and how general the effects are across groups, tests and contexts.

We propose that one criterion for successful compensation research in the future is the acknowledgement of both vertical and horizontal modes of knowledge generation and integration. Without this, compensation research may turn out to be too disability/ability specific, task specific, and context specific, creating a less coherent knowledge base in the area. The concept of working memory fares well when it comes to such overall efforts, as it represents a mechanism that has vertical as well as horizontal explanatory power.

REFERENCES

Amedi, A., Raz, N., Pianka, P., Malach, R., & Zohary, E. (2003). Early "visual" cortex activation correlates with superior verbal memory performance in the blind. *Nature Neuroscience, 6*, 758–766.

American Psychiatric Association. (1994). *Diagnostic and statistical manual of mental disorders – DSM-IV* (4th ed.). Washington, DC: APA.

Andersson, J., & Rönnberg, J. (1995). Recall suffers from collaboration: Joint recall effects of friendship and task complexity. *Applied Cognitive Psychology, 9*, 199–211.

Andersson, J., & Rönnberg, J. (1996). Collaboration and memory: Effects of dyadic retrieval on different memory tasks. *Applied Cognitive Psychology, 10*, 171–181.

Andersson, J., & Rönnberg, J. (1997). Cued memory collaboration: Effects of friendship and type of retrieval cue. *European Journal of Cognitive Psychology, 9*, 273–287.

Arnold, P., & Heiron, K. (2002). Tactile memory of deaf-blind adults on four tasks. *Scandinavian Journal of Psychology, 43*, 73–79.

Bäckman, L., & Dixon, R.A. (1992). Psychological compensation: A theoretical framework. *Psychological Bulletin, 112*, 259–283.

Baron-Cohen, S. (2000a). The cognitive neuroscience of autism: Implication for the evolution of the mental male brain. In M. Gazzaniga (Ed.), *The cognitive neurosciences* (2nd ed.; pp. 544–545). Cambridge, MA: MIT Press.

Baron-Cohen, S. (2000b). The extreme male brain theory of autism. *Trends in Cognitive Science, 6*, 248–254.

Baron-Cohen, S., & Wheelwright, S. (2003). The friendship questionnaire: An investigation of adults with Asperger syndrome or high-functioning autism, and normal sex differences. *Journal of Autism and Developmental Disorders, 33*, 509–517.

Bellugi, U., Bihrle, A., Neville, H., Jernigan, T., & Doherty, S. (1992). Language, cognition, and brain organization in a neurodevelopmental disorder. In M. Gunnar & C. Nelson (Eds.), *Developmental behavioral neuroscience* (pp. 201–232). Hillsdale, NJ: Lawrence Erlbaum Associates, Inc.

Burton, H., Snyder, A.Z., Diamond, J.B., & Raichle, M.E. (2002). Adaptive changes in early and late blind: A fMRI study of verb generation to heard nouns. *Journal of Neurophysiology, 88*, 3359–3371.

Cornoldi, C., & Vecchi, T. (2000). Mental imagery in blind people: The role of passive and active visuospatial processes. In M.A. Heller (Ed.), *Touch, representation and blindness* (pp. 143–181). Oxford, UK: Oxford University Press.

Courtin, C. (2000). The impact of sign language on the cognitive development of deaf children: The case of theories of mind. *Journal of Deaf Studies and Deaf Education, 5*, 266–276.

Dahlgren, S.-O. (2002). *Why does the bus stop when I am not getting off? How children with autism, Asperger syndrome and dysfunction in attention, motor control and perception (DAMP) conceptualise the surrounding world.* Doctoral thesis, Department of Psychology, Göteborg University, Sweden.

Daneman, M., & Carpenter, P.A. (1980). Individual differences in integrating information between and within sentences. *Journal of Experimental Psychology: Learning, Memory and Cognition, 9*, 561–584.

Dixon, R.A. (1996). Collaborative memory and aging. In D.J. Herrman, M.K. Johnson, C.L. McEvoy, C. Herzog, & P. Hentzel (Eds.), *Basic and applied memory research: Theory in context* (pp. 359–383). Mahwah, NJ: Lawrence Erlbaum Associates, Inc.

Dixon, R.A., & Bäckman, L. (1995). Concepts of compensation: Integrated, differentiated, and Janus-faced. In R.A. Dixon & L. Bäckman (Eds.), *Compensating for psychological deficits and declines: Managing losses and promoting gains* (pp. 3–19). Hillsdale, NJ: Lawrence Erlbaum Associates, Inc.

Dixon, R.A., & Bäckman, L. (1999). Principles of compensation in cognitive neurorehabilitation. In D.T. Stuss & G. Winocur (Eds.), *Cognitive neurorehabilitation* (pp. 59–72). New York: Cambridge University Press.

Dixon, R.A., & Cohen, A.-L. (2001). The psychology of aging: Canadian research in an international context. *Canadian Journal on Aging, 20*, 124–148.

Elbert, T., Sterr, A., Rochstroh, B., Pantev, C., Muller, M.M., & Taub, E. (2002). Expansion of the tonotopic area in the auditory cortex of the blind. *Journal of Neuroscience, 22*, 9941–9944.

Emmorey, K., Klima, E., & Hickok, G. (1998). Mental rotation within linguistic and non-linguistic domains in users of American sign language. *Cognition, 68*, 221–246.

Emmorey, K., & Kosslyn, S.M. (1996). Enhanced image generation abilities in deaf signers: A right hemisphere effect. *Brain and Cognition, 32*, 28–44.

Gayan, J., & Olsson, R.K. (2003). Genetic and environmental influences on individual differences in printed word recognition. *Journal of Experimental Child Psychology, 84*, 97–123.

Gobet, F. (1998). Expert memory: A comparison of four theories. *Cognition, 66*, 115–152.

Griffith, S., & Frith, U. (2002). Evidence for an articulatory awareness deficit in adult dyslexics. *Dyslexia, 8*, 14–21.

Gustafson, S. (2002). Cognitive abilities and print exposure in surface and phonological types of reading disability. *Scientific Studies of Reading, 5*, 351–375.

Hanakawa, T., Honda, M., Okada, T., Fukuyama, H., & Shibasaki, H. (2003). Neural correlates underlying mental calculation in abacus experts: A functional magnetic resonance imaging study. *Neuroimage, 19*, 296–307.

Hugdahl, K., Ek, M., Takio, F., Rintee, T., Tuomainen, J., Haarala, C., & Hämäläinen, H. (2003). Blind individuals show enhanced perceptual and attentional sensitivity for identification of speech sounds. *Cognitive Brain Research, 19*, 28–32.

Hulme, C. (2002). Phonemes, rimes, and the mechanisms of early reading development. *Journal of Experimental Child Psychology, 82*, 58–64.

Johansson, O., Andersson, J., & Rönnberg, J. (2000). Do elderly couples have a better prospective memory than other elderly people when they collaborate? *Applied Cognitive Psychology, 14*, 121–133.

Johansson, O., Andersson, J., & Rönnberg, J. (2005). Compensating strategies in collaborative remembering in very old couples. *Scandinavian Journal of Psychology*, *46*, 349–359.

Joseph, R.M., & Tanaka, J. (2003). Holistic and part-based face recognition in children with autism. *Journal of Child Psychology and Psychiatry, 44*, 529–542.

Keysar, B., Linn, S., & Barr, D.J. (2003). Limits on theory of mind use in adults. *Cognition, 89*, 25–41.

Klingberg, T., Fernell, E., Olesen, P., Johnsson, M., Gustafsson, P., Dahlström, K., Gillberg, C.G., Forssberg, H., & Westerberg, H. (2006). *Computerized training of working memory in children with Attention Deficit Hyperactivity Disorder. A controlled, randomised, double-blind trial.* Manuscript submitted for publication.

Klingberg, T., Forssberg, H., & Westerberg, H. (2002). Training of working memory in children with ADHD. *Journal of Clinical and Experimental Neuropsychology, 24*, 781–791.

Lessard, N., Pare, M., Lepore, F., & Lassonde, M. (1998). Early-blind human subjects localize sound sources better than sighted subjects. *Nature, 395*, 278–280.

Lotze, M.S., Tan, H.R., Braun, C., & Birbaumer, N. (2003). The musician's brain: Functional imaging of amateurs and professionals during performance and imagery. *Neuroimage, 20*, 1817–1829.

Luna, B., Minshew, N.J., Garver, K.E., Lazar, N.A., Thulborn, K.R., Eddy, W.F., & Sweeney, J.A. (2002). Neocortical system abnormalities in autism – an fMRI study of spatial working memory. *Neurology, 59*, 834–840.

Lunner, T. (2003). Cognitive function in relation to hearing aid use. *International Journal of Audiology, 42*, 49–58.

Lyxell, B. (1989). *Beyond lips: Components of speechreading skill.* Unpublished doctoral thesis, Department of Psychology, University of Umeå, Sweden.

Lyxell, B. (1994). Skilled speechreading: A single case study. *Scandinavian Journal of Psychology, 35*, 212–219.

Magnussen, S., Andersson, J., Cornoldi, C., De Beni, R., Endestad, T., Goodman, G., Helstrup, T., Koriat, A., Larsson, M., Melinder, A., Nilsson, L.G., Rönnberg, S., & Zimmer, H. (2006). What people believe about memory. *Memory, 14*, 595–613.

Maguire, E.A., Valentine, E.R., Wilding, J.M., & Kapur, N. (2003). Routes to remembering: The brains behind superior memory. *Nature Neuroscience, 6*, 90–95.

Marschark, M., Green, V., Hindmarsh, G., & Walker, S. (2000). Understanding theory of mind in children who are deaf. *Journal of Child Psychology and Psychiatry, 41*, 1067–1073.

McCullough, S., & Emmorey, K. (1997). Face processing by deaf ASL signers: Evidence for expertise in distinguishing local features. *Journal of Deaf Studies and Deaf Education, 2*, 212–222.

Meudell, P.R., Hitch, G.J., & Boyle, M.M. (1995). Collaboration in recall: Do pairs of people cross-cue each other to produce new memories? *Quarterly Journal of Experimental Psychology, 48a*, 141–152.

Murphy, C., & Cain, W.S. (1986). Odor identification: The blind are better. *Physiology and Behavior, 37*, 177–180.

Muter, V., & Diethelm, K. (2001). The contribution of phonological skills and letter knowledge to early reading development in a multilingual population. *Language Learning, 51*, 187–219.

Neville, H.J., & Lawson, D. (1987). Attention to central and peripheral visual space in a movement detection task. III. Separate effects of auditory deprivation and acquisition of a visual language. *Brain Research, 405*, 284–294.

Newman, A.J., Bavelier, D., Corina, D., Jezzard, P., & Neville, H.J. (2002). A critical period for right hemisphere recruitment in American Sign Language processing. *Nature Neuroscience, 5*, 76–80.

Olesen, P., Westerberg, H., & Klingberg, T. (2003). Increased prefrontal and parietal activity after training of working memory. *Nature Neuroscience, 7*, 75–79.

Paul, B.M., Stiles, J., Passarotti, A., Bavar, N., & Bellugi, U. (2002). Face and place processing in Williams syndrome: Evidence for a dorsal-ventral dissociation. *NeuroReport, 13*, 1115–1119.

Perner, J., Frith, U., Leslie, A.M., & Leekam, S.R. (1989). Prospects for a cognitive neuropsychology of autism: Hobson's choice. *Psychological Review, 97*, 122–131.

Peterson, C.C., & Siegal, M. (1999). Representing inner worlds: Theory of mind in autistic, deaf, and normal hearing children. *Psychological Science, 10*, 126–129.

Premack, D. G., & Woodruff, G. (1978). Does the chimpanzee have a theory of mind? *Behavioral and Brain Science, 1*, 515–526.

Prigatano, G.P., & Klime, S. (2003). What do patients report following memory compensation training? *Neurorehabilitation, 18*, 47–55.

Pugh, K.R., Mencl, W.E., Jenner, A.R., Lee, J.R., Katz, L., Frost, S.J., Shaywitz, S.E., & Shaywitz, B.A. (2001). Neuroimaging studies of reading development and reading disability. *Learning Disabilities Research and Practice, 16*, 240–249.

Reed, T. (2002). Visual perspective taking as a measure of working memory in participants with autism. *Journal of Developmental and Physical Disabilities, 14*, 63–76.

Robinson, B., Mervis, C.R., & Robinson, B.W. (2003). The roles of verbal memory and working memory in the acquisition of grammar by children with Williams syndrome. *Developmental Neuropsychology, 23*, 13–31.

Roder, B., & Rosler, F. (2003). Memory for environmental sounds in sighted, congenitally blind and late blind adults: Evidence for cross-modal compensation. *International Journal of Psychophysiology, 50*, 27–39.

Roder, B., Rosler, F., & Neville, H.J. (2001). Auditory memory in congenitally blind adults: A behavioral-electrophysiological investigation. *Cognitive Brain Research, 11*, 289–303.

Rönnberg, J. (1993). Cognitive characteristics of skilled tactiling: The case of GS. *European Journal of Cognitive Psychology, 5*, 19–33.

Rönnberg, J. (1995a). Perceptual compensation in the deaf and blind: Myth or reality? In R.A. Dixon & L. Bäckman (Eds.), *Compensating for psychological deficits and declines: Managing losses and promoting gains* (pp. 251–274). Mahwah, NJ: Lawrence Erlbaum Associates, Inc.

Rönnberg, J. (1995b). What makes a skilled speechreader? In G. Plant & K. Spens (Eds.), *Profound deafness and speech communication* (pp. 393–416). London: Whurr.

Rönnberg, J. (1999). Cognitive and communicative perspectives on physiotherapy: A review. *Advances in Physiotherapy, 1*, 37–44.

Rönnberg, J. (2003a). Cognition in the hearing impaired and deaf as a bridge between signal and dialogue: A framework and a model. *International Journal of Audiology, 42*, 68–76.

Rönnberg, J. (2003b). Working memory for speechreading and poorly specified linguistic input: Applications to sensory aids. *Hearing Review*, May, 26–31.

Rönnberg, J. (2003c). Working memory, neuroscience and language: Evidence from deaf and hard of hearing individuals. In M. Marschark & P. Spencer (Eds.), *The handbook of deaf studies, language, and education* (pp. 478–489). Oxford, UK: Oxford University Press.

Rönnberg, J., Andersson, J., Andersson, U., Johansson, K., Lyxell, B., & Samuelsson, S. (1998). Cognition as a bridge between signal and dialogue: Communication in the hearing impaired and deaf. *Scandinavian Audiology*, *27*, 101–108.

Rönnberg, J., Andersson, J., Samuelsson, S., Söderfeldt, B., Lyxell, B., & Risberg, J. (1999). A speechreading expert: The case of MM. *Journal of Speech, Language and Hearing Research*, *42*, 5–20.

Rönnberg, J., Rudner, M., & Ingvar, M. (2004). Neural correlates of working memory for sign language. *Cognitive Brain Research*, *20*, 165–182.

Rönnberg, J., Söderfeldt, B., & Risberg, J. (2000). The cognitive neuroscience of signed language. *Acta Psychologica*, *105*, 237–254.

Samuelsson, S. (2000). Converging evidence for the role of occipital regions in orthographic processing: A case of developmental surface dyslexia. *Neuropsychologia*, *38*, 351–362.

Samuelsson, S., Gustavsson, S., & Rönnberg, J. (1996). The development of word decoding skills in young readers. *Scandinavian Journal of Educational Research*, *40*, 325–332.

Samuelsson, S., Gustavsson, S., & Rönnberg, J. (1998). Visual and auditory priming in developmental dyslexia: A double dissociation. *Dyslexia*, *4*, 16–29.

Schultz, R., Gauthier, I., Klin, A., Fulbright, R.K., Anderson, A., Volkmar, F., Skudlarski, P., Lacadie, C., Cohen, D., & Gore, J. (2000). Abnormal ventral temporal cortical activity during face discrimination among individuals with autism and Asperger symdrome. *Archives of General Psychiatry*, *57*, 331–340.

Sovik, N., Samuelstuen, M., & Flem, A. (2000). Cognitive and linguistic predictors of text comprehension. *European Journal of Psychology of Education*, *15*, 135–155.

Stanovitch, K.E. (1980). Toward an interactive compensatory model of individual differences in the development of reading fluency. *Reading Research Quarterly*, *16*, 32–76.

Stanovitch, K.E., Siegel, L.S., & Gottardo, A. (1997). Converging evidence for phonological and surface subtypes of reading disability. *Journal of Educational Psychology*, *89*, 114–127.

Stein, J. (2003). Visual motion sensitivity and reading. *Neuropsychologia*, *41*, 1785–1793.

Tager-Flusberg, H., Plesa-Skwerer, D., Faja, S., & Joseph, M. (2003). People with Williams syndrome process faces holistically. *Cognition*, *89*, 11–24.

Tallal, P., Merzenich, M.M., Miller, S., & Jenkins, W. (1998). Language learning impairments: Integrating basic science, technology, and remediation. *Experimental Brain Research*, *123*, 210–219.

Tantam, D., Monagham, L., Nicholson, & Stirling, J. (1989). Face recognition in young children: When the whole is greater than the sum of its parts. *Visual Cognition*, *5*, 479–496.

Teunisse, J.-P., & Gelder, B. (2003). Face processing in adolescents with autistic disorder: The inversion and composite effects. *Brain and Cognition*, *52*, 285–294.

Tinti, D.C., & Cornoldi, C. (2004). *Visual experience is not necessary for survey spatial cognition: Evidence from blindness*. Manuscript submitted for publication.

Tinti, D.C., Galati, M.G., Vecchio, R., De Beni, R., & Cornoldi, C. (1999). Interactive auditory and visual images in totally blind persons. *Journal of Visual Impairment and Blindness*, *93*, 579–583.

Vicari, S., Belluci, S., & Carlesimo, G.A. (2003). Visual and spatial working memory dissociation: Evidence from Williams syndrome. *Developmental Medicine and Child Neurology*, *45*, 269–273.

Vicente, K.J., & Wang, J.H. (1998). An ecological theory of expertise effects in memory recall. *Psychological Review*, *105*, 33–57.

Wegner, D.M., Raymond, P., & Erber, R. (1991). Transactive memory in close relationships. *Journal of Personality and Social Psychology*, *61*, 923–929.

Wellman, H.M., Cross, D., & Watson, J. (2001). Meta-analysis of theory-of-mind development: The truth about false belief. *Child Development*, *72*, 655–684.

Wilson, B. (2002). Towards a comprehensive model of cognitive rehabilitation. *Neuropsychological Rehabilitation*, *12*, 97–110.

Wilson, M., & Emmorey, K. (1997a). A visuospatial "phonological" loop in working memory: Evidence from American Sign Language. *Memory and Cognition*, *25*, 313–320.

Wilson, M., & Emmorey, K. (1997b). Working memory for sign language: A window into the architecture of the working memory system. *Journal of Deaf Studies and Deaf Education*, *2*, 121–130.

Wilson, M., & Emmorey, K. (1998). A "word length" for sign language: Further evidence for the role of language in structuring working memory. *Memory and Cognition*, *26*, 584–591.

World Health Organization. (1993). *The ICD-10 classification of mental and behavioural disorders*. Geneva: WHO.

11 Metacognitive aspects of memory

Asher Koriat and Tore Helstrup

COGNITIVE AND METACOGNITIVE PROCESSES

People routinely engage in a variety of metacognitive processes when they learn new material or when they receive information that they are likely to use in the future. The more complex the material studied or the information received the more elaborate are the monitoring and control processes in which they engage. Even a simple prospective memory task in which we have to carry out a few errands may require some planning that takes into account many cognitive considerations. For example, we might decide to begin with the chore that, according to our judgement, is the one we are most likely to forget. As we complete these errands, we must "cross them out" from our mind, and of course, we might change our original plan when we are suddenly reminded of an extra errand. All these activities require not only planning our behaviour but also managing and orchestrating many cognitive operations along the way. Deficient monitoring may result either in omission errors (e.g., missing a chore or an appointment), repetition (e.g., telling the same story once again; Koriat, Ben-Zur, & Sheffer, 1988) or over-checking to make sure that a planned action has already been performed (e.g., checking that we have locked the door, see Koriat & Ben-Zur, 1988).

Successful learning (as well as teaching) requires a great deal of knowledge about the capacities and limitations of the cognitive system, about the effectiveness of different learning strategies and the effort that they require, and so on. In particular, a learner must have a realistic assessment of his or her abilities and competence. The work in developmental psychology has indicated that not only is it important that learners know the benefits of different learning strategies, but it is also crucial that they can and do implement them (Dufresne & Kobasigawa, 1989).

The effective self-management of learning and remembering requires the on-line monitoring of one's knowledge during different phases of the process and the adaptive regulation of various cognitive operations. Thus, in everyday life we learn and rehearse new information, we retrieve information from memory and make use of it, we consult our knowledge as we try to solve problems and to plan our activities, we consider alternative courses of actions in terms of their benefits and costs, and finally we choose to behave in one way or another. While engaging in these various cognitive processes, however, we also observe ourselves as we do so, inspecting the course of these processes, and regulating our thoughts and actions accordingly.

Thus, a distinction may be drawn between cognitive and metacognitive processes. In the terminology of Nelson and Narens (1990, 1994) this distinction amounts to that between an object level and a metalevel. The object level includes the processes that are traditionally subsumed under the rubric of information processing – encoding, rehearsing, retrieving and so on. The metalevel is assumed to supervise the processes that take place at the object level, to regulate them and navigate them towards one's own goals.

We shall clarify this distinction using the example of a student preparing for an upcoming examination. As the student prepares for the exam, he or she makes use of a variety of cognitive processes: reading and text processing, making sense of the material by relating it to information retrieved from memory, engaging in inferential reconstructive processes designed to fill in some of the gaps encountered, organizing the materials in his or her mind, and trying to memorize it. In parallel, however, he or she engages in metacognitive processes, monitoring these cognitive processes and regulating their course according to a variety of considerations.

Metacognitive processes include two general functions – monitoring and control (Nelson & Narens, 1990). The monitoring function refers to the reflective processes involved when we observe and supervise our cognitive processes on-line and evaluate their ease, progress and success. For example, the student must assess on-line the degree to which he or she has mastered the material in order to decide whether he or she needs to continue studying or "knows" the material and is ready for the exam.

The control function refers to the regulation of the cognitive processes, and includes a variety of higher-order operations that initiate, modify, and regulate the course of basic processes. Thus, in the course of learning the student needs to choose what learning strategy to use, how much time to allocate to different parts of the materials, which parts of the materials to restudy, and when to stop studying and move on to other activities. Such regulatory control operations are normally guided by the output of the monitoring operations. However, they are also based on the students' goals and on their beliefs about cognition. For example, as will be discussed later, learners normally allocate more study time to the items that are judged to be difficult than to those that are judged to be easy. Of course, this strategy is adaptive if the goal is to achieve a homogenous level of competence across all items (Nelson & Leonesio, 1988). However, when the goal set is relatively easy (e.g., to recall only a few of the items), participants focus on the easier items (Thiede & Dunlosky, 1999). The same is true when learning occurs under time pressure (Son & Metcalfe, 2000). Thus, the allocation of time and effort during study is affected not only by feedback from on-line monitoring (e.g., realizing that a piece of material is difficult to comprehend) but also by goals and situational constraints. In addition, control processes are also guided by prior knowledge and beliefs: In preparing for an exam, students would choose a learning strategy that they believe to be the most effective for study under the particular conditions (e.g., expecting open-ended questions vs. expecting forced-choice questions in the test (Mazzoni & Cornoldi, 1993). But they may relinquish a particular strategy if they find it to be ineffective.

Of course, monitoring and control processes would also be involved during the exam itself. In choosing which questions to answer (when the student has that option), in allocating time between different questions, and in the "self-scoring" of one's performance before handing in the test (Koriat & Goldsmith, 1998).

The example of the student preparing for (and taking) the exam also illustrates an important principle: The student's success in the exam will depend not only on cognitive skills but also on metacognitive skills, that is, on the ability to monitor one's degree of comprehension and competence during study, to allocate study time and effort effectively to different parts of the materials, and to choose and implement useful learning strategies that take into account both the qualities of the material and the nature of the expected exam. Of course, it also depends on the ability to engage in effective monitoring and control processes during the exam itself. For example, when monitoring is deficient, students may experience an "illusion of knowing", and may stop studying prematurely (and later be surprised to receive a low grade on the test). They might also choose or write down an answer in the exam that is clearly wrong (even though they might "know" the correct answer, but either do not know that they know it or do not try hard enough to look for it). Thus, metacognitive skills are no less important than cognitive skills in determining actual performance (Bjork, 1999; Koriat & Goldsmith, 1998).

We should stress that the distinction between cognitive and metacognitive processes is not sharp. First, the same type of process may sometimes subserve a cognitive function while in other times it may be used in the context of a supervisory, metacognitive level. Second, in many cases it is difficult to specify whether a particular process belongs to the "object level" or to the "meta level". However, the rough distinction between cognitive and metacognitive levels is useful to retain. We shall now examine some of the work on metacognitive processes.

THE INTEREST IN METACOGNITIVE PROCESSES

There has been an upsurge of research on metacognition in recent years. This interest derives from the recognition of the role that metacognitive processes play in many aspects of behaviour. For example, extensive work in developmental psychology, stimulated by Flavell (1979), supports the idea that developmental changes in memory performance are due in part to the development of metacognitive knowledge and metacognitive skills.

Discussions of intelligence assume that metacognitive skills, such as the ability to plan how to perform a certain task and to monitor one's own success in doing so, are central to intelligence (Sternberg, 1986). In the area of forensic psychology there have been many issues concerning metacognition, such as the reliability of witnesses' reports and the extent to which witnesses can monitor the accuracy of their reports (Perfect, 2002). Of course, in memory research, questions about metacognition emerge in many different contexts such as the determinants of memory accuracy (Koriat, Goldsmith, & Pansky, 2000), the processes underlying source monitoring and source confusions (Johnson, 1997), fluency attributions and misattributions (Kelley & Jacoby, 1998), false memories and misinformation effects and how they can be escaped (Israel & Schacter, 1997), and so forth. There has also been increased interest in the neuropsychological study of brain-damaged patients demonstrating intrusions, false recognitions and confabulations (Buckner, 2003; Burgess & Shallice, 1996; Schacter, Norman, & Koutstaal, 1998). In parallel, there has also been a great deal of research in recent years on monitoring and control processes in old age (Hertzog, Kidder, Powell-Moman, & Dunlosky, 2002; Kelley & Sahakyan, 2003).

In addition, however, the interest in metacognition may also reflect a shift from the traditional behaviouristic view in which people's behaviour is assumed to be driven by the impinging stimuli towards a more active view in which the person is assumed to have some degree of control over cognitive processes and behaviour, and to regulate his or her behaviour towards particular goals (see Koriat, 2000a, b).

This view presents a methodological dilemma. For example, we know that self-initiated monitoring and control processes take place during memory testing, and that these processes affect memory performance. Thus, the accuracy of what is reported from memory is in part under the person's control (Koriat & Goldsmith, 1996a, b). How should such intervening processes on the part of the subject be handled? Traditionally, memory researchers tended to treat subject control as a nuisance factor that should be either eliminated (e.g., by using forced-choice tests in order to minimize subjects' decision to volunteer or withhold an answer) or partialled out (e.g., by using a correction for guessing). Indeed, Nelson and Narens (1994) noted that although subject-controlled processes are not explicitly acknowledged in most theories of memory, "there is an implicit acknowledgment on the part of investigators concerning the importance of such processes. The evidence for this is that investigators go to such great lengths to design experiments that eliminate or hold those self-directed processes constant via experimental control!" (p. 8). Thus, the implicit assumption underlying traditional memory research is that subject-controlled processes conflict with the desire for experimental control.

However, in contrast to the tendency of laboratory studies of memory to exert strict experimental control and to minimize the contribution of self-regulation, in everyday life, people typically have great freedom in controlling and regulating various aspects of learning and remembering: During learning they are free to choose which encoding strategies to use, how to allocate their learning resources and when to terminate study. Similarly, when attempting to retrieve a piece of information from memory, they are free to decide whether to continue searching for that information or to give up, and whether to volunteer a candidate answer that comes to mind or withhold it lest it might be wrong. Metacognitive researchers share the assumption that such self-controlled processes constitute an integral part of memory functioning (Barnes, Nelson, Dunlosky, Mazzoni, & Narens, 1999; Goldsmith & Koriat, 1999), and should be incorporated in the experimental study of cognition rather than being eliminated or partialled out.

Of course, there are many processes that occur automatically, outside the person's consciousness and control. Evidence for the occurrence of such processes has accumulated in recent years (see Bargh, 1997). Some of these seem to involve the kind of monitoring and control operations that have been discussed by researchers in metacognition (e.g., Reder, 1988). There is still disagreement whether such processes that occur without conscious control should also be subsumed under the topic of metacognition (see Spehn & Reder, 2000).

In what follows we shall examine some of the findings on monitoring and control processes in learning and remembering. Research in this area has focused on five different questions. First, what are the bases of metacognitive judgements? Second, how accurate are these judgements? Third, what are the factors that are responsible for the accuracy and inaccuracy of monitoring? Fourth, what are the principles governing the link between monitoring and control? Finally, what are the consequences of monitoring-based regulation on actual memory performance? We shall begin by discussing some of these questions with regard to monitoring and control processes during learning.

MONITORING AND CONTROL PROCESSES DURING STUDY

We normally engage in a variety of monitoring processes in the course of learning and remembering. Consider a prospective memory situation in which we have to remember to perform some act in the future. For example, my wife reminds me "don't forget, we have an appointment tomorrow at 8 with the insurance person". What do I do then? Typically, I may try to assess the probability that I will remember or forget the appointment. On the basis of that assessment (which takes into account my schedule on that day, my beliefs about how good I am at remembering appointments, etc.), I may decide either to take some special measure so as not to forget, or to simply do nothing about it, being sure that I will remember it anyway. Of course, whether I eventually show up for the appointment depends not only on my memory, but also on my metamemory, that is, on the ability to correctly assess the probability of future recall and to allocate encoding resources accordingly.

The bases of judgements of learning

How do we assess the likelihood of recalling a piece of information in the future? How do students monitor their degree of comprehension and mastery as they study new material? One common and straightforward theory – the direct-access theory – is that learners can access the memory trace that is formed during study, and can make judgements of learning (JOLs) by taking a reading of the strength of the memory trace (Cohen, Sandler, & Keglevich, 1991). For example, in studying a list of words, a learner is assumed to detect the increase in encoding strength that occurs as more time is spent studying each word. In fact, the learner can then stop studying when a desired strength has been reached. Of course, this direct-access model can also explain the accuracy of JOLs: If JOLs monitor encoding strength, they should be accurate in predicting future recall because recall also varies with memory strength.

In contrast to this model, several authors subscribe to the cue-utilization view of JOLs (e.g., Begg, Duft, Lalonde, Melnick, & Sanvito, 1989; Benjamin & Bjork, 1996; Koriat, 1997). According to this view, JOLs are inferential in nature: Learners have no way of monitoring the strength of the memory directly but must utilize a variety of cues and beliefs to reach a reasonable assessment of future recall. Thus, they may take into account the perceived difficulty of the study items, the ease with which they come to mind during study, the number of study repetitions and the encoding strategies used, the type of memory test expected, one's beliefs about one's own memory efficacy, and so on.

An important distinction that has been proposed in discussing the bases of JOLs is between experience-based and theory-based JOLs (Koriat, 1997). Experience-based JOLs are assumed to rely on mnemonic cues that derive from the on-line processing of the studied items. These cues, such as encoding and retrieval fluency, give rise to a sheer experience of knowing, which can serve as a basis for the reported JOLs. Indeed, evidence has accumulated suggesting that JOLs reflect the learner's monitoring of the ease with which studied items are processed during encoding (Begg et al., 1989; Koriat, 1997; Matvey, Dunlosky, & Guttentag, 2001). Begg et al., for example, reported results suggesting that the effects of several attributes of words (e.g., concreteness-abstractness) on JOLs are mediated by their effects on ease of processing. Other researchers have emphasized retrieval fluency rather than encoding fluency, arguing that JOLs are based on the ease and probability with which the to-be-remembered items are retrieved during learning (Benjamin & Bjork, 1996). Using cue-target paired-associates, Matvey et al. (2001) found that JOLs increased with increasing speed of generating the targets to the cues at study, and Hertzog, Dunlosky, Robinson, and Kidder (2003) also found that JOLs increased with the success and speed of forming an interactive image between the cue and the target. Taken together, these results support the view that JOLs are based on the fluency of perceiving or retrieving targets at study.

Turning next to theory-based judgements, there is little doubt that people make use of their a-priori theories about memory in making JOLs. Theory-based JOLs rely on the deliberate application of metacognitive beliefs or theories about one's memory skills and about the way in which various factors can affect memory performance (see Dunlosky & Nelson, 1994; Koriat, 1997; Mazzoni & Kirsch, 2002). For example, in making JOLs, people may take into account beliefs about how good they are in retaining certain kinds of information (e.g., names, faces) and how different learning strategies may affect memory performance. For example, JOLs appear to draw on the belief that generating a word is better for memory than reading it (Begg et al., 1989; Matvey et al., 2001). The contribution of metacognitive beliefs has been spelled out most clearly by developmental psychologists (e.g., Flavell, 1979; see Koriat, 2002) in the context of children's memory functioning, but such beliefs clearly influence adults' metacognitive judgements as well (see Koriat, 1997).

It should be stressed that unlike theory-based JOLs, which rely on an analytic, deliberate inference, experience-based JOLs are based on non-analytic, contentless cues such as encoding and retrieval fluency. These cues are typically used unconsciously, and their effects are automatic. The non-analytic basis of metacognitive judgements is responsible for the phenomenal quality of the feeling of knowing as an immediate, unexplained intuition, similar to that which is associated with the experience of perceiving (see Kahneman, 2003).

Dissociations between predicted and actual recall

The clearest evidence in support of the idea that JOLs are based on inference from cues comes from observed dissociations between JOLs and actual recall performance. Benjamin, Bjork, and Schwartz (1998) had participants answer several questions and then assess the likelihood that they would be able to recall the answer in a free-recall test. They found that the more rapidly participants retrieved an answer to a question the higher was their estimate that they would be able to recall that answer at a later time. In reality, however, the opposite was the case. These results imply that the accuracy of JOLs is not guaranteed (as might have been the case if JOLs were to monitor memory strength), but depends on the validity of the cues on which these judgements are based.

Another type of dissociation has been recently observed by Koriat, Bjork, Sheffer, and Bar (2004). They had participants study a list of paired associates and make JOLs for tests that were expected either immediately after study, a day after study or a week after study. Assuming that JOLs monitor processing fluency during study, then they should be expected to exhibit insensitivity to the expected time of testing. Indeed, whereas actual recall dropped considerably with retention interval, JOLs were entirely indifferent to the expected retention interval. The result showed dissociation between JOLs and recall such that JOLs matched closely actual recall for immediate testing, whereas for a week's delay they were considerably inflated.

It is interesting to note that when a new group of participants was asked to estimate how many words learners would recall after each of the three retention intervals, their estimates matched very closely the first group's actual recall, exhibiting a clear forgetting function. This finding suggests that in making theory-based predictions, participants draw upon their beliefs about forgetting, but do not do so when their predictions rely on their immediate subjective experience.

The validity of JOLs in predicting recall

Although, as noted above, dissociations have been observed between JOLs and recall under some circumscribed conditions, these are the exceptions rather than the rule. By and large learners are moderately accurate in predicting recall success. As early as 1966, Underwood showed that participants can estimate with some accuracy which items should be easier to learn and which should be difficult to learn. In addition, learners can monitor their degree of mastery of studied material on line (e.g., Dunlosky & Nelson, 1994; Mazzoni & Nelson, 1995): They can estimate roughly the percentage of items that they will recall (absolute accuracy), and can also say which items they will recall and which they will not (relative accuracy). In most studies, relative accuracy (or "resolution") has been indexed by the within-person gamma correlation between JOLs and recall (Nelson, 1984). This correlation reflects the degree to which a learner can discriminate between what he will recall and what he will not.

However, there are situations in which monitoring is particularly poor. An example is when monitoring concerns one's own performed actions (e.g., Cohen et al., 1991; Koriat, Ben-Zur, & Druch, 1991). Thus, when participants perform a series of mini-tasks (so called Self-Performed Tasks, or SPTs; see Chapter 3) and asked to indicate the likelihood of recalling these tasks in the future, the accuracy of their predictions tends to be much poorer than that of monitoring the recallability of different words in a studied list.

Evidently, it is important to seek procedures that can improve JOL accuracy. Two such procedures have been found to be effective across several experiments. The first is repeated practice studying the same list of items. Several experiments confirmed that the accuracy of JOLs in predicting future recall improves with repeated study–test cycles of the same list of items (King, Zechmeister, & Shaughnessy, 1980; Koriat, Sheffer, & Ma'ayan, 2002; Mazzoni, Cornoldi, & Marchitelli, 1990). Koriat (1997) proposed that this improvement occurs because (1) with increased practice studying a list of items, learners shift from basing JOLs on the pre-experimental attributes of the items towards greater reliance on mnemonic cues (e.g., processing fluency) associated with the study and retrieval of these items, and (2) mnemonic cues tend to have greater validity in predicting recall than pre-experimental cues, being sensitive to the actual processing of the items.

The second procedure that was found to improve JOL accuracy is that of soliciting JOLs not immediately after studying each item, but a few trials later. In paired-associate learning, delayed JOLs, prompted by the cue alone, have been found to be considerably more accurate than immediate JOLs or delayed JOLs prompted by the entire cue-target pair (Dunlosky & Nelson, 1992; Nelson & Dunlosky, 1991). Presumably, the condition in which JOLs are delayed and cued by the stimulus alone approximates the eventual cued-recall test. Indeed, Nelson, Narens, and Dunlosky (2004) reported evidence that in making delayed JOLs, participants rely heavily on the accessibility of the target. When JOLs are solicited immediately after study, the target is practically always retrievable, and hence its accessibility has little diagnostic value. Koriat and Ma'ayan (2005) also observed that whereas immediate JOLs rely primarily on the the ease with which the item is encoded, as JOLs are further delayed they tend to be based primarily on the ease with which the target comes to mind, which is a better predictor of later cued recall.

Illusions of knowing during learning

Everyday experience suggests that students sometimes exhibit an illusion of competence, holding unduly high expectations about their future performance (see Dunning, Johnson, Ehrlinger, & Kruger, 2003; Metcalfe, 1998). What are the mechanisms that can instil such illusions?

Bjork (1999) discussed several conditions of learning that tend to enhance performance during learning but impair long-term retention. These conditions, according to Bjork and Bjork (1992), facilitate "retrieval strength" but not "storage strength". As a result learners may experience an illusion of competence, resulting in inflated predictions about their future performance. For example, whereas massed practice generally results in better performance than spaced practice in the short term, spaced practice yields considerably better performance in the long term (e.g., Bahrick, 1979). Therefore massed practice causes learners to overestimate their future performance (see Zechmeister & Shaughnessy, 1980). Indeed, in Simon and Bjork's (2001) study, massed (blocked) practice inflated participants' predictions of their future performance: Participants asked to learn each of several movement patterns under blocked conditions predicted better performance than they did when those patterns were learned under random (interleaved) conditions, whereas actual performance exhibited the opposite pattern.

Koriat and Bjork (2005) also described a condition that has the potential of creating an illusion of competence during learning: Because JOLs are made in the presence of information that is absent but solicited during testing, the failure to discount the effects of that information when making JOLs can instil an illusion of competence. Koriat and Bjork presented evidence suggesting that such illusions occur when the target (or answer) presented during study activates aspects of the cue (or question) that are not likely to come forward during testing when the cue (or question) appears alone.

In sum, the cue-utilization approach to JOLs has the advantage of explaining the conditions that lead to accurate and inaccurate JOLs. The results obtained thus far suggest that JOLs are sensitive to mnemonic cues that are revealed on-line during encoding. The advantage of cues such as encoding and retrieval fluency is that they are generally sensitive to a variety of factors that affect actual recall, such as level of processing, prior presentation, and exposure duration. Hence they are generally diagnostic of future memory performance. Under some conditions, however, these cues can also mislead metacognitive judgements. In general, JOLs will be accurate to the extent that processing fluency at the time of making JOLs incorporates the same demands as later recall (see Benjamin et al., 1998; Groninger, 1979). Conditions that produce an illusion of competence tend to involve different demands at study and test.

On-line control processes during learning

As noted earlier, much of the work in metacognition assumes a causal effect of monitoring on control. Thus, we might expect learners to use their monitoring judgements during study as a basis for the controlled, strategic regulation of learning. A classic demonstration of this idea is the relationship between JOLs and study time in self-paced learning: When learners are allowed to control the amount of time spent on each item, they generally allocate more time to items that are judged to be difficult to learn than to those that are judged to be easy to learn (for a review see Son & Metcalfe, 2000). This observation has been taken to indicate that learners use their JOLs as a basis for regulating the allocation of study time, investing more effort in the study of difficult items in order to compensate for their difficulty (Nelson & Leonesio, 1988).

Dunlosky and Hertzog (1998) proposed a discrepancy-reduction model according to which learners specify a desired level of memory strength that they wish to reach – a level that was referred to as the "norm of study" (Le Ny, Denhiere, & Le Taillanter, 1972). As they study the material, they monitor continuously the increase in memory strength that occurs as more time is spent studying each item, and cease study when the pre-set norm of study has been reached.

Son and Metcalfe (2000), who reviewed the literature regarding the relationship between item difficulty and self-paced study time, indeed found that in 35 out of 46 published experimental conditions, learners exhibited a preference for studying the more difficult materials. However, as noted earlier, there are exceptions to this rule. For example, Thiede and Dunlosky (1999) presented participants with an easy goal: to learn a list of 30 paired-associates with the aim of recalling at least 10 of those. When participants indicated which items they wished to study, they were more likely to choose the easier items rather than the more difficult items. Thiede and Dunlosky proposed a model in which there is a superordinate level of control, which concerns pre-study and planning decisions that are made in order to maximize the efficiency of study and minimize the effort invested in it. Son and Metcalfe also showed that under high time pressure, participants tend to invest more study time in items that are judged as easy rather than on those that are judged as more difficult.

These results suggest that people adopt an adaptive strategy, choosing to focus on the easier items when time pressure is strong or when they have an easy goal. Presumably students preparing for an exam will do the same when they do not have enough time to spend studying or when they only want to pass the exam rather than receiving a high grade. The adaptive, goal-driven nature of study time allocation is also revealed by studies indicating that learners invest more study time when they expect a recall test than when they expect a recognition test (Mazzoni & Cornoldi, 1993), and more time when the instructions stress memory accuracy than when they stress speed of learning (Nelson & Leonesio, 1988).

An important question that emerges concerns the effectiveness of the policy of study time allocation for enhancing memory performance. Unlike expectations from the discrepancy-reduction model (Dunlosky & Hertzog, 1998), Metcalfe and her associates (Metcalfe, 2002; Metcalfe & Kornell, 2003) observed that learners allocated most time to medium-difficulty items and studied the easiest items first. In parallel, they observed that when study time was manipulated by the experimenter rather than self-paced, medium-difficulty items benefited more from increased presentation duration than did easy or difficult items. These results were taken to suggest that learners adopt an effective strategy of study time allocation when allowed to pace their study.

MONITORING PROCESSES DURING REMEMBERING

We shall turn next to the monitoring and control processes that occur during retrieval. As early as 1970, Tulving and Madigan claimed that one of the truly unique characters of human memory is its knowledge of its own knowledge. They argued that genuine progress in memory research depends on understanding how the memory system not only can produce a learned response or retrieve an image but also can, rather accurately, estimate the likelihood of its success in doing it.

Ever since this statement was made, a great deal of work has been conducted on the feeling of knowing (FOK) that sometimes accompanies the search for a memory item. William James has provided a poetic description of the feeling that accompanies the tip-of-the-tongue (TOT) state, when we struggle to retrieve an elusive name or word from memory. The TOT state is interesting because it combines two seemingly inconsistent features: The person is unable to retrieve the sought target, but at the same time has a strong feeling of knowing, and can sometimes monitor the emergence of the elusive target into consciousness.

The bases of feelings of knowing when recall fails

The discrepancy between subjective and objective indices of knowledge naturally raises the question: How do we know that we know? When we fail to retrieve a name from memory, how do we know that it is "there"? As with JOLs solicited during study, we can distinguish between two general explanations for the basis of the FOK that is sometimes experienced when recall fails. One explanation is based on the idea of direct access. Hart (1965) proposed that FOK judgements are based on accessing a special memory-monitoring module that can directly inspect the information stored in memory to determine whether the solicited target is stored in memory or not. Thus, whenever a person is required to recall a target, the monitoring module is activated to make sure that the target is present in store before attempting to retrieve it. Such a monitor, then, can save the time and effort looking for a target that is not in store. The important feature of the direct-access model is that it also offers a straightforward explanation for the accuracy of the FOK: If the FOK directly monitors the presence of the target in memory, then it ought to serve as a valid predictor of actual memory performance. In fact, if this view is endorsed, it should be the inaccuracy of the FOK that would need explanation.

More recent approaches, however, assume that FOK judgements are inferential in nature. Two types of inferential processes have been assumed to underlie FOK judgements. First, these judgements may be based on beliefs and information retrieved from memory. For example, a person may remember an episode in which she has used the word or name that she now fails to recall. Such information-based judgement typically involves a conscious and deliberate inference. Second, FOK judgements may be based on a sheer subjective feeling, as when a person "senses" that a name is on the tip of the tongue. It has been argued that FOK judgements that are based on subjective experience are also inferential in nature because the feeling that one knows is itself a product of implicit heuristics (Koriat & Levy-Sadot, 1999). These heuristics, like those underlying JOLs, may occur below full consciousness to influence and shape subjective experience and the feeling of knowing. Thus, it has been proposed that rememberers have no priviledged access to information that they fail to retrieve, but must infer the presence of that inormation in memory on the basis of what they can retrieve (Koriat, 1993).

Two heuristic-based accounts have been proposed to underlie experience-based FOK judgements; the cue familiarity and accessibility accounts. According to the cue-familiarity hypothesis, FOK is based on the familiarity of the pointer that serves to probe memory, not on the retrievability of the target itself (Metcalfe, Schwartz, & Joaquim, 1993; Reder, 1988). Thus, a rapid preliminary FOK is routinely and automatically elicited by the familiarity of the terms of a memory question, and this FOK governs question-answering strategy. Indeed, in several studies, the advance priming of the terms of a question (assumed to enhance the familiarity of the question) was found to enhance speeded, preliminary FOK judgements without correspondingly raising the probability of recall or recognition of the answer (Reder, 1988; Schwartz & Metcalfe, 1992). Additional support for the cue-familiarity account comes from studies using a proactive-interference paradigm (Metcalfe, Schwartz, & Joaquim, 1993), and also from studies of arithmetic problems (Reder & Ritter, 1992; Schunn, Reder, Nhouyvanisvong, Richards, & Stroffolino, 1997). Consistent with this account is also the finding of Glucksberg and McCloskey (1981) that increasing the familiarity of questions for which participants do not know the answer increases the latency of "don't know" responses to these questions.

According to the accessibility account, in contrast, FOK is based on the overall accessibility of pertinent information regarding the solicited target (Koriat, 1993, 1994). Even when retrieval fails, people may still retrieve a variety of partial clues and activations, such as fragments of the target, semantic and episodic attributes, and so on. These partial clues may induce the subjective feeling that the target is stored in memory, and that it will be recalled or recognized in the future. An important assumption of the accessibility account is that participants have no direct access to the accuracy of the partial clues that come to mind, and therefore utilize the accessibility of correct and wrong partial clues indistinguishably.

Support for the accessibility account comes from a study that examined the nature of word definitions that consistently induce a TOT state (Koriat & Lieblich, 1977). The results suggested that the critical factor is the overall amount of partial information they tend to precipitate, regardless of whether that information is correct or not.

Koriat (1993) had participants study a nonsense string and then attempt to recall as many of the letters as they could, and make FOK judgements regarding the probability of recognizing the correct string among lures. The results indicated that FOK judgements increased with the number of letters that participants reported regardless of the accuracy of these letters. Thus, FOK increased as a function of the number of correct letters and also as a function of the number of wrong letters reported. When the number of letters reported was held constant, FOK judgements also increased with the ease with which information came to mind, as reflected in the latency to initiate recall.

If FOK judgements increase with the accessibility of both correct and incorrect partial information, why are they nevertheless accurate in predicting *correct* recall or recognition of the target? Koriat (1993) argued that this is because much of the information that comes spontaneously to mind is correct. That is, when a piece of information comes spontaneously to mind during remembering, it is much more likely to be correct than incorrect. Therefore, the total amount of partial information accessible is a good cue for recalling or recognizing the *correct* target.

Dissociations between knowing and the feeling of knowing

The assumption that FOK judgements are inferential in nature, being based on a variety of cues, implies that they need not be always accurate. Indeed, the findings supporting the cue-familiarity account of the FOK demonstrate a dissociation such that the advance priming of the cue enhances FOK judgements without correspondingly affecting recall. A similar dissociation, consistent with the accessibility account, was reported by Koriat (1995) using different classes of general-information questions. Such questions typically bring to mind more correct (partial or complete) information than incorrect information. Hence, FOK judgements based on that information are expected to be correct by and large, as was found to be the case. However, for a minority of questions – so-called deceptive questions (Fischhoff, Slovic, & Lichtenstein, 1977) – people tend to produce predominantly incorrect information (e.g., "What is the capital of Australia?", "In which US state is Yale University located?"). For such deceptive questions FOK judgements made following recall failure were found to be *negatively* correlated with subsequent recognition memory performance, presumably because these questions bring to mind partial clues that are predominantly wrong. Thus, FOK judgements tend to be accurate as long as the questions bring to mind more correct than incorrect partial information.

In sum, there is sufficient support for the idea that FOK judgements are based on mnemonic cues such as cue familiarity, partial information about the target, and the ease with which information comes to mind. In fact, there is evidence for a two-stage model in which both cue familiarity and accessibility are assumed to contribute to the FOK, but whereas the effects of familiarity occur early, those of accessibility occur later, and only when cue familiarity is sufficiently high to drive the interrogation of memory for potential answers (Koriat & Levy-Sadot, 2001; Vernon & Usher, 2003).

As far as the accuracy of FOK judgements is concerned, these judgements are accurate by and large in predicting future recall and recognition (Schwartz & Metcalfe, 1994). However, their accuracy varies with the validity of the cues on which they rest.

The control effects of feelings of knowing

Positive feelings of knowing generally drive memory search: When people feel that they know the answer to a question, they try harder to look for it than when they feel that they do not know the answer (Barnes et al., 1999; Costermans, Lories, & Ansay, 1992; Gruneberg, Monks, & Sykes, 1977).

People also spend more time searching for a solicited target when they experience a TOT feeling than when they do not (Schwartz, 2001).

More generally, Reder (1988) argued that preliminary FOK judgements guide the selection of strategies that people use to answer questions or solve problems. For example, Reder and Ritter (1992) had participants make fast judgements whether they knew the answer to an arithmetic problem and could retrieve it directly, or whether they had to compute it. "Know" judgements were found to increase with increasing frequency of previous exposures to the same parts of the problem, not with availability of the answer. Thus misled FOK judgements can misguide the decision to retrieve or compute the answer.

The regulation of memory retrieval is affected not only by FOK judgements but also by other considerations. For example, when participants are penalized for slow responding, they retrieve answers faster but produce more incorrect answers (Barnes et al., 1999).

RETROSPECTIVE CONFIDENCE IN ONE'S MEMORY PRODUCTS

Even after retrieving an answer from memory or choosing an answer from among distractors, we can generally monitor the likelihood that that answer is correct.

The bases of subjective confidence and its accuracy

Much of the work in this area has been conducted in the framework of judgment and decision making using forced-choice questions. The typical finding is that people are generally overconfident in the correctness of the answers that they choose (Lichtenstein, Fischhoff, & Phillips, 1982). Part of this overconfidence is possibly due to a confirmation bias: In making their confidence judgements, people selectively review the evidence that entered into making the choice, focusing on the evidence that favours the chosen answer and discounting the evidence against it (Koriat, Lichtenstein, & Fischhoff, 1980). However, this bias may also stem in part from a biased selection of items by experimenters, with an overrepresentation of challenging "deceptive" items (Gigerenzer, Hoffrage, & Kleinbölting, 1991).

While subjective confidence may be based on an analytic process in which the overall support for the chosen or produced answer is consciously evaluated, there is evidence that it may also rest on such mnemonic cues as the ease with which the answer has been reached. Indeed, it has been observed that the more effort and the longer the deliberation needed to reach an answer, the lower is the confidence in that answer (e.g., Costermans et al., 1992; Nelson & Narens, 1990; Robinson, Johnson, & Herndon, 1997). Kelley and Lindsay (1993) specifically showed that when priming speeds up the emergence of an answer, confidence judgements also increase accordingly. This effect occurred even for incorrect answers. Typically, however, correct answers are associated with shorter latencies than incorrect answers, so that latency of responding is generally a valid diagnostic cue for the correctness of the answer.

The strategic regulation of memory accuracy

How does subjective confidence affect behaviour? Clearly, the more confident a person is in the correctness of an answer or a decision, the more he or she is likely to commit oneself to it. A good example is the case of a person on the witness stand. According to the conceptual framework proposed by Koriat and Goldsmith (1994, 1996a, b), an eyewitness who is sworn to tell the truth and nothing but the truth, must monitor the subjective likelihood that a memory response that comes to mind is correct, and then determine whether to volunteer that response or not. The decision to volunteer or withhold a candidate answer is assumed to depend on the confidence associated with that response relative to a control threshold that is pre-set on the basis of the relative utility of providing as complete a report as possible versus as accurate a report as possible. A response is provided if its associated confidence exceeds the threshold but is withheld otherwise. The results on the whole supported this model. First, several results suggest that the decision to volunteer or withhold an answer is based almost entirely on the subjective confidence in the correctness of that answer, when other factors are held constant. Thus, the within-subject correlation between confidence and volunteering averaged .95 or more. Furthermore, rememberers were found to rely heavily on their subjective confidence even when the accuracy of subjective confidence was very limited. Thus, monitoring is a critical determinant of control.

Second, when rememberers were allowed freedom to choose whether to volunteer an answer or not, their memory accuracy was much higher than when they were forced to answer each and every question. This finding can explain the impression that peoples' reports are more accurate under everyday, naturalistic conditions than in the laboratory (e.g., Neisser, 1988). Clearly, in everyday life people are generally allowed much more freedom in reporting information from memory than is the case in the laboratory. How do rememberers enhance the accuracy of their report? They do so by screening out answers that are associated with low confidence, and to the extent that confidence is diagnostic of accuracy, they can thereby enhance the accuracy of what they report. However, because monitoring effectiveness is typically not perfect, the enhanced accuracy comes at the expense of memory quantity performance, because participants also sacrifice some of the correct answers. The implication is that as long as monitoring effectiveness is not perfect, eyewitnesses cannot both "tell the whole truth" and "tell nothing but the truth". Only when monitoring is perfect can a person volunteer all correct responses that come to mind and withhold all incorrect responses. When monitoring is not perfect a quantity–accuracy tradeoff would be observed, the magnitude of which should decrease with increasing monitoring effectiveness.

Third, under free-report conditions, participants' screening policy was found to vary with the incentives for accuracy. When participants were given high incentives for accuracy (e.g., a high penalty for wrong answers) they were more conservative in their reporting, and in fact achieved a higher memory accuracy performance but at a greater expense in memory quantity. Thus, memory accuracy (unlike memory quantity, see Nilsson, 1987) seems to be under the control of the rememberer.

Koriat and Goldsmith's model has been found to apply to adults as well as to children. In a study that included school-age children (Koriat, Goldsmith, Schneider, & Nakash-Dura, 2001) it was found that even second- to third-grade children used the option of free report effectively to enhance the accuracy of what they reported. Furthermore, they exhibited sensitivity to accuracy incentive, achieving higher memory accuracy performance when accuracy incentive was high than when it was low. These results have implications for the dependability of children's testimony in legal settings.

The conceptual framework of Koriat and Goldsmith (1996b) was also extended to incorporate another means by which people normally regulate the accuracy of what they report: the control over grain size (Goldsmith, Koriat, & Weinberg-Eliezer, 2002). Thus, when not completely certain about the time of an event, a person may simply report that it occurred "early in the morning" rather than "at 7:30 am". Neisser (1988) pointed out that when he solicited responses to open-ended questions the participants tended to provide answers at a level of generality at which they were not likely to be mistaken. Indeed, Goldsmith et al. (2002) observed that when participants are given the option to control grain size, they may choose to sacrifice informativeness (degree of precision) for the sake of accuracy, and will tend to do so when their subjective confidence is low. By regulating the grain size of their answers people may be able to achieve a relatively high level of accuracy even when a great deal of information has been forgotten.

In sum, in everyday life people have great freedom in reporting an event from memory: they can choose what perspective to adopt, what to emphasize and what to skip, how much detail to provide, and so on. The results obtained so far suggest that they regulate their reporting flexibly and effectively to achieve certain goals. It is our view that such strategic regulation processes are part and parcel of memory, and must be incorporated into memory research.

In concluding this chapter we should note that there are many other aspects of metacognition that have not been covered here and that are quite common in everyday life. One is source monitoring and reality monitoring (Johnson, 1997). We can remember when and where we last met a certain person. Sometimes reality monitoring is difficult: I may wonder whether I actually performed a certain action or only planned to do it. Obsessive-compulsive people may go back several times to check whether they have locked the door because by the third or fourth time they are not certain any longer whether they checked that the door was locked or only intended to do so (Reed, 1985). The confusion between reality and imagination is probably responsible for the imagination inflation effect (Garry & Polaschek, 2000): Imagination sometimes leads to memories for events that have not happened, and increases confidence that these events have actually taken place.

Metacognitive processes also occupy an important role in problem solving. For example, in the course of attempting to solve a problem people can sometimes judge whether they are on the right track to the solution (Carlson, 1997). Metcalfe and Wiebe (1987), for example, distinguished between incremental problems and insight problems. They found that feelings of warmth increased gradually as the problem neared completion. This, however, was only true for incremental problems, whereas insight problems are usually solved suddenly, without any subjective warning signals.

To sum up, learning and remembering in everyday life typically entail many metacognitive processes that are used by people to optimize their performance and to adapt to a variety of circumstances. Children gradually learn more about their memory skills and memory limitations; they acquire new strategies and learn about the usefulness of these under different conditions. Their success in school and their ability to solve problems depend heavily on the efficient evaluation of their performance and on the self-management of strategies of learning and remembering. However, such skills are also critical for adult performance, and many problems in real life derive from deficient metacognitive skills rather than from deficient cognitive skills. Thus, deficient monitoring can be hazardous in many real-life situations, as when a driver overestimates his ability to overtake a car. Similarly, illusions of knowing and overconfidence can result in failures and frustrations. Thus, the study of metacognition can have important theoretical as well as practical implications.

CONCLUSION

In this chapter we have outlined several threads of research in metacognition that are concerned with the processes that occur during encoding, during retrieval and during memory reporting. We have shown how these lines of research bring to the fore the importance of self-assessment and self-regulation during various stages of information processing. While demonstrating the operation of these processes we have also attempted to stress their contribution to effective memory functioning. Effective monitoring of one's knowledge and effective regulation of one's cognitive processes represent an essential component of adaptive functioning, and affect one's memory performance.

Clearly, however, the experimental study of metacognition has so far incorporated only a fraction of the complexity of metacognitive processes that occur constantly in everyday life: when we plan and carry out a series of errands, monitoring their completion as we go; when we solve simple problems, such as a crossword, deciding where to start, what strategy to adopt, and how to probe our memory for the solution; when we prepare a talk, trying to adopt the perspective of the audience, and so on and so forth. Clearly people in everyday life have a much greater freedom in regulating their learning and memory processes than participants have in the metacognitive experiments described in this chapter. If we are to understand the complex dynamics of memory processes, we must allow investigation of the broad variety of monitoring and control processes that take place in everyday life.

REFERENCES

Bahrick, H.P. (1979). Maintenance of knowledge: Questions about memory we forgot to ask. *Journal of Experimental Psychology: General, 108*, 296–308.

Bargh, J.A. (1997). The automaticity of everyday life. In R.S. Wyer Jr (Ed.), *Advances in social cognition, Vol. 10* (pp. 1–61). Mahwah, NJ: Lawrence Erlbaum Associates, Inc.

Barnes, A.E., Nelson, T.O., Dunlosky, J., Mazzoni, G., & Narens, L. (1999). An integrative system of metamemory components involved in retrieval. In D. Gopher & A. Koriat (Eds.), *Attention and performance XVII: Cognitive regulation of performance: Interaction of theory and application* (pp. 287–313). Cambridge, MA: MIT Press.

Begg, I., Duft, S., Lalonde, P., Melnick, R., & Sanvito, J. (1989). Memory predictions are based on ease of processing. *Journal of Memory and Language, 28*, 610–632.

Benjamin, A.S., & Bjork, R.A. (1996). Retrieval fluency as a metacognitive index. In L. Reder (Ed.), *Implicit memory and metacognition* (pp. 309–338). Hillsdale, NJ: Lawrence Erlbaum Associates, Inc.

Benjamin, A.S., Bjork, R.A., & Schwartz, B.L. (1998). The mismeasure of memory: When retrieval fluency is misleading as a metamnemonic index. *Journal of Experimental Psychology: General, 127*, 55–68.

Bjork, R.A. (1999). Assessing our own competence: Heuristics and illusions. In D. Gopher & A. Koriat (Eds.), *Attention and performance XVII: Cognitive regulation of performance: Interaction of theory and application* (pp. 435–459). Cambridge, MA: MIT Press.

Bjork, R.A., & Bjork, E.L. (1992). A new theory of disuse and an old theory of stimulus fluctuation. In A.F. Healy, S.M. Kosslyn, & R.M. Shiffrin (Eds.), *Essays in honor of William K. Estes, Vol. 2: From learning processes to cognitive processe* (pp. 35–67). Hillsdale, NJ: Lawrence Erlbaum Associates, Inc.

Buckner, R.L. (2003). Functional anatomic correlates of control processes in memory. *Journal of Neuroscience, 23*, 3999–4004.

Burgess, P.W., & Shallice, T. (1996). Confabulation and the control of recollection. *Memory, 4*, 359–411.

Carlson, R.A. (1997). *Experienced cognition.* Mahwah, NJ: Lawrence Erlbaum Associates, Inc.

Cohen, R.L., Sandler, S.P., & Keglevich, L. (1991). The failure of memory monitoring in a free recall task. *Canadian Journal of Psychology, 45*, 523–538.

Costermans, J., Lories, G., & Ansay, C. (1992). Confidence level and feeling of knowing in question answering: The weight of inferential processes. *Journal of Experimental Psychology: Learning, Memory, and Cognition, 18*, 142–150.

Dufresne, A., & Kobasigawa, A. (1989). Children's spontaneous allocation of study time: Differential and sufficient aspects. *Journal of Experimental Child Psychology, 47*, 274–296.

Dunlosky, J., & Hertzog, C. (1998). Training programs to improve learning in later adulthood: Helping older adults educate themselves. In D.J. Hacker (Ed.), *Metacognition in educational theory and practice* (pp. 249–275). Mahwah, NJ: Lawrence Erlbaum Associates, Inc.

Dunlosky, J., & Nelson, T.O. (1992). Importance of the kind of cue for judgments of learning (JOL) and the delayed-JOL effect. *Memory and Cognition, 20*, 374–380.

Dunlosky, J., & Nelson, T.O. (1994). Does the sensitivity of judgments of learning (JOLs) to the effects of various study activities depend on when the JOLs occur? *Journal of Memory and Language, 33*, 545–565.

Dunning, D., Johnson, K., Ehrlinger, J., & Kruger, J. (2003). Why people fail to recognize their own incompetence. *Current Directions in Psychological Science, 12*, 83–87.

Fischhoff, B., Slovic, P., & Lichtenstein, S. (1977). Knowing with certainty: The appropriateness of extreme confidence. *Journal of Experimental Psychology: Human Perception and Performance, 3*, 552–564.

Flavell, J.H. (1979). Metacognition and cognitive monitoring: A new area of cognitive-developmental inquiry. *American Psychologist, 34*, 906–911.

Garry, M., & Polaschek, D.L.L. (2000). Imagination and memory. *Psychological Science, 9*, 6–9.

Gigerenzer, G., Hoffrage, U., & Kleinbölting, H. (1991). Probabilistic mental models: A Brunswikian theory of confidence. *Psychological Review, 98*, 506–528.

Glucksberg, S., & McCloskey, M. (1981). Decisions about ignorance: Knowing that you don't know. *Journal of Experimental Psychology: Human Learning and Memory, 7*, 311–325.

Goldsmith, M., & Koriat, A. (1999). The strategic regulation of memory reporting: Mechanisms and performance consequences. In D. Gopher & A. Koriat (Eds.), *Attention and performance XVII: Cognitive regulation of performance: Interaction of theory and application* (pp. 373–400). Cambridge, MA: MIT Press.

Goldsmith, M., Koriat, A., & Weinberg-Eliezer, A. (2002). Strategic regulation of grain size memory reporting. *Journal of Experimental Psychology: General, 131*, 73–95.

Groninger, L.D. (1979). Predicting recall: The "feeling-that-I-know" phenomenon. *American Journal of Psychology, 92*, 45–58.

Gruneberg, M.M., Monks, J., & Sykes, R.N. (1977). Some methodological problems with feelings of knowing studies. *Acta Psychologica, 41*, 365–371.

Hart, J.T. (1965). Memory and the feeling-of-knowing experience. *Journal of Educational Psychology, 56*, 208–216.

Hertzog, C., Dunlosky, J., Robinson, A.E., & Kidder, D.P. (2003). Encoding fluency is a cue used for judgments about learning. *Journal of Experimental Psychology: Learning, Memory, and Cognition, 29*, 22–34.

Hertzog, C., Kidder, D.P., Powell-Moman, A., & Dunlosky, J. (2002). Aging and monitoring associative learning: Is monitoring accuracy spared or impaired? *Psychology and Aging, 17*, 209–225.

Israel, L., & Schacter, D.L. (1997). Pictorial encoding reduces false recognition of semantic associates. *Psychonomic Bulletin and Review, 4*, 577–581.

Johnson, M.K. (1997). Identifying the origin of mental experience. In M.S. Myslobodsky (Ed.), *The mythomanias: The nature of deception and self-deception* (pp. 133–180). Hillsdale, NJ: Lawrence Erlbaum Associates, Inc.

Kahneman, D. (2003). A perspective on judgment and choice: Mapping bounded rationality. *American Psychologist, 58*, 697–720.

Kelley, C.M., & Jacoby, L.L. (1998). Subjective reports and process dissociation: Fluency, knowing, and feeling. *Acta Psychologica, 98*, 127–140.

Kelley, C.M., & Lindsay, D.S. (1993). Remembering mistaken for knowing: Ease of retrieval as a basis for confidence in answers to general knowledge questions. *Journal of Memory and Language, 32*, 1–24.

Kelley, C.M., & Sahakyan, L. (2003). Memory, monitoring, and control in the attainment of memory accuracy. *Journal of Memory and Language, 48*, 704–721.

King, J.F., Zechmeister, E.B., & Shaughnessy, J.J. (1980). Judgments of knowing: The influence of retrieval practice. *American Journal of Psychology, 93*, 329–343.

Koriat, A. (1993). How do we know that we know? The accessibility model of the feeling of knowing. *Psychological Review, 100*, 609–639.

Koriat, A. (1994). Memory's knowledge of its own knowledge: The accessibility account of the feeling of knowing. In J. Metcalfe & A.P. Shimamura (Eds.), *Metacognition: Knowing about knowing* (pp. 115–135). Cambridge, MA: MIT Press.

Koriat, A. (1995). Dissociating knowing and the feeling of knowing: Further evidence for the accessibility model. *Journal of Experimental Psychology: General, 124*, 311–333.

Koriat, A. (1997). Monitoring one's own knowledge during study: A cue-utilization approach to judgments of learning. *Journal of Experimental Psychology: General, 126*, 349–370.

Koriat, A. (2000a). Control processes in remembering. In E. Tulving & F.I.M. Craik (Eds.), *The Oxford handbook of memory* (pp. 333–346). London: Oxford University Press.

Koriat, A. (2000b). The feeling of knowing: Some metatheoretical implications for consciousness and control. *Consciousness and Cognition, 9*, 149–171.

Koriat, A. (2002). Metacognition research: An interim report. In T.J. Perfect & B.L. Schwartz (Eds.), *Applied metacognition* (pp. 261–286). Cambridge, UK: Cambridge University Press.

Koriat, A., & Ben-Zur, H. (1988). Remembering that I did it: Processes and deficits in output monitoring. In M. Gruneberg, P. Morris, & R. Sykes (Eds.), *Practical aspects of memory: Current research and issues, Vol. 1* (pp. 203–208). Chichester, UK: Wiley.

Koriat, A., Ben-Zur, H., & Druch, A. (1991). The contextualization of memory for input and output events. *Psychological Research, 53*, 260–270.

Koriat, A., Ben-Zur, H., & Sheffer, D. (1988). Telling the same story twice: Output monitoring and age. *Journal of Memory and Language, 27*, 23–39.

Koriat, A., & Bjork, R.A. (2005). Illusions of competence in monitoring one's knowledge during study. *Journal of Experimental Psychology: Learning, Memory and Cognition, 31*, 187–194.

Koriat, A., Bjork, R.A., Sheffer, L., & Bar, S.K. (2004). Predicting one's own forgetting: The role of experience-based and theory-based processes. *Journal of Experimental Psychology: General, 133*, 643–656.

Koriat, A., & Goldsmith, M. (1994). Memory in naturalistic and laboratory contexts: Distinguishing the accuracy-oriented and quantity-oriented approaches to memory assessment. *Journal of Experimental Psychology: General, 123*, 297–315.

Koriat, A., & Goldsmith, M. (1996a). Memory metaphors and the real-life/laboratory controversy: Correspondence versus storehouse conceptions of memory. *Behavioral and Brain Sciences, 19*, 167–228.

Koriat, A., & Goldsmith, M. (1996b). Monitoring and control processes in the strategic regulation of memory accuracy. *Psychological Review, 103*, 490–517.

Koriat, A., & Goldsmith, M. (1998). The role of metacognitive processes in the regulation of memory performance. In G. Mazzoni & T.O. Nelson (Eds.), *Metacognition and cognitive neuropsychology: Monitoring and control processes* (pp. 97–118). Mahwah, NJ: Lawrence Erlbaum Associates, Inc.

Koriat, A., Goldsmith, M., & Pansky, A. (2000). Toward a psychology of memory accuracy. *Annual Review of Psychology, 51*, 481–537.

Koriat, A., Goldsmith, M., Schneider, W., & Nakash-Dura, M. (2001). The credibility of children's testimony: Can children control the accuracy of their memory reports? *Journal of Experimental Child Psychology, 79*, 405–437.

Koriat, A., & Levy-Sadot, R. (1999). Processes underlying metacognitive judgments: Information-based and experience-based monitoring of one's own knowledge. In S. Chaiken & Y. Trope (Eds.), *Dual process theories in social psychology* (pp. 483–502). New York: Guilford Press.

Koriat, A., & Levy-Sadot, R. (2001). The combined contributions of the cue-familiarity and accessibility heuristics to feelings of knowing. *Journal of Experimental Psychology: Learning, Memory, and Cognition, 27*, 34–53.

Koriat, A., Lichtenstein, S., & Fischhoff, B. (1980). Reasons for confidence. *Journal of Experimental Psychology: Human Learning and Memory, 6*, 107–118.

Koriat, A., & Lieblich, I. (1977). A study of memory pointers. *Acta Psychologica, 41*, 151–164.

Koriat, A., & Ma'ayan, H. (2005). The effects of encoding fluency and retrieval fluency on judgments of learning. *Journal of Memory and Language, 52*, 478–492.

Koriat, A., Sheffer, L., & Ma'ayan, H. (2002). Comparing objective and subjective learning curves: Judgments of learning exhibit increased underconfidence with practice. *Journal of Experimental Psychology: General, 131*, 147–162.

Le Ny, J.F., Denhiere, G., & Le Taillanter, D. (1972). Regulation of study-time and interstimulus similarity in self-paced learning conditions. *Acta Psychologica, 36*, 280–289.

Lichtenstein, S., Fischhoff, B., & Phillips, L.D. (1982). Calibration of probabilities: The state of the art to 1980. In D. Kahneman, P. Slovic, & A. Tversky (Eds.), *Judgment under uncertainty: Heuristics and biases* (pp. 306–334). New York: Cambridge University Press.

Matvey, G., Dunlosky, J., & Guttentag, R. (2001). Fluency of retrieval at study affects judgments of learning (JOLs): An analytic or nonanalytical basis for JOLs? *Memory and Cognition, 29*, 222–233.

Mazzoni, G., & Cornoldi, C. (1993). Strategies in study time allocation: Why is study time sometimes not effective? *Journal of Experimental Psychology: General, 122*, 47–60.

Mazzoni, G., Cornoldi, C., & Marchitelli, G. (1990). Do memorability ratings affect study-time allocation? *Memory and Cognition, 18*, 196–204.

Mazzoni, G., & Kirsch, I. (2002). Autobiographical memories and beliefs: A preliminary metacognitive model. In T.J. Perfect & B.L. Schwartz (Eds.), *Applied metacognition* (pp. 121–145). Cambridge, UK: Cambridge University Press.

Mazzoni, G., & Nelson, T.O. (1995). Judgments of learning are affected by the kind of encoding in ways that cannot be attributed to the level of recall. *Journal of Experimental Psychology: Learning, Memory, and Cognition, 21*, 1263–1274.

Metcalfe, J. (1998). Cognitive optimism: Self-deception or memory-based processing heuristics? *Personality and Social Psychology Review, 2*, 100–110.

Metcalfe, J. (2002). Is study time allocated selectively to a region of proximal learning? *Journal of Experimental Psychology: General, 131*, 349–363.

Metcalfe, J., & Kornell, N. (2003). The dynamics of learning and allocation of study time to a region of proximal learning. *Journal of Experimental Psychology: General, 132*, 530–542.

Metcalfe, J., Schwartz, B.L., & Joaquim, S.G. (1993). The cue-familiarity heuristic in metacognition. *Journal of Experimental Psychology: Learning, Memory, and Cognition, 19*, 851–864.

Metcalfe, J., & Wiebe, D. (1987). Intuition in insight and noninsight problem solving. *Memory and Cognition, 15*, 238–246.

Neisser, U. (1988). Time present and time past. In M.M. Gruneberg, P. Morris, & R. Sykes (Eds.), *Practical aspects of memory: Current research and issues, Vol. 2* (pp. 545–560). Chichester, UK: Wiley.

Nelson, T.O. (1984). A comparison of current measures of the accuracy of feeling-of-knowing predictions. *Psychological Bulletin, 95*, 109–133.

Nelson, T.O., & Dunlosky, J. (1991). When people's judgments of learning (JOLs) are extremely accurate at predicting subsequent recall: The "delayed-JOL effect." *Psychological Science, 2*, 267–270.

Nelson, T.O., & Leonesio, R.J. (1988). Allocation of self-paced study time and the "labor-in-vain effect". *Journal of Experimental Psychology: Learning, Memory, and Cognition, 14*, 676–686.

Nelson, T.O., & Narens, L. (1990). Metamemory: A theoretical framework and new findings. In G. Bower (Ed.), *The psychology of learning and motivation: Advances in research and theory* (pp. 125–173). New York: Academic Press.

Nelson, T.O., & Narens, L. (1994). Why investigate metacognition. In J. Metcalfe & A.P. Shimamura (Eds.), *Metacognition: Knowing about knowing* (pp. 1–25). Cambridge, MA: MIT Press.

Nelson, T.O., Narens, L., & Dunlosky, J. (2004). A revised methodology for research on metamemory: Pre-judgment Recall And Monitoring (PRAM). *Psychological Methods, 9*, 53–69.

Nilsson, L.-G. (1987). Motivated memory: Dissociation between performance data and subjective reports. *Psychological Research, 49*, 183–188.

Perfect, T.J. (2002). When does eyewitness confidence predict performance? In T.J. Perfect & B.L. Schwartz (Eds.), *Applied metacognition* (pp. 95–120). Cambridge, UK: Cambridge University Press.

Reder, L.M. (1988). Strategic control of retrieval strategies. In G.H. Bower (Ed.), *The psychology of learning and motivation: Advances in research and theory, Vol. 22* (pp. 227–259). San Diego, CA: Academic Press.

Reder, L.M., & Ritter, F.E. (1992). What determines initial feeling of knowing? Familiarity with question terms, not with the answer. *Journal of Experimental Psychology: Learning, Memory, and Cognition, 18*, 435–451.

Reed, G.F. (1985). *Obsessional experience and compulsive behavior: A cognitive-structural approach*. Orlando, FL: Academic Press.

Robinson, M.D., Johnson, J.T., & Herndon, F. (1997). Reaction time and assessments of cognitive effort as predictors of eyewitness memory accuracy and confidence. *Journal of Applied Psychology, 82*, 416–425.

Schacter, D.L., Norman, K.A., & Koutstaal, W. (1998). The cognitive neuroscience of constructive memory. *Annual Review of Psychology, 49*, 289–318.

Schunn, C.D., Reder, L.M., Nhouyvanisvong, A., Richards, D.R., & Stroffolino, P.J. (1997). To calculate or not to calculate: A source activation confusion model of problem familiarity's role in strategy selection. *Journal of Experimental Psychology: Learning, Memory, and Cognition, 23*, 3–29.

Schwartz, B.L. (2001). The relation of tip-of-the-tongue states and retrieval time. *Memory and Cognition, 29*, 117–126.

Schwartz, B.L., & Metcalfe, J. (1992). Cue familiarity but not target retrievability enhances feeling-of-knowing judgments. *Journal of Experimental Psychology: Learning, Memory, and Cognition, 18*, 1074–1083.

Schwartz, B.L., & Metcalfe, J. (1994). Methodological problems and pitfalls in the study of human metacognition. In J. Metcalfe & A.P. Shimamura (Eds.), Metacognition: Knowing about knowing (pp. 93–113). Cambridge, MA: MIT Press.

Simon, D.A., & Bjork, R.A. (2001). Metacognition in motor learning. *Journal of Experimental Psychology: Learning, Memory, and Cognition, 27*, 907–912.

Son, L.K., & Metcalfe, J. (2000). Metacognitive and control strategies in study-time allocation. *Journal of Experimental Psychology: Learning, Memory, and Cognition, 26*, 204–221.

Spehn, M.K., & Reder, L.M. (2000). The unconscious feeling of knowing: A commentary on Koriat's paper. *Consciousness and Cognition, 9*, 187–192.

Sternberg, R.J. (1986). *Intelligence applied*. New York: Harcourt Brace Jovanovich.

Thiede, K.W., & Dunlosky, J. (1999). Toward a general model of self-regulated study: An analysis of selection of items for study and self-paced study time. *Journal of Experimental Psychology: Learning, Memory, and Cognition, 25*, 1024–1037.

Tulving, E., & Madigan, S.A. (1970). Memory and verbal learning. *Annual Review of Psychology, 21*, 437–484.

Underwood, B.J. (1966). Individual and group predictions of item difficulty for free learning. *Journal of Experimental Psychology, 71*, 673–679.

Vernon, D., & Usher, M. (2003). Dynamics of metacognitive judgments: Pre- and postretrieval mechanisms. *Journal of Experimental Psychology: Learning, Memory, and Cognition, 29*, 339–346.

Zechmeister, E.B., & Shaughnessy, J.J. (1980). When you know that you know and when you think that you know but you don't. *Bulletin of the Psychonomic Society, 15*, 41–44.

12 Self-referent beliefs about memory and actual performance: Relationships with age and sex

Lars-Göran Nilsson and
Maria Larsson

As noted by Cohen (1996), one of the characteristic features of everyday memory research is its emphasis on the functional aspects of memory. By tradition, everyday memory research employs two different kinds of method. The first relies on data from self-reports and thus relies on introspective evidence; the second comprises experimental methods, which may be more or less naturalistic. Subjective reports of specific memory abilities such as memory for routes or faces may provide valuable information regarding an individual's experience of learning and remembering in their daily life. Given that beliefs and expectations about one's own memory abilities may affect everyday behaviour (e.g., preferences about life in general, decisions about family economy such as pension plans and loans for housing, long-term planning about education and life careers), it is of interest to study what people think about their memory abilities.

Many people today are concerned about what they experience as a declining memory function as they grow older, and they often worry that such a decline might be an early sign of dementia. More commonly than before, not only older persons, but also middle-aged people, visit memory clinics to have their memory examined in neuropsychological tests. Is the experienced forgetfulness just an expression of normal ageing or is it a neurodegenerative development in progress that eventually will end up in dementia? Is there a decrease of memory function already in middle age? If so, when does it start? Does it hold for all forms of memory? Are there differences between men and women?

These questions are serious ones for those concerned. A great deal of research is currently being done on early markers of impending dementia. With regard to cognitive markers, research has indicated that impairments in episodic memory are reliable pre-clinical markers of dementia (Small, Fratiglioni, Viitanen, Winblad, & Bäckman, 2000). In this chapter we look at whether self-perceptions of memory functioning may serve as a reliable indicator of a declining memory in objective terms (i.e., measured by standardized laboratory tests).

The structure of the chapter is as follows. First, we specify what we think is general consensus in the scientific community regarding the conceptualization of memory. We then describe the Betula project, an ongoing longitudinal prospective study of memory, health, and ageing, from which the data used in the present study have been taken. This is followed by a review and discussion of available knowledge regarding self-perception of memory and its relationship with objective measures of memory. Finally, we present and discuss the results of the present study.

CONCEPTUALIZATION OF MEMORY

The question has been posed whether it matters if memory is a single, unitary entity or whether there are several different forms of memory that need to be considered when we are dealing with memory function in adulthood and old age.

For many years it has been known, on the basis of clinical and neuropsychological studies, that certain groups of patients experience great difficulties in certain types of memory test, whereas their performance in other tests is at the same level as that of the normal population. In recent years, brain imaging studies have confirmed these observations by showing that specific brain structures are activated for certain tasks and other brain structures for other tasks (Cabeza & Nyberg, 2000; Nyberg & Tulving, 1996). On the basis of such findings, attempts have been made to classify memory into different memory systems.

The classification of memory by Tulving (1972, 1983, 1987, 1991) in different memory systems has been proven to be a fruitful way to organize what is known today about memory function in normal ageing. Tulving initially (1972) proposed distinguishing between one type of memory that would account for representations of personally experienced events that had occurred at a certain time and place and another type for general knowledge. He coined the term episodic memory for the first type. Episodic memory is used for the encoding of personal experiences and conscious recollection of events and episodes of one's own past; it operates at a conscious level and retrieval is explicit rather than implicit. Episodic memory is the only memory system that, at the time of retrieval, operates backwards in time. The rememberer has to travel back in time to a given episode in order to access the information needed. In this sense, episodic memory is strongly dependent on contextual cues for proper access to the to-be-remembered information. Tulving (1972) contrasted this form of memory with memory for general knowledge, denoted *semantic memory*. In retrospect, it might be argued that this term is not ideal. For example, it gives the impression that it only comprises the meaning of words, (e.g., hot is the opposite of cold). As it has come to be used, however, the meaning of semantic memory is that of general knowledge that does not require a mental journey back in time to a given episode when this knowledge was acquired. In contrast to episodic memory, retrieval from semantic memory is implicit and is not dependent on contextual information.

Eventually, Tulving's classification of memory came to include five different forms of memory. These five separate but interacting components of memory are procedural memory, perceptual representation system, working memory, semantic memory, and episodic memory (Tulving, 1983, 1987, 1991). Although the first three systems of Tulving's classification are dealt with further here, a brief description is presented for general orientation. *Procedural memory* is about the acquisition and use of various kinds of behavioural skills. It operates at an automatic level and its output is non-cognitive. The acquisition of most procedural skills such as walking, swimming, dancing or cycling is gradual and slow. Forgetting is not a problem; in most cases one can perform skills adequately although they have not been practised for many years. The *perceptual representation system (PRS)* is used to identify objects in the surrounding world; it operates at an automatic and unconscious level. Tasks assessing PRS are usually referred to as implicit, because the instructions given do not require the subject to think back to a previous episode. These tasks are usually referred to as priming tasks. The third memory system concerns memory for the present. It is usually referred to as *short-term memory*, primary memory or working memory (Baddeley, 1992). While the term short-term memory was most commonly used some three or four decades ago, working memory is usually used now, because it captures the active role played by this memory system in its current processing of information. Thus, this memory system makes it possible to hold and process information that is at the focus of consciousness. Storage is short-lived and temporary and it operates fully at a conscious level.

In this chapter we focus on age and sex effects in episodic and semantic memory functions. We will take the opportunity to highlight two possible subsystems of each of these. Specifically, on the basis of structural equation modelling, Nyberg et al. (2003) recently proposed that episodic memory can be subdivided into recall and recognition and semantic memory into vocabulary and fluency. Thus, objective test scores in tasks that assess episodic and semantic memory and respective subsystems will be related to self-evaluations of memory ability.

Previous research has demonstrated that age and sex are potent variables in determining level of performance in objective assessment of memory by means of laboratory tests (Herlitz, Nilsson, & Bäckman, 1997; Nilsson et al., 1997). The general findings in these and other studies are that performance in memory tests declines as people grow older and that memory performance, in at least some tests of memory, is generally better in women than in men. The decrease in performance as a function of age and the superiority in memory performance in women have been demonstrated for episodic memory tasks rather than semantic memory tasks. To the best of our knowledge, no systematic studies have reported whether self-reports about memory also vary as functions of age and sex.

The data used here to illustrate the effects of age and sex on objective and subjective memory emanate from an ongoing longitudinal study on memory, ageing and health (Betula; Nilsson et al., 1997, 2004). We turn next to a brief description of this study.

THE BETULA STUDY

This study was launched in 1988 and aimed to (1) explore the development of memory and health in adulthood and old age, (2) detect early cognitive signs of dementia and identify possible risk factors for dementia, and (3) determine pre-morbid memory functioning in individuals who, during the course of the project, would be the victims of accidents or would develop diseases that would affect the central nervous system.

Design and participants

The overall design of the Betula project was described in Nilsson et al. (1997, 2004). Only a brief summary is given here. Four waves of data collection have taken place to date: T1 (1988–1990), T2 (1993–1995), T3 (1998–2000) and T4 (2003–2005). Five samples (S1–S5) of participants were randomly selected from the population register of Umeå, a city in northern Sweden with about 110,000 inhabitants. The age range range of the samples was 35–80 years.

The data to be reported here are from S1, when these participants were tested at T2, which was the first time a reasonably detailed questionnaire had been used to assess subjective aspects of memory. Of the 1000 partici-pants of S1 tested at T1, 862 returned to testing at T2; 53 participants had died between T1 and T2, 28 individuals had become demented, 38 were unwilling to participate at T2 or could not participate because of hospital-ization or other illness, and 19 could not be reached because of an unlisted telephone number or because they had moved from Umeå. Additionally, for the data to be reported here, special care was taken to specifically include only normally ageing individuals without the potential influence of an impending dementia disease. To this end, a rather conservative decision was taken to include only subjects who were *not* diagnosed as demented a further 5 years later (at T3). During the period from T2 to T3, 44 persons in S1 had been diagnosed as demented and were therefore excluded from analysis in the present study. Demographic information about the individuals partici-pating in the present study is presented in Table 12.1. A 3 (age) × 2 (sex) analysis of variance (ANOVA) revealed that years of formal education dif-fered between age cohorts, $F(2, 782) = 197$, $p < .0001$, $\eta^2 = .34$. For this reason, this variable was used as a covariate in all the analyses reported in the present study.

Table 12.1 Demographic variables

	Age cohort					
	35–45	N	50–60	N	65–85	N
Age						
Male	39.8 (4.10)	132	55.5 (4.10)	122	71.7 (5.27)	118
Female	40.0 (4.10)	138	54.5 (4.08)	143	71.8 (5.81)	135
Education						
Male	13.4 (3.42)	132	9.43 (3.56)	122	8.43 (3.57)	118
Female	13.6 (3.28)	138	9.42 (3.46)	143	7.57 (2.42)	135

Table 12.2 Memory tasks

Episodic memory
Recall tests
1. Sentence learning with encoding enactment (16 items at study) – (a) free recall, (b) two cued recall tests, (c) yes/no recognition, (d) source recall.
2. Sentence learning without encoding enactment (16 items at study) – (a) free recall, (b) two cued recall tests, (c) yes/no recognition, (d) source recall.
3. Word recall tests with and without concurrent card sorting at study or test (12 items) – (a) no card sorting at study and test, (b) card sorting at study only, and (c) card sorting at test only.
4. Memory for activities.

Recognition tests
1. Face recognition – yes/no response option (16 items at study, 32 items at test).
2. Name recognition – four-alternative forced choice of first and last name (16 items at study).
3. Recognition of nouns – enacted and non-enacted conditions.

Semantic memory
Knowledge test
1. Vocabulary (30 items).

Fluency tests
1. Word fluency, initial letter A.
2. Word fluency, initial letter M, five-letter words.
3. Word fluency, initial letter B, names of professions.

Note
The episodic memory composite comprised all tests listed under the recall and recognition categories. The semantic memory composite included the vocabulary test and three fluency tests.

Tests and questionnaire

A detailed description of the cognitive tasks in the Betula test battery was presented in Nilsson et al. (1997). The tasks used in the present study are listed in Table 12.2. As the table shows, two types of task comprise the episodic memory composite measure: recall and recognition. The semantic memory composite includes vocabulary and word fluency performance. The

Table 12.3 Questions assessing subjective memory

1. I have difficulties remembering regular telephone numbers.
2. I have difficulties deciding who a person is although I realize that I know this person.
3. I can have a word on the tip of my tongue but cannot produce the word.
4. I do not know where I have put objects such as glasses, although I have just recently used them.
5. I am on my way to do something but have to stop to return to the original place to remember what I was about to do.
6. I have lost objects because I have forgotten to take them with me when I left.
7. Does anyone in close relation to you (family, friends) think that you have a poor memory?
8. How well does your memory function now as compared to five years ago?

Note
Items 1–7 were rated on a scale ranging *never, seldom, sometimes, often, usually*. Item 8 was rated on a scale ranging *much better, somewhat better, similar, somewhat worse, much worse*.

questionnaire comprising the eight items used to assess subjective memory is presented in Table 12.3. For statistical reasons, the nominal variables for Items 1–7 (*never, seldom, sometimes, often, usually*) and Item 8 (*much better, somewhat better, similar, somewhat worse, much worse*) were transformed to values 1–5.

SUBJECTIVE RATING OF MEMORY

Previous research has demonstrated that knowledge of one's own memory capabilities may be positively related to objective memory performance as measured by memory tests in late life (Johansson, Allen-Burge, & Zarit, 1997; Wahlin, Maitland, Bäckman, & Dixon, 2003), although the correlations are modest (see Hertzog & Hultsch, 2000 for an overview). Typically, the correlations between measures of self-ratings of memory efficacy and objective memory performance tend to vary in the range of .2 to .3 in normally aged adults (Cavanaugh & Poon, 1989; Zelinski, Gilewski, & Anthony-Bergstone, 1990). These modest relationships suggest that individuals are capable of a certain degree of accuracy in monitoring their own memory changes. In support of this notion, Johansson et al. (1997) presented findings showing that reported decline in memory was significantly related to actual decline over a 2-year interval in a group of very old adults. For those experiencing symptoms of dementia, the relationship is typically much weaker (Kaszniak, 1996), suggesting that persons suffering from dementia have problems in accurately monitoring their actual memory ability.

To the best of our knowledge, however, less is known about the relationship between subjective and objective measures of memory over a longer period of the life span. For example, is this relationship a characteristic feature of late life only or can such a relationship also be found in middle-aged and younger elderly individuals? Little is known either about potential sex differences in self-referent beliefs about memory functions. Since there are significant sex differences in memory performance as measured by objective memory tests, it would be of interest to know whether such differences are also reflected in self-perceptions of memory skill.We also wished to explore whether there are interactions between age and sex for the subjective ratings of memory, and if the degree of the subjective-objective memory relationship may vary as a function of age and sex.

OBJECTIVE MEMORY PERFORMANCE AND SELF-RATING

We report the results of the present study in two steps. First, we examine the age and sex factors as determinants of objective and subjective memory. Second, we examine the correlation between episodic and semantic memory and their subsystems on the one hand, and the subjective ratings for each of the eight questions in the questionnaire on the other.

Memory performance expressed as composite scores for episodic and semantic memory is illustrated in Figure 12.1. To facilitate comparisons between memory systems, all data to be reported were transformed into z-scores.

As can be seen in the top graph in Figure 12.1, there is a dramatic decrease in episodic memory performance as a function of age. The data were subjected to a 3 (age) × 2 (sex) ANCOVA with number of years of formal education as a covariate. Means and standard errors are based on collapsed data for successive age cohorts, 40–50, 55–65 and 70–85, respectively. The main effect of Age was highly significant, $F(2, 771) = 87.4, p < .001, \eta^2 = .19$. The main effect of Sex was also statistically significant, $F(1, 771) = 33.7, p < .001$, $\eta^2 = .04$, but there was no Age × Sex interaction, $p = .68$. The results regarding the age variable are in line with those obtained in many other laboratories. Excellent reviews summarizing this large body of studies can be found in Bäckman, Small, and Wahlin (2001), Craik and Jennings (1992), and Hultsch and Dixon (1990). Likewise, the female superiority in episodic memory agrees with previous findings (Halpern & LaMay, 2000; Herlitz et al. 1997; Maitland, Herlitz, Nyberg, Bäckman, & Nilsson, in press; Voyer, Voyer, & Bryden, 1995). The data for semantic memory are shown in the bottom graph of Figure 12.1. The analysis revealed a reliable age effect in semantic memory, indicating an improvement in performance from the youngest age group (40–50 years of age) to the middle group (55–65 years of age), and thereafter a decline in performance for the oldest group (70–85 years of age). This inverted U-shape function for semantic memory has previously been demonstrated for T1 data from the Betula Study (Nilsson, 2003). The 3 (age) × 2 (sex) ANCOVA revealed a significant main effect of Age, $F(2, 785) = 22.3, p < .001, \eta^2 = .05$, no significant main effect of Sex, $p = .07$, and no Age × Sex interaction, $p = .12$.

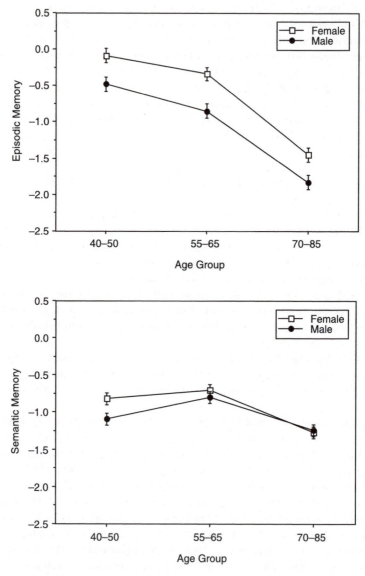

Figure 12.1 Mean actual performance in *z*-scores as a function of age and sex for episodic and semantic memory.

For the recall subcomponent of episodic memory, the data pattern is very similar to that of the episodic memory composite and is therefore not presented in a figure. The same type of ANCOVA as above revealed a significant main effect of Age, $F(2, 773) = 98.7$, $p < .001$, $\eta^2 = .20$, a significant main effect of Sex, $F(1, 773) = 23.3$, $p < .0001$, $\eta^2 = .03$, but no Age × Sex interaction, $p = .43$. For the recognition subcomponent, the main effect of age was again significant, $F(2, 782) = 37.4, p < .001, \eta^2 = .09$, as was the main effect of Sex, $F(1, 782) = 29.8, p < .001, \eta^2 = .04$. The Age × Sex interaction did not reach statistical significance, $p = .96$.

Where the subcomponents of semantic memory are concerned, chronological Age has a significant impact on both fluency, $F(2, 789) = 20.1, p < .001, \eta^2 = .05$, and vocabulary, $F(2, 795) = 16.6, p < .001, \eta^2 = .05$. For fluency, the age effect reflected a gradual decrease in performance from the youngest to the oldest age group, very much like the function described in Figure 12.1 for episodic memory. For vocabulary, there was an inverted U-shaped function similar to that found for the composite score of semantic memory, with an increase in performance from the youngest to the middle age group followed by a decrease in performance for the oldest group. The main effect of Sex was significant for fluency, $F(1, 789) = 6.00, p < .05, \eta^2 = .01$, showing a female superiority, but not for vocabulary ($p = .87$). The Age × Sex interaction was non-significant for both of these variables ($ps < .25$).

Two types of scale were used for the subjective ratings. For items 1–7, the scale included the following steps: (1) *never*, (2) *seldom*, (3) *sometimes*, (4) *often*, and (5) *usually*. A composite score was computed by adding the individual scores of the seven items and by z-transforming the sums. These ratings express the frequency with which participants experience that they have memory problems and we will refer to this score as subjective frequency. Item 8 included the following steps: (1) *much better*, (2) *somewhat better*, (3) *similar*, (4) *somewhat worse*, and (5) *much worse*. This measure expresses how the participants experience that their memory has changed as compared to 5 years previously. We will refer to z-transformed scores of Item 8 as subjective change.

The data for the two types of subjective memory rating were analysed by a 3(age) × 2 (sex) ANCOVA, using years of formal education as the covariate. The analysis of the data for subjective frequency, depicted in the top graph of Figure 12.2, reveal a significant main effect of Sex, $F(1, 776) = 5.82, p < .05, \eta^2 = .01$, indicating that men experienced more memory problems than women. The main effect of Age was non-significant, $p = .11$. There was a tendency towards an interaction between Age and Sex, $F(2, 776) = 2.63, p < .10, \eta^2 = .01$. For subjective change shown in the bottom graph of Figure 12.2, the analysis revealed a significant main effect of Age, $F(2, 776) = 25.3, p < .001, \eta^2 = .06$, indicating that subjective experience of memory change become more frequent with increasing age. That is, the older adults believe that their memory has declined significantly in comparison with their proficiency 5 years previously. The main effect of Sex and the Age × Sex interaction did not reach significance ($p = .86$, and $p = .11$, respectively).

In the following tables showing correlations between objective and subjective memory measures, a high negative correlation indicates good monitoring of how one's own memory is functioning, the latter being measured by the objective tests used in this study.

The overall correlations between the subjective and objective memory

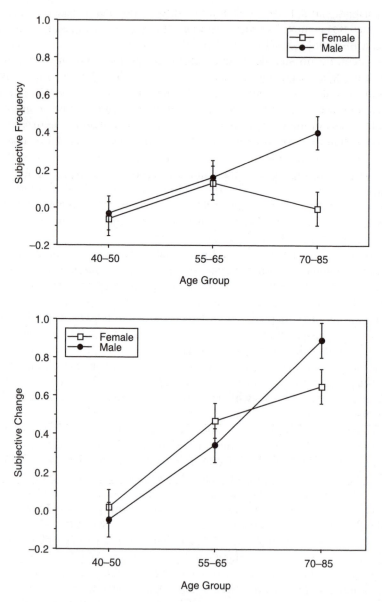

Figure 12.2 Mean ratings in *z*-scores as a function of age and sex for items assessing frequency of memory problems and changes in memory functioning.

measures show that subjective change correlates significantly with the episodic memory composite ($r = -.11, p < .01$), and the recall subcomponent ($r = -.11, p < .01$). The relationships between subjective change and the three semantic memory scores were all non-significant, as were the relationships between subjective frequency and all episodic and all semantic memory scores. When the correlational data are broken down into three different age cohorts and separately for men and women, an interesting picture emerges. The data for women are presented in Table 12.4 and those for men in Table 12.5. As can be seen, there are no significant correlations for women. For men it can be seen that subjective change correlates negatively with both recall and recognition in the oldest group only, suggesting that old men do indeed have good insight into the fact that their episodic memory is declining (see top graph of Figure 12.1). For men aged 55–65 years, there are also significant correlations between subjective change and both fluency and vocabulary. These positive

Table 12.4 Correlations between objective and subjective measures of memory for women

Subjective measures	Objective measures			
	Episodic		Semantic	
	Recall	Recognition	Fluency	Vocabulary
40–50 years				
Frequency	–.07	–.02	–.12	–.02
Change	–.09	–.13	–.08	–.02
55–65 years				
Frequency	.04	.11	–.05	.01
Change	–.04	–.08	–.11	–.05
70–85 years				
Frequency	.06	.02	.13	.15
Change	–.08	.03	.16	–.03

Table 12.5 Correlations between objective and subjective measures of memory for men

Subjective measures	Objective measures			
	Episodic		Semantic	
	Recall	Recognition	Fluency	Vocabulary
40–50 years				
Frequency	–.05	–.03	–.06	–.01
Change	–.03	–.02	–.07	–.06
55–65 years				
Frequency	–.02	–.04	.09	.16
Change	.21	.10	.24*	.25*
70–85 years				
Frequency	–.10	–.09	.04	.02
Change	–.22*	–.28*	–.11	–.16

*p < .05

correlations indicate that their relatively high scores in semantic memory (see bottom graph of Figure 12.1) are accompanied by high ratings about how their memory has changed over the last 5 years. These high ratings mean that these men realize that their memory is declining. All in all, we interpret these positive correlations for 55–65-year-old men and negative correlations for 70–85-year olds as pointing in the same direction, namely a growing insight into declining memory function.

For the analyses on the relationships between self-perceived change in memory functioning with actual memory performance, we also computed the actual objective change scores of episodic and semantic memory over a 5-year test interval (i.e., T2–T1) for men and women in the individual age groups. The results indicated that the subjective experience of memory change among older men correlated significantly with actual episodic memory change over a 5-year interval ($r = -.24$, $p < .05$). This finding again suggests that older men are capable of retrospectively perceiving a real memory change over time (cf. McDonald-Miszczak, Hertzog, & Hultsch, 1995). No other correlations were reliable.

DISCUSSION

In line with previous research, this study demonstrated a gradual age-related deterioration in episodic memory performance, whereas age had a less pronounced effect on proficiency in semantic memory tasks (e.g., Nilsson, 2003; Nilsson et al., 1997). Furthermore, corroborating previous findings, female superiority in episodic memory but not in overall semantic memory performance was observed (Herlitz et al., 1997). It is also noteworthy that none of the statistical analyses revealed any significant interactions between age and sex, which replicates results obtained elsewhere (Herlitz et al., 1997). Not surprisingly, the data on subjective ratings in our study demonstrated that old people, and men in particular, experience more memory difficulties than younger individuals.

As noted above, previous research has shown that self-referent beliefs about cognitive functioning often show modest relationships, with correlations varying between .2 and .3 in normal ageing (see Hertzog & Hultsch, 2000, for an overview). Using a large population-based sample, the work discussed here has shown that self-perceived memory change over a 5-year interval correlated significantly, although modestly, with an actual change in episodic recollection of information. In contrast, self-reports that tapped the frequency of memory problems proved to be unrelated to all of the memory tasks tested.

The significant correlations demonstrated between objective and subjective measures of memory for old participants are in line with the data patterns obtained in some of earlier research (Johansson et al., 1997; Wahlin et al., 2003). We also addressed the relationship between belief in one's own performance and actual memory performance in a longitudinal context in terms of one question: How well is your memory functioning now as compared with 5 years ago? The results indicated that older males were particularly good at identifying greater memory problems. The fact that these correlations for old men are stronger than those for middle-aged and young-old participants suggests a greater sensitivity of old men to any strengths and weaknesses that can be assessed by objective memory tests. To the best of our knowledge, this has not been demonstrated in previous studies. Future studies are needed to determine whether this superiority among elderly men is a reliable finding.

The results of subjective ratings of health may shed some light on this new finding. It has been suggested (Wahlin, personal communication) that subjective medical health may take on a different meaning in ageing men and women. Indeed, it is well known that women are more prone to self-rate their health status as poor (Gijsbers van Wijk & Kolk, 1997). The reports of ill health among the participants may also reflect differential survival rates in men and women (Brayne, Matthews, McGee, & Jagger, 2001). As has frequently been observed, women become sick while men tend to die (Nathanson, 1977). Thus, in men, self-reported health status may more accurately describe newly acquired ill health with more immediate functional consequences than would be the case among women, among whom the duration of diseases is known to be longer (Brayne et al., 2001) and ageing-related decrements in self-reported health status may be associated with less dramatic functional consequences. Importantly, it is also known that underreporting of disease is more common among men than women (Gijsbers van Wijk & Kolk, 1997). Thus, to the extent that the ill health actually reported by the male participants reflected more serious conditions than the same subjective estimates as made by women, the sex by health interaction effects obtained in this study may follow logically. By the same token, it might be argued that the memory difficulties reported by men in the present study reflect more serious conditions than the subjective estimates by women.

ACKNOWLEDGEMENTS

The Betula Study is funded by the Bank of Sweden Tercentenary Foundation (1988–0082:17), the Swedish Council for Planning and Coordination of Research (D1988–0092, D1989–0115, D1990–0074, D1991–0258, D1992–0143, D1997–0756, D1997–1841, D1999–0739, B1999–474), the Swedish Council for Research in the Humanities and Social Sciences (F377/1988–2000), and the Swedish Council for Social Research (1988–1990: 88–0082, and 311/1991–2000).

REFERENCES

Bäckman, L., Small, B., & Wahlin, Å. (2001). Aging and memory: Cognitive and biological processes. In J.E. Birren & K.W. Schaie (Eds.), *Handbook of the psychology of aging* (5th ed., pp. 349–377). New York: Academic Press.

Baddeley, A. (1992). Working memory. *Science*, *255*, 556–559.

Brayne, C., Matthews, F.E., McGee, M.A., & Jagger, C. (2001). Health and ill-health in the older population in England and Wales: The Medical Research Council Cognitive Function and Ageing Study (MRC CFAS). *Age and Ageing*, *30*, 53–62.

Cabeza, R., & Nyberg, L. (2000). Imaging cognition II: An empirical review of 275 PET and fMRI studies. *Journal of Cognitive Neuroscience*, *12*, 1–47.

Cavanaugh, J.C., & Poon, L.W. (1989). Metamemorial predictors of memory performance in young and older adults. *Psychology and Aging*, *4*, 365–368.

Cohen, G.C. (1996). *Memory in the real world*. Hove, UK: Psychology Press.

Craik, F.I.M., & Jennings, J.M. (1992). Human memory. In F.I.M. Craik & T.A. Salthouse (Eds.), *Handbook of the psychology of aging* (pp. 51–110). Hillsdale, NJ: Lawrence Erlbaum Associates, Inc.

Gijsbers van Wijk, C.M.T., & Kolk, A.M. (1997). Sex differences in physical symptoms: The contribution of symptom perception theory. *Social Science and Medicine*, *45*, 231–246.

Halpern, D.F., & LaMay, M.L. (2000). The smarter sex: A critical review of sex differences in intelligence. *Educational Psychology Review*, *12*, 229–246.

Herlitz, A., Nilsson, L.-G., & Bäckman, L. (1997). Gender differences in episodic memory. *Memory and Cognition*, *25*, 801–811.

Hertzog, C., & Hultsch, D.F. (2000). Metacognition in adulthood and old age. In F.I.M. Craik & T.A. Salthouse (Eds.), *Handbook of aging and cognition* (pp. 417–466). Mahwah, NJ: Lawrence Erlbaum Associates, Inc.

Hultsch, D.F., & Dixon, R.A. (1990). Learning and memory in aging. In J.E. Birren & K.W. Schaie (Eds.), *Handbook of the psychology of aging* (3rd ed., pp. 258–274). San Diego, CA: Academic Press.

Johansson, B., Allen-Burge, R., & Zarit, S. (1997). Self-reports on memory functioning in a longitudinal study of the oldest old: Relation to current, prospective, and retrospective performance. *Journal of Gerontology: Psychological Sciences*, *52B*, P139–P146.

Kaszniak, A.W. (1996). Preparing for treatment of the elderly: Assessment. In S.H. Zarit & B. Knight (Eds.), *A guide to psychotherapy and aging: Effective interventions in a life stage context* (pp. 163–220). Washington, DC: American Psychological Association.

Maitland, S.B., Herlitz, A., Nyberg, L., Bäckman, L., & Nilsson, L.-G. (2004). Selective sex differences in declarative memory. *Memory and Cognition 32*, 1160–1169.

McDonald-Miszczak, L., Hertzog, C., & Hultsch, D.F. (1995). Stability and accuracy of metamemory in adulthood and aging: A longitudinal analysis. *Psychology and Aging*, *10*, 553–564.

Nathanson, C.A. (1977). Sex, illness and medical care: A review of data, theory and method. *Social Science and Medicine*, *11*, 13–26.

Nilsson, L.-G. (2003). Memory function in normal aging. *Acta Neurologica Scandinavica*, *107* (Suppl 179), 7–13.

Nilsson, L.-G., Adolfsson, R., Bäckman, L., de Frias, C., Molander. B., & Nyberg, L. (2004). Betula: A prospective cohort study on memory, health and aging. *Aging, Neuropsychology and Cognition, 11*, 134–148.

Nilsson, L.-G., Bäckman, L., Erngrund, K., Nyberg, L., Adolfsson, R., Bucht, G., Karlsson, S., Widing, M., & Winblad, B. (1997). The Betula prospective cohort study: Memory, health, and aging. *Aging, Neuropsychology, and Cognition, 4*, 1–32.

Nyberg, L., Maitland, S.B., Rönnlund, M., Bäckman, L., Dixon, R., Wahlin, Å., & Nilsson, L.-G. (2003). Selective adult age differences in an age-invariant multi-factor model of declarative memory. *Psychology and Aging, 18*, 149–160.

Nyberg, L., & Tulving, E. (1996). Classifying human long-term memory: Evidence from converging dissociations. *European Journal of Cognitive Psychology, 8*, 163–183.

Small, B.J., Fratiglioni, L., Viitanen, M., Winblad, B., & Bäckman, L. (2000). The course of cognitive impairment in pre-clinical Alzheimer's disease: Three- and six-year follow-up of a population-based sample. *Archives of Neurology, 57*, 839–844.

Tulving, E. (1972). Episodic and semantic memory. In E. Tulving & W. Donaldson (Eds.), *Organization of memory* (pp. 382–403). New York: Academic Press.

Tulving, E. (1983). *Elements of episodic memory.* Oxford, UK: Clarendon Press.

Tulving, E. (1987). Multiple memory systems and consciousness. *Human Neurobiology, 6*, 67–80.

Tulving, E. (1991). Concepts of human memory. In L.R. Squire, N.M. Weinberg, G. Lynch, & J.L. McGaugh (Eds.), *Organization and locus of change* (pp. 3–32). New York: Oxford University Press.

Voyer, D., Voyer, S., & Bryden, M.P. (1995). Magnitude of sex differences in spatial abilities: A meta-analysis and consideration of critical variables. *Psychological Bulletin, 117*, 250–270.

Wahlin, A., Maitland, S.B., Bäckman, L., & Dixon, R.A. (2003). Interrelations between subjective health and episodic memory change in Swedish and Canadian samples of older adults. *International Journal of Aging and Human Development, 57*, 21–35.

Zelinski, E.M., Gilewski, M.J., & Anthony-Bergstone, C.R. (1990). Memory Functioning Questionnaire: Concurrent validity with memory performance and self-reported memory failures. *Psychology and Aging, 5*, 388–399.

13 Memory pathways: Involuntary and voluntary processes in retrieving personal memories

Tore Helstrup, Rossana De Beni, Cesare Cornoldi and Asher Koriat

THE PATHWAY METAPHOR

How do memories emerge into consciousness? How are they searched for and recovered? How are retrieved memories validated and how are they "reported" to oneself or to others? In this chapter we shall use a pathway metaphor to address these questions, focusing on the retrieval of episodic memories of a personal nature.

The pathway metaphor assumes that the rememberer stands at the cross-road between two paths, one leading *to* memory and the other leading *from* memory. The path leading *to* memory brings the individual into his or her memory system, like a pathway taken when a person arrives either by chance or as a result of a premeditated excursion into a garden with familiar flowers and animals. The pathway metaphor also implies that if we want to access a particular memory, we have to reach out for it; we have to submit a description to our memory that specifies what we are looking for (Norman & Bobrow, 1979) and try to locate something that roughly meets that description. Thus, we have to specify a path *to* the intended memory.

On the other hand, making use of the retrieved memory, integrating the information retrieved, reporting it privately to oneself (e.g., thinking, feeling) or publicly (e.g., in words or in actions) is like specifying a path leading *from* memory. It is like bringing back from the garden some of the flowers we collected there.

Thus, to retrieve memories is to travel mentally along two paths. When retrieving memories, one can be said to find oneself at the crossroads where paths *to* and *from* memories intersect. In a sense one must negotiate with one's memory, conducting a transaction that involves both taking and giving.

Certainly, there are many memory paths. We shall contrast two paths *to* episodic memories; voluntary and involuntary. These two paths are typically, although not exclusively, associated with two different modes, respectively – re-experiencing and factual recollection. The two paths *from* episodic memories are also associated with two modes; editing versus not editing. The editing of one's memories reflects a process that takes place in making use of one's memories, that is, in specifying a path *from* one's own memories. Unedited memories are used as they are, whereas edited memories are scrutinized before use.

The combination of the two paths may be understood in terms of the degree to which the paths *to* and *from* memory are controlled by the person. Typically, controlled access to one's memories, that is, deliberately searching for specific events or episodes, is associated with the exercise of deliberate editing processes in reporting these memories to oneself or to others. On the other hand, involuntarily retrieved memories, which emerge in the absence of an intention to remember, are typically experienced and reported with only a moderate degree of controlled metacognitive editing. However, instances in which involuntary memories are edited and others in which voluntary memories are transmitted with little editing are not uncommon.

In this chapter we discuss the retrieval of episodic memories in an everyday perspective using the pathway metaphor, in which the rememberer is seen to stand between the paths that lead to one's memories and those that lead from them.

INVOLUNTARY AND VOLUNTARY MEMORIES

Much of the experimental study of memory has focused on controlled, voluntary memory retrieval. When participants are first presented with some material and are later asked to recall it, they typically engage in a controlled, deliberate search for the material. Furthermore, they know that their performance will be scored in terms of certain criteria, so their search is guided by the attempt to satisfy these criteria. Such is the case, for example, in university examinations. A student who is asked to answer test questions or to pick the correct answer from among several alternatives would typically struggle to probe his or her memory for the correct answer.

In everyday life, in contrast, there are many cases in which memories come to us, so to speak, without any deliberate effort being made by us. Such memories are generally referred to as involuntary memories (or "mind popping", "thoughts that come unbidden", "involuntary remembering", etc.). Consider the following personal example concerning the retrieval of a memory episode.

Last January, when leaving Norway, two of us had a series of highly activated memories of past episodes and scenes (e.g., the visit to the Vigeland chapel, the snow at the top of a nearby hill, the fireworks at a friend's home, the meeting with an industrial psychologist on a dark terrace, having lunch at the Centre for Advanced Studies, and Norwegian folk music). These experienced episodes popped one after the other into our minds as we talked, without any logical sequence. The recency of these events may have made their memories more accessible than other events. However, when we arrived back home and were questioned by our relatives, we engaged in a more controlled, voluntary survey of our memories, guided by the specific questions posed: What exactly had we eaten at the home of our friends? What was the name of the hill? The products of the controlled memory search tended to be more logically organized than the products of our involuntary remembering.

We may liken the experience associated with involuntary memory to that of a fisherman standing on the bank of a river, waiting passively for a fish to catch itself on the hook. In contrast, the experience associated with voluntary memories may be likened to that of a hunter who is out there actively searching for an animal, systematically exploring the terrain, taking advantage of various clues that may lead him to his prey.

Obviously, the distinction between voluntary and involuntary memories is not sharp. Memory processes typically involve a mixture of the two modes of retrieval. Even when a controlled inspection of our memory is initiated in response to a query by an acquaintance ("What did you do when you were in Norway?" "What did you do on the last evening before your return home?"), certain aspects of the stored episodes may suggest themselves more readily than others, and new memory associations open up. Thus, the controlled travel through one's memories may be diverted by involuntary memories despite our attempt to stay on the same memory path. Of course, the controlled search may also be guided by general knowledge of the event (e.g., that it used to get dark early; that we were with our friends) and also by abstract semantic knowledge (we know that the end of the year is at midnight, we know that snow is common in the Scandinavian winter, etc.). Controlled, voluntary memories are generally submitted to an editing process in order to ensure that they satisfy certain criteria such as accuracy. The editing process becomes more stringent when a public report is involved. Involuntary memories, in contrast, jump into our minds as "unedited" raw data. Of course, some editing is likely to take place when we recount them.

The distinction between voluntary and involuntary memory was made, in fact, by Ebbinghaus (1885/1964; see Berntsen, 1998). He made a distinction between memories that occur "with apparent spontaneity and without any act of the will" and memories that are called back "into consciousness by an exertion of the will" (pp. 1–2). Thus, involuntary memories are those that emerge spontaneously, sometimes unexpectedly, without any intent to conjure them up. Voluntary memories, in contrast, emerge in response to a controlled, goal-directed search, typically prompted by some requirement, and guided by the need to satisfy some general criterion.

THE STUDY OF INVOLUNTARY MEMORY

Despite the prevalence of experiences of involuntary memory in everyday life, little systematic research has been carried out on the memories that emerge into consciousness without any intention to remember. The reasons, perhaps, lie in the difficulty of applying traditional experimental methods to this area of investigation. Nevertheless a few studies have borrowed methods from autobiographical memory research to investigate several aspects of involuntary memories. For example, Berntsen (1996) used a diary method to study involuntary autobiographical memories in their everyday context. She asked participants to record at most two involuntary memories each day (participants were free to choose which; prior tests had indicated that participants typically report five or six occurrences daily on average when they are not restricted to reporting only two). Later on, Berntsen (1998) used cue words or short sentences (e.g., "riding a bike") that had been found to elicit involuntary memories in her diary study as prompts for eliciting voluntary memories in another group of participants. This allowed her to compare voluntary and involuntary autobiographical memories.

While Berntsen (1996, 1998) focused on autobiographical memory, Kvavilashvili and Mandler (2004) focused on the involuntary retrieval of semantic memory, such as the spontaneous emergence into memory of a word or a tune, unaccompanied by additional contextual information. Their method was based on diaries and questionnaires that examined the nature and frequency of such memories. They found that these memories often occur without any apparent cue while people are engaged in relatively automatic activities. One interesting observation was that even a brief encounter with new words or names was sufficient to produce an involuntary memory at a later point, sometimes with no conscious recollection of having encountered these words or names before. Thus, reading someone's name in a newspaper was sufficient for that name to pop up.

The studies of Berntsen and of Kvavilashvili and Mandler confirm that memories often pop up without intention during our everyday activities. The involuntary memories reported are usually very short-lived. A question of interest is whether more extended episodes can also emerge into consciousness without active, deliberate search and maintenance. Some negative memories have a relatively long duration in time and recur in spite of the person's effort to avoid them (Spence, 1988). However, involuntary memories with more pleasant overtones that have relatively long durations may also occur. Such memories have been reported to be a source of pleasure and personal value (Salaman, 1982).

DISTINCTIVE CHARACTERISTICS OF INVOLUNTARY MEMORIES

What are the distinctive characteristics of involuntary memories? As mentioned above, Berntsen (1998) compared the involuntary memories reported by one group with the voluntary memories produced by another group of participants in response to cue words derived from the involuntary memories reported by the first group. She found several systematic differences. Some differences can also be gleaned from other studies. First, a notable feature of involuntary memories is their personal content. Berntsen observed that involuntary memories were more frequently related to specific episodes than were voluntary memories (89% versus 63%, respectively), suggesting that involuntary memories do not simply capture schematic knowledge. Rather they often concern events or episodes from one's personal life. However, impersonal semantic knowledge also sometimes emerges involuntarily. Thus, as Kvavilashvili and Mandler (2004) noted, sometimes words, melodies or names pop up without intention in the course of our daily activities: We suddenly "hear" a song playing in our ear. Similarly, a name that we have been struggling to recall may suddenly pop into our head as if from nowhere. However, it is quite unlikely that we would spontaneously remember that "canaries are birds" or that "a sofa is a piece of furniture".

Involuntary memories are typically associated with certain phenomeno-logical properties: a richer preservation of the original emotional and sensory features, a strong perception of vividness of the event and a feeling of "re-experiencing" the event. The memory sometimes has a perceptual quality. We re-experience an event or episode rather than retrieve its verbal content or its gist. Thus, spontaneous retrieval may produce memories more closely corresponding to the original experience. This is unlike voluntary memories, which tend to be more selective and more focused.

Another distinctive feature concerns the retention interval: Berntsen found that involuntary memories tend to be more recent than voluntary memories. Most of the involuntary memories reported were about events that had taken place during the previous year (and at most during the past 3 years), whereas most of the voluntary memories referred to events that had happened over the past 4 years.

Involuntary memories also seem to differ from voluntary memories in their organization: When an event or episode come spontaneously to mind, its emergence into consciousness does not usually follow a logical, sequential organization. Rather, different facets of the event may pop up associatively into memory, without any clear order. One image may trigger another. The emergence of involuntary memories is relatively rapid, as though different features of an episode were being accessed in parallel. This is in contrast to voluntary memories, whose retrieval tends to be slow, sequential and labori-ous. Because voluntary memories are self-initiated, their retrieval is often guided by top-down programmes that constrain the sequence in which they are conjured up.

We might have expected involuntary memories to concern events that had been frequently retrieved. Surprisingly, the available evidence suggests that involuntary memories generally concern events that had hardly been recol-lected previously, including some that perhaps could not have been accessed voluntarily. Thus, Berntsen (1998) observed that in approximately 45% of involuntary memories, people reported that they had "never talked or thought about them before" whereas this only happened with less than 10% of voluntary memories. Thus, the memories that occur spontaneously are not necessarily the most activated, nor those that have been recently refreshed.

Indeed, Proust (1919) also noted that sometimes involuntary retrieval captures memories that otherwise would never come to mind.

THE ACTIVATION OF INVOLUNTARY MEMORIES

In the previous section we discussed the distinctive features of involuntary memories that occur spontaneously without deliberate memory search and retrieval. It is natural to ask what the precipitating conditions that bring memories *to* us without any intention on our part to recall them are.

As noted by Kvavilashvili and Mandler (2004), involuntary memories are more likely to occur when we are not engaged in intentional cognitive activities. Such memories would seem to emerge when we are in a relaxed state, in which attention is diffuse rather than focused. Involuntary memories also occur when controlled processes are mostly aimed at eliminating disturbing thoughts (see Berntsen, 1998).

With regard to the precipitating cues, these cues are frequently internal, emotional and/or sensory rather than verbal. Environmental context, mood and smell can prime involuntary memories (see, e.g., Chapters 3 and 4). The relationship between the cue and the memory is often complex and indirect. In many cases, however, we are completely unaware of any precipitating cue.

Presumably the pathways to involuntary memories are associative in nature. This may explain why some basic factors such as body posture and mental state (a reclining posture, fatigue, drugs) may precipitate such memories. The occurrence of spontaneous memories is quite frequent in clinical situations such as psychoanalytic psychotherapy. The attempt to report what comes to mind first in response to a cue word often produces involuntary memories. People under the effects of hallucinogenic drugs also often report having vivid involuntary re-experiences of past events. These drugs seem to be optimal for the emergence of involuntary memories as they reduce controlled, rational thinking and suspend editing operations, thereby enhancing the effects of internal cues. In some sense, dreams also represent the emergence of fragmented involuntary memories and are illustrative of a re-experiencing process that occurs with little editing. When suddenly awakened, the person still has in mind some of these non-edited fragments. However, when asked later to report the dream, he or she may engage in an editing process, putting together the dream fragments and trying to build a coherent story. Similarly, people under the effects of alcohol are more inclined to have involuntary memories. However, in that case social aspects become more dominant in the production of these memories.

We sometimes react with surprise to the unexpected emergence into consciousness of clear events and images from the past. This reaction may be due not only to the fact that such memories are unexpected, but also to our failure to trace the path that led us to them. Sometimes the spontaneous emergence of unexpected memories may evoke an unpleasant feeling because it occurs outside of our control. The psychoanalytic assumption of psychological determinism has led theoreticians ever since Freud to assume that many behaviours that appear to us to be random occurrences (such as slips of the tongue) actually derive from processes of which we are not aware. Freud (1920/1975) put special emphasis on the defensive, unconscious origin of involuntary behaviours, and promoted the view that such behaviours reflect intentions and desires that the person would rather deny. He described the processes whereby mental elements are associated and then emerge into consciousness in a disguised form. In particular, he stressed the idea that the processes that are outside our awareness and control tend to follow associative and illogical rules, such as when such processes take off from the sound of a word rather than from its meaning. However, as Berntsen (1998) reported, this does not seem to be the general rule, because involuntary memories are not associated with more negative emotions than are involuntary memories.

However, with regard to the precipitation of involuntary memories, an important class of such memories that deserves particular attention is that of post-traumatic memories, in which the memory of traumatic events keeps popping out not only in the absence of any intention to retrieve the events but also against the person's will. Such painful memories tend to impose themselves repeatedly. This recurrence against the will reflects a failure of control, because the person generally fails to avoid these memories or stop them when they start flowing into consciousness. Such unpleasant re-experiences may also contain a great deal of detail, so that one might feel flooded by the re-experiencing of the event, which takes over cognitive control.

Presumably, because traumatic memories are emotionally charged, they may be primed even by weak cues. It is also possible that the repeated re-experience of painful memories produces a spread of activation that increases the number of elements that can prime these memories.

In explaining the recurrent emergence into consciousness of painful thoughts and memories, Freud (1905/1953) emphasized the nature of these thoughts and memories as ones that the person is struggling to expel from consciousness. In contrast, recent research by Wegner and his associates (e.g., Wegner, Schneider, Carter, & White, 1987; Wenzlaff & Wegner, 2000) focused on the process of thought suppression itself as a source of recurrences of ruminative thoughts and traumatic memories. That body of research suggested that, in general, thought suppression is counterproductive, reinforcing the state of mind that one is trying to avoid. Perhaps, then, it is the struggle to avoid thinking about a painful event that makes the memory of that event come to mind. As we have seen, however, involuntary remembering is not confined to negative events (Berntsen, 1998).

INVOLUNTARY MEMORIES AND REMEMBERING BY RE-EXPERIENCING

The discussion of involuntary memory brings to the fore an important distinction between two modes of remembering: re-experiencing and factual recollection. In the "re-experiencing" mode, the phenomenological quality of memory is such that the person feels as if he or she is experiencing the event again in the same manner "as if he/she were still there". This is what Tulving (2002) referred to as "travel back in time", when the person remembers past happenings by mentally travelling back into the past. This type of remembering was assumed by Tulving to be specifically linked to the episodic memory system as this system is understood today. For example, the patient KC studied by Tulving is assumed to have lost his episodic memory as a result of brain injury. However, KC can still report information about the past in a factual, declarative way, without the phenomenological experience of travelling back in time. It is his "autonoetic" consciousness, his memory of personal episodes, that is impaired.

Thus, the re-experiencing mode is associated with a reinstatement of many contextual aspects of the event, including its "when" and "where" as well as its personal and emotional significance. The event is sometimes "seen" from the same perspective as that which the person occupied when witnessing the event. One remembers oneself as the observer rather than as part of the observed event (Nigro & Neisser, 1983). Unlike this mode, the declarative, "noetic" mode involves recollecting the factual content without an impression of experiencing the event. For example, we may recall that we spent last Christmas in Oslo without recollecting any specific contextual information associated with that memory.

Very often, involuntary memories are re-experiences, and may involve various degrees of detail and precision. However, they need not always be so. As noted earlier, involuntary recall may involve specific elements of our life such as a song or a name, which come to mind without being associated with a well-defined episode, or without a feeling of re-experiencing. However, the re-experience mode seems to be characteristic of many involuntary memories, for example when we are in a certain place and, without any intention, an episode associated with that place pops into our mind in a very vivid, emotionally intense way, and we have the impression that the episode is still continuing.

Although re-experiencing is more dominant in involuntary memories it also characterizes many acts of controlled, voluntary remembering, such as when several family members try to actively recall a family event. In a non-social context, too, re-experiences can be voluntary. One may actively provide oneself with triggering cues in order to recreate a certain past experience. Some controlled retrieval strategies actually involve the attempt to voluntarily reinstate the original context and to try to feel the same way one felt when experiencing the episode (Fisher & Geiselman, 1992; Smith, 1979). It is unclear whether one must suspend voluntary control in order to have the feeling of re-experiencing the episode.

In everyday life we enjoy reactivating pleasant experiences. Although it is difficult to re-experience on demand, there are various ways to increase the likelihood of inducing re-experiences. We may mentally or physically try to reinstate previous "stimulus conditions" (the encoding specificity principle or state-dependent memory, Bower, 1981; Tulving & Thomson, 1973), consult diaries or old photos, or get together with old friends to share a shared past (see Chapter 8). Thus, there exist methods of controlling or influencing the occurrence of re-experiencing. However, once re-experiencing takes place, it will tend to unfold "automatically".

Re-experiences can take all gradations of positive and negative emotional shades. The positive ones are particularly satisfying because they reinstate pleasures, rather than merely reminding one of them. Nostalgia may have an overtone of indulgence, but is widely recognized as an attractive memory condition.

CONTROLLED, VOLUNTARILY RETRIEVED MEMORIES

Most "formal" situations in which memory is involved entail voluntary, controlled retrieval. The best examples are achievement tests, in which students must probe their memories for a solicited piece of information. In fact, most laboratory studies on memory, like those involving free recall tasks, paired associates tasks and general information questions, attempt to tap voluntary retrieval. In terms of the pathway metaphor, voluntary memories involve building a path *to* our memories. In everyday life too, controlled recall is common, but it may also be private, as when one thinks back on previous experiences without intending to give a memory report. One example is when one is walking alone, or reflecting about one's past before going to sleep.

Each recollection is presumably coloured by previous recollections, and affects subsequent recollections. Important episodes are certainly recollected several times. Frequently recollected episodes become schematized. Schematization presumably implies a dilution of the distinction between experienced and inferred information (Bartlett, 1932; Neisser, 1967).

As will be discussed later, voluntary retrieval involves a variety of metacognitive processes that monitor and control the course of remembering, assessing the truth value of the retrieved information, regulating recall, filling up the gaps and engaging in reconstructive processes.

Voluntary retrieval generally serves some function. Obviously, in achievement tests the goal of the person is to provide the *correct* answer. The same is true of many TV games. Personal, private search of one's memory is also often driven by the desire to ascertain what "really" happened. And most clearly, accuracy is perhaps the most important criterion in court, when juries must evaluate the reliability of eyewitness testimony. Thus, in many real-life situations the focus is on veridicality or accuracy (Koriat & Goldsmith, 1996).

However, as Neisser aptly argued:

> It is not the case that all memory-based behaviors focus on accurate reproduction; other dimensions of the performance may be much more important. The aim of telling a joke, for example, is to tell it *effectively*; whether you tell it just as you heard it is of no consequence at all. A singer of epic tales "repeats" a familiar story, but not with a view to reproducing some prior performance; rather, his intent is to impress and entertain his present audience (Lord, 1960; Rubin, 1995). Actors do indeed memorize their lines, but getting the words right is the least, most insignificant part of their task. Experimental subjects tend to focus on accuracy when they recall a story for the benefit of the experimenter, but other dimensions become more important when they discuss the same story with a peer (Hyman, 1994).
>
> (Neisser, 1996, p. 204)

Thus, controlled recollections have some function, and that function generally dictates what the person focuses on, what perspective one adopts in "scanning" one's memory and reporting it, how much detail one communicates, etc. (Goldsmith & Koriat, 1999). Little such selection is assumed to take place in involuntary memory.

Because controlled retrieval of episodic events is carried out with some goal in mind, there is greater pressure on producing as consistent and complete an account as possible. This is particularly so when a public report is required. Thus, the quest for coherence and completeness is characteristic of voluntary memories, whereas involuntary memories can be quite fragmentary. When remembering is controlled, there is a desire to fill in the gaps and to tell oneself and others a coherent story.

In sum, intentional recall is top-down, active and goal-directed. It often involves processes of problem solving, similar to those that take place in solving a riddle (Koriat, 2000).

INTERACTIONS BETWEEN CONTROLLED AND AUTOMATIC PROCESSES IN REMEMBERING

The example we used at the beginning of the chapter shows how the typical process of retrieval of episodic personal memories may involve not only deliberate, goal-directed retrieval processes, but also a series of memories that pop up involuntarily. Sometimes memories appear in unexpected ways and we follow the lead of these memories to engage in controlled retrieval processes. Once a memory episode involuntarily comes to mind, we try to verify it complete it and monitor its source, and this, of course, entails controlled operations.

Sometimes people have a specific goal that directs the search in memory, but then memory starts to wander and to be guided by its own products in a data-driven fashion. For example, Palladino and De Beni (2003) asked people of different ages to create a mental image of an autobiographical memory in response to a cue word. They found that the image created was progressively enriched, especially in the case of the elderly, by further autobiographical elements that were not strictly associated with the cue word.

It is very likely that all controlled remembering also entails automatic processes. As we search our memory, there are "suggestions from below" that we decide to follow or ignore (Koriat, 2000). Because there is no simple algorithm for retrieving the correct episode, we must reconstruct it from various elements of it that are suggested to us by our memory. Automatically activated features and elements can facilitate controlled retrieval but can also block it and divert it from its course. It has been proposed, for example, that some of the difficulties that we encounter in reaching for a word that is on the "tip of our tongue" derive in part from the interfering effects of "blockers" or "interlopers" that come to mind during the search for the elusive word (Burke, MacKay, Worthley, & Wade, 1991; Jones, 1989).

THE ROLE OF INVOLUNTARY MEMORIES IN EVERYDAY LIFE

In everyday life, memory, in both its intentional and unintentional aspects, serves different functions (Glenberg, 1997; Neisser, 1976, 1978). One remembers in order to solve various tasks, e.g., to answer questions, find one one's way to desired goals, write a story, etc. Sometimes we have the phenomenological experience of remembering, as in cases of episodic memory, when we have the experience of travelling back in time. At other times we may not be conscious that we are solving a problem by memory support, or are relying on our memory while travelling through the town. When paths to memory are open and used, we are not always fully conscious of using these paths. It has been observed (Antrobus, Singer, & Greenberg, 1966) that free thoughts and daydreaming, which involve involuntarily retrieved material from memory, represent a large portion of our everyday time.

Remembering in everyday life generally occurs in the context of many other processes such as perceiving, planning, thinking, deciding and acting. Very rarely does it occur in isolation. Hence the paths to one's past will normally be opened while one is travelling concurrently along other mental paths leading to other goals.

We venture the hypothesis that many artistic products draw their psychological importance from their re-experiential function. The most valued musical works evoke re-experiencing. Not only biographies and autobiographies purport to recreate the past; novels are also indirect narratives of the past. Novels and biographies present the reader with the past seen from the author's perspective, but they also allow the reader to re-experience his or her own past through identification with the story characters. References are often made to Proust's reconstruction of his past, the loss of which is threatened. Proust's aim was to overcome time in the sense of bringing back at least some psychologically important experiences as they were originally experienced.

Re-experiences are functionally important because they provide an opportunity for reconsidering our past, for better understanding of what happened, including our own thoughts and actions, and for re-evaluating that past. Re-experiences may bring forward information that was previously not much reflected on. On re-inspection of re-experienced information, problems may be solved, a process that may also affect creative mental imagery (Finke & Slayton, 1988). Re-experiencing may also produce insights regarding old information, in the same way that perceptual reorganizations may create insights concerning novel information.

In concluding this section we wish to point out the relevance of re-experience in the context of forensic psychology. Re-experiences and involuntary memories may provide memory information that is difficult to retrieve by deliberate search. When remembering is not under deliberate strategic control, it must be induced indirectly. The evidence suggests that the chances of involuntary memories emerging are greater under relaxed and unfocused conditions. It also appears that there is an intimate link between the precipitating cues that elicit an involuntary memory and the content of that memory. Eyewitnesses might succeed in recovering relevant information when successfully induced to re-experience the event involved. This may be the dynamics behind successful "hypnosis", drug-induced relaxations or techniques inducing context reinstatement (e.g., cognitive interviews, Fisher & Geiselman, 1992). However, there is no guarantee that re-experiences are completely veridical. One's perceptions may sometimes be mistaken and the same is true with regard to re-experienced memories.

VOLUNTARY MEMORIES IN EVERYDAY LIFE

Intentional remembering may sometimes be an effortful and laborious process. Fortunately, there are pieces of information that we can access almost without effort, particularly when the information has been well rehearsed. In that case the phenomenological experience is similar to that of directly accessing the solicited information. Such direct accessing is an economic and efficient way of retrieving memories. Quickly accessed information is also quite likely to be correct (Robinson, Johnson, & Herndon, 1997).

Sometimes direct access may fail. A good example is the "tip-of-the-tongue" state, when we are convinced that we know a name but cannot recall it. We are all familiar with the frustration and irritation that accompanies such blocked retrievals, when controlled efforts to find the elusive name are unsuccessful.

Retrieving episodes and events from the distant past is sometimes very laborious. Unfortunately, not much is known about the retrieval of complex, real-life events because much of the laboratory research on memory has focused on relatively simple tasks (Koriat, 2000). In attempting to retrieve a personal episode from the distant past, a person typically retrieves fragments of the episode and scenes one after the other and tries to use them as cues for additional details. Very often the process looks like that of solving a puzzle when too many pieces are missing. In such cases, a serious problem facing the rememberer is that of source and reality monitoring (Mitchell & Johnson, 2000): Does this fragment belong to this event or does it belong to another event? Did this segment of the event really take place? The problem is thus that of linking the pieces that belong to the same past event and reconstructing a sensible story.

Several techniques have been described for probing one's own memory. However, most of these techniques can help retrieval when they are used during encoding. They are based on associating the to-be-remembered information with specific cues, which can later be used to support memory retrieval. A good example is the method of loci (see Cornoldi & De Beni, 1985). Other techniques apply to retrieval, such as the alphabetical cueing procedure for recalling names or words. However, more intricate search and retrieval strategies have been described (see Koriat, 2000). Some of these techniques have been incorporated into the cognitive interview (Fisher & Geiselman, 1992).

When it comes to the recollection of personal autobiographical events, such recollection is often carried out within a social (e.g., family) setting. In such cases, support obtained from others who have witnessed the event may help not only in cueing one's memory for more details, but also in validating one's own memories.

In sum, intentional remembering is quite prevalent in everyday life. We can generally access episodic memories, particularly when they are integrated into personal schemata. Search processes can be used to recover temporarily blocked episodic memories. Effortful retrieval generally requires laborious monitoring and control processes.

PATHWAYS FROM MEMORY: HOW THE RETRIEVED EPISODE IS VALIDATED AND EVENTUALLY COMMUNICATED

In our pathway metaphor, the processes by which retrieved memories can be brought to consciousness and/or expressed can be described as pathways *from* memory. So far we have discussed the paths *to* memory. We discuss now the paths *from* memory. In general, a retrieved memory episode may be communicated directly in a largely unedited form, or it may be "edited" according to our personal interests or according to the goals of communication.

Non-edited paths from memory

Many retrieved pieces of information that we report, mostly from semantic memory, are largely unedited. Answers to everyday memory questions may usually be based on information directly accessed, for example, when we state our name, and give our address or telephone number. Episodic facts may also be reported unedited. Editing requires time, so that pressure of time may not allow sufficient opportunities for editing. This is part of the rationale behind lie-detection methods. So far research has not detected reliable verbal or nonverbal cues to deception (Vrij, 2000; Vrij & Mann, 2004). However, it has been argued, for instance by psychoanalytic theory, that bodily gestures and reactions ("body language") may open doors to memories and motivations of which the clients themselves are unaware.

Edited paths from memory

Memory editing is almost always the rule even when we are not aware of it. For example, consider the simple laboratory task of free recall. We generally assume that in this task the participant reports all the words that he or she can recall from a previously presented list of words. However, research has shown that some editing goes on even in this simple task (Koriat & Goldsmith, 1996). First, participants operate under the assumption that there is no point reporting again a word that has already been reported. Therefore, for each word that comes to mind they must presumably monitor whether they have already produced that word before, and only then decide whether to report it. When output monitoring is rendered difficult (e.g., by asking participants to report the items verbally rather than write them down), the proportion of report repetitions increases (Gardiner, Passmore, Herriot, & Klee, 1977). Koriat, Ben-Zur, and Sheffer (1988) observed that elderly people are deficient in output monitoring (remembering what they said or did), which is responsible, perhaps, for their greater tendency to tell the same story over again or to take a medicine more often than needed. In a free-recall task, the elderly group was found to recall about half of the words the younger group remembered, but their probability of repeating some of these words was double that of the younger group.

A second type of evidence for the occurrence of editing in free recall comes from the proportion of errors of commission made. Even when there are no explicit instructions about guessing, participants assume that they are expected not only to reproduce a large proportion of the studied words but also to be accurate. Indeed, when participants are specifically instructed to be less "inhibited" they report more words, but the majority of these are errors of commission (Bousfield & Rosner, 1970). Koriat and Goldsmith (1996) showed that the accuracy of free-recall reports is delicately tuned to the accuracy incentives used: Participants were quite accurate (making few false recalls) when they expected to win one Israeli *shekel* for each correct answer but lose the same amount for each wrong answer. However, they were more conservative in their reporting, and also more accurate, when the penalty for incorrect reports increased. Thus, control processes operate even in simple laboratory tasks.

Of course, when it comes to memory in real life, there is greater need to edit one's memories during reporting. First, the amount of information involved is usually extremely large, and one must be very selective, attempting to squeeze the information into some sort of manageable description. In addition, some structuring and organization needs to be imposed on the data.

Second, and no less importantly, memory reporting, as indicated earlier, generally has a goal and a function, and these typically guide the editing and constructive process. We must take into account the expectations and knowledge of the receiver of the communication, must choose where to start, what features to emphasize and what to ignore, what level of detail to supply, etc.

In addition to a general "editorial" policy, specific decisions must be made with regard to each item that comes to mind, whether to report it or not, and how to report it. In the case of a person on a witness stand, the "official" criteria are generally clear: i.e., "to tell the truth, the whole truth and nothing but the truth". This is a heavy requirement, because as Koriat and Goldsmith (1996) demonstrated, people can rarely meet all three requirements and must generally sacrifice some correct answers for the sake of enhancing the overall accuracy of what they do report (the quantity–accuracy trade-off). One compromise that people sometimes use is to report an uncertain piece of information at a level of generality at which the report is less likely to be wrong (control over the "grain size of the report"; Goldsmith, Koriat, & Weinberg-Eliezer, 2002). At any rate, eyewitnesses must monitor on-line the accuracy of what comes to mind in order to decide whether to include it in the report or omit it (see Chapter 11).

Of course, other types of editing may take place, involving slight or more serious modifications. The report may be embellished or improved in order to make it appear more convincing. It may be attenuated and diluted when the person is uncertain. Some of the editing may actually take place unwittingly and unconsciously. This might result, for example, in a tendency to focus more on pleasant than unpleasant aspects of autobiographical memories (see Chapter 8).

THE INTERACTION BETWEEN PATHS TO MEMORY AND PATHS FROM MEMORY

The distinction between edited and non-edited memories can be considered in conjunction with the distinction between involuntary and voluntary retrieval processes, thus offering a more complete description of how the memory of a personal episode finally turns out. As noted earlier, involuntary memories are typically not edited. Such non-editing may be against the remembering person's will or intention, as has been shown to be the case for involuntary traumatic memories, but it need not always be so (Berntsen, 1996, 1998). The existence of non-edited memories is well known in folk psychology, and is often utilized in works of art. Descriptions of the stream of consciousness that break grammatical rules may sometimes signal a more personal protagonist level than descriptions that follow ordinary rules (cf. Joyce's description of Bloom's thoughts; Joyce, 1922/1960). When composers include unexpected natural sounds into their compositions, this technique may be intended to suggest different levels of musical interpretation. The techniques of Impressionism serve a similar function, for example, to indicate a "truer", more direct depiction than that conveyed by a photograph-like painting.

Memory editing has been well documented in everyday experience. Such editing is partly regulated by conversational conventions à la Grice (1967, 1975). It is also regulated by metacognitive beliefs and knowledge about memory and by social norms (Austin, 1962; Yzerbyt, Lories, & Dardenne, 1998). For instance, there is a vast difference between telling memories to superiors (bosses) and to inferiors (employees, pupils). Memories are reported differently in unconventional and conventional settings (in a bar or a party compared to the court or a school classroom).

In novels, we may contrast the style of the author when an event is neutrally described as an "objective" event, with when that event is described as seen from the hero's point of view. A comparison of news reporting, gossiping and story-telling reveals different editorial practices. We make daily use of similar rules or "mechanisms" when reporting episodic memories. One reason might be that such editorial practices are socially based (Middleton & Edwards, 1990). We have learned how to remember. In school we are instructed how to tell a story – how to report memorized information. Young children probably start with what we have referred to as direct access, i.e., unedited memory reporting, but they gradually learn how to edit their memory reports (cf. Stein, Ornstein, Tversky, & Brainerd, 1997).

To be "impulsive" and report "the first thing that comes to mind" is not generally regarded as the most intelligent or proper way of behaving. We expect the memory report to be organized enough to be comprehensible to oneself or to others. Memory editing is a decision-making process (Hastie & Dawes, 2001). It is no coincidence that signal-detection methods are so suitable for memory analysis. In fact, these methods take into account the fact, noted earlier, that people not only have different abilities to recognize old information but also different criteria for deciding when to give a positive response. Memories are also rejected or accepted in terms of how they fit with an overarching report schema (Alba & Hasher, 1983).

The literature on human memory abounds with illustrations of organizational principles. Chunks are created to help encoding and rehearsal. Irrelevant information is filtered out. New information is stored in familiar categories. Memories are reported in clusters, and so on (Tulving & Donaldson, 1972). Our reference to memory editing is thus only a reminder of a basic memory principle that may also be of interest during encoding (e.g., Koriat & Pearlman-Avnion, 2003). Memories tend to be encoded and subsequently reported in edited versions.

As we noted, memory editing is usually intentional, and is recognized to be so by the remembering person and by those who eventually receive the memory report. Metamemory research has stressed conscious and deliberate monitoring and control processes (Nelson, 1996; Nelson & Narens, 1990). However, some researchers also stress the idea that metacognitive processes can occur without the person's conscious control (Reder, 1988; see also Chapter 11).

Table 13.1 summarizes the four possible combinations of the different paths *to* and *from* memory. All four combinations are possible. The fact that some combinations are more likely than others is a result of the features of the different paths as described earlier. Category A represents spontaneous pop-out memories that are often manifested in behavioural indices. Metacognitive operations are minimal. Category B represents situations with a goal-directed memory search that is not directed towards memorial report, and hence incorporate little editing. This is, perhaps, the least frequent category because voluntary memories are typically edited. However, voluntary rapid retrieval may also occur with little editing. In consequence, people sometimes report something that they later regret having reported. This occurs in mental states when metacognitive processes are suspended or relaxed, or, perhaps, under pressure of time.

The C category includes verbally reported involuntary memories, reflections on spontaneous memories and other cases in which the remembering persons reorganize their involuntary memories. Small talk and confidential talk represent social situations in which one exchanges "memorial opinions".

Table 13.1 Combinations of pathways *to* and *from* memory

	Pathways to memory	
Pathways from memory	*Involuntary*	*Voluntary*
Non-edited	A	B
Edited	C	D

Biographical memory contributions, such as Proust's literary project or autobiographical descriptions, tend to fall into this memory class.

The pathway combination in the D category represents the typical memory situation. This category is representative not only of typical laboratory memory experiments but also of "everyday memory" in folk parlance. Here the memory report is intended to answer specific search questions. The memories are voluntary by intention.

For each of the four cells in Table 13.1 there should be separate entries for intrapersonal and interpersonal memory situations. Here we merely offer some brief comments. The A category probably is most frequent and typical of intrapersonal than of interpersonal memory situations. The opposite probably applies to category D.

To a large extent, interactions between pathways to and from memory will reflect personal choices. We shall comment upon some of these. A person might experience satisfaction and pleasure when involuntary episodic memories pop into his or her mind. Enjoying this process, he or she might want to prolong the re-experience and prefer not to intervene. That person might let the retrieval process flow unedited and try not to focus attention on potentially disturbing situational factors. In this case the triggering of the re-experience may have started off involuntarily, but the person intentionally tries to prolong the unedited memory flow. Unpleasant re-experiences, on the other hand, may result in the person being overwhelmed by traumatic feelings that make active strategic intervention difficult. Sometimes the person may be able to intervene and stop the re-experiencing process by diverting attention to other situational aspects, by efforts to re-edit the re-experiences, or by shifting to remembering by recollection.

A person engaged in edited voluntary retrieval may produce some useful cues that trigger unedited re-experiences. Here an initial controlled process leads to non-strategic processing. On the other hand, when thinking back on certain life episodes or reporting these to another person (e.g., a therapist), a person may come to realize that edited reporting may be a more suitable alternative (e.g., child to parents, witness in court).

These are only some of the many interactive possibilities between pathways *to* and *from* memory. In terms of metacognitive functions, the person serves as a kind of shunt between the retrieval pathways to episodic memories. In everyday situations one often starts with specific intentions about how and what one wishes to report, only to realize that what one comes up with is quite different. A musician may play a piece from memory but at the same time try to convey a personal interpretation based on involuntary memories. Sudden impulses that are triggered by re-experience are controlled by a kind of edited memory processing.

PATHWAY COMBINATIONS AND METACOGNITION

The coordination and control of our memorial pathways corresponds to what is currently referred to as "metamemory" or "metacognition". These terms are commonly employed to refer to the processes involved in monitoring and regulating one's own cognitive processes (Cornoldi, 1995, 1998; Koriat & Goldsmith, 1996; Nelson, 1996; Nelson & Narens, 1990). Current discussions of metacognition generally assume that people have some control over cognitive processes and can regulate learning and remembering in accordance with various goals (see Chapter 11; Helstrup, 2002, 2005a, b). Nelson and Narens (1990; see also Nelson, 1996) proposed a framework that postulates a feedback loop between metacognitive monitoring and metacognitive control: Metacognitive monitoring is used to oversee the operation of basic information-processing operations and to monitor their results and success, whereas metacognitive control is used to regulate these processes in a top-down fashion.

The metacognitive perspective assumes that there is some degree of self-control over the processes of learning and remembering. In terms of the pathway metaphor, this implies that pathway selection and pathway combinations are partly under personal control. It is recognized, however, that some of the processes can occur automatically and can be controlled by unconscious cognitive mechanisms. Thus, remembering can sometimes occur automatically, as is illustrated by the occurrence of involuntary memory, but recollection and editing normally entail self-regulation. However, it is sometimes possible to self-cue one's own re-experiences. For instance we may pay visits, mentally or physically, to old locations with the result that the re-visit triggers a re-experience. This is a form of controlled re-experience. Re-experiences may then undergo editing, but they also may be left unedited.

Metacognition also involves knowledge and beliefs about one's own memory as well as about memory in general. This knowledge is useful not only for the regulation of one's own cognitive processes but also for guiding communication with other people. Communication generally implies a great deal of shared knowledge and beliefs. For instance, rules like those described by Grice (1967, 1975), as well as other rules, govern the way in which we report our memories.

Everyday memory should thus not be seen exclusively as a private mental phenomenon. We share our past, just as we share our present, with others. Remembering everyday episodes has an important social function, and many of these episodes also have a social content. Because much of our metacognitive knowledge is shared, memory control is also performed through social channels. Control factors are especially important when it comes to understanding reports of mental events such as experiences or memories.

An important issue in everyday memory is how to understand the extent to which social and emotional factors affect memory processes. Emotional factors at the reporting stage are perhaps among the most influential factors affecting metacognitive control. Our emotional attitude to the recipient of a message should greatly influence our report procedures. Emotions may influence the pathways both to and from memory. From the perspective of the recipient of a memory report, the emotional state of the reporter will influence the degree of confidence that recipient will have in that report. Emotions thus seem to play a central role in everyday memory, far more so than in the memory tasks studied under standard laboratory conditions.

INVOLUNTARY MEMORY AND VOLUNTARY FORGETTING

As we have seen, evidence at hand unambiguously supports the idea that memories at times pop up without warning or deliberate search (Berntsen, 1996, 1998; Spence, 1988). Two practical questions naturally arise. How can we avoid unwanted memories and how can we obtain the desired ones?

Some psychotherapeutic techniques incorporate tools devoted not only to the facilitation of memory re-experiences but also to overcoming unwanted re-experiences that can be highly debilitating. It would seem that re-experiences are difficult to probe directly. However, they can be induced indirectly by reinstating some of the triggering cues.

Apparently, one way of reducing the impact of involuntary memories is by attempting to "erase" them. Several authors have stressed that forgetting should be critical for adaptation to a changing world. People must be able to discard out-of-date information in order to avoid errors and interference, and in order to update the contents of their memories (E.L. Bjork, Bjork, & Anderson, 1998; Hasher, Tonev, Lustig, & Zacks, 2001; Wessel & Wright, 2004; Wright, Loftus, & Hall, 2001; Wright, Mathews, & Skagerberg, 2005). How efficient are people at deliberately forgetting a specific piece of con-sciously registered information? Research indicates that when people are instructed to forget a previously learned piece of information, they are often successful in reducing or eliminating the interference of that information with the subsequent retrieval of to-be-remembered information. The underlying mechanism seems to involve inhibiting the retrieval of the to-be-forgotten information.

There are indications, however, that the information that was to be forgot-ten remains in memory: When memory is tested through recognition or relearning, or when it is tested through indirect measures of memory such as priming, performance on the to-be-forgotten items is typically comparable to that of to-be-remembered items (Basden, Basden, & Gargano, 1993; E.L. Bjork & Bjork, 1996). In fact, recent evidence suggests that although the retrieval of to-be-forgotten information is inhibited, the indirect influence of that information may actually be greater in certain situations than those of intentionally remembered information. This occurs because the failure to recollect the forgotten information prevents the rememberer from mitigating the undesirable indirect influences of the forgotten information (E.L. Bjork

& Bjork, 2003). The implication of this line of research, then, is that involuntary memories cannot be warded off completely through directed forgetting.

Of course, there are other methods of avoiding involuntary memories: For example, re-experiencing may be stopped by diverting one's attention away from the original experience, but because this does not erase the underlying memory, it may emerge spontaneously at some later time. Alternatively, involuntary memories can be prevented by redirecting one's recollection, as when we call forth new search cues that may induce us to conceive of the recollected episode in a different way.

Another means would be to avoid unedited direct access to memories, trying instead to re-edit the recollected episodes. Social feedback on re-edited memory reports will help to build up new memory schemata.

In sum, voluntary forgetting is an important tool that is used in everyday life to avoid the emergence of unwanted memories. However, directed forgetting does not erase the underlying memory but only inhibits its expression. Other strategies may be used to protect against the spontaneous emergence of undesired memories. Such strategies may entail a reconstruction and re-evaluation of the original episode.

CONCLUSIONS

The pathway metaphor was intended as a way to provide a tool for thinking about the retrieval of episodic memories. However, it can be argued that retrieval is also a metaphor in its own right (see Chapter 1). The notion of retrieval seems to build on a memory trace concept: "Something" is retrieved that corresponds to the trace. Our double-path metaphor (to and from memory) suggests that memories must first be re-established and developed before they can be called forth. Conceptualized in this way, retrieval is a two-stage finding-and-reporting process in which finding and reporting interact. Memories are not traces, but are more like mental products or achievements.

The interaction is performed by the remembering person. Although memory retrieval can occur privately, it often takes place in a social context. Episodic memories are typically reported in a social context, and practical memory applications must take this fact into account.

REFERENCES

Alba, J.W., & Hasher, L. (1983). Is memory schematic? *Psychological Bulletin, 93*, 203–231.

Antrobus, J.S., Singer, J.L., & Greenberg, S. (1966). Studies in the stream of consciousness: Experimental enhancement and suppression of spontaneous cognitive processes. *Perceptual and Motor Skills, 23*, 399–417.

Austin, J.L. (1962). *How to do things with words*. Oxford, UK: Clarendon Press.

Bartlett, F.C. (1932). *Remembering*. Cambridge, UK: Cambridge University Press.

Basden, B.H., Basden, D.R., & Gargano, G.J. (1993). Directed forgetting in implicit and explicit memory tests: A comparison of methods. *Journal of Experimental Psychology: Learning, Memory, and Cognition, 19*, 603–616.

Berntsen, D. (1996). Involuntary autobiographical memories. *Applied Cognitive Psychology, 10*, 435–454.

Berntsen, D. (1998). Voluntary and involuntary access to autobiographical memory. *Memory, 6*, 113–141.

Bjork, E.L., & Bjork, R.A. (1996). Continuing influences of to-be forgotten information. *Consciousness and Cognition, 5*, 176–196.

Bjork, E.L., & Bjork, R.A. (2003). Intentional forgetting can increase, not decrease, residual influences of to-be-forgotten information. *Journal of Experimental Psychology: Learning, Memory, and Cognition, 29*, 524–531.

Bjork, E.L., Bjork, R.A., & Anderson, M.C. (1998). Varieties of goal-directed forgetting. In J.M. Golding & C.M. MacLeod (Eds.), *Intentional forgetting: Interdisciplinary approaches* (pp. 103–137). Hillsdale, NJ: Lawrence Erlbaum Associates, Inc.

Bjork, R.A. (1970). Positive forgetting: The noninterference of items intentionally forgotten. *Journal of Verbal Learning and Verbal Behavior, 9*, 255–268.

Bjork, R.A. (1989). Retrieval inhibition as an adaptive mechanism in human memory. In H.L. Roediger & F.I.M. Craik (Eds.), *Varieties of memory and consciousness* (pp. 309–330). Hillsdale, NJ: Lawrence Erlbaum Associates, Inc.

Bousfield, W.A., & Rosner, S.R. (1970). Free vs. uninhibited recall. *Psychonomic Science, 20*, 75–76.

Bower, G. (1981). Mood and memory. *American Psychologist, 36*, 129–148.

Burke, D.M., MacKay, D.G., Worthley, J.S., & Wade, E. (1991). On the tip of the tongue: What causes word finding failures in young and older adults? *Journal of Memory and Language, 30*, 542–579.

Cornoldi, C. (1995). *Metacognizione e apprendimento*. Bologna, Italy: Il Mulino.

Cornoldi, C. (1998). The impact of metacognitive reflection on cognitive control. In G. Mazzoni & T.O. Nelson (Eds.), *Metacognition and cognitive neuropsychology* (pp. 139–159). Mahwah, NJ: Lawrence Erlbaum Associates, Inc.

Cornoldi, C., & De Beni, R. (1985). Effects of loci mnemonic in memorization of concrete words. *Acta Psychologica, 60*, 11–24.

Ebbinghaus, H. (1964). *Memory: A contribution to experimental psychology*. New York: Dover Publications. [First published 1885]

Finke, R.A., & Slayton, K. (1988). Explorations of creative visual synthesis in mental imagery. *Memory and Cognition, 16*, 252–257.

Fisher, R.P., & Geiselman, R.E. (1992). *Memory-enhancing techniques for investigative interviewing*. Springfield, IL: C. Charles Thomas.

Freud, S. (1953). Fragment of an analysis of a case of hysteria. In J. Strachey (Ed.), *The standard edition of the complete works of Sigmund Freud, Vol. 7*. London: Hogarth Press. [First published 1905]

Freud, S. (1975). Beyond the pleasure principle. In J. Strachey (Trans.), *The standard edition of the complete psychological works of Sigmund Freud, Vol. 18* (pp. 7–67). London: Hogarth Press. [First published 1920]

Gardiner, J.M., Passmore, C., Herriot, P., & Klee, H. (1977). Memory for remembered events: Effects of response mode and response-produced feedback. *Journal of Verbal Learning and Verbal Behavior, 16*, 45–54.

Glenberg, A. (1997). What memory is for. *Behavioral and Brain Sciences, 20*, 1–55.

Goldsmith, M., & Koriat, A. (1999). The strategic regulation of memory reporting: Mechanisms and performance consequences. In D. Gopher & A. Koriat (Eds.), *Attention and performance XVII: Cognitive regulation of performance: Interaction of theory and application* (pp. 373–400). Cambridge, MA: MIT Press.

Goldsmith, M., Koriat, A., & Weinberg,-Eliezer, A. (2002). The strategic regulation of grain size in memory reporting. *Journal of Experimental Psychology: General, 131*, 73–95.

Grice, H.P. (1975). Logic and conversation. In P. Cole & J.L. Morgan (Eds.), *Syntax and semantics, Vol. III: Speech acts* (pp. 26–40). New York: Seminar Press.

Hasher, L., Tonev, S.T., Lustig, C., & Zacks, R.T. (2001). Inhibitory control, environmental support, and self-initiated processing in aging. In M. Naveh-Benjamin, M. Moscovitch, & R.L. Roediger, III (Eds.), *Perspectives on human memory and cognitive aging: Essays in honour of Fergus Craik* (pp. 286–297). Hove, UK: Psychology Press.

Hastie, R., & Dawes, R.M. (2001). *Rational choice in an uncertain world*. London: Sage.

Helstrup, T. (2002). Læring i et kognitivt perspektiv (Learning from a cognitive perspective). In I. Bråten (Ed.), *Læring. I sosialt, kognitivt og sosial-kognitivt perspektiv* (pp. 103–130). Oslo, Norway: Cappelen Akademisk Forlag.

Helstrup, T. (2005a). Cognitive control by what or whom? In W. Østreng (Ed.), *Synergies. Interdisciplinary communications 2003/2004*. Oslo, Norway: Center for Advanced Study.

Helstrup, T. (2005b). *Personlig kognisjon*. Bergen, Norway: Fagbokforlaget.

Hyman, I.E. (1994). Conversational remembering: Story recall with a peer versus for an experimenter. *Applied Cognitive Psychology, 8*, 49–66.

Johnson, H.M. (1994). Processes of successful intentional forgetting. *Psychological Bulletin, 116*, 274–292.

Jones, G.V. (1989). Back to Woodworth: Role of interlopers in the tip-of-the-tongue phenomenon. *Memory and Cognition, 17*, 69–76.

Joyce, J. (1960). *Ulysses*. London: Bodley Head. [First published 1922]

Koriat, A. (2000). Control processes in remembering. In E. Tulving & F.I.M. Craik (Eds.), *The Oxford handbook of memory* (pp. 333–346). New York: Oxford University Press.

Koriat, A., Ben-Zur, H., & Sheffer, D. (1988). Telling the same story twice: Output monitoring and age. *Journal of Memory and Language, 27*, 23–39.

Koriat, A., & Goldsmith, M. (1996). Monitoring and control processes in the strategic regulation of memory accuracy. *Psychological Review, 103*, 490–517.

Koriat, A., & Pearlman-Avnion, S. (2003). The memory organization of action events and its relationship to memory performance. *Journal of Experimental Psychology: General, 132*, 435–454.

Kvavilashvili, L., & Mandler, G. (2004). Out of one's mind: A study of involuntary semantic memories. *Cognitive Psychology, 48*, 47–94.

Lord, A.B. (1960). *The singer of tales*. Cambridge, MA: Harvard University Press.

Middleton, D., & Edwards, D. (Eds.) (1990). *Collective remembering*. London: Sage.

Mitchell, K.J., & Johnson, M.K. (2000). Source monitoring: Attributing mental experiences. In E. Tulving & F.I.M. Craik (Eds.), *The Oxford handbook of memory* (pp. 179–195). London: Oxford University Press.

Neisser, U. (1967). *Cognitive psychology*. New York: Appleton-Century-Crofts.

Neisser, U. (1976). *Cognition and reality*. San Francisco, CA: Freeman.

Neisser, U. (1978). Memory: What are the important questions? In M.M. Gruneberg, P.E. Morris, & R.N. Sykes (Eds.), *Practical aspects of memory* (pp. 3–24). London: Academic Press.

Neisser, U. (1996). Remembering as doing. *Behavioral and Brain Sciences, 19*, 203–204.

Nelson, T.O. (1996). Consciousness and metacognition. *American Psychologist, 51*, 102–116.

Nelson, T.O., & Narens, L. (1990). Metamemory: A theoretical framework and some new findings. In G.H. Bower (Ed.), *The psychology of learning and motivation* (pp. 125–173). New York: Academic Press.

Nigro, G., & Neisser, U. (1983). Point of view in personal memories. *Cognitive Psychology, 15*, 467–482.

Norman, D.A., & Bobrow, D.G. (1979). Descriptions: An intermediate stage in memory retrieval. *Cognitive Psychology, 11*, 107–123.

Palladino, P., & De Beni, R. (2003). When mental images are very detailed: Image generation and memory performance as a function of age. *Acta Psychologica, 113*, 297–314.

Proust, M. (1919). *Du coté de chez Swann*. Paris: Gallimard. The first volume of *A la recherché du temps perdu*.

Reder, L.M. (1988). Strategic control of retrieval strategies. In G.H. Bower (Ed.), *The psychology of learning and motivation: Advances in research and theory, Vol. 22* (pp. 227–259). San Diego, CA: Academic Press.

Robinson, M.D., Johnson, J.T., & Herndon, F. (1997). Reaction time and assessments of cognitive effort as predictors of eyewitness memory accuracy and confidence. *Journal of Applied Psychology, 82*, 416–425.

Rubin, D.C. (1995). *Memory in oral traditions: The cognitive psychology of epic, ballads, and counting-out rhymes*. London: Oxford University Press.

Salaman, E. (1982). A collection of moments. In U. Neisser (Ed.), *Memory observed* (pp. 49–63). San Francisco, CA: Freeman.

Smith, S.M. (1979). Remembering in and out of context. *Journal of Experimental Psychology: Human Learning and Memory, 5*, 460–471.

Spence, D.P. (1988). Passive remembering. In U. Neisser & E. Winograd (Eds.), *Remembering reconsidered: Ecological and traditional approaches to the study of memory* (pp. 311–122). New York: Cambridge University Press.

Stein, N.L., Ornstein, P.A., Tversky, B., & Brainerd, C. (Eds.) (1997). *Memory for everyday and emotional events*. Mahwah, NJ: Lawrence Erlbaum Associates, Inc.

Tulving, E. (2002). Episodic memory: From mind to brain. *Annual Review of Psychology, 53*, 1–25.

Tulving, E., & Donaldson, W. (1972). *Organization of memory*. London: Academic Press.

Tulving, E., & Thomson, D.M. (1973). Encoding specificity and retrieval processes in episodic memory. *Psychological Review, 80*, 352–373.

Vrij, A. (2000). *Detecting lies and deceit*. New York: Wiley.

Vrij, A., & Mann, S. (2004). Detecting deception: The benefit of looking at a combination of behavioural, auditory and speech content related cues in a systematic manner. *Group Decision and Negotiation, 13*, 61–79.

Wegner, D.M., Schneider, D.J., Carter, S.R., & White, T.L. (1987). Paradoxical effects of thought suppression. *Journal of Personality and Social Psychology, 53*, 5–13.

Wenzlaff, R.M., & Wegner, D.M. (2000). Thought suppression. *Annual Review of Psychology*, *51*, 59–91.

Wessel, I., & Wright, D.B. (Eds.) (2004). *Emotional memory failures*. Hove, UK: Psychology Press.

Wright, D.B., Loftus, E.F., & Hall, M. (2001). Now you see it, now you don't: Inhibiting recall and recognition of scenes. *Applied Cognitive Psychology*, *15*, 471–485.

Wright, D.B., Mathews, S.A., & Skagerberg, E.M. (2005). Social recognition memory: The effect of other people's responses for previously seen and unseen items. *Journal of Experimental Psychology: Applied*, *11*, 200–209.

Yzerbyt, V.Y., Lories, G., & Dardenne, B. (Eds.) (1998). *Metacognition: Cognitive and social dimensions*. London: Sage.

Author index

Subject index

Note: page numbers in *italic* denote references to figures/tables.